Miltiadis Zermpoulis
Dreaming Big in Post-War Greece

Culture and Social Practice

I dedicate this book to the memory of my grandparents, Stefanos and Kleopatra Karaiskakis.

Miltiadis Zermpoulis holds a PhD in social anthropology from the Department of Balkan, Slavic and Oriental Studies at the University of Macedonia in Thessaloniki, Greece. Between 2017 and 2021 he worked for a migrant organization in North Rhine-Westphalia, Germany. Since June 2021 he has been working as a research associate and deputy head at the Institute for Transcultural Competence at Police Academy of the Free and Hanseatic City of Hamburg. His academic interests include material culture, anthropology of space, state culture, social classes, post-colonial theories, ethnic/religious minorities and migration.

Miltiadis Zermpoulis

Dreaming Big in Post-War Greece

Neighborhood, Life Style, and Everyday Practices in the City of Thessaloniki

[transcript]

This dissertation was submitted as a doctoral thesis to the Department of Balkan, Slavic and Oriental Studies at the Faculty of Economic and Regional Studies at the University of Macedonia in 2019.

Bibliographic information published by the Deutsche Nationalbibliothek
The Deutsche Nationalbibliothek lists this publication in the Deutsche Nationalbibliografie; detailed bibliographic data are available in the Internet at http://dnb.d-nb.de

Cover layout: Jan Gerbach, Bielefeld
Cover illustration: © DEI Historical Archive
Proofread: Anthie Kyriakopoulou & Giorgos Azis
Translated by Anthie Kyriakopoulou & Giorgos Azis

https://doi.org/10.14361/9783839464915
Print-ISBN 978-3-8376-6491-1
PDF-ISBN 978-3-8394-6491-5
ISSN of series: 2703-0024
eISSN of series: 2703-0032

"[...] It was an introverted city. After that decade of bloodshed, people were swallowing again silently the gloom of every day. On their clothes, latches seemed to be hanging from buttons, locking their bodies in jackets and gloomy skirt suits, to make sure they wouldn't move graciously and wouldn't live. They rarely ever smiled and even when they did so, it was only to comply with the order of a photographer on the esplanade. Their faintly smiling lips were hardened. Oily brilliantine and stiff hair-sprayed hair were a shy attempt to achieve a poor and scrawny beauty.

Their joy had now been localized. Their past grace and nobility had been burned in the fear of recent memory. In a way, they were all turning peasants. Former bourgeois Israelites had been burned in the fumes of the camps in Poland; most of those who survived left for Athens and Palestine. The famine memory was turning all other bourgeois, who stayed there and did not leave for the capital, into peasants. Real peasants, too, were coming with the intention to stay forever in the injured city armpits. The provinces, wounded by civil stabbings, were vomiting their people like infected blood. No wealthy people had been left; only those making money and thousands of labourers. They all wished to forget: the former their guilt, the latter their memories; most of them had buried their family members with their own hands. They wished to forget, fall asleep not to remember anymore; this is maybe why they loved so much the lulling noise of the concrete mixer in the construction sites, mixing the concrete blend and sending it so high up to reach the newly built framework of the apartment buildings.

These were now sweeping away the detached houses with metopes and tiles, those compassionate houses of the old city that had their walls torn by bullets, those houses that made them remember."

"[...] And all those big trees with the apartments appeared broken down from the very moment of their creation: narrow corridors like catacombs, dark entrance doors with eyes, such and such family, air shafts, spotty stairs with mosaic patterns, slow old-fashioned lifts with a red eye in the darkness of the corridors. Smell of sizzled onion and peppers, sounds from a whispering radio, smoker's cough, because those waiting for the lift were coughing to dispel the evil, as if this coughing could change the burnt-out light bulb in the corridor."[1]

---

1   Excerpt from the novel by Isidoros Zourgos (2005), *In the Shadow of the butterfly*, Pataki editions. I would like to thank the author and the publisher for allowing me to use this excerpt in this publication. This extract has been translated from Greek into English for the purposes of this publication.

Contents

Acknowledgements

This study would have never been completed without the unreserved support and trust of the informants from the center of Thessaloniki and the district of Kato Toumba, who opened their apartments to me and allowed me to spend a considerable amount of time with them. These people, of whom unfortunately some are no longer alive, shared openly their story with me and guided me around the "innermost places" of their life. I express my deep gratitude to them.

I warmly thank Professor Fotini Tsibiridou, supervisor of my thesis, for her initial help and support in the choice of this subject and her constant subsequent trust in me and in this project, throughout the study. I also thank her for the moral support as well as the intellectual feedback and guidance she offered to me during all these six years of research and writing. But I also wish to thank her for all these 19 years, during which she has accompanied and supported me in the journey of personal and scientific accomplishment.

I particularly thank Professor Emerita Effie Voutira, who paved the way for me to discover and perceive deeper the social and cultural dimensions of the field, of which we both used to be part, since we were born and raised there. The borderline between Toumba and the city center has never been so clear-cut after all, as it has been proved by our personal biographies and the way we cooperated within the context of this study. I wish to thank Assoc. Professor Alexandra Bakalaki for her useful advice at the outset of this study not to see *petty bourgeoisism* as something negative and perceive in advance its negative conceptualization within the context of postwar Greek society. Besides, she lived in a neighboring district and, as she disclosed to me, quite often she admired the way of living of these people, which was particularly vivid and full of imagination and creativity. Thanks to Pelagia Astreinidou and Professor Emeritus Kostas Kotsakis for the interesting discussions at their place in Ano Poli, which helped me understand better the material of the fieldwork. I warmly thank them for the guidance, advice and pertinent suggestions.

In addition, I wish to thank DAAD, the German Academic Exchange Service, for funding my research from 01.09.2015 to 28.02.2017. Without their financial support this study would not have been completed. I thank the University of Hamburg and the Institute for Anthropological Studies in History and Culture for the benefits and their contribution to writing a large part of this thesis.

I wish to thank Dr. Kerstin Poehls, supervisor within the context of my grant and stay in Hamburg; Professor Emerita Waltraud Kokot for trusting me and sharing with me all the material of her fieldwork on Kato Toumba, which she performed in 1980; Sonja Windmüller, Professor for European Ethnology and Folklore at the Christian-Albrechts University in Kiel, for teaching me to pay attention to what informants give me in the field. I also wish to thank the Professors and colleagues who encouraged me throughout my research and helped me continue and complete it: Professor Christina Koulouri, Assoc. Prof. Georgios Angelopoulos, Assoc. Prof. Anna Stavrakopoulou, Asst. Prof. Giorgos Mavrommatis, Professor Dieter Haller, Professor Emerita Regina Schulte, Eleni Ioannidou, Professor Emerita Vilma Chastaoglou and Professor Emeritus Filippos Oraiopoulos.

I wish to thank Stella Drakou and all staff of the Historical Archive of *DEI* in Thessaloniki and Maria Mavroeidi from the Historical Archive of *DEI* in Athens for their support and constant help; the employees of the office of City Plan in the department of public property, which hosts the archive of Social Welfare.

I thank my parents, Fani and Zermpoulis Zermpoulis who did everything to help me focus completely on this research. Finally, my husband Martin Krekeler for his respect and love.

Despite careful inquests, all errors are mine.

List of Greek words and acronyms used in the text

antiparochi	formal, legally binding agreement involving a flats-for-land exchange between the signing parties
DEI	Greek Public Power Corporation
EAM	National Liberation Front
EAP	Refugee Settlement Commission
EDA	United Democratic Left Party
Enosis Kentrou	Centre Union Party
EPON	United Panhellenic Organization of Youth
ERE	National Radical Union: Greek political party formed in 1956 by Konstantinos Karamanlis
ethnikofron	Greek term associated in the early post-war decades with the non-leftist middle classes to designate a person with national consciousness. It is used as an opposite for "communist", who was considered as a "traitor", an "enemy of the homeland" in the Greek civil war and post-civil war context.
EYATH	Thessaloniki Water Supply and Sewerage Corporation
KKE	Communist Party of Greece
koukoues	supporter of the Communist Party of Greece
mikromesaioi	lower middle classes
noikokyraioi (or *noikokyrides* – also in singular *noikokyris* or *noikokyraios* when referring to a man or *noikokyra* and *noikokyraies/noikokyres* in plural when referring to a woman)	term describing the identity of middle-class members successfully managing their household issues
noikokyremenos	tidy and neat
noikokyrio	household

PASOK	Panhellenic Socialist Movement, social-democratic political party
prokommenos	diligent
prokopi	prosperity, progress, diligence
Pronoia	Welfare service
Syriza	Coalition of the Radical Left – Progressive Alliance, left-wing political party in Greece
tourkosporos	offensive term to describe a Greek from Asia Minor

Preface

After the end of the Nazi occupation and the subsequent Civil War, the foundation and safeguarding of the Western bourgeois liberal orientation of the country and its inhabitants emerged as the dominant desire and need for different sides of the social body of the winners. The success of this objective was an outcome of the class-based reshaping of the Greek society. In particular, the lower middle class and middle class, which formed the body of post-war nation-state socially, culturally, and ideologically, were empowered.

Top-down policies and bottom-up simple everyday practices contributed decisively to the fulfillment of this objective. Post-war governments sought and facilitated mass urbanization of the hitherto predominantly agricultural Greek society, as well as economic migration of a large part of the Greek population to Western Europe countries. The main purpose of the policies implemented in the post-war period was the radical transformation and modernization of the everyday way of living. The first three post-war decades were dominated by the slogan of change at all levels of everyday life. This political slogan quickly became the slogan of the people that wanted to forget the hardships of the war. "Dreaming big" was a necessity and a way to overcome the dystopia of the previous years of Nazi occupation and the civil war that followed.

This thesis comes into dialogue with Marxist-inspired critical studies that prevailed during the post-war era and tried to describe the phenomenon of *petty bourgeoisism*[1]. From an anthropological point of view and with the tools of ethnography, this thesis will fill gaps and meanings of the lived experiences brought to Greece by the modernization programs.

This study has adopted a mainly emic approach, highlighting the behaviors and lived experiences of informants in the field, along with the micro-histories that came to light through the study of the archives in the city of Thessaloniki.[2] It focuses

---

1   This term is a neologism created by the author. It is the translation of the Greek term "Μικροαστισμός". It does not refer to the class of petty bourgeoisie itself, but to the mentality developed within Greek middle classes. It will appear in italics throughout the text.

2   The need for such an approach to the study of the Greek middle classes that focuses on the lived experiences and behaviors of the people themselves has recently been pointed out by Pa-

specifically on the impact and meanings of the social and political transformation after the civil war, with the victory of the Conservatives in the political stage and the promotion of "technologies of political surveillance and compliance" (Foucault, 1987, pp. 11–37) in the everyday life of the city.[3] As an ethnography of material reality (Buchli, 2002; Miller, 2005; Gialouri, 2012), the study focuses on commonplace practices, relationships, and daily routines and habits of the inhabitants of the city involving material objects. The multiple meanings of materiality in the everyday life of a city are sought.[4]

This study pertains to the type of anthropology called "anthropology at home"; its specific characteristic is the researcher's level of difficulty in recognizing practices and modalities that look familiar and straightforward (Hastrup, 2008; Kuper, 2008). The anthropologist must, in this case, work with greater reflection about the types of normality s/he identifies in the field (Kuper, 2008; Gkefou-Madianou, 2008). In any case, this study follows the methodologies and considerations of an ethnography of/for the city (Pardo & Prato, 2018; Tsibiridou, 2018; Giannakopoulos & Giannitsiotis, 2010).

The ethnographic research was initiated in summer 2012 in the old historical center of the city, in the context of a pilot program by the non-profit company *SARCHA*. In the context of that program, I tried to help a small group of architects who were interested in redesigning an already built environment through a bottom-up approach, taking into account the conflicts, perceptions and meaning-making of

---

nagiotopoulos in his book *Περιπέτειες της Μεσαίας τάξης. Κοινωνιολογικές καταγραφές στην Ελλάδα της ύστερης Μεταπολίτευσης* [Adventures of the middle classes. Sociological records in Greece of the late political transition] (2021, p. 23).

3   I am referring to the practices of the post-war Conservative governments described as the "parastate of the rightism", and the financial and political trusteeship imposed during the post-war period by the Marshall Plan (see Tsoukalas, 1981, 2005; Mouzelis, 1978; Charalambis, 1985, 1989; Dordanas, 2006; Panourgia, 2013).

4   Concerning the concept of modernization, it is important to mention at this point that it occurs mainly bottom-up, from the Thessaloniki informants themselves. Of course, as far as the primary material used in the thesis and the secondary bibliography are concerned, the 1950s and 1960s are linked to the goals of modernization and development both on the level of government and that of everyday life and mentality. In particular, Kyriakidou-Nestoros (1993b, pp. 249–250) describes the 1960s as the decade of prosperity, during which Thessaloniki succeeds in having the highest productivity rates in the country in the secondary and tertiary sectors and sees an even greater increase in its population. Certainly, the call for modernization and development as opposed to the Civil War following the end of the Nazi occupation must be understood in the ideological context of US interventionism in Greek society already since the era of the Truman doctrine. According to Panourgia (2013, p. 61), the Post-War Reconstruction that is funded by the Marshall Plan (1947) inaugurates the start of the Cold War, allowing for foreign influences to protect the modernization project of Western capitalism against the Soviet threat through technologies of surveillance and compliance.

space that anthropology can bring to the surface. I tried to highlight the relationships that were identified in the field between people, buildings, and other material objects, and which act on multiple networks and create different places beyond the apparent place of interaction. In this case, the space referred to an old market of used goods, a bazaar in the city center. This first ethnographic research allowed me to realize the differentiation between the old urban center and the main field of Kato Toumba to the east of the city, from 2012 to 2015. The comparison between the two areas helped me understand the differences in the cultural and political boundaries of these two areas of the city; these differences are found in traumatic experiences from the past and shape the present of the inhabitants through personal and collective memory.

After the completion of this research project in summer 2012, I started the fieldwork in Kato Toumba from the neighborhood I grew up in. By summer 2014, I had met 90 informants. Among them, there were people who constituted the second generation of refugees from Asia Minor (1923), informants who had migrated to Germany in the 1950s and returned to the city at the beginning of 1970s, native and old inhabitants of Thessaloniki as well as domestic migrants who had moved during and after the Civil War to Thessaloniki, abandoning villages and towns of the broader area of Macedonia.[5]

In 2015, with a scholarship from the German Academic Exchange Service (DAAD) and the scientific support of the University of Hamburg and the Institute for Anthropological Studies in History and Culture, I extended my research to informants still living in Germany. My scholarship and stay in Germany contributed to the initiation and completion of the writing of my thesis, mainly due to the distance from the field.

In the first chapter entitled *"Methodology issues and theoretical starting points"*, the methods and theoretical tools used in the research are described in detail. Moreover, the theoretical pathways and inquiries that eventually led to the selection of the specific methods, but also to the selection of the subject itself, are presented, to provide sufficient explanation of the scientific approach adopted for the topic of the thesis.

The second chapter entitled *"Introduction: 'Transformation' and 'Petty bourgeoisism'. Greek class distinctiveness and theories of 'underdevelopment'"* provides a historical

---

5   See Kyriakidou-Nestoros (1993b) on the importance of studying the gradual shaping and development of refugee consciousness in the *longue durée* from generation to generation, and the interesting socio-cultural context in which this refugee consciousness is formed and re-signified in Thessaloniki before and after the Nazi occupation and Civil War. The constant refugee flows towards the city, the loss of its Jewish inhabitants, the polar opposites "locals-refugees" are those that ultimately constitute the lived experience and mentality of the residents of post-war Thessaloniki (Kyriakidou-Nestoros, 1993b).

overview of the theories and official discourses about the post-war social transformation and, especially, the phenomenon of a burgeoning middle class in juxtaposition to the economic development of the country, mainly during the first decades after the war. This chapter presents the context in which the experiences of change and ascent/growth of the informants were shaped bottom-up, as well as the official discourses developed top-down, which tried to describe the social and cultural conditions that characterized their practices and behaviors as the "miracle or ascent of the *noikokyraioi*" or conversely as "underdevelopment and *petty bourgeoisism*". Through the theories of material culture, space, shaping of gender-based identities, and a post-colonial anthropological reading of social class in the contemporary glocal context, an effort is made to problematize the traditional association of the post-war expansion of the middle class, and, especially, the "extensive *petty bourgeoisism*" as a phenomenon and mentality that permeates horizontally all classes, with the characteristics of an "underdeveloped, peripheral country of the Mediterranean".

In the third chapter entitled "*Poverty, refugeeism and material adaptation. Homes and people in a dynamic relationship*", I focus on the material world, in and through which the informants of Toumba experience change and transition from the status of the poor and despised refugee to the condition of the "worthy and successful *noikokyris*". Toumba is represented as a predominantly refugee settlement through lived experiences in contrast to the different experiences of "native" informants from the city center. The aim is to make the results of the policies of refugee integration into the Greek state visible, and, also, on a more general level, to highlight the modalities with which different layers of society responded to the specific post-war context, which in itself aimed at the mass urbanization of the Greek population.

In the fourth chapter entitled "*Things in post-war home: modernity, innovation and becoming a noikokyra/noikokyris*", a prominent role is given to objects and their stories, which confirm the lived experiences of a successful integration and participation in a "contemporary and modern", according to words used by my informants, way of living that prevailed in Thessaloniki from the mid-1960s onward. The informants, through their different choices of lifestyle (migration to Germany, uninsured labor, purchases of durable goods, etc.) in the context of "development", try to become part of a gender-based, social, political, and economic normality.

In the fifth and final chapter of the thesis entitled "'*Modern' state, 'noikokyraioi' citizens and local shades of 'corruption'*", I try to discuss concepts such as corruption, clientelism and, more specifically, the concept of the illegal as opposed to the legally appropriate, which are connected to the phenomenon of *petty bourgeoisism* in the post-war era, by using material from archival research and oral interviews from the point of view of the theories of the state and its relation to citizens. The Greek state was placed under financial supervision many times in its history due to its weakness to reform and develop in accordance with the example of other states of the western liberal world. This "underdevelopment" was associated with "inherent" characteristics of the Greek society and the Greek political system, which are themselves linked to corruption, the clientelist state, and the non-bourgeois style of the everyday life of its citizens as a result of its Ottoman past. By providing specific examples, this chapter tries to highlight the lack of consistency between the above-mentioned concepts and practices, opting for cultural dimensions and interpretations of practical behaviors as they are shaped and reproduced in the context of post-war capitalist development and the political economy of the Cold War.

The book is completed with the *"Conclusions"*. In this chapter, the main points of the arguments brought forth in this study are summarized. This study concludes that the shaping of a Greek middle class and its post-war expansion was not a result of top-down policies only and does not relate exclusively to experiences of failure, fear of "proletarianization", social exclusion, corruption, consumerist spending, and "bad taste". The acting subjects who identify themselves as *noikokyraioi* are different from one another, with different biographies and behaviors. They are mainly men and women living in an environment that is open to influences, not only from the Greek society, but also from the broader political, social and cultural environment in which they move and by which they are influenced. The upward social mobility or, better, the need for progress was expressed in the post-war era not only by the Greek society, but also by all societies coming out of the Great War wounded. In the context of the economic crisis threatening Greece since 2010, the informants, as members of the middle class that this crisis seems to threaten, use the positive experiences of the past as well as the difficult years of both the World and Civil Wars to resist it, while at the same time they develop new, inter-generational ways and strategies for their social reproduction.

1. Methodology issues and theoretical starting points

The investigation of the ways and habits through which middle class behaviors crystallize and manifest set a series of methodological issues and conceptual definitions from the outset. The issue of the historical period and the definition of *petty bourgeoisism* as a social phenomenon and mentality of a past era concerned the modernization process of a share of the population of Thessaloniki, but also raised questions of conceptualization and understanding of the phenomenon in the ethnographic present.[1] At the same time, while petty-bourgeois habits and mentalities are widespread in the past, they are recognized as a self-explanatory legacy in the present. Admittedly, the epistemological quiver for the meanings of *petty bourgeoisism* has been particularly poor and not updated at all (Liakos, 2004; Potamianos, 2015; Dertilis, 2015; Papanikolaou, 2018; Aranitou, 2018; Panagiotopoulos, 2021).

In other words, since *petty bourgeoisism* as a social phenomenon is identified and located bibliographically in the first post-war decades (Tsoukalas, 1977, 1981, 2005; Charalambis, 1989; Stathakis, 2000; Karapostolis, 1984; Mouzelis, 1978; Dertilis, 2015; Potamianos, 2015; Kondylis, 1991, 2011), how could then a classic ethnography in the present showcase remnants of past practices and habits? How could oral testimonies and memories of past practices be released from present corrections? How did *petty bourgeoisism* legacies from the past, feeding or passing into the present, link to the pressure suffered by middle class in the circumstance of the Greek crisis? These were some of the questions that puzzled me, raising concerns and ambivalence towards the goals of the field research and expected results.[2]

However, the circumstance of the global financial crisis, which in Greece took the form of shutoff of construction activities, provided a creative gap for the field research. The constant building that characterized Greek cities until that moment suddenly stopped with over taxation of property and implementation of strict austerity measures, while the lower middle class that lived within this context and around

---

1   See Kyriakidou-Nestoros (1993b, 1993a), Potiropoulos (2001), Deltsou (1995), Papataxiarchis (2003), Skouteri-Didaskalou (1988) on the importance of highlighting the historical context in the sense of *longue durée*, in the analysis of cultural representations comprised in the ethnographic field.

2   Op. cit.

this particularity started losing their comparative advantage. Thus, rebuilding narrations in the present hit by a crisis, which marked an imperative and violent change for a lot of people in Greece, reminding past times of poverty, deprivation and exclusion, provided a unique opportunity in the research and crisis circumstances, in order to depict the new subjectivities that were being shaped. At this point, it is very important to remember the words of Kyriakidou-Nestoros about the importance of oral testimonies as sources for reconstructing the past and understanding it in the present:

> "Personal testimonies of refugee history cannot be historical testimonies by themselves. But when they are integrated into the history of the era, when they are cross-checked with respective written testimonies, when available, or with more oral ones – indeed, in the maelstrom of archival records, our historians may sometimes forget the importance of an eyewitness – it is only then that the personal testimonies of oral history may reveal their true importance: first, they provide shades in the picture drawn by historical facts, making it lively and real, then – and this is even more important – they shed light to those aspects of history that without oral testimonies would remain in the dark – because not everything can be listed, especially when it comes to the everyday life of ordinary people and how they silently consume history. In the history of mentalities – if we admit that the change levers cannot be found only at the elite level – personal testimonies of ordinary people have a lot to tell us." (Kyriakidou-Nestoros, 1993b, p. 239) [3]

However, a central issue in this study has been the conceptualization and use of the term *petty bourgeoisism*, both as a descriptive category in the field and as an analytical category in the text. This term had a negative connotation and was a heterodetermination, which characterized a group of people with specific characteristics that had already been described and established in cinema, television, and literature (Mylonaki, 2012; Papanikolaou, 2018; Paschalidis & Vamvakas, 2018). This problem was solved with participant observation, but mainly thanks to the way in which interviews were eventually conducted in the field. Participant observation, but also the methodological tools of oral history that I opted for to conduct the interviews, brought up terms and conceptualizations that were different from those that had been showcased by Greek Sociology and Political science. The new terms and conceptualizations that arose from the ethnography in Thessaloniki were closely linked to biographies and the experience of financial crisis that threatened the social reproduction of the classes I was studying. Moreover, my own presence in the field, but also my personal biography, had an impact on the performance of all participants of the survey, highlighting interesting aspects of each subjectivity reproduced in the field. This emphasis on observation differs, according to Karen O'Reilly (2007), from

---

3   Translator's exact translation from Greek.

simple participation. The researcher participates and observes at the same time, being and not being part of the collectivity that is being studied. According to the same author, the social world is not simple and unidimensional, existing as an objectivity depending directly on our ideas, but a result of interaction, feedback, conceptualization, action and interpretation. "[...] the social world is constructed and reconstructed through its members." (O'Reilly, 2007, p. 103)

Finally, according to Deltsou and Tsibiridou (2016), in a globalized environment with realities expressed and intermediated in multiple ways, the exercise of ethnography cannot be limited to a dry participant observation. The representations of everyday lived experience, which produces a cultural meaning, require and need a precise and detailed deconstruction, using methods and approaches that problematize and identify the diffusion of power. Deltsou and Tsibiridou (2016) stress the importance of a socio-semiotic approach regarding representations, but also the uses and practices of life. Focusing the observation not only on how people lived their reality, how they speak and what they say in the field, but also on how they question, criticize and finally interact with polysemic meanings, reinforces the effort for more reflective and critical ethnography.

I started building the theoretical background for the subject of this study already during my postgraduate studies. While studying historical anthropology I got acquainted with the methodology for the study of microhistories highlighting the everyday life of a rising German bourgeoisie of the 18th and 19th century. The postgraduate seminars by Professor Emerita Regina Schulte at the University of Bochum within the framework of the subject of contemporary and modern history aimed at raising awareness of a different kind of history. The latter was developed in Germany in the 1980s, at the initiative of some few 'revolutionary',[4] within the context of that period, groups of historians, who aimed at integrating into the big narration of the event-based history subjects and groups that had been excluded from the formal narration (Van Laak, 2003). Historians like Jörg Wollenberg, Lutz Niethammer and Gert Zang will lay the foundations of oral history and history from below in Germany. This new form of history, mainly with the foundation of the association for social history of Mainz in 1983 and of pan-German history workshop later, is seen in a negative way by the historians of the traditional approach, while its representatives are called "barefoot historians".[5]

---

4   Revolutionary in the sense that they were the first ones to propose the use of oral testimonies beyond the written documents that had been exclusively used in the scientific field of History until the end of the 1970s. This group of historians tried to distinguish themselves from the prevailing history of big men that represented big state events and write a modern social history, which would focus on everyday life, work, ways of living, living conditions, family life, etc.

5   See *Kleiner Überblick über die Vereinsgeschichte*, Verein für Sozialgeschichte Mainz, accessed October 21, 2022, http://www.sozialgeschichte-mainz.de/wir-ueber-uns/vereinschronik.html

This history draws elements from the theories and methods of cultural and social anthropology. It was developed initially mainly in America, but also in Great Britain as a separate scientific field, to give voice to experiences of people and groups mainly from the working class in the post-war era. It showed the importance of different sources, such as letters and autobiographies, but also oral testimonies, in understanding basic aspects of managing human life and everyday life, such as death, illness, childhood, gender-based identities, experience of work, etc. (Wierling, 2003; Brüggemeier & Kocka, 1985).

More specifically, dealing with the study of the everyday life of the German bourgeoisie from the point of view of historical anthropology allowed me to become acquainted with correspondence and mainly with the specifics of personal written texts. These more intimate sources showcased in the best way the human, everyday and subjective element within the context of an early national class establishment, triggering my interest and wish to study the respective aspects of the Greek bourgeoisie, mainly that of the Greek diaspora. The absence of a similar archive, like the one in Germany, made it difficult to complete this project, showing from the outset how specific was the shaping of the Greek bourgeoisie experience for the low classes.[6] In one of the numerous discussions I had with my future supervisor Fotini Tsibiridou, the issue of the Greek post-war *petty bourgeoisism* emerged emphatically, together with the need to study anthropologically the different social classes that appeared decidedly in the public discourse through cinema and literature but had been almost absent from the Greek academic qualitative research until that moment.

I knew from the beginning that what I was mostly interested in was to showcase experiences of both cultural and social change, mainly as a result of the policies implemented towards the end and especially after the civil war in Greece, to preserve the capitalist and western character of the country.[7] The fear of communism and the ghost of civil ideological and social conflict shaped characteristic subjectivities

---

6   In Greece, personal archive collections are limited and concern specific upper-middle-class families that played an important part in Greek history, on whom there is a large number of studies. However, more personal collections including journals, correspondence of the involved bourgeois and other such texts, like the ones collected in Germany due to the specific tradition of the German bourgeoisie particularly during the period of its economic prevalence, are not available.

7   See also the interesting study by Panourgia (2013) about how specific groups of people and ideologies have been progressively associated since the end of the 19th century with the concept and content of "dangerous citizen" within the framework of implementation of biopolitical surveillance technologies aiming at the protection and further development of the capitalist system in Greece.

and mentalities, which, due to their contingency and volatility[8], could be showcased and described within the framework of the methodology of oral history and cultural anthropology.[9] As Karen O'Reilly points out, ethnography is "iterative-inductive research" (2007, p. 3), in the sense that it is shaped in the long run, during the field research but also through the experiences collected by the researcher, who takes each time a decision about the methods and techniques to be applied, depending on their suitability on a case-by-case basis.

In the wake of the study by Paul Thompson (2008), *Voice of the Past: Oral History*, a turning point in Britain's oral history, I tried to prepare my relationship with what I was looking for in the field. I built a questionnaire aiming at the reconstruction of an autobiographical narration,[10] mainly from Thompson's point of view, a comprehensive life story, but also a collection of biographical elements, which would help in the future indexing of the interviews of eyewitnesses (2008).

However, when I entered the field, I had many more problems to deal with, maybe also because I was not a stranger; this was not an unknown field I was entering for the first time, but the place and neighborhoods where I grew up and shaped my character. My choice to have different research fields in the city was probably the most appropriate solution, as in this way I could exit and enter different social and cultural spatialities, familiar and non-familiar ones. "Multi-sited" field research in an urban environment allowed for comparison and reflection on the dynamics of space and material reality through an interactive relationship, but provided also a framework for shaping the different subjectivities and social contexts (Marcus, 2008, pp. 67–108).[11] Following the theoretical model introduced by George Marcus, known as "Multi-Sited" Ethnography, I followed the tracks of microhistory, human beings themselves and their experiences, as these were lived and reconstructed within the framework of our interaction (Marcus, 1995).

Many theorists of oral history focused on the issue of "intersubjectivity", in the sense that during this interaction subjectivities are reconstructed and reshaped by both sides (Abrams, 2014, pp. 82–89). Both the narrator and the researcher participate in the conversation and in the social interaction, carrying experiences, memories, assumptions, gender-based standards and representations, which influence

---

8   In the sense that mentalities and subjectivities shaped as a result of a historic and social reality evolve and are constantly transformed integrating different elements and features within the framework of different social and cultural imperatives and needs.

9   On the methods of oral history that help study invisible aspects of history, for which there are no written sources and formal archives, see also Kyriakidou-Nestoros (1993b) and Niethammer (1980).

10   See also the interesting study on memory that narrates the history of urban space in Van Boeschoten et al., (2016).

11   On the interweaving of space and time see Nitsiakos (2003); on the spatial approaches of culture see Giannakopoulos and Giannitsiotis (2010).

communication and its content. In her exceptional text on the post-war generation of Italy, Luisa Passerini (1987) stresses the psychoanalytic dimension in recomposing a life narration. Fragments of experiences and memory are recalled composing a story, which certainly does not remain unaffected by emotions, repulsions, desires and disappointments of both the narrator and the researcher (Abrams, 2014, pp. 53–79). The narration takes place in a different context in the present and recomposes pieces of experiences codified in different social contexts and shaped by broader collectivities in the present and past (op.cit.).

It was impossible to remain unconcerned in this research, which was self-referential for a long period, by my own relationship with Toumba, my family and its history. In the dystopian environment of the Greek crisis[12], I found myself discussing about things that I had repelled, as I lived in a different cultural context for many years,[13] realizing in the headlines of German newspapers the tragic end of a society as I knew it or at least as I thought I knew it. In her very interesting introduction on ethnography, Loshini Naidoo refers to the method of "auto ethnography" (2012, p. 3) as a "critical ethnography" that goes beyond the objectives of "reflexive ethnography", whose only aim is to highlight by means of a critical analysis the power relations and injustice that may prevail in a culture. In "auto ethnography", researchers use their personal story, to propose a different narration in relation to the hegemonic discourses prevailing in the culture that is being studied and to challenge in this way the power structures preserved and reproduced by the prevailing narration (pp. 4–5).

My first contact with this subject started, therefore, as an "auto ethnography"[14] (Naidoo, 2012), from my parental home and my grandmother, my mother's mother, who was born in Kato Toumba in 1933 as the fourth child to a left-wing family of workers, refugees from Asia Minor. The endless transcriptions of the interviews with my grandmother created a new relationship between us, a confessional one; quite often, recalling her stories and experiences was bringing me in front a very different self from the one I knew as a child. It was the self of "self-presentation", as characteristically mentioned by Herzfeld, who, in good part, as we will see also later on,

---

12   Of particular interest are a series of cultural texts (literature, cinema etc.) produced during the period of the Greek financial crisis, which describe, according to Dimitris Papanikolaou, the transition from family-frame to family-short circuit, indirectly problematizing the dystopic present of the crisis in that structural part of the Greek society that was formerly described and lived as a shelter and place of security and balance. Within the context of the financial crisis, several young people are forced, due to unemployment, to go back to their parental homes, where they have to deal with the social rigidity and dysfunctionality of the traditional petty bourgeois Greek family (2018).

13   From 2005 to 2010 I studied and worked in North Rhine-Westphalia in Germany.

14   At this point, I would like to thank Prof. Emerita Voutira for suggesting this ethnographic approach.

was the result of strategies of normalization of refugees in the specific context of post-war growth and modernization, which favored the biggest possible expansion of the middle class.[15] My grandmother's sense of self, which was shaped and depicted through those interviews, was quite influenced by the fact that the person she was speaking to was no longer her little grandson, but a social scientist from Germany, as she used to say, who could handle calmly and in perfect confidentiality a lifetime's moments of a girl who grew up during the Nazi occupation with a communist father. Child labor, the neighborhood's outcry for the imprisoned father, her sister's death of tuberculosis and poverty highlighted aspects of a family story that paved the way for shaping my own subsequent subjectivity, as her grandson. My return to the Greece of crisis in 2011 after six years of absence in Western Germany, my mandatory enlistment in the infantry battalion of the Greek force of Cyprus, but also the beginning of the field survey in the city center of Thessaloniki in 2012 and in Kato Toumba in 2013 urged me to reconsider my own sense of self and reflect on the establishment of my own subjectivity, which had been shaped within the context of my family's need to participate after the war in the fight for upward social mobility passing through social recognition. In particular, in the context of the Greek crisis, the association of the middle class and Greek administration with corruption, the clientelist state and its incapacity to become European created my emphatic need, knowing well our family story, to propose a different version against these hegemonic discourses, which, in the 1950s as well as nowadays, allow for the implementation of harsh economic measures, in order for the country to meet the requirements of a voracious capitalism taking advantage of such self-awareness.[16]

My choice to start psychoanalysis in parallel with the field research during my stay in Thessaloniki allowed me very quickly to gain an overview over the management of the feelings I had to deal with on a daily basis in the city. A city that could not accept me back. Every day, I had to deal with the question of why I had chosen to go back to a country that "was dying"[17], to borrow the insightful title of the book by Dimitris Dimitriadis (2003), abandoning the Promised Land, as Germany was seen at that moment by my informants and colleagues. The psychoanalytic process allowed me to set limits between the observer and the person who participates in the

---

15   See also Potiropoulos (2003) on the process of integrating refugees into Greek society but also the significant contribution of Alki Kyriakidou-Nestoros to the shift of social research towards the study of cultural adaptation of refugees of 1922, at the level of mentality and ideology (as cited in Potiropoulos, 2001, p. 263).

16   See Herzfeld (2019, 2008) on the detailed categories of self-presentation and self-awareness suggested for the study of the Greek paradigm; see also Aranitou (2018).

17   Translated into English by the translator directly from the Greek text.

culture that is being studied and to manage the emotional impact of the research results on myself.[18]

Very soon I realized that the questionnaire could not help me, as it often blocked the flow of a spontaneous conversation and interaction with the people I met. I started writing in the research diary every detail that could help me understand the way in which the informants saw me in the field, but also the way in which they recomposed volatile and contingent subjectivities on the occasion of our encounter.[19]

Even the refusal to meet me within the framework of the research in Kato Toumba could complement the experience of the consent of an informant, in order to spend some time together at the informant's personal place: "My child does not want to meet you. What are the neighbors going to say? A widow that allows a man to enter her home? Let's better discuss here", she says, "at Eleni's place".[20]

In addition to the notes, the informants quite often gave me things to take with me or spoke to me almost always through things they bought or made after the end of the civil war. Without ever having worked on theories of material culture prior to this study, I realized that in this specific field and for this generation of people who grew up without IKEA, belongings contributed to establishing a different sense of self and a unique individualization of the experience they wished to tell. These informants were not familiar with what Abrams (2014, p. 54) describes as a confessional cultural context of the western world,[21] since most of them were influenced by the

---

18   See also Luisa Passerini (1987) on the role of her personal psychoanalysis within the context of her study on the post-war generation of students in Italy, to which she belonged too, the generation of 1968. As pointed out by Joan Wallach Scott in her introductory note on the English translation of Passerini's book *Autoritratto di gruppo*: Passerini "uses interviews not to collect facts, not to clarify what did and did not happen in the past, but to explore the ways in which the relationship between private and public, and personal and political is negotiated. It is this negotiation that produces identity and the sense of belonging to a collectivity, be it "women", "the working class", or the generation of 1968". (Passerini, 2004, pp. xii–xiii).

19   See also Zermpoulis (2017) on the use of personal belongings and specifically of family photo albums aiming at the performative reproduction and shaping of subjectivity during the interview. The subjectivity is described as volatile and contingent, as it is spontaneous and open to the randomness of the moment and the impact of the researcher's presence, but also the use of things during the interview. Quite often, the researcher is invited to take a picture of the informants at their home following their suggestions, while the family heirlooms used to decorate the home are called forth by the subject to shape and reproduce, during the interview, a personal narration justifying the subject's choices and way of living.

20   Excerpt from an interview in Toumba. All excerpts of interviews and conversations with informants were originally in Greek. They were translated into English by the translator.

21   More specifically, Abrams (2014, pp. 54–55) mentions that in the countries of the developed western world people live in a confessional cultural context, in which the disclosure of aspects of the self considered private until now is normalized through the public consump-

characteristic feature of the Greek middle classes, who avoid referring to what is taking place in the domestic realm. "Others", seen always as a whole, represent a threat, seeking an opportunity to bring dishonor and disillusion the family image that represents every home as a unit in Greece. Besides, the phrase "one should not air one's dirty laundry in public"[22] is rather well known and still influences the second generation, meaning the children of my informants, who were born at the beginning of 1950s and are suspicious towards the modern social media and the modalities in which the private suddenly becomes public.

The people with whom I spoke opened up to me at their place and mainly in those areas of their home which served to show their relatively public or better their social image.[23] A living room illuminated with huge chandeliers, where there was dark carved furniture and numerous decorative objects was almost always the place where I met my informants. The sense of self they wished to recompose during our meeting was going through belongings, which also helped the process of remembering and recalling fragments of memory, as they were linked with the most important family moments. As Abrams points out, human beings codify, which then makes it easier to invoke important life events, but without reproducing the feelings they experienced at that moment (Abrams, 2014, pp. 126–127). According to Serematakis (2018, p. 110), memory is sensorial and intertwined with matter, reaching us in bits and pieces, not as a whole. Seremetakis stresses that memory, both private and public, is invested in materialities, places and things that have the potential to evoke specific emotions (op. cit.).

The theories of material culture and in particular the theoretical analytical tool of "materiality" (Miller, 2005) helped me understand the modalities in which the identity of *noikokyris* is shaped and reproduced in the private and public urban space through the contact with the belongings a *noikokyris* uses and possesses. The material world of *noikokyraioi* informants is the context, as described by Ervin Goffmann (1975), in which they perceive themselves but also the "frame", according to Sir Ernst Hans Josef Combrich (1979), in which their action is shaped.[24]

---

tion of interviews of celebrities, personal references of the popular press to successes and tragedies, and systematic focus of the media on the private life of those exposed to public view.

22 English translation of the Greek idiomatic expression "*τα εν οίκω, μη εν δήμω*" (translator's note). This popular phrase has been used also by Skouteri-Didaskalou in her well-known study (1984, pp. 77–110) for the particular interweaving of the private and public sphere, especially regarding women and the association of Greek women with home and family.

23 On the terms "perform" and "performance", in the sense of the social action itself, which is defined by a ritual repetition determining also the subject, see Butler (2009).

24 As we will see also in Chapter I, texts *Frame analysis* by Goffmann and *The sense of Order: A Study in the psychology of Decorate Art* by Gombrich influenced the establishment of Miller's theory on "materiality" (as cited in Gialouri, 2012, p. 28).

In her very interesting study about security issues, but also their link with modern life in Greece, Bakalaki (2003) highlights the importance of belongings and home within the framework of a *noikokyremenos* (tidy) way of living, as this has been shaped historically, but also within the context of change experienced by people in Greece in the post-war period due to the economic growth. The anthropologist explains that home and belongings in the context of modernization of the country are linked to the modern subject who must, as a real *noikokyris*, deal with the risks entailed by this growth and change. The home and belongings that the *noikokyris* must safeguard by buying expensive and modern security systems express this very transition of the subject from poverty and necessity to the wealth and prosperity of modern life.

As we will see in the next chapters, the informants do not feel petty bourgeois or simply *noikokyraioi*.[25] *Noikokyraios* (man or woman) is an identity with specific gender-based features, which is inextricably linked with the policies of the Greek nation-state, the appropriate everyday urban life and the desirable or sought-after way of living of a people that reproduces behaviors, which can be explained on the basis of the "crypto-colonial" (Herzfeld, 2002) version of the western capitalist three-thousand-year-old Greek nation, but also of the segmentation that characterizes the Greek national process of homogenization (Papataxiarchis, 2006b, 2006c).[26]

---

25 The term "petty bourgeois" is thoroughly analyzed in Chapter II *"INTRODUCTION: 'Transformation' and 'Petty Bourgeoisism'. Greek class distinctiveness and theories of 'underdevelopment'"*. Regarding the terms *noikokyris* and *noikokyra*, these are used literally and refer to the person that manages his/her household issues. In particular the female term *noikokyra* refers to a woman who does not work and is in charge of tasks that in the Greek context of patriarchy are associated with her gender-based identity, see also: Skouteri-Didaskalou (1984) and Bakalaki (1994). Almost all informants of this generation had a positive view of women's dedication to "household issues". A woman's work outside the household automatically meant that "paterfamilias" could not fulfill the obligations that corresponded to his gender. Characteristic descriptions are provided by Renée Hirschon (2006) in her field research in Piraeus, but also by Kokot (1994, 1996) in Kato Toumba. However, as we will see also in Chapter IV of the thesis *"Things in post-war home: modernity, innovation and becoming a noikokyra/noikokyris"*, the gender-based identity in the context of class perception of *noikokyraioi*, as this is shaped in the post-war era and results from ethnographic examples, differs from that of cultural representations of the Greek ethnography of 1960s and 1970s (Campbell, 1964; Friedl, 1962, 1963). The *noikokyraies-noikokyres* of Toumba are women, who, through their social and financial practices and strategies in the public sphere, bring the two spheres together with the aim of the best possible achievement of the goal in the context of the household code (Papataxiarchis, 2006a), which is the increase of profit for their family.

26 From the point of view of ethnographies of post-colonial criticism one could approach these subjects as derivatives of the intertemporal impact of the "foreign" financial and cultural forces in Greece, mainly as a result of the constant interaction and cultural interplay in terms of copying (e.g. as a "mimic man", as this is described in Bhabha, 1994, p. 86), with domestic but also foreign (mainly European) elites (see also Papailia, 2016).

The *noikokyraioi*, at least as they result from this ethnography in Thessaloniki, are *ethnikofrones*[27] and perceive themselves mainly in the context of serving the duties undertaken upon their birth, within the system of Greek patriarchy and ethnocentric objective setting for constant progress and prosperity of the nation.

The Greek ethnography of the second generation of anthropologists (Papataxiarchis, 2006b) is very important for the investigation of the shaping of gender-based identities, as this has been shaped historically through the feminist criticism and the theoretical transition, as characteristically mentioned by Bakalaki, from "Anthropology of Women to Anthropology of Genders"[28] (Bakalaki, 1994, p. 34). The gender-based identities of the middle classes of *noikokyraioi* must be seen on the basis of the specific model of the Greek *noikokyrio*, as this was analyzed by Greek and foreign ethnographers of the Greek paradigm (Papataxiarchis, 2006a; Dubisch, 2019; Salamone & Stanton, 2019; Hirschon, 2006). The Greek household and, therefore, the Greek family, is socially and culturally readjusted and reproduced in the post-war and cold-war context of Thessaloniki, functioning as a "financial business", aiming, by means of the code of complementarity underpinning it, at increasing the profit (Papataxiarchis, 2006a; Salamone & Stanton, 2019; Bakalaki, 2003), not only of itself, but also of the post-war Greek state.

In 2013, I visited for the first time the archive of *DEI*[29] in Thessaloniki, without knowing exactly what I was looking for. The fact that the electrification of the whole country was one of the leading goals of the American programs for the reconstruction of the Greek economy played an important part in taking this decision. However, the constant reference of the people I met in the field to the experience of getting and using household appliances during the first post-war decades and in particular the association of these practices with the identity of the "modern" subject played an even more important part in taking this decision. In particular, the mnemonic narrations that recomposed the social impact that this acquisition had rendered necessary the choice to study the way in which this service of the state managed so quickly to become part of the social memory, of the cultural and financial change that my informants experienced during the first post-war decades. The electrification and fashionable household electrical appliances facilitate the fulfillment of the big post-war dream.

---

27   It is a Greek term associated in the early post-war decades with the non-leftist middle classes to designate a person with national consciousness. This word is used as an opposite for "communist", who was considered as a "traitor", an "enemy of the homeland" in the Greek civil war and post-civil war context.

28   Translator's exact translation from Greek.

29   This is a transcription of the Greek acronym "ΔΕΗ", referring to the Greek Public Power Corporation (translator's note).

In May 2015, after the completion of the field ethnographic research in Thessa-loniki, I decided to study the archive of *Pronoia*[30], which was kept in the City Planning Office of the Region of Central Macedonia. I made this choice because I was interested in the planning itself of the material reality of Toumba by *EAP* (Refugee Settlement Commission) and in how the state itself managed the cultural and social integration of Christian refugees few years after the integration of the city itself into the Greek state.[31] This choice aimed by no means at shaping a full picture of the field, as I did not believe, and still do not believe, in closed and fixed cultural systems that can be represented in the ethnographic text (see also Gkefou-Madianou, 2008, 1999; Clifford & Marcus, 1986; Deltsou, 1995).

My approach respects the volatility and contingency of the research findings, but also the partial nature of the research results (O'Reilly, 2007; Marcus & Fisher, 1986; Gkefou-Madianou, 2008). Besides, the basic aim in the choice of the methods was to organize a small-scale qualitative survey, to understand specific practices and behaviors of human beings, in the different social and cultural contexts in which they took and still take place, following the encouragement of the great sociologist of social functions of memory Maurice Halbwachs (2013).

Finally, in August 2015, I earned a scholarship from the German Academic Exchange Service (DAAD) and returned to Germany and more specifically to the Department of Cultural Anthropology of the University of Hamburg. My stay quite far from the field, the department itself and my colleagues there helped me start the analysis of the ethnographic material and of the ninety interviews that I had collected and transcribed in Greece. The circumstance of my personal encounter with the anthropologist who did the first field research in Kato Toumba in the 1980s, Waltraud Kokot, Professor at the Department of Ethnology of Hamburg, who generously shared with me the whole material of her own ethnographic research to be processed and integrated into mine, was particularly important.

---

30   Transcription of the Greek named entity *"Πρόνοια"*, which means "Welfare" (translator's note).

31   This spatial dimension of the experience of refugeeism and its association with the shaping of a refugee consciousness in three generations, as this was studied by the postgraduate research program of Kyriakidou-Nestoros (1993a), is very important because the "new" place of settlement is a special place, a "significant place in the map" as Skouteri-Didaskalou (as cited in Potiropoulos, 2003, p. 15) put it, a place connecting "before" with "after", explaining the particular identity of refugees (Potiropoulos, 2003, p. 16).

2. Introduction: "Transformation" and *"Petty Bourgeoisism"*
Greek class distinctiveness and theories of "underdevelopment"

The end of the Second World War finds the country in ruins. A large part of its building stock and infrastructure has been destroyed (Antonopoulou, 1991, p. 174). The political climate in post-war Greece is quite tense. The conservative political forces that prevailed with the intervention of the British and, subsequently, of the Americans fear the potential prevalence of the left-wing ideology that inspires and leads the popular masses, which emerged through *EAM*[1] and the national resistance movement during the Nazi occupation (Mazower, 2000, pp. 14–31; Panourgia, 2013, p. 61; Voglis, 2014, pp. 102–135). The clash between left and right-wingers will lead the country into a long period of civil strife, with its well-known post-war repercussions that shaped the political culture and the relationship between citizens and the state (Antonopoulou, 1991; Dertilis, 2016; Iatridis, 1984; Mazower, 2000, pp. 14–31; Panourgia, 2013; Voglis, 2014).

In 1947, and as the Civil War rages in the country, the Greek government, in cooperation with the government of the United States, chooses to follow the way of the capitalist countries and joins the American program for the reconstruction of the devastated by war Europe (Voglis, 2014, pp. 248–251). The program of the American General and Secretary of State George C. Marshall (1948) will be the catalyst for the final establishment of the two opposite sides of the Cold War, which had already started (Giannoulopoulos, 1992, p. 103; Panourgia, 2013, p. 61). The main goal of the Americans was the strengthening of the military and economic cooperation of the European countries, which would act as a rival to the policies of the Soviet Union (Voglis, 2014, p. 250). On the occasion of the European Recovery Program (1947), the creation of supranational economic and military entities by the capitalist countries

---

1 Acronym for "National Liberation Front", in Greek: *Ethniko Apeleftherotiko Metopo (Εθνικό Απελευθερωτικό Μέτωπο)* (translator's note).

will soon be under way, like those of the European Economic Community (EEC) and the North Atlantic Treaty Organization (NATO). [2]

The Greek political forces and the representatives of the US aid seek to achieve significant structural changes and institutional reforms through the Marshall Plan. Their objective is the complete economic and social transformation of the Greek state.

2.1 Discourses of development and reconstruction

The arguments for the rapid industrialization and the proposals for a successful transformation of the Greek agricultural economy into a capitalist one seem to develop already in the pre-war period[3] and intensify after the end of the Second World War (Chatziiosif, 1993, pp. 23–33; Antonopoulou, 1991, pp. 55–71; Dertilis, 2015, p. 35; Aranitou, 2018).

The rhetoric of development through the formation of heavy industry can be found across the ideological spectrum of the political elites of the country since the interwar period already.[4]

For many, the US aid appears to be a great opportunity in this political and economic context. The country would be able to claim through foreign investments a different position in the global division of labor (Stathakis, 2000, pp. 46–48). According to the new model of development, the agricultural model of the Greek economy and the limited manufacturing production that dominated in the pre-war years should transform into a capitalist mode of production based on big capital accumulation and export-oriented industrialization (Giannitsis, 1985).

However, to grasp the background and the importance of this post-war aspiration, it is useful to briefly mention the history of these choices. As previously indicated, already since the end of the 19th century, the political and social elites of the country had sought to achieve its structural reconstruction through the promotion

---

2   Giannoulopoulos (1992, p. 106).

3   See the interesting study by Potamianos (2015) on the lower middle-class of *noikokyraioi* of Athens from 1870 to 1920.

4   I am, specifically, referring to the proposal by the TEE President Anargyros Dimitrakopoulos (1938) *"On reconstruction"*, the proposal by Dimitris Batsis and the Communist Party of Greece (1945) for the development of heavy industry through the exploitation of natural resources and the native workforce, the article by Admiral Andreas Chatzikiriakos (1936) on the establishment of a metal industry and the serving of the Greek arms industry, the Zolotas report (1948) on the sustainability of the Greek economy, and, finally the Varvaresos report (1952) which moved to the opposite direction of a more liberal income and credit policy. See Chatziiosif (1993, pp. 23–33), Karagianni and Nikolaou (1993, pp. 95–114); Liodakis (1993, pp. 77–94).

of plans for the creation of heavy and productive industries. More specifically, according to studies on the economic and political history of Greece, in the last quarter of the 19th century and the first decades of the 20th century, the first major economic transformation of the Greek economy is observed. It mainly consists of indirect investments or foreign capital penetration, the export-led commercialization of the agricultural production, and the development of manufacturing production (Mouzelis, 1978, pp. 38–50; Dertilis, 2015, p. 75). In addition, the tariff policy implemented by the Greek governments during this period seems to have helped in this direction, since it contributed to reducing imports of consumer goods and raw materials that were now supplied domestically (Antonopoulou, 1991, pp. 50–55).

This first economic transformation, combined with the consequences of the more than double increase in the territory and population of the country at the end of the 19th and the beginning of the 20th century, triggered important changes in both the political and social shaping of Greece during that era (Tsitselikis, 2006; Potamianos, 2015; Dertilis, 2015). The resulting inequalities were expressed in class terms: new classes and ideas appeared, threatening the established pre-capitalist social schemes. The progressive urbanization but also the social mobility observed in the beginning of the 20th century due to changes in the economy contribute to the appearance of new lower middle-class strata that are concentrated in the capital. According to Potamianos (2015) and Dertilis (2015), the great inequality in taxation, resulting from the political choice of supporting the agricultural strata and the upper bourgeoisie, will lead to popular reactions that culminate in the Goudi coup (1909) (Dertilis, 2015, pp. 845–847). According to Potamianos, the Greek petty bourgeois of that period will, for the first time, express themselves in a unified manner trying to defend the interests of their social class, which the author describes as the class of *noikokyraioi*, professionals and manufacturers or traditional petty bourgeoisie following the distinction made by Poulantzas (1985) differentiating them from the new lower middle-class strata of salaried employees (Potamianos, 2015, pp. 1–14).

Potamianos (2015) refers specifically to Athens, which, from 1870 to 1920, grew enormously, resulting in the formation of these new classes described also by Poulantzas, which are also associated with the transformation of the capitalist mode of production. More specifically, according to the author (2015, p. 38), during that era Athens became the administrative center of the country, where 15% of public employees lived and worked. According to him, besides an admin worker city, Athens was many other things as the seat of the palace and capital of high society social life, attracting at the end of the 19th century the bourgeois families from the countryside and abroad; Athens was also the seat of the stock exchange and big banks, university and numerous schools, health services, technical companies and scientific institutions. Therefore, based on the distinction made by Poulantzas (1985), Potamianos (2015) believes that this new petty bourgeoisie, the salaried strata of Athens, is the result of the expanded reproduction of the capitalist mode of production that threatens the presence of the traditional strata; for this reason, they try to organize themselves in order to defend their interests in a structured way and avoid their complete extinction. [5]

In the very interesting study by Aranitou (2018, p. 127) on the consequences of the economic crisis for the traditional Greek lower middle-class from 2009 to date, the class of *noikokyraioi* is a "clear legacy" of pre-war Greece and reestablishes itself in the post-war era as a result of that specific historical circumstance. Panagiotopoulos (2021, pp. 99–100) notes the absence of a historical sociology of the middle classes in Greece. According to him, such a sociology would give the opportunity to study the social dimensions of this phenomenon at the level of lived experiences. Panagiotopoulos wonders whether what we call the "middle class" in Greece has its "sociological ancestors" in the old middle class of the *noikokyraioi* of the late 19th century and early 20th century and the class that was caught between the conservative urban elitism and the rural tradition, the Athenian modernism and the working-class laicism, in Greece of social modernism and the new collective identities and the cursed of the metropolitan margin that clearly coexist, e.g. in the 1960s (2021, p. 99).

The Great Depression of 1929 and the fact that Greece, contrary to the rest of Europe, will be at war for almost the entire 1940s, will lead to the abrupt end of the above developments. The initial hopes and expectations fostered by the quite promising Truman Doctrine (1947) as well as the first four-year reconstruction plan of America will suddenly come to an end, when international developments will force the United States to differentiate its policy in Europe. The central agencies implementing the Marshall Plan decided not to disturb, more so after the Korean War, the delicate balance between France, Great Britain, and Germany (Stathakis, 1993, pp. 41–56). Thus, the main goal of the American program should be the restarting of the economic system that was destroyed by the war, making Germany the economic and defense regulator inside Europe, especially after the capitulation to France in the context of the Schuman Plan (Giannoulopoulos, 1992, p. 130; Chatziiosif, 1993, pp. 28–29). Within this context, most of the reconstruction programs implemented in post-war Greece focused on the application of stabilization policies and not on the structural reconstruction of the Greek economy (Stathakis, 1993, pp. 41–56).

Initially the economy of the country went into recession due also to the conservative policies of the US programs. From 1952 and onwards the rise to power of General Papagos, an unprecedented policy of liberalization of the Greek market was implemented, aiming at rapidly attracting foreign investments. Many scholars present the specific legal and institutional framework that was established in that period

---

5   On the distinction between a new and a traditional lower middle-class made by Poulantzas, see also in Aranitou (2018, pp. 93–106).

as "colonial", since it was particularly favorable for foreign investors, at the expense mainly of the small-scale commercial production, which was, until then, the model of development of the Greek economy (Mouzelis, 1978, pp. 272–283; Antonopoulou, 1991, p. 57).

These measures were particularly destructive for the agricultural populations, while still consistent with the framework of national planning seeking rapid urbanization and modernization, in order to disrupt the radicalization of the countryside (Aranitou, 2018, p. 124).[6] The complete lifting of economic protectionism, which had been established in the pre-war years, but also the disruption of any economic assistance in the form of subsidies for agricultural production forced a large part of the population to abandon the countryside and find their way to the big urban centers, mainly Athens (Tsoukalas, 1981, p. 115; Antonopoulou, 1991, p. 57). Already by 1951, the share of the agricultural production in the Gross Domestic Product dropped significantly by 20%-30% (Antonopoulou, 1991, p. 73). This percentage will progressively decrease in favor of industrial production and, especially, the development of the service sector. This is of course directly linked to the choice of the Greek state to proceed with a radical social transformation and the overturning of the Greek model of small-scale commercial and agricultural production against the advice of American technocrats to choose a conservative and stability-oriented income and monetary policy. However, the capital investments sought by the Greek government will not happen until, at least, the early 1960s, when the completion of the reconstruction programs of the metropolitan European states will open the first round of investments (Charalambis, 1989, pp. 186).

The decade of the 1950s is notably important for the first major public investments that took place in infrastructure projects, transportation, communication and, primarily, energy. One of the biggest projects is the electrification of the country, which will contribute to the development of the secondary sector during the next decade (Antonopoulou, 1991, pp. 91–92). In the 1950s, the Greek economy shows a very high GDP growth rate of 6.6%, except for the period 1957–1960, which is characterized by a lower GDP growth rate due to the decrease in manufacturing production and a balance of payments deficit (op.cit.).

However, the period of the greatest possible development and transformation of the Greek society was that of the 1960s (Stathakis, 2000, pp. 43–65; Charalambis, 1989, pp. 190–191; Karapostolis, 1983, pp. 120–121). During that period and especially towards its end, the Greek economy showed enormous growth rates, with its GDP skyrocketing to 8.7% (Mouzelis, 1978, p. 179; Antonopoulou, 1991, p. 88). It is worth noting that in public discourse this development is comparable to that of Japan and

---

6   This change was considerably influenced by the massive cleansing of the mountain villages that had taken place in the previous years and led to the large-scale displacement of the rural population of the country, see Voglis (2014, p. 321).

is considered by many as an economic miracle. During that period, a large inflow of foreign capital, mainly American, is observed, which is invested in the production of capital goods (metals, chemical products, metallic structures, etc.) (Mouzelis, 1978, p. 278; Antonopoulou, 1991, pp. 97–105). It is worth mentioning that, while industrialization begins and major companies have the largest share of domestic industrial production in relation to their investment in Greece, this will not have the expected multiplier effect on the Greek economy. However, industrial production in Greece increases, especially if we compare it with the recession in the agricultural sector. In particular, the growth rate of industrial production first reaches 9.5% in the 1960s, while towards the end of the decade and until the first oil crisis of 1973–74 it hits 13.5% (Antonopoulou, 1991, p. 92).

These developments are taken together with the demographic transformation of Greek society, in which, for the first time in its history, the percentage of the urban population out of the total Greek population is larger than that of the agricultural one, since by 1971 65% of the population lives in urban or semi-urban areas of the country (Karapostolis, 1983, p. 109). Of particular interest is the fact that, in the period of 1968–1976, the countries described as "peripheral" by the Dependency Theory, which makes a distinction between core and periphery, demonstrate higher growth rates in industry than the so-called "metropolitan" countries. Greece, specifically, which is placed by the majority of scholars among the countries of peripheral development, shows, as mentioned earlier, an increase of 13.5%, when the corresponding percentage for the "metropolitan" countries is 5.3% and for the other "peripheral" countries is 8.2% (Antonopoulou, 1991, pp. 92–93). According to Antonopoulou (1991), this is linked to the global division of labor and the post-war policy of "metropolitan" countries to de-industrialize and focus on the development of high technology (op.cit.).

Following the interpretative scheme of "peripheral modernization", "metropolitan countries" invest a big capital, not in the form of state loans for the strengthening of the economy as in the 19th century, but as direct investments in the economy of the "developing" world through the establishment of multinational companies. Such investment practices were based on the logic of development theories, according to which, the change in the mode of production of the "traditional" countries to an exclusively capitalist one with capital-centered structures would lead to the "modernization" of their societies, as it happened in Western Europe at the end of the 19th century (Ferguson, 2005, pp. 166–181).

Undoubtedly, as the aforementioned historical overview and, to some extent, the figures and statistics reveal, Greece saw a rapid development and increase of its living standards, while its infrastructure and administration were modernized and improved to satisfactory compared to the pre-war and war years. According to a relevant study by Karapostolis (1983) on the consumer behavior of the Greeks in the 1960s, private consumption in Greece increased dramatically, mainly because of the increase in the average disposable income and the lifestyle transformation of the majority of the Greeks, among whom the urban lifestyle became the predominant one. What is interesting in the social research conducted by Karapostolis is that its empirical data contradict those analyses derived from the Marxist model rendering consumption patterns and practices dependent on the position of the social subjects in the relations of production. More specifically, Karapostolis (1983) holds that, in the 1960s, a convergence is observed in a series of expenditures between the popular and higher strata, leading to the development of similar consumer practices. In a few words, Karapostolis stresses the massive petty bourgeoisification of society in terms of the ways and possibilities of people to consume in that era.

Nevertheless, some neo-Marxist Greek theorists (Tsoukalas, 1981, 2005; Mouzelis, 1978) interpret this kind of development as "underdevelopment" (Mouzelis, 1978).

2.1.1 "Underdevelopment" in Greece

From the 1970s to the end of the 1990s, Greece is placed by social and political scientists, such as Charalambis (1989), Mouzelis (1978) and Tsoukalas (1981), within the broader framework of peripheral development countries characterized by "underdevelopment" and "foreign dependence". This theory, which seems to have a significant degree of influence on studies trying primarily to analyze the post-war Greek world (Liakos, 2004, pp. 360–415; Panagiotopoulos, 2021, p. 96), positions itself critically on one hand and on the other hand dialogues with the respective theories of development that are characterized by an evolutionary and structural-functionalist conceptual perspective (Ferguson, 2005, pp. 166–181).

According to this theory, the Greek manufacturing production faces a problem of "articulation" and "assembly" (Mouzelis, 1978, pp. 85–144; Giannitsis, 1985, pp. 17–22; Giannoulopoulos, 1991, p. 369) vis-à-vis the remaining production of both the secondary sector and the small commercial production. The resources of the small commercial production go to heavy industry through an unequal taxation system, and the already modernized sector cannot incorporate the more traditional sectors of the economy into its own model of development by means of reinvestment. For as long as Greece does not manage to build an industry, like the one developed in Western Europe in the 19th century, it is condemned to foreign dependency, a parasitic *petty bourgeoisism* linked to the enlargement of the tertiary sector of the economy and the small, commercial and agricultural production, and, finally, an "illegitimate" parliamentarianism born by a clientelist system balancing inequalities and preventing the manifestation of social tensions (Mouzelis, 1978, pp. 90–96; Tsoukalas, 2005, pp. 17–52, 1981, pp. 102–139; Charalambis, 1989).

In this context of "underdevelopment", Greece demonstrates social, cultural, and political characteristics at the level of the superstructure of a "dependent peripheral economy" (Tsoukalas, 1981; Mouzelis, 1978; Filias, 1974). The "apparent", according to (neo)Marxist analysts, economic progress and improvement in indicators such as growth rate, GDP per capita, and standard of living are mainly based on undeclared resources and non-productive or "parasitic" activities developed extra-institutionally in the Greek society and linked to the phenomenon of "underdevelopment" (op.cit.).

More specifically, the agricultural masses arriving to Athens and, to a lesser degree, to Thessaloniki in the early 1950s do not manage to find work in the domestic manufacturing production, which until the end of this decade shows a declining trend. These social strata become active in commerce and the service sector in general, expanding what they think is an unproductive tertiary sector, while a large part of them work in the also "unproductive" and "parasitic" construction sector (Tsoukalas, 1981; Mouzelis, 1978; Filias, 1974; Charalambis, 1989).

From the mid-1950s, a large percentage of the population that cannot survive in urban centers as a consequence of "underdevelopment" is led to emigration. A "peripheral country" is sending cheap labor to a "metropolitan country". The remittances from migrants and the development of tourism, especially towards the end of the 1950s, contribute to the increase of undeclared resources in the "peripheral country", covering thus itself against the balance of payments liabilities created as a result of the limited exports of industrial goods.

In parallel, and already from the 1950s, the great need for housing caused by the rural flight leads to the progressive development of the construction sector. In the post-war era, and contrary to other European countries, housing construction will be based almost exclusively on a system of self-financing, which is favored by the extensive land fragmentation in Greece and the private savings of a rising middle class (Papamichos, 2000, pp. 79–86). The dynamics of this sector will contribute to the parallel development of industry and, especially, the sector that provides the reconstruction effort with the necessary materials, without any need for equipment or imports of raw materials (Giannitsis, 1985, pp. 17–18).

Construction through the *antiparochi*[7] system will not lead to a significant capital accumulation; however, it will allow for a surplus redistribution to take place among all the actors participating in the construction of an apartment building in the form of low or high incomes for many years (Antonopoulou, 1991, pp. 187–192). According to Antonopoulou (1991, p. 182), this system will not create "big capitalists", but will contribute to the improvement of the living standards of those involved, while the remittances from migrants and marine workers, which are heavily invested in the construction sector, will make it the "locomotive" of the Greek economy until the burst of the financial crisis in 2010.

---

7   The *antiparochi (αντιπαροχή)* is a formal, legally binding agreement involving a flats-for-land exchange between the signing parties (translator's note).

Due to the particular political conditions of the peculiar Democracy of the post-war era, this development was characterized by an unfair and violent distribution of wealth and power (Elefantis, 2002), which, according to the social scientists of "underdevelopment", benefited mainly the strata connected to the sectors supporting it. In fact, these strata are, in ideological terms, either connected to or tolerating such policies when tempted by the profit-making development (Charalambis, 1989).

2.1.2   Middle class as parasitic and extra-institutional mobility

In this specific socio-political context, a new middle class is shaped; it is characterized by a "parasitic" and "extra-institutional" upward mobility (Tsoukalas, 1977, 1981, 2005; Charalambis, 1985, 1989; Mouzelis, 1978). Greece presents the characteristics of a mass democracy that follows the post-war Fordist model of development, which is characterized by the enlargement of the middle class and, especially, its lower middle-class strata. Concerning their cultural practices, these strata are distinguished by their pointless and conspicuous consumption as well as their lack of bourgeois education and culture (Karapostolis, 1983; Kremmydas, 1993:16; Tsoukalas, 1981, pp. 115–128). In Greece, and according to Greek scholars (Axelos, 2010; Kondylis, 2011; Dertilis, 2015; Kostis & Dertilis, 1991), the shaping of this class presents different features due to the Greek class distinctiveness, or the lack of a "Western-style" bourgeoisie that drew its characteristics from its financial outlook and the lifestyle of its industrial magnates.

2.1.3   On *petty bourgeoisism*: from criticism to connotations

The discourse[8] developed in the social sciences and humanities from the 1970s onwards links the economic "underdevelopment" of Greece to the appearance of a widespread *petty bourgeoisism*. As a mentality, *petty bourgeoisism*[9] is not interpreted in classist terms only but is shaped on the basis of an ideology that helps sustain its reproduction and is directly linked to the "inherent" characteristics of the political, social and economic shaping of modern Greece (Potamianos, 2015, p. 7; Aranitou, 2018, pp. 119–149). This *petty bourgeoisism* mentality is substantialized and described as an inherent attribute, the deeper essence of a people trying to become European

---

8   By the term "discourse" I mean the discourses that, from time to time, were expressed publicly at an academic level or at the level of the political and social opinion. Such discourses unfolded from specific political and ideological starting points.

9   More specifically, Aranitou (2018, p. 127) states that, as a phenomenon, *petty bourgeoisism* concerned not only the urban centers, but the entire territory. As a mentality, *petty bourgeoisism* was massively adopted, acquiring thus an "ideological content" in the context of the subsequent analysis of the aspects of the Greek transformation.

and developed,[10] but its very essence, its Ottoman past and its dependence on another essence, that of the West, prevent them from finding a free and authentic pace. This is exemplified by the viewpoint of Diamantouros, who proposed the use of the term "cultural dualism" to better understand the particularity of the Greek social shaping (Diamantouros, 2000, as cited in Aranitou, 2018, p. 144). According to this author, a large part of the Greek society is dominated by an "obsolete culture" (op.cit.). This culture is characterized by its "anti-European spirit, widespread xenophobia, localism, introversion, a sense of inferiority towards the West, etc." (op.cit.). The mentality of the Greek society is mainly paternalistic, and this is why it failed to integrate into the modern environment of capitalist market, remaining deeply pre-capitalist (op.cit.). According to Diamantouros (2000, p. 41, as quoted in Aranitou, 2018, p. 145), the obsolete culture does not concern the entirety of the Greek society, but is limited to the traditional lower middle-class strata, which are held responsible for the low productivity and competitiveness of the Greek economy. Diamantouros (2000, p. 53, as quoted in Aranitou, 2018, p. 146) emphasizes that this social group finds the reforms repulsive due to its identification with the old and obsolete practices of its long Ottoman legacy.

Aranitou (2018, pp. 152–153) considers that the politico-ideological public discourses criticizing the social/economic organization of the country, which started already before the crisis, paved the way for the implementation of the strict policies in the era of memoranda, whose goal was, again, the structural transformation of the socio-economic organization of Greece. Aranitou (2018) brings back to the discussion of social and political sciences the topic of class as well as the problematic of the Marxist analysis in relation to a multilayered middle class that, on an abstract and theoretical level of analysis, would disappear in favor of the working class when the capitalist mode of production solely prevailed (2018, p. 55). Following the analysis by Aranitou, the treatment of the historical juncture in Marxist texts and, in particular, the analysis by Poulantzas on the differentiation between "traditional" and "new" petty bourgeoisie helps us understand the ways in which the middle class, and especially the "new" one, managed to reproduce themselves in the developed world during the post-war era as a result of the political, economic, and social choices of the post-war urban middle class (2018, pp. 93–106). Panagiotopoulos (2021, pp. 91–92) points out that recently during the years of the financial crisis (2010–2018) there has been a special focus on the Greek "middle class". According to him, for the first time the middle class is being named as such in public discourse, replacing other names, usually with negative and derogatory meanings that the specific social space used to take on (op.cit.). This is certainly linked to the fact that this class was particularly

---

10   On the theories making a distinction between the contemporary Western world and the more traditional pre-capitalist societies, but also on the critique leveled against such linear and evolutionary approaches and analyses, see Deltsou (1995).

threatened during this period and thus there was a need for its social history to be read more in its modern dimension than through the scheme of the underdeveloped petty-bourgeois country of the semi-periphery (op.cit.). As Panagiotopoulos aptly observes, Greek society and social formation in Greece should not be exoticised and treated as something different from the countries of central Europe (2021, p. 100). It seems that the morphological developments that took place in advanced capitalism are not unfamiliar to Greek society, given that what Panagiotopoulos describes as a "western (petty bourgeoisation) trend" seems to be similar to the historical development of middle classes in Greece (op.cit).

Of particular interest on the same topic is the text by Bakalaki (2008, pp. 519–571) in the collective volume on the anthropological theory and ethnography by Gkefou-Madianou (2008), which attempts to soften the extreme ambiguity that, according to many theorists, permeates the Greek culture: it seems to hover between the opposite poles of, on one hand, a European-Western Greece or one that aspires to become European-Western and, on the other hand, a Greek state with native (*Rhō-maïika*) characteristics linked to the agrarian culture or the stigma of Ottoman influence.[11] By comparing the official discourses on gender and especially the issue of the education of women, which were developed in the 19th century in both Europe and Greece, with the discourses from below as highlighted by the ethnographic research in Greece from the 1960s onwards, the anthropologist demonstrated the existence of convergences, consistencies and resonances instead of diametrical oppositions between them. Bakalaki stresses that the opposition between the West and Greece is rather an artefact one, since Greek official discourses on gender seem to converse with and are influenced by similar perceptions in Europe already from the first years of the Greek state. The native practices and conceptualizations of gender represented in the ethnographic texts of foreign scholars in Greece are not so native as they might think; instead, they seem to be interiorized representations of perceptions disseminated in the agrarian world by the dominant domestic bourgeoisie already in the 19th century (2008, pp. 519–581).[12]

---

11   See also Deltsou (1995) on the non-existence of this line of separation, whereby the village or rural Greece is placed in total contrast to and having a lack of communication with the urban centers of the country. In the spirit of *longue durée*, she demonstrates in her ethnography on Nikiti the social and economic relations of local inhabitants with the great port cities of the Mediterranean, as they were shaped already since the 14th century. This society transformed and developed specific socio-economic relations and normalities as a result of the adaptation of its inhabitants to different political and cultural systems, starting with the Eastern Roman (Byzantine), later the Ottoman and, ultimately, the Greek administration.

12   On the predicament of the disadvantaged position of Greece vis-à-vis an, ever more developed, Europe, and how it is reproduced in the way in which Greeks associate the increase in crime in contemporary Greece with the increase in immigration from the neighboring Balkan countries, see also Bakalaki (2003, pp. 209–229. The Greeks, by associating crime

In the context of the relationship between the Greek cultural distinctiveness and the West,[13] it is worth noting the extract from the introductory chapter "Faux urbanism" by the philosopher Panagiotis Kondylis (1995, 2011), which describes the Greek bourgeoisie as lagging behind the, what he calls, Western bourgeoisie:

> "That loose and heterogeneous social grouping, which was occasionally called 'bourgeoisie' in Greece, embodied with its various components different attributes of the bourgeois morals and ethics – never all of them and at the same time. In addition, it never managed to create a native and independent bourgeois culture with a wider social diffusion, although it adopted, again each time with different components, in a more or less superficial and incoherent manner, individual elements of the European bourgeois culture. [...] For reasons we will explain immediately, its meaning expanded to incorporate – with positive or negative connotations, depending on individual sympathies – the 'wealthy citizens', the 'plutocrats', the '*noikokyraioí*', the 'reactionaries' or the 'enemies of socialism'."[14] (Kondylis, 2011, p. 12)

In the next chapters, I will present in more detail the "rhetoric"[15] in Herzfeld's terms (1992), that is the official discourses on the Greek phenomenon of *petty bourgeoisism*, their transformations and, finally, their modern usages in public discourse that helped create a public identity, against which the informants are measured in the glocal context of a crisis threatening the reproduction of social life and that of the

---

with the "hungry and underdeveloped immigrants" threatening the riches that are stored in the homes of "Greek development", repulse the Greek past and experience change in terms of approaching the developed and modern West (Bakalaki, 2003, p. 219).

13   See also regarding such approaches Panagiotopoulos (2021, p. 204).

14   Translator's exact translation from Greek.

15   In his interesting study on Western bureaucracy (1992), Herzfeld uses the term "rhetoric" to describe the ways in which public discourses, charged with a specific symbolic and ideological content, influence the everyday actions of people. For example, a public employee in Crete does not have the same priorities at work as a British public employee, since different stereotypical rhetorics influence both the actions of the employees themselves and the ways in which they are perceived by their recipients (1992, pp. 82–83). Particularly, the rhetoric of an organized and impartial Western Weberian bureaucracy viewed in terms of cultural intimacy has defined the way in which we think about the state apparatus of the industrialized Western countries (1992, pp. 10–21). The use of Herzfeld's theoretical framework for rhetoric, in the sense that discourses are produced and shape the way in which we think and act under specific circumstances, will help us understand how particular discourses on *petty bourgeoisism*, when treated as a metonym for wrong and counterproductive mentality, influence how we see the Greek middle class, while justifying and interpreting practices that discredit the entire Greek society as less Western, or not completely capitalist, and underdeveloped. In addition, of similar interest is the text on "social poetics" by the same author and its particular usefulness in the study of the Greek culture (Herzfeld, 2008).

Greek post-war social transformation.[16] My goal is to problematize the concepts of class, modernization and *petty bourgeoisism* as they were shaped in Greek social theory, and to show that, through an anthropological approach to class (Kalb, 2015, pp. 1–28), it is possible to perceive the practices whereby my informants, as social and cultural subjects, reproduce or aspire to "safeguard" in the future the acquired right of a "middle-class" society to which they believe they belong.[17] The European "crisis" in public discourse and the discourses of the informants seem to threaten this class position and the substantialized "class of the *noikokyraioi*", an ideal type reborn in terms of substance and expanded during the 1960s.[18] This decade appears

---

16   Very interesting and important for understanding the significance of such polarizing, hegemonic discourses that seem to reconstruct through specific social practices antagonistic and
separate, social and cultural spaces and identities, such as the village vs the city, the modern – urban vs the traditional – rustic, and even the refugee culture vs the native culture, are
the ethnographies of Nikiti by Deltsou (1995), of Michaniona by Potiropoulos (2003), and of
Cherso Kilkis by Karalidou (2008).

17   According to Aranitou (2018, p. 16), the mainstream analysis – and pursuit – presents the
disappearance, or collapse, or shrinking of the middle class sometimes as a tragedy and at
other times as a vindictive targeting and success of specific neoliberal policies. In this context and as far as the small business entrepreneurship, the main expression of the traditional
petty bourgeoisie, is concerned, the small size must be discarded as unproductive and an
impediment in furthering economic development (op.cit.). In other words, the departure
from the logic of "Think small first: A Small Business Act for Europe" and the replacement
of this logic by policies with a priority on business growth is suggested (op.cit.).The deep
crisis of the model of socio-economic organization, which was expressed as a debt crisis in
Greece at the end of 2009, had as a result the adoption of policies that put into doubt the
general framework of reproduction of the Greek middle class (2018, p. 17). According to her,
these policies appeared and, subsequently, were concretized as the only solution for the
country to exit the crisis (op.cit.). It is about a series of "reforms", by which a structural and
comprehensive change of the development model of the last decades in the country was attempted, thus transforming the structure of the Greek society (op.cit.). Aranitou emphasizes
that, for the first time in the post-war period, these measures threatened the reproduction
of the new as well as the traditional petty bourgeoisie, which constitute the mainstay of
the Greek economy. As a result of that, the country's GDP decreased by 25% in 4 years, unemployment rose to 28% in 2015, while, finally, its public debt increased to a level above
the permissible limit in Europe (2018, pp. 17–18). The author ascribes to the Troika, the International Monetary Fund, the private companies and, finally, the legal firms promoting
said measures a rather "eclectic" and "superficial" analysis of the fundamental characteristics of the transformation and historical development of the Greek societal model. Finally,
she draws attention to the fact that, despite the arbitrary conclusions about the collapse of
the traditional middle class in Greece, this class managed to hold on and, in contrast to the
corresponding middle classes of the Western world, to stay inside the democratic context of
social and cultural representation and "away from the alarm bells of the Far Right and anti-
European nationalism" (2018, pp. 20–21).

18   On the ways that such national or national-religious substances are produced and re-pro-
duced in the context of colonization, and for the developments in the post-colonial world,

in their discourses as the period of realization of what today is threatened by the crisis. The social subjects narrate their life stories and strategies by which they overcame the poverty of occupied and post-war Thessaloniki and managed to reach and taste ways of life that, in the pre-war years, seemed unreachable. These subjectivities were shaped progressively through the disciplinary technologies of the self (Foucault, 2006, p. 141) in the context of an institutional transformation that, at the level of discourse[19] and everyday life, aimed at westernization and modernization.[20]

The *noikokyraioi*[21] informants are social subjects that position themselves critically or awkwardly vis-à-vis the phenomenon of *petty bourgeoisism*. If we take into

---

see the very interesting and informative article by Tsibiridou (2017). In particular, the author highlights that, to understand the modalities with which the new subjectivities are formed in the post-colonial world, one has to delve into the ideal types and transformations of every tradition in different historical moments, and she continues: the understanding of behaviors and policies cannot be achieved if one does not convey as a whole the experiences of subjects that are adopted selectively and lived as embodied experiences (2017, p. 131).

19   "We belong to the West (Translator's exact translation from Greek)" speech by Konstantinos Karamanlis in the Greek parliament on 12/06/1976, see relevant video from the Greek parliament: https://www.youtube.com/watch?v=-51DbXntgll.

20   Panagiotopoulos (2021, pp. 99–110) distinguishes three historical periods concerning the consolidation of the middle classes in Greece, a small old middle class of *noikokyraioi* at the end of the 19th century, the post-war middle classes, as a middle class model, that were formed dynamically after the war with the multi-family housing of *antiparochi* and the long period of reconstruction, and finally the new middle class as the dominant social force after the end of the dictatorship (1974). What is interesting in Panagiotopoulos's analysis is his view that in the post-war middle class, as in the rest of the Western world, the working class and the householders came together to enjoy the same goods of social modernization and modern city life (2021, p. 101). As he points out, this same new culture will be shared by social groups that were previously not related (2021, p. 102).

21   It is worth noting the use of the term by Evangelos Averoff, especially during the period of the pre-election campaign against the threat of the coming victory of the Socialists and Andreas Papandreou, when New Democracy appeared as the "party of the *Noikokyraioi*", see "Η γενναία υπέρβαση που χρειάζεται η Νέα Δημοκρατία [The brave overcoming that New Democracy needs]," To Vima, published October 2015, https://www.tovima.gr/2015/10/10/opinions/i-gennaia-yperbasi-poy-xreiazetai-i-nd/. About the political ideology of Evangelos Averoff see Vamvakas and Panagiotopoulos (2014, pp. 3–6). It is also interesting to see how it is nowadays reproduced on different occasions that are linked to the policies of New Democracy, like the one of a former Member of the Greek Parliament and Deputy Minister in 2012 who belonged to the specific Party and, after his expulsion in that same year, he founded his own party and joined the Independent Greeks (ANEL) in 2014: "The 'Party of the *Noikokyraioi*' became the 'Party of the Fateful'!! I am sorry for the dreadful state of affairs to which this historic Party has fallen, and towards which many of us in the Christian Democratic Party feel as 'flesh of its flesh' aiming to 'carry the torch' of its timeless ideas and values (translator's exact translation from Greek), "Νίκος Νικολόπουλος: Το κόμμα των νοικοκυραίων έγινε κόμμα των μοιραίων [Nikos Nikolopoulos: The party of the *Noikokyraioi* became the party of the Fateful]", The Best, published November 2015, http://www.thebest.gr/news/index/view

account the hegemonic dimension of the knowledge and the mechanisms of resistance against, or subversion of, the negative discrimination contained in *petty bourgeoisism* (Foucault, 1987, pp. 51–69), the discourses on the said phenomenon produced by Greek social theorists in the post-war period are used by the informants themselves to maintain a differentiating distance from a term that was associated with the Greek maladministration and the tacky mimicry of Western bourgeoisie. Herzfeld has argued that the "binary oppositions" often benefit those who use them and bring them through their discourses and acts to the field (2008, p. 498). But specifically this extreme ambivalence[22] that characterizes the Greek culture should, according to Herzfeld (1982, 1987, as quoted in Bakalaki, 2008, p. 522), be dealt with in the field by the ethnographer through a more accurate study, in both a specific and more general context, of the practices and ways in which informants reproduce it in their discourses. Bakalaki argues that, as far as Greek hegemonic discourses are concerned, we must be very careful since, as Herzfeld (1987, p. 112, as quoted in Bakalaki, 2008, p. 563) maintains, the local elite "reproduced domestically and to their benefit the hierarchical relationship of Greece with Europe" (Bakalaki, 2008, p. 563). The fact that, while in public discourse but also in the discourse of the of Marxist sociology analysis in Greece, the term *noikokyraios* tends to be a synonym for a negatively laden petty bourgeois lifestyle, subjects use it in the context of a crisis to defend their threatened class position, is quite interesting.[23]

The above finding makes us think about the power of discourse and the domineering mechanisms of knowledge, produced by intellectuals who studied and

---

Story/364633. For the various political parties' description of the middle classes in Greece, see Panagiotopoulos (2021, p. 96).

22   According to Herzfeld, the official Greek nationalism has Europe as its model and struggles to be a part of it, and it is this image the country aims to project outwards. Alternatively, there is the native *Rhōmaíikos (Romaic)* self, which Greeks are aware of, manage between themselves, and always try to guiltily hide from the outsiders (Herzfeld, 1982, 1987, as quoted in Bakalaki, 2008, p. 522).

23   Panagiotopoulos (2021, p. 100) clarifies that the small 19th-century class of the *noikokyraioi* as a social group may still remain at the core of modern middle classes, but it never carried its cultural load and mores as it grew. In the present ethnography, it is interesting how my informants born mainly in the 1930s but also in the following decades of the 1940s, 1950s and 1960s associate the Greek middle class with the culture, mores and aspirations of the *noikokyraioi*, using this term as a self-definition in opposition to the term petty bourgeois. The *Noikokyraioi* are associated with the dream of a modern and contemporary life characterized by economic robustness and security through intergenerational mutual support, the fulfillment of their dreams for future generations through the doctrine of "looking up" and loyalty to the Greek state.

worked in the context of a hegemonic state as well as foreign culture[24], and the use and reproduction of such knowledge at the level of mass culture (Bourdieu, 1999, pp. 53–75). The *noikokyraioi*, as they crystallized in the analytical framework of the Greek middle classes, strive in the midst of a crisis to reproduce in their family context (Donner, 2015, pp. 131–148) the terms and conditions of their stay in the position that they so painstakingly captured, recovered or maintained in the post-war years.

For this reason, and before we continue with the everyday practices, habits, and way of living of the *noikokyraioi*, we must review the conceptualization of the "class" category in the post-war Greek context.

2.2 The analytical category of "class" and its use in the post-war Greek context

The two important late 19th-century theories that establish the conceptual framework for the class analysis of social formation and help us understand the establishment of class subjectivities in the social field, are developed in the texts by Karl Marx (Marx & Engels, 1962; Marx, 2009) and Max Weber (2006). The two intellectuals coincide in that they place economic production at the center of their analysis to comprehend the transformation of society and the shaping of the modern world, which differs from medieval feudalism (Westwood, 2002, pp. 45–62; Carrier, 2015, pp. 28–40).

Industrial capitalism, at least as it is experienced in his era and initially described by Marx in *The Communist Manifesto* (1964) and subsequently in his more mature studies (Marx & Engels, 1962; Marx, 1964a, 1964b, 1964c), transforms relations of production on the basis of new social relations, which themselves are shaped as a result of the reconstruction of the British economy (Westwood, 2002, pp. 12–13). The major change in this new mode of production is the advantageous position of the English capitalist "bourgeoisie" in relation to the workers due to the total control of the means of production by the former (Carrier, 2015, pp. 28–29).

Following the classical analyses of Marxist theory (Wolf, 1984; Wright, 1978; Poulantzas, 1975; Balibar, 1995, Carrier & Kalb, 2015; Westwood, 2002), the owners of the means of production produce profit-surplus to their benefit by appropriating the labor power of the workers. In this relationship, and due to his/her lack of capital or property, the worker must provide his/her labor power to the capitalist in exchange for a salary to reproduce the means and conditions of his/her existence.

---

24   For example, the majority of these intellectuals, before they began to work at Greek universities, lived and studied in France, Germany, and the United States, see Liakos (2004, p. 360).

The reproduction of this essential inequality crystallizes in the social construction of class, which can represent and protect its interests through politics (Carrier, 2015, pp. 28–40; Poulantzas, 1975). Politics becomes the second field in which the economic class becomes socially visible, acquires conscience and fights for its interests against the others (op.cit.).

In his effort to adapt Marxist theory to a structural – functionalist perspective, Althusser (2006, pp. 86–111) developed the theory of "ideological state apparatuses" which can contribute to the reproduction of the hegemonic bourgeois ideology in the superstructure. It is about a hegemony that, according to Gramsci (2006, pp. 71–85), keeps the subaltern strata of civil society under the influence of bourgeois capitalists, resulting in them being unable to become part of the working class, which could overthrow bourgeois domination through a counter-hegemony.

Poulantzas (1975, 1978) emphasizes the "relational" character of the struggle (Westwood, 2002, p. 47). Classes are shaped socially, in relation to other classes, and it is the experience of everyday life and social conditions that, following Thompson (1966, pp. 9–14), bring them together and can lead them to the revolution. These two interpretations by Poulantzas and Gramsci, depicting a Marxist-inspired social inequality, highlight even more the contingent nature and procedural transformation of an economic class into a social one. The social class does not precede in time, nor is it unified, but it is the outcome of social relations, experiences of inequality and their political handling in political economy terms within the specific historical and social context (Westwood, 2002, pp. 46–47).

On the other hand, the Weberian theory of classes is trilateral and concerns the inequalities that are shaped at three levels: those of the market, culture and administration (Westwood, 2002, p. 48; Collier, 2015, p. 28). As far as the interwar German economy is concerned, these are differences depending on the salaries and individual market positions. In parallel, Weber refers to the existence of German social classes that differentiate themselves due to their adherence to a "moral" hierarchization, in which the economic factor is not always relevant (Westwood, 2002, p. 49). One has a distinct position due to his/her individual lifestyle, moral stance, consumption, etc. The "Stände" (status groups) of Weberian theory distinguish themselves at the level of a cultural hierarchization and are capable of claiming at the level of politics more rights that can enable their social reproduction (op.cit.). According to Carrier, the different approaches reflect the different experiences of the two 19th-century men (Carrier, 2015, pp. 28–29). More specifically, during Marx's lifetime, or even earlier, the shaping and development of capitalism in England as well as the first reactions against it took place, from the Luddite movement (1811–13) to the revolutions of 1848 that broke out in a large part of Western Europe and became the triggering event for the writing of *The Communist Manifesto* (2015, pp. 28–29).

On the contrary, and as emphasized again by Carrier (2015, p. 29), Weber writes at the end of that century and, therefore, sees something different from what Marx saw and described in his writing. In Weber's time, the Wilhelmine federal state of Germany (1871) is founded as a result of the Bismarckian system, which, however, has a very different political system from the one of the established British parliamentarianism. In addition, Germany does not yet have that level of capital accumulation, which would lead to a heavy industrialization similar to that of Great Britain in the beginning of the 19th century (Berstein & Milza, 1997, pp. 150–162). In Germany, the social strata are distinguished by cultural and social criteria and therefore not necessarily only by economic ones. As we read in Aranitou (2018, p. 44), by the term "class" Weber means "every group of people that are in the same class situation", namely who have the same economic "opportunities" in the market as a result of their capitals and social status. It is, therefore, about the cultural dimension of class, which does not directly depend on the relations of production, a premise that had a significant impact on the sociological analyses of class distinction with regards to the practices of consumerism (Westwood, 2002, pp. 48–49).

2.2.1 Without a bourgeoisie

The two philosophical currents mentioned above seem to lay the foundations for the study of the post-war Greek world through the analytical category of class. Next, we will try to problematize the discourses on *petty bourgeoisism*, as they are inspired by the above philosophical perspectives and in their effort to comment on or interpret the long-term modernization and transformation of a Greek society without a bourgeoisie.

In Greece, the first historian who treats the topic of the Greek revolution in a Marxian perspective is Nikos Svoronos, who, together with K. Th. Dimaras and the Enlightenment School, will provide the starting point of a new approach to the analysis of the modern as well as pre-revolutionary Greek world (Liakos, 2004, p. 363). By placing the "new" Greek history in the European discussion regarding the 19th century and the rise of nationalisms, the French Annales School and the *longue durée* framework of analysis, they attempt to answer the leading question of Greek historiography in the 20th century about why this specific country and under which circumstances developed a different kind of modernity (Liakos, 2004, p. 362).

More specifically, and as far as post-war Greek historiography is concerned, an interpretative scheme is chosen to make the political and cultural development of the country depend on the economic one. By being an agricultural country until, at least, the 1960s, Greece is unable to transform its mode of production to a purely capitalist one and witness the much-desired development of Western countries. However, as Dertilis points out, twice in the 170 years of existence of the national state, the state apparatus managed to grow and significantly transform the economy, with the inevitable result of generating inequalities, which will manifest in the form of social protests and conflict.[25] The first period seems to open up wounds which potentially lead to two big civil conflicts: the National Schism (1914–17) and the Civil War (1944–49). The second and broader transformation of the Greek economy in the 1960s leads, despite its consumerist euphoria and the privileges it confers to the new "lower middle-class" strata,[26] to social upheaval and protests due to a weak Greek growth, which, mainly at the end of the 1950s, cannot serve the already shaped petty-bourgeois ideology that is characterized by its continuous demand for economic and social progress. This discontent of the lower strata is expressed politically with the significant increase in *EDA* (United Democratic Left) Party affiliation in 1958, the election of *Enosis Kentrou* (Centre Union Party) in the middle of the next decade, and the political complications resulting from the inability to meet said expectation, which will eventually lead to the Dictatorship in order to safeguard the post-civil-war balance of powers.

The important issue put forward by scholars of the Greek paradigm is the finding that there is no "bourgeoisie" with the cultural characteristics of the urban classes as described by Elias (2000) in his monumental study on the "civilizing" process, which refers mainly to Germany and France.

The Greek specifics, both in terms of class ambiguity and Greece's relation to Western European culture, refers mainly to the relationship between this country

---

25   It is interesting to study the last and more mature perspective of Dertilis regarding an alternative modernity that seems to better describe the example of Greek growth by emphasizing the contribution of inherent, structural characteristics of the Greek formation, such as the international/diasporic networks, the Greek family, the developed tertiary sector etc., which themselves contribute over time to the survival of a state apparatus that has a standard of living among the highest in the world (Dertilis, 2015, p. 6, 2016).

26   According to Aranitou, the discourse on many strata or classes, instead of one middle class, has to do with the reflection and criticism which was developed around the Marxist analysis and its predictions that the lower middle class would always stay small and eventually disappear. Contrary to this prediction, the middle class evolved to become the backbone of society, being the most populous class among Western social formations in the post-war period. More importantly today, she notes, when there are so many and different professions, new skills, and a great diversification of living standards, the discourse about one, unified middle class becomes even more difficult to maintain (2018, pp. 58–61). See also Panagiotopoulos (2021, pp. 31–43).

and a specified entity perceived as the West[27] / Western urban culture[28], whose inherent characteristic in natural evolutionary terms is the continuous progress and prosperity in all fields (Said, 1978; Appiah, 2016). This entity always stands on the opposite side of another entity, that of the East, whose inherent characteristic is its backwardness and traditional organization. Of course, this conceptual opposition reminds us of Orientalism (Said, 1978), a rhetoric of power that shapes European self-consciousness from the late Medieval Ages and, mainly, from the 19th century onwards, and which was founded as the polar opposite of a spectral, non-Western, world characterized by primitivism, underdevelopment and backwardness (Gazi, 1999, p. 238; Athanasiou, 2016, p. 12). Like Greece, and according to Anderson's theory of imagined communities (1991), the East is shaped as an essence through "spectral" conceptualizations made by native or foreign academics that have worked in universities of Central and Western Europe, and North America.[29]

Greece is always between these two entities, while at the level of public and academic discourse it tries to transform itself into a healthy an equal part of the Western culture.[30] These dominant discourses converse with and are influenced by international schools of thought and theories of post-war development, which are uncritically introduced into the native, academic and political discourse, while they are progressively incorporated into the mass culture in ethno-orientalist (Gazi, 1999, p. 244) or self-colonialist terms through their reproduction in printed and electronic

---

27   Prompted by his fieldwork in Crete, Herzfeld (1992, 2002, 2008) makes some very interesting observations regarding the conceptualization of Western culture and its use in the local political and cultural context by cultural policies. Of special interest for this analysis by Herzfeld (1992, 2002, 2008) are the concepts of Western rhetoric as a kind of blood-tied family, and the comparisons between ethnogenesis and kinship – family relations in the pre-capitalist society. It is also interesting to note the concept of Herzfeld on the crypto-colonialism of the Greek world as a consequence of the hegemonic discourses of a superior and better organized West, or even of a better Greece as represented by Ancient Greeks. Modern Greeks constantly measure and compare themselves against the entity of the West and those better ancestors, and this comparison always leads to the conclusion of them and their culture being weak (Herzfeld, 2002).

28   On the concept of "culture" and the anthropological turn to cultural critique to avoid Western and Eurocentric cultural interpretations see Gkefou-Madianou (1999, 2008, 2009).

29   See Papailias (2016, pp. 26–27) on the way in which the Greek society was first studied as "Europe's Other" in the context of the need for knowledge production that would be necessary for the successful outcome of the post-war programs of Great Britain and the United States, which aimed to "develop" the post-colonial "Third World" and post-war Europe through the provision of economic aid and expertise. The difficulty of anthropologists to continue their research in the former colonies drives them to the discovery of the "internal Other", "transposing Africa to Europe" (2016, p. 27).

30   On the ways in which these positivistic and orientalist dualisms are reproduced in the contemporary context of global neoliberal hegemony, see Tsibiridou (2017).

media, as Herzfeld (2002) very aptly presents in his example of nationalism in Greece and Thailand.

Taking into account the above distinctions and assumptions, post-war Greek historiography, but also social research in/on Greece in general, focus on either an economic and political analysis highlighting the ambiguous class distinction, clientelist system, foreign dependence and populism, or the study of the "honor-shame" dichotomy, which is considered a dominant one in the wider Mediterranean world.[31] With these conceptual tools, relevant studies attempt to record the paradigm of the Greek particularity and cultural diversity (Papataxiarchis, 2006b; Papailias, 2016, p. 27).

Against this backdrop, the first ethnographies are carried out; according to Avdela, they seem to influence the legal documents of the period that aim to modernize the Greek society and are evolutionary (Avdela, 2002, p. 211; Papailias, 2016, p. 27). Moreover, in the years to follow, the Greek phenomenon will be incorporated in the broader conceptual framework of the Mediterranean cultures and their difference vis-à-vis the example of Western Europe (Papataxiarchis, 1992, pp. 44–49, 2006b, p. 26; Avdela, 2002, pp. 212–234).[32] Initially, and because of the focus placed on the agricultural and mountainous populations through the substantialized honor-shame category of analysis introduced by Campbell (1964), a meaningful analysis of the class distinctiveness of specific groups will be averted. A decade later, in her ethnography about mountainous Evia entitled "Portrait of a Greek mountain village", Campbell's student Du Boulay (1974) will differentiate herself from this conceptual scheme of social values and will introduce the concept of *prokopi* that refers to the gradual, urban transformation noted by Du Boulay in the Greek society at the end of the 1960s (Avdela, 2002, p. 221).

> "As powerful as the tendency to compete and confirm oneself might be, the theoretical power of the ideal of *noikokyris*, in which one progresses by exclusively minding one's own business, ensures [the existence of] a strong sanction against an excessive competition and the search for vindication, and today it almost totally limits the tendency of male honor to express itself through physical violence and long-standing enmity." (Du Boulay, 1974, pp. 111–178, as quoted in Advela, 2002, p. 221)

The critique from an anthropological perspective put forward by anthropologists such as Herzfeld (1987), Papataxiarchis (2003) and Bakalaki (2008), attempts to prob-

---

31   See the emblematic study of John Campbell (1964) "Honour, Family, and Patronage: A Study of Institutions and Moral Values in a Greek Mountain Community".

32   According to Papailias (2016, p. 27), Greece was chosen by many European researchers in the post-war era for the additional reason of being the only country in the Balkans that remained a capitalist one.

lematize the social research in post-war Greece. At a first level, the role of the first anthropologists that come with the American and British missions to study the particularity of the Greek economic retardation and help with the success of the American reconstruction program is evaluated (Avdela, 2002, pp. 212–224). In parallel and under the prism of the crisis of representation in anthropological theory and the devaluation of the grand narratives in social sciences, field researchers abandon the ideologisms of the past about the general stereotypes of the whole Greek particularity as well as the analytical categories of class and social organization (Tsibiridou, 1999, pp. 163–182).

As long as the public discourse on society deals with or reproduces stereotypical assumptions about the Greek *petty bourgeoisism*, fieldwork research in Greece seems to ignore them and what this hegemony might mean for the lives concerned. However, at the same time, contemporary social theory inspires, and provides analytical tools for a more in-depth and critical study of culture, as habits take shape and reproduce themselves under the weight of hegemonism and the legacies of the past (Clifford & Marcus, 1986; Gkefou-Madianou, 2008, pp. 11–66, 1999, pp. 327–370).

The lower middle-class is associated in international literature with those strata that, due to their economic position in the capitalist mode of production, are constantly on the threshold since their reproduction is constantly threatened owing to their limited economic capabilities (Potamianos, 2015, p. 2; Aranitou, 2018, pp. 36–42).

The enduring expectation of upward social mobility and the constant fear for a possible proletarianization are some of the negative characteristics attributed to this class and are based mainly on the critique of the "unconscious worker" by Marx, in which the petty bourgeois acquire the "negative image of an ideal proletariat" (Potamianos, 2015, pp. 2–3). It is worth noting the fact that they, especially regarding the French lower middle-class or its other European equivalents, are collectively attributed with behaviors and lifestyles that are usually characterized by strong conservatism, individualism, and a bad replication of upper-class manners (pp. 6–29).

Particularly important is the contribution of the French anthropologist Pierre Bourdieu (2006, 2008), who tries to combine for the first time [the terms of] economy and culture with regard to the contradictions he encounters in the post-war French social formation (Westwood, 2002, pp. 49–50). Bourdieu places at the center of the Marxist analysis of social inequality the importance of culture in social distinction. The habitus, in which one is born, together with the possession of various kinds of capital shape the taxonomic taste that, in the form of a complete lifestyle, distinguishes subjects in terms of a natural continuity. Bourdieu's social subject can transform economic capital into cultural or other forms of capital to secure the reproduction of his/her social existence, depending on the needs as they are shaped in the social field of competition. The petty bourgeois, who are between the popular strata they strive to distinguish themselves from and the bourgeoisie whose position and taste they wish to attain, feel particularly insecure and make sure to reproduce the "taste for necessity" [with which they aspire] to achieve an intergenerational social mobility through economic and educational strategies (Bourdieu, 2008, p. 374). The freedom and security characterizing the taste of the bourgeoisie turn into fear for the petty bourgeois: although they possess the symbolic cultural goods, they ignore the legitimate way of using them (2008, pp. 108–109). The petty-bourgeois strata are forcefully deprived of things and pleasures and are possessed by the fear of making the wrong choice or adopting the wrong behavior (2008, p. 255). Overall, they are characterized by the imitation syndrome and a tendency to present everything in a dimension that is different from the real one, in their effort to enter spaces and lifestyles that are totally unknown to them. Finally, they tend to construct from the materials of the legitimate culture an average culture distinguished by heterogeneous choices for tastes that are extraneous to each other (2008, p. 368).

Next, we will deal with the normative, conformist, punitive and inspirational discourses that are undermined by the petty bourgeois who suffer criticism. The fieldwork experience prompts us to mention here some widespread hegemonic discourses on Greek *petty bourgeoisism* to make visible the discursive framework of predispositions either from the perspective of those being researched or the perspective of the researcher.

2.2.2 Ideotype of Greek *petty bourgeoisism*

In a recent interview (Paridis, 2015) to the online newspaper Lifo entitled "*Petty bourgeoisism* is the only ideology produced by Greece", the Dean of the University of Sydney and Professor of Modern Greek and Byzantine studies, Vrasidas Karalis, used the same interpretative scheme from the 1970s to describe the maladministration of Greek society and the bad Greek mentality, which, according to the Professor, was exploited by *Syriza*[33] to win the elections.

> "The big migration of the 1950s and 1960s left the country in the hands of the petty bourgeois. People pertaining to this volatile formation between urban and working class live in insecurity and fear, as they are anxious about losing privileges earned by making compromises and concessions. Unfortunately, *petty bourgeoisism* is the only ideology produced by Greece, to which the country remains prisoner up to this day. Will the new generation be able to overcome it in the future and recognize at last the historical position of the Greek society? Who knows? Maybe one of the most unexpected consequences of the crisis is that people will

---

33   Syriza is the abbreviation used for the Coalition of the Radical Left-Progressive Alliance, a left-wing political party in Greece.

manage to become independent of the big despotic codes that are responsible for these phobic and fragile identities of theirs. This is the quest, but who knows if this will ever happen. We, people of the diaspora, are always optimistic."[34] (Paridis, 2015)

In Greece, the scientific and non-scientific discussion about *petty bourgeoisism* is also associated with greed and the ardent desire for upward social mobility; the failure of the Greek economy to enable it leads to consumerist refilling (Karapostolis, 1983, p. 269). Thus, according to Karapostolis (1983) we pass from the "tolerance of deprivation", which mainly characterized the popular strata during the war, to the post-war "universal claim to well-being and direct acquisition of cultural goods that the previous regime of absolute poverty deprived them of" (1983, p. 280). According to Dertilis (2015, p. 8), the claim to economic and social advancement in Greece is a cross-class ideology characterizing society already in the 19th century. According to the author, the Greek society moves in between the polar opposites of the prosperous and thriving Greeks, who are possessed by the syndrome of a better and superior future for themselves and their family members, and the "slacker mob"[35], a characterization that Dertilis borrows from Seferis to highlight the catastrophic consequences of a Greek chauvinism that does not allow for *prokopi* [to take place] (Dertilis, 2015, p. 3). In his interpretative scheme, the historically unjust taxation of the lower city strata, already from the end of the 19th century and, even more so, during the 1960s, led to a "policy of *antiparochi*", whose aim was to appease the dissatisfaction of the petty bourgeois. This policy led these strata to adopt specific cultural practices in their relationship with the state. More specifically, these strata that were appointed to the public sector in return for their electoral allegiance are distinguished by their corruption practices, gift-taking, and extra-institutional multiple-job holding,[36] which allow them to cope with the inequality created by their over taxation (Dertilis, 2015, pp. 846–847).

Dertilis specifically mentions that especially after 1960, and despite the establishment of an income tax, the various governments and administration had the authority and duty to control absent-mindedness, corruption, parallel employment of civil servants and tax evasion. The opposite occurred. The institutional bodies dealt with those illegalities, both big and small, with indifference, tolerance and impunity, which led to a larger, social, universal tolerance. Another balancing element concerned the benefits that the petty-bourgeois strata reaped from their trespassing of

---

34   Op. cit.

35   Translator's exact translation form Greek.

36   Holding multiple jobs (in Greek: *πολυπραγμοσύνη*) is, also, a cultural characteristic attributed to the entirety of the Greek people and refers to the political economy of the post-Byzantine period [when] the non-Muslim populations were forced into performing multiple occupations due to their insecure [social] position in the Ottoman empire (Dertilis, 2015).

public and forest land with the overt acquiescence of the state; and from the successive legalization of illegal buildings in the 20th century (2015, p. 847).

It is obvious that the cultural characteristics of the petty bourgeois shape a way of doing, a lifestyle characterized by corruption, illegality, circumvention of the state, which, as a unified entity, tolerates these practices to compensate for its unequal stance in favour of the upper classes and the rural populations. In particular, after the 1960s, the predominance of the urban population over the rural one creates the phenomenon of a widespread *petty bourgeoisism* characterizing the entirety of the Greek world. *Petty bourgeoisism* is no longer classist but becomes a "way of living" and a "value system" for the largest part of the population (2015, p. 849).

More specifically, according to Dertilis, the advance at all costs, even in semi-legal or illegal ways, began establishing itself as a common practice and becoming increasingly acceptable by the Greek society in its entirety. From the 1990s onwards, this practice was encompassed by the *porfyra*[37] of the "neoliberal" ideology, leading to a frenzy of lawlessness, *omnium bellum contra omnes*, and a deep and inescapable crisis (2015, p. 849).

In that same logic, Kondylis (1995), as an opponent of the Greek Marxist sociologists and the proponents of neoliberal modernization, who use concepts that are only meaningful to him in the economic, political, and social context of Western Europe, emphasizes the petty bourgeoisification of the "loose", heterogeneous, and powerless Greek bourgeoisie.

> "Afterall, the issue of classist policy was not pressingly raised in a country where the gradual decomposition of patriarchal structures created a big mass of petty bourgeois as the main component of the social body, who could as well belong to a right-wing, a liberal, or a left-wing party. Whoever can be called the Greek petty bourgeoisie, such as the businessmen, the bankers, the ship owners, and some parts of the self-employed, were as a rule politically dispersed in different parties, preferably those that, at any given time, were the two biggest ones. The different groups comprising this 'loose' class satisfied their demands with essentially the same clientelist methods as simple voters [did] [...]." (Kondylis, 2011, p. 31)[38]

This association of a historically classist position, related mainly to the transformation of capitalism and the inequalities it generated at the end of the 19th and beginning of the 20th century, with an entire nation that behaves and acts in an unconventional way vis-a-vis the ethos and values of an imaginary western bourgeoisie was completed with the appearance of the private media and, mainly, television in the

---

37   The *porfyra* (in Greek: πορφύρα) was a velvet robe made by silk and worn by the Byzantine Emperors (translator's note).

38   Translated from the original in Greek.

1990s.[39] *Petty bourgeoisism* emerged as the most well-known negative public image in Greece, with which no one wanted to be identified, yet used daily to criticize the dysfunctions of the Greek state and society by comparing them with an imaginary, perfect and unified, public administration system[40] in the West of the Enlightenment and Renaissance. The Greek petty bourgeois and their practices became news headlines that critically commented on the inability of the Greek society to modernize and complete itself according to the standards and specifications determined by its participation in the European Union and, later, the European monetary union. The Greek petty bourgeoisie was the favourite subject, not only of the Greek literature and cinema in the 1960s and 1970s, but also of the first Greek tv series that appeared in private television in the early 1990s and consolidated the image of the Greek petty bourgeois: the *Afthairetoi* [arbitrary people] (1989–1991) written by Vasilis Nemeas and directed by Nikos Koutelidakis (1992–1993), the *Mikromesaioi* [low middle classes] and the *Retire* [Penthouse] by Giannis Dalianidis (1990–1992), to name a few. These series, as well as many others in the following period, managed to become popular due to making representations of all negative cultural characteristics of the modern big city inhabitant in Greece, with which the viewers probably identified themselves in the context of a "cultural intimacy" [or] the familiarization with practices seen as being problematic, and ultimately offering, following Herzfeld (1997, p. 8), convincing cultural explanations for the obvious deviations from the ideal common good by reproducing it.

Texts like the one by journalist and writer Malvina Karali (2015) entitled "Does the President watch porn?", which aimed at criticizing the election of Kostis Stefanopoulos as President of the Hellenic Republic, are particularly telling of the transformations and usage of rhetoric on *petty bourgeoisism*, as it was developed in the 1970s and 1980s, in the modern public discourse (Karali, 2015).

---

39   Of particular interest is the fact that the results of my research converge with the findings in Aranitou (2018) in that, from the 1990s, there was a production of discourses that paved the way for the imposition of memoranda that would change once and for all the problematic pathology of the Greek post-war arrangement, the cause of the crisis. According to the author, the intensity and content of the policies that were implemented since 2009 had a historical continuity and connection to everything that came before them on the level of political and public discourse (2018, pp. 142–149). However, this study places the beginning of this discussion earlier, since it is an ultimately structural one with regard to the discourses on the "Greek specifics" and the constant need for modernization and integration of the "Oriental" Greeks in the, already modernized, body of western family.

40   See Herzfeld (1997) for an exceptional analysis of state culture and, particularly, the reproduction of the logic of a unified public administration through "deficient behaviors and practices" of bureaucrats and citizens that, according to the Weberian tradition, becomes apparent on the level of rhetoric as perfect, efficient, and whole.

"These dudes, the petty bourgeois, never consider committing suicide because their life belongs to God, but, in essence, because they do not decide neither for their life, nor for their death. Wherever it suits them they have no memory, but by envisioning the future, they do not live a present of *prokopi*. They make long-term dreams that, as a rule, are caught up by death. They build walls. They buy small plots of land. They do not look for purses, because they rarely fall in love and, as with all idiots, they never feel powerless. They tremble before their obligations, but they finally marry a very patient [woman/girl] who was annoyed by them for years and does not even want to shit on them anymore. They have two brats, because "one equals none". Or three, if the first two are girls. And of course, they love call girls, whom they ask after fucking: "How did you end up like this?" No, the petty bourgeois do not have a teddy bear. [They have] only trash. In food, in ideas, in lifestyle, in actions. I know the Brotherhood from the inside and from the outside (...). [The petty bourgeois] trembles to be cheated and is always cheated. [The petty bourgeois] dodges. [The petty bourgeois] falsifies. [The petty bourgeois] postpones. [The petty bourgeois] pretends. [The petty bourgeois] asks for everything and gives nothing. [The petty bourgeois] pretends to be fair. [The petty bourgeois] denies the paternity tests to escape [paying] alimony, in the close presence of a petty provincial lawyer who is calm and honest, ready to tarnish the poor thing. The petty bourgeois does not look for trouble. Therefore, he can never be a revolutionary, thus a *palikari*[41]. [The petty bourgeois] is not disliked for being too much, [he] is sickening as a side road. [The petty bourgeois] thinks that [he] is a diplomat and solves Gordian Knots, but [he], essentially, untangles himself and drives people around him crazy. No one is more dangerous than those quiet, calm little people, the petty bourgeois." (Karali, 2015)[42]

2.3 Fieldwork in Kato Toumba

The area of Kato Toumba in Thessaloniki was chosen as a research field on purpose, since my goal when designing my research was to further study the findings of the ethnographic fieldwork by German Anthropologist Waltraud Kokot (1994, 1996). According to her, the inhabitants of Toumba, who in the beginning were almost entirely refugees from Asia Minor, started to change by the end of the 1970s. This change was linked to an important spatial change that resulted from the transfer to Toumba of the [administrative and legal] practice of *antiparochi*, which was exclusively implemented in the city center during the 1950s and 1960s, and the repatriation of migrants from the countries of Western Europe and, especially, Western Germany. It

---

41   *Palikari* in Greek means a courageous and honest person.

42   Translated excerpt, see op. cit.

was, therefore, the result of the reflux of immigration due to the first oil crisis in 1973 as well as a consequence of internal migration, which had already started in the last years of the Civil War and referred to the policies "on the relocation of rebel-hit populations" to urban settings.

According to Waltraud Kokot's research (1994, 1996), the city center coming closer to the refugee settlement of Kato Toumba is observed, not only practically, in terms of the expansion of the city and its transport connectivity, but also on the cultural level of interpretation. Her informants feel that the line separating the Toumba of poor refugees from the city center of the Bayatides[43] is being undone, and Toumba is transforming into a wealthy, interstitial Eastern suburb that, together with the refugee [settlement of] Panorama, the refugee [settlement of] "Muddy Kalamaria", and its [urban] competitor Kapsida (Pylaia), will be the counterpoint to the industrial, Western Thessaloniki of the working-class/popular strata (Kokot, 1994, pp. 25–33). As she conferred to me in our meetings, which we held in 2015–2016 in Hamburg in the context of my fieldwork there, Kokot also chose the specific period because she was looking for a purely urban population in her desire to differentiate herself from an Anthropology of Greece that, until then, was concerned with rural populations. The paradigm of Toumba was the most suitable one in a city that had lost the largest part of its pre-war population and, particularly, the majority group of Sephardic Jews. The latter were closely connected to the production of space that the post-war reconstruction, based on *antiparochi*, would replace and [thus] change the class map of the city.

Both in the context of [my] fieldwork research and for [my] writing needs, the analytical categories focus on the study of the dynamic subject-object relation and are based, in good part, on the theories of material culture. In the context of the "cultural turn" that mainly characterizes the Anglo-Saxon anthropology after the 1980s, I follow the de-symbolization of the Geertzian version of culture as a system, and I emphasize the voluntary action of the subject in the context of the everyday life practices (Gialouri, 2012).

On the other hand, the analytical category of class helps us understand how the research subjects in Thessaloniki associate the decoration and consumption practices in the post-war context with their "middle class" position and the upward [social] mobility that they aspired [to have] in the post-war years. Both the analytical category of class and the system of reference to this specific historical conjuncture, in which the post-war subjectivity is produced, are useful analytical tools that, combined with the important findings from the theory of materiality (Miller, 1998, 2001, 2005, 2010), can [help] interpret the discourses on "the destruction of the class of the *noikokyraioi*". These discourses are expressed by the informants in the modern, eco-

---

43   This term is used in Thessaloniki to describe the old, native residents of Thessaloniki.

nomic and political, context of the globalization of capitalism and the consequences of neoliberal policies that are implemented in the global South.

In a very interesting historical review of the theoretical trends in the American and British Anthropology, Dutch Anthropologist Don Kalb (2015, pp. 1–28) highlights the need to turn to new anthropologies of class and their production in the, constantly changing, global capitalist system. An approach of classes in terms of static positions in the relations of production, which would reproduce the known class categories of the proletarians, the petty bourgeoisie etc. [as] the result of the social relations at the end of the 19th century, would not help in understanding the inequalities that the transformation of capitalism creates across time (p. 15).

According to him, Anthropology must distance itself from the interpretative, symbolic Anthropology of the school of Franz Boas as well as from an exclusively post-structuralist, "culturalist" Anthropology that aimed at describing the native culture without it being viewed within the context of a greater glocal vision and a social system of inequality that permeates and, ultimately, influences cultural representations. Don Kalb suggests an "Anthropological political economy" (Kalb, 2015, p. 10) that, according to him, has its roots in the US rebellions of the 1960s and 1970s, the revolutions against colonialism in the Third World as well as in British Anthropology after World War II. With this term, he refers more to an Anthropology that is not limited to the local, but will [instead] incorporate the local to the global, view social subjects within a global system of inequality and oppression that influences social relations, gender and their social position (pp. 7–16).

Class subjectivity and its transformation should be studied across time in the glocal socio-political context of its formation, putting emphasis on the contingency and relational condition of class, which will not be limited to the discursive expression promoted by the linguistic turn, but will deepen the experience and practice of subjects that partake of the constantly changing social relations on the level of everyday life (Kalb, 2015, pp. 4–5). According to him:

> "Capitalism is a dynamic bundle of contradictory but interdependent, spatialized social relationships of inequality, power and extraction, and the mythologies that are associated with them. It is these social relationships that underpin the anthropological notion of capitalism as simultaneously a mode of production, a mode of accumulation, a mode of social reproduction, a mode of the production of space, a mode of being and a mode of becoming." (Kalb, 2015, p. 14)

And he continues:

> "In anthropological hands, then, class is less an already-defined position that determines both consciousness and action, and more an invitation to discover people's shifting historical, situated and antagonistic social interdependences." (Kalb, 2015, p. 16)

In this research, I consciously chose to use the term "middle classes" that is used in the Greek and European public spheres, more so in the contemporary socio-political context of the economic crisis and the transformation of the national Fordist capitalism to a globalized post-Fordist capitalism of a unified market that is defined both on the level of the nation-state and that of the multinational state-like formations. The international discourses on the threatened weakening of the post-war middle classes, as a result of the neoliberal policies that, due to the crisis, reduce the post-war [welfare] state, limit and transform the national state (Appadurai, 1996), are co-articulated with the corresponding discourses on the Greek middle classes and, particularly, the class mentality of the *noikokyraioi*.

In the Greek context of today's "post-construction" crisis of empty apartments and stores that are called upon to pay the debt of the country and guarantee its stay in the European economic community, the informants from Thessaloniki, as small owners, small businessmen, and pensioners from the neighborhood of Toumba and the city center with their children unemployed or working in the, negatively evolving, public and private sector of the country, aim to maintain the status of the [economically] robust and proud *noikokyraios*[44] depending on their available capitals. Their grandchildren do not prefer to stay in the apartments that they built for them but aspire to reproduce in the global metropolises of "real" development the middle-class status and lifestyle of European Greece, [and] of the Greek Olympic Games and modernization. Ferguson (2005, pp. 166–181), by attempting to problematize the concept of "alternative modernity", as it was developed in the context of postcolonial studies, with regard to the example of post-colonial Africa, raises the issue of a development nostalgia on the part of his informants, [among whom] those who can abandon the underdeveloped periphery and experience through the strategy of migration the lifestyle of the advanced metropolis do so in view of the insufficient infrastructure and inefficient state apparatus.[45]

The grandchildren of the informants from Thessaloniki, who are in display together with their, post-war produced, degrees on the dining tables of the good living rooms, abandon the city *en masse* even before the crisis [started] and choose for their master [programs] the best-known world metropolises, where they try to integrate with the support of their families. The post-war living rooms, with their chandeliers, their Persian carpets and solid wood (massif) carved buffets with the lion paws, which used to remain closed to contribute to the furthering of social *prokopi*, opened sometime after the 1990s [following] the fashion of open spaces. And while the walls that separated them from the rest of the spaces were torn down, they might close again in the conjuncture of today's deep economic crisis, maybe even to disappear.

---

44   Singular for *noikokyraioi* (translator's note).

45   On immigration policies see Goldin, Cameron and Balarajan (2013).

Finally, [my] choice of the term *noikokyraioi*, although a problematic analytical category for statistical and quantitative approaches, must be used in an anthropological study where there is an interest in the way the subjects are self-determined, giving meaning to a Greek middle class that is contingent, contradictory, highly diversified, and multi-layered, trying to reproduce itself intergenerationally through *noikokyremenes*[46] practices.

2.4 Modernization, urbanization and ideological "civilizing"[47]: an anthropological reading

In the field, I constantly heard about the "State of Karamanlis"[48] that, although unfair and violent, managed to lead the divided Greek society into a road parallel to those of the Northern and Western European countries. "He made us into a state",[49] they told me, even if their leftist backgrounds and the exile of their parents inhibited such an admission. What does the phrase "he made us into a state" mean, though? How can a society be organized and administered in the form of a state regime?

In her highly enlightening paper on state culture, Aretxaga (2003) highlights that many scholars like Appadurai (1996), who saw the liberalization of the market and the globalization of capitalism in the 1980s and, especially from the 1990s onwards, the shrinking or, even, disappearance of the state, were refuted. The "hollowed-out" character of the state [gives it] the capacity to "sustain ethnic conflicts, processes of insurgency and counterinsurgency, war economies, international interventions, refugee camps, and torn societies" and, in this way, survive and reproduce itself across time as a form of organizing and commanding power (p. 394).

Papataxiarchis (2006c) introduces the "regime of otherness" as a structural [element of] the Greek state apparatus to interpret the practices with which otherness was acted upon through time, both on the level of everyday life and [that of] the official state discourse, in the modernizing Ottoman state and the modern Greek state form that replaced it. In the Greek paradigm, in particular, otherness has a way of being incorporated in the unified perspective of the modern Greek state through striving practices of "segmental reasoning" (p. 410). The hegemonic ideology of nation-

---

46   Tidy and neat, worthy of someone who is a *noikokyraios* (translator's note).

47   This is a term commonly used by informants in the field. This term is also used in state archives such as that of *DEI* to describe this post-war change in Greek society. The word "civilized" is always associated with the European and Western way of living.

48   Konstantinos Karamanlis (1907–1998) served as Prime Minister of Greece in the first post-junta governments during the second half of the 1970s (translator's note).

49   See Bakalaki (2003, p.217) on the negative way in which the Greeks view the Greek state, especially in what concerns the interests of their households.

alism and anti-communism, which characterizes the Venizelian[50] state and later, after the civil war, the state of Karamanlis with its "para-constitutions" (Elefantis, 2002; Charalambis, 1989; Mouzelis,1978; Panourgia, 2013), produces through discourses and practices the "other" that threatens the westernization and modernization of the homeland (Papataxiarchis, 2006c, pp. 431–436; Panourgia, 2013). Venizelos and Karamanlis often symbolize in the discourses and everyday decoration practices of the informants[51] the very idea of the modernized Greek and Western capitalist state, which links to a specific ideological narrative whereby Greece must modernize/transform its state apparatus according to the Weber-inspired Western state in order to become again a worthy member of the Western world, to which it is supposed to belong by descent.

The statuettes of Venizelos or the busts of Karamanlis, which I came across in the apartments of my informants, were "performances of the state" (Mitchell, 2006) that rendered visible the state – citizen relation. However, as we saw with the anthropological studies in the post-colonial states of Africa, Asia, and India, the culture of the Western colonial nation-state used local elites, traditions, and rituals that "put power on a disguise" to penetrate and make itself tangible among the local populations (Gledhill, 2013; Nustad & Krohn-Hansen, 2005). In the post-war Greek context of the American reconstruction and European integration, the "divided power" (the army, the Palace, the political parties, the people, the American technocrats, the European community etc.) struggles to acquire a unified form on the levels of discourse and everyday experience to control antagonistic forces that threaten its consolidation. Divided pieces of a broken political system are glued back together on the basis of a crypto-colonial (Herzfeld, 2002) version of the Western, 3000-year-old, Greek nation to become the "mask" of the unified idea of the state (Abrams, 1988, p. 77). The vision of modernization and westernization is the adhesive substance that will allow the Greek nation to remain faithful to the ideals and principles that it passed on to the West. The "leftists", as other "dangerous citizens" (Panourgia, 2013), threaten the reproduction of the pre-war model of state apparatus and the coalescence of the country with the countries of the capitalist world, thus they are exiled and re-educated in concentration camps from a state that possesses the "meta-capital" (Bourdieu, 1999). In the constitution of this modern world, which is designed in a legal context,[52] spatially (Ferguson & Gupta 2002, pp. 981–1002) as well as on the levels of

---

50   Eleftherios Venizelos (1864–1936) was a politician and Prime Minister in Greece.

51   We will later see how the informants decorate their offices as well as the interior spaces of their apartments with statuettes and busts of the persons that, in their discourses, are identified with the development and modernization of the Greek state.

52   See the interesting writing by Avdela (2002, p. 29) on the transformation of criminal justice law with the aim of delegitimizing family and gender-based violence, and especially the crimes based on the cultural context of the "underdeveloped Mediterranean countryside". According to the writer, in the 1950s and 1960s an effort is being made to control the

rhetoric, public and private discourse, mass culture, and education (Herzfeld, 1992; Bourdieu, 1999), many individual actors produce and reproduce the state, as social subjects [that are involved] in the daily reproduction of its idea – either by fighting against it or serving it, in the context of social life (Gupta, 2006; Herzfeld, 1992).

The idea of the modern Greek state, particularly in a city that is incorporated in it later in the 20th century, is produced not only in the figures and statistics that affirm post-war development, but also in the buildings that are built according to the principles of modernism[53] to house the schools that will teach national history, the museums that will narrate national continuity, the polytechnic school of the Aristotle University that will build the modern Greek city, the buildings of the services that will contribute to the "civilizing" and modernization of the "underdeveloped" and "primitive" countryside and, finally, the modern apartment that will house the re-baptized modern subject, who has now all the means for a modern life. The imposing modern buildings of *DEI* and *EYATH*[54] embody and promise the modernization of the Greek household. The state of Karamanlis and Junta is associated with the bathrooms that many acquire inside their houses, the electrical switches and plugs, the asphalt paving of everyone's neighborhood roads. The post-war state is experienced daily through the consumption practices of the modern, constituting the post-war subjectivity of the *noikokyraios* [that belongs] to a multi-layered middle class, which, however, shares more or less the same values and goods (Karapostolis, 1983; Bakalaki, 2003, pp. 214–216) rendering them hegemonic for the lower working-class strata until at least the 1970s, when the access of the country to the European Union and its gradual participation as a European force in the globalized market will transform the terms and practices of reproduction for the next generations.

---

emotion linked to honor by expanding its meaning. Both in the post-war Greek press, the academic discussions, the cinema, and on the level of justice administration honor is separated from violence, sexuality, and gender-based identity (p.33). Avdela considers that these practices led to the ideological triumph of the version of authoritarian modernity promoted during this period by the winners of the war. The Greek family [that is characterized by] mutual understanding and acceptance, as presented in popular magazines like Thesaurós (Θησαυρός), Romántzo (Ρομάντζο), Ginaíka (Γυναίκα), and Pántheon (Πάνθεον) as well as the Greek cinema, must contribute to the modernization and progress of the Greek society (pp. 235–242).

53   On the modernist buildings and the role of Patroklos Karantinos due to his pre-war tenure in the Ministry of capital city administration and, in the post-war years, in the Ministry of Education see Giakoumatos (2003, pp. 393–532) and, especially, on the case of Thessaloniki Kolonas (2012).

54   *DEI (ΔΕΗ)* are the abbreviated initials for the Public Power Corporation and, in the same way, *EYATH (EYAΘ)* refers to the Thessaloniki Water Supply and Sewerage Corporation (translator's note).

2.5 Space and objects in the discourses and practices of the *noikokyraioi* from Thessaloniki

In the sense attributed to it by the studies of the space turn (Low & Lawrence-Zúñiga, 2007) as a built environment and space totality through which cultural behaviors and practices manifest themselves and take place, space is a very important analytical field-tool for this research in order to realize the ways in which the way of living of the *noikokyraioi* is produced and reproduced in Thessaloniki.[55]

The political and economic change in the first post-war decades drastically changed the city landscape and neighborhood. Public and private spaces are transformed in the context of development policies and the city is soon converted to a vast construction site for many years. My informants link the economic crisis, which places a burden to their everyday reality during the research, to the stopping of the familiar sound of the cement mixer and the absence of scattered reconstruction materials that occupied for months part of the public space in the neighborhood. "Nothing is being built anymore" is the common response to the question on the reconstruction and rebuilding years of the 1960s. According to Stavridis (1990, 2006), space does not exist as a reception box of actions but is an element of their development.

Action is always developed and interpreted with reference to a network of spatial-temporal correlations. The practices and relations that developed in the spatial context of rebuilding are those that transformed today's acting subjects, who are nostalgic of the familiar noises and images that constitute for them development and modernization. The characteristic picture of Konstantinos Karamanlis, who, as Minister of Public Works, touches the tool for the removal of the railway lines, inaugurating in 1954 the coming of the modern age that would be distinguished by the use of modern city buses and the car, is a milestone in the collective memory and, ultimately, in the memory of the city's reconstruction and modernization. The collective memory of the modern that refers to the public space is intertwined with the experiences and practices that take place in the neighborhood as well as the more intimate space of home where I meet my informants. The emotions, everyday life, and social relations did not happen only in those "spaces of change", but the acting gendered subjects, as a cultural product of the authoritarian and taxonomic schemes of their time, built and formed those spaces "objectifying", according to Daniel Miller (2005), interesting subjectivities.

In the collective volume she published on home, Irene Cieraad (1999), following a bibliographical review of the Anglo-Saxon approach to home as a domestic space,

---

55   On the social dimension of space and the meaning of the spatial constitution of reality for the subjects see Giannakopoulos and Giannitsiotis (2010).

emphasizes the importance of researching its meaning beyond the symbolic dimensions of the spatial / domestic taxonomy and decoration taking place in it. Where and how meaning is produced and how this is, ultimately, interpreted by the acting subject is something that should concern modern qualitative studies on domestic space. In particular, following the theories of material culture, the combination of meaning and practices producing it can lead us to useful conclusions about the action of the materiality of the home as an assemblage of different materials that intertwine, according to Latour (1993; 2005), in collectivities and networks that are, ultimately, indicative of the kind of practices and behaviors developed in their context. Home, as a structure and context, in which the acting subject is constituted socially and culturally through embodied practices, particularly preoccupied Bourdieu (2006) in his theory of practice. The socialization of both Kabyle Berbers and French citizens of different class and tribal origins takes place inside the structuring structures of the public, social space and that of home, which imposes itself normatively as a totality of objects and transforms the social subject at the moment that he/she comes into contact with it. Specific objects, spaces, and domestic structures act as carriers for the expectations of the social group within which people grow.

In addition, the concept of the "humility of things" that Miller (1987, pp. 85–108, as quoted in Miller, 2005, p. 5) introduced, influenced by the studies of Erving Goffman (1975) on the importance of "context/frame" for the action itself and those of E.H. Gombrich (1984) on the "sense of order", confirm the abovementioned theories on the importance that the material world has as a set of rules, a foundation upon which everything social is based and with which it interacts (Miller, 2005, p. 18).

The *noikokyraioi* from Toumba and the center of Thessaloniki invite me to the homes of reconstruction and open their good living room to me, which after 40 years has remained intact due to its proper "non-use" that was imposed by the normative content in which the need to acquire it was produced. The informants narrate not only by having as a background the objects they consumed in the post-war years, as a result of their economizing and their right choices, but also through them.[56] The objects are moved and used performatively for the narration to an informant that they believe he can appreciate.[57] As Anat Hecht says:

"A house encompasses an array of different materials, from furniture and fixtures to ornaments and décor, collectively creating a dwelling experience that

---

56   On the importance of the Greek home and wealth that was acquired in the post-war years, especially in the context of the European modernization and progress by which the Greek society and state are timelessly possessed, see Bakalaki (2003, pp. 214–215).

57   On the autobiographical narrations of a classist and familial continuity in the context of a unified, multilayered post-war society that the informants from Thessaloniki perform through the usage of family heirlooms and, especially, family photographs, see Zermpoulis (2017).

is greater than the sum of its parts. For these are more than mere 'things', they are a collection of appropriated materials, invested with meaning and memory, a material testament of who we are, where we have been, and perhaps even where we are heading. They are what tranforms our house into our home, a private cosmos that houses our memories of bygone times, as well as our hopes for what is yet to come. They bind our past with our present and our possible futures, thereby framing and reflecting our sense of self." (Hecht, 2001, p. 123)

For Chevalier, "to lose a home is to lose a private museum of memory, identity and creative appropriation" (Chevalier, 1996, 1998, as quoted in Hecht, 2001, p. 123). Through their practices of decoration, household management, hospitality, and consumption of objects from the post-war Greek and Western modernism, the inhabitants of Thessaloniki produce and re-produce the particular intimacy of a Greek middle class that constitutes and goes along with the identity of the *noikokyraios*.[58]

The constitution of a national intimacy through the production and consumption of a specific aesthetic in the space of the home and its association with hegemonic policies of the various bourgeoisie has been of concern to many social scientists. A characteristic example is the work by Orvar Löfgren (1987) "*Deconstructing Swedishness: Culture and Class in Modern Sweden*" on the Swedish bourgeoisie, upon which newer studies have been based like the one by Keith Murphy (2013) "*A cultural geometry: Designing political things in Sweden*", which explains the ways and mechanisms whereby modern Swedishness is being designed and reproduced, and how the particular furniture products promise to their owner the ideals of intimacy of the Swedish middle class globally. In her writing on the policies of modernization and social change in Great Britain, Judy Attfield (1999, pp. 73–82) shows in an easy-to-understand way how, irrespective of the posterior negative evaluation of the housing policies of the state to modernize and democratize the household life as failures, the inhabitants of Harlow New Town adapted the architectural modernism to their own needs and traditions by creating different versions of a domestic modernism.

Cieraad (1999, pp. 31–53) shows us how in the Netherlands a window without curtains is associated with the post-war empowerment of women as well as the modern and democratic way of living openly in the city. The showcase window of post-war Dutch society stands on the opposite side of the late 19th-century window that was covered with heavy curtains to protect the venerable and moral wife, highlighting the liberal stance of society towards issues of privacy and sexuality.

---

58   On the association of home with the gender-based cultural identities of *noikokyris* and *noikokyra*, and the cultural values linked to home as a proof of economic and social success in the context of the country's transition from poverty and backwardness to its successful integration into what is called the modern world, see Bakalaki (2003, p. 214).

Finally, of interest are three studies on the ways in which the modern subject of the post-Soviet era is gradually reconstructed through the consumption of a "spectral" Western modernism in combination with the revival of, pre-Soviet as well as Soviet, modern and traditional ways of living.

In her very interesting piece of work *Ethno-baroque: Materiality, aesthetics and conflict in modern-day Macedonia*, anthropologist Rozita Dimova (2006) shows the processes and ways of the construction of an insecure Macedonian nationalism based on the experiences and feelings of loss and lack of a once privileged class of people, mainly as a result of the economic and political change taking place in the country after 1991, by making use of the theories of material culture. The ability of the, formerly "poor and uncivilized", ethnic Albanians of Macedonia to consume the modern and the luxurious by migrating to the countries of the West changes their spatial and social perception by the, formerly privileged and ethnically Macedonian, working class, forming new cultural and national subjectivities.

In the Romanian countryside of the post-Soviet era, following the ethnography of Vintila Mihailescu (2014, pp. 83–107) *"Something nice. Pride Houses, Post/Peasant Society and the Quest for Authenticity"* subjects build "traditional" farmhouses also characterized as "Pride Houses", using however luxurious materials from the globalized free market of the capitalist world that most of the time are not suitable for the topography and architecture of the region, objectifying in this way a nationally authentic self and the identity of the winner.

To end, according to the interesting ethnography by Ferhevary (2002) *"American Kitchen, luxury Bathrooms and the search for a 'Normal' Life in Post-Socialist Hungary"*, the middle-class Hungarians consume the "normal" lifestyle, mainly through the interior decoration and furnishing of their apartments, wishing, thus, to distinguish themselves from the still "abnormal", "non-western", "uncivilized" Soviet public space. What is interesting in this ethnography, as in the previous two, is that the specific practices of modernization or consumption of the modern were cultivated by the Soviet governments themselves in their effort to improve the standards of living. The middle-class Hungarian, following this ethnography, experiences the "normal/civilized" European lifestyle as the authentic version of the Hungarian lifestyle, associating it with the pre-Soviet era of a spectral western Hungarian society without the mediation of Communism.

3. Poverty, refugeeism and material adaptation
Homes and people in a dynamic relationship

In this chapter, I will present the different forms of dwelling of my informants, to show the modalities in which subjects progressively establish the world in which they seek to live. As mentioned also in the introduction, this way is not independent of political developments and economic transformations, the refugee status in an emerging and constantly changing national formation, like the one of the Greek state in the beginning of the 20th century.

The change in the sense of domesticity at the different homes and the experiences through life stories in the cultural and social context of post-war Thessaloniki are used in this chapter to highlight the interaction between the material world and active subjects.

As mentioned earlier, social theory has thoroughly dealt with the conceptualization of home and its role in shaping subjects through identification processes.[1] The relationship between a house and the person who lives in it and shapes it is a determining one for both. They interact within a personal and everyday relationship. By using at this point the theoretical reflection of Lefebvre (1991) about the production of space, we could consider the house itself as the embodiment of an idea and the result of specific political and social choices and practices in a specific time and place. This leads many theorists to considering that the house as materiality subjects the person who lives in it to specific behaviors and practices (Hurdley, 2006, p. 719).

However, it is also worth mentioning the importance of its use and dwelling, the lived everyday experience in the house and the small and silent "strategies", according to de Certeau (1988, pp. 115–130), with which the subject acts and shapes the space to make it personal and intimate.

Anthropologist Sophie Chevalier (1999, pp. 83–94) in her study of the role of mass consumption objects in shaping subjects during the industrial and post-industrial period in France, reaches, through the excellent scheme of two houses of the average French citizen, very important conclusions, which challenge previous theoret-

---

1   For example, see Cieraad (1999); Miller (2001); Hurdley (2006); Bachelard (1994); Csikszent-
     mihalyi (1999); Blunt and Dowling (2006).

ical points of view referring to the alienation of the working class because of the uniform and isolated way of dwelling in the cities, far from their traditional way of living in the countryside. According to this ethnography, the different history of the French society regarding progress and industrialization pace compared to Great Britain resulted in the strong association of French city residents with the countryside even during the post-war era, when families tried to keep at all costs the family house in the countryside, as this was the embodiment of their family identity and genealogical continuity. Houses and their objects, even when the people who made them meaningful and perceived the affinities that connected them had passed away, continued to play an important part in shaping the subjects who inherited them, through discursive practices that associated them with the subjects of the past. Although all these objects were mass production ones, they now embodied specific social relationships, meanings, people and circumstances, which made it possible to continue family life and tradition and rendered spaces absolutely personal and unique (Chevalier, 2002, p. 849).

The study of the material culture advocates, as we saw earlier, the focus on things and everyday practices around them, to understand the behaviors and mentalities taking place in different social, economic and cultural contexts.[2] Several anthropologists, mainly after the 1980s, who recognize in the subject not only the role of a passive consumer of material goods but also that of a producer, opt for this direction. More specifically, by the concept of "producer" they mean mainly the physical "action" of the individual and the production of meaning and specific values over the material things, as a result of the use and daily practices they develop (Gialouri, 2012, pp. 25–35).

Anthropologist Daniel Miller raises from the outset, within the context of the discussion about consumption, the importance of practice and meanings produced during the use of material things. Miller recognizes the impact of the material culture on shaping specific behaviors and practices, providing a set of rules on which society is organized. The material culture works silently, which means that the less one perceives the outside world the more is influenced by it (Miller, 2005, p. 5). This viewpoint is based on older studies (Goffman, 1975; Gombrich, 1979), in which the material world and the ideas it represents provide the framework within which the subject socializes, meaning that the subject's practices, lifestyle and normality comply unconsciously with preexisting ("structured" and "structuring", according to Bourdieu) structures. Miller (2005, pp. 8–10) relies mainly on the Hegelian philosophy and the concept of "dialectic" of subject and object.

---

2   On Sweden see Frykman and Löfgren (1987) and Murphy (2013). On Great Britain see Attfield (2006), Miller (2008) and Hurdley (2006). On Italy see Arvidsson (2001). On Cyprus see Navaro-Yashin (2009). On Norway see Gullestad (1984) and Garvey (2001). And, finally, on France see Bourdieu (2006, 2008) and Chevalier (1999).

In the well-known "Master/Slave Dialectic" that Hegel treats in the *Phenomenology of Spirit* (Hegel, 2006), it becomes clear that subjects perceive themselves fully and can reach self-consciousness only through substantial contact and rupture with the outside world (meaning the entirety of the cultural production) that has determined their existence (Kojevve, 1947; Miller, 2005, pp. 8–10). A slave formulates objects, the outside world, not to meet own needs, but to be consumed by his/her master. This practice educates the slave and through this circumstance he/she shapes a slave's consciousness, which he/she experiences as normality (op.cit.).

A slave being subordinated to his/her master recognizes and respects the value of individual freedom, which, however, he/she does not experience for himself/herself; this is an advantage vis-à-vis his/her master, who, being unable to recognize and respect another person's autonomy, reaches a deadlock (Kojevve, 1947; Miller, 2005, pp. 8–10). What is at stake for the subordinated person in this dialectic relationship is to refuse this circumstance through the example of the master's life and express own wishes in relation to things (outside world), refuse, destroy or formulate them, but this time for own consumption, in order to find out his/her real self through this interaction (Kojewe, 1947, p. 41). According to Hegel, this very relationship of refusal with the object formulates and renders the manufacturer autonomous (op.cit.).[3]

Based on a Hegelian "philosophy of practice", Miller refuses a Marxian-type disapproval of consumption (Miller, 1987, pp. 19–33, 2005, pp. 8–10, as cited in Gialouri, 2012, pp. 26–27). According to Miller, consumption must be seen as a necessary condition of "refamiliarization (Aufhebung)" with the object preceded with the necessary "alienation (Entäusserung)" (op.cit.). During the "lifting" process, the subject is humanized through labor itself (op.cit.). Thus, the subject by formulating objects formulates himself/herself, while discovering a part of consciousness in them, which is disclosed during a "productive" consumption process (op.cit.).

Home both as materiality and as articulation of specific ideologies and imaginary schemes in space has been dealt with also in critical geography. Alice Bunt and Robyn Dowling (2006) in their collective volume on home as a place of expression of the sense of "domesticity" describe in detail the theories and analytical tools in which home has been approached over time by philosophers, social geographers, sociologists, psychologists, historians and anthropologists. According to them, home is not only the building in which a person lives (op.cit.). The sense of experience, meaning being at a place that feels like home, a shelter in terms of interiority, security and continuity may penetrate national boundaries in practical terms, but a person still feels like living in there, often performing familiar national practices (Bunt & Dowling, 2006; Petridou, 2001, pp. 87–104). According to Bunt and Dowling:

---

3   See Kojewe (1947, p. 41), "The forming activity (the work) is the pure being-for-itself. The product of work is the worker's production; it is the realization of his project, of his idea. It is him that is realized in and by this product."

"Home, [...], is a *place*, a site in which we live. But, more than this, home is also an idea and an imaginary that is imbued with feelings. These may be feelings of belonging, desire and intimacy (as, for instance, in the phrase 'feeling at home'), but can also be feelings of fear, violence and alienation [...]. These feelings, ideas and imaginaries are intrinsically spatial. Home is thus a *spatial imaginary*: a set of intersecting and variable ideas and feelings, which are related to context, and which construct places, extend across spaces and scales, and connect places [emphasis by the Author]." (Bunt & Dowling, 2006, p. 2).

According to Tim Putnam, home is located at the "core" of a world in which humans place and perceive themselves as subjects (Putnam, 1999, p. 144). The sense of "domesticity" through specific practices is empodied in the construction of a house, which not only reflects the subject's personal feelings and experiences, but is also subject to specific and predetermined "household policies" promoted by hegemony and power factors, but also action and resistance to them from below (Bunt & Dowling, 2006, p. 6).[4] State, economy, fashion, social environment, but also personal aspirations, experiences, social memory, class, gender and imagination of the subjects themselves influence the way in which humans build and subsequently experience home (McCracken, 1989; Cieraad, 1999; Miller, 2001; Blunt & Dowling, 2006; Buchli, 2010).

As we saw in the previous chapter, home and property were from the start the main policy of development and economic transformation of post-war Greek state. It is a development policy, a technology of normalization and violent modernization, which invested in the sector of extended construction, encouraging mainly in law and taxation terms the practice of *antiparochi*.[5] In the post-war period, in the liberal Greek state medley, policies focused on the modernization of the infrastructure of big cities, but also on home ownership through the purchase of apartments in new buildings that were massively constructed, initially in the center of big cities (Burgel, 1976; Maloutas, 1990; Oikonomou, 1987; Oikonomou, 1999, 2008).

---

4   On the implementation of technologies of hegemony and power in the context of neoliberal policies in the public space of the city, but also policies of reaction, counter-hegemonic rhetorics and new pluralist cosmopolitan policies, see Tsibiridou (2017), Deltsou and Tsibiridou (2017).

5   At this point, I wish to thank Professor Chastaoglou, Professor of Architecture at the Aristotle University of Thessaloniki, who, during a meeting I had with her in 2015 in her office, explained to me that *antiparochi* is not a law, but a practice of the market itself. However, it is common to present it in the Greek literature as a law. For example, in her latest piece of work on middle class, Aranitou (2018) reproduces this tradition by mentioning: "built in very small plots of old houses and based on the *antiparochi* law, the newly built buildings contributed to the creation of a new model with shops to rent on the ground floor and apartments on the other floors, contributing also spatially to the expansion of small enterprises in urban settings [Translated from the Original in Greek]." (2018, p. 130)

Moving from the old home, where they were born and raised, to a new apartment, mainly in the middle of the 1960s, the informants felt *"noikokyraioi"*, "modernized" and "humanized".[6] The demolition of the old home and the acquisition of the coveted modern apartment represents the final step in a course of daily arduous and expensive instances of what was modern and nationally accepted, but also of practices aiming at being part of a fantasy of the European "civilized" world, which differentiates them from the non-western, the "non-civilized", the *non-noikokyraioi* others.

In this chapter, an effort is made to analyze the discourses, conceptualizations and specific everyday practices of the subjects during the first decades of their life, the ones that preceded the 1960s, which seem to have shaped the informants' post-war practices and choices. The home where they were born and raised is the place where the need for the new was shaped; it was embodied with the help of *antiparochi* in the post-war apartment: there the subjects as successful *noikokyraioi* recall the past and worry about the present.

By comparing the discourses of informants from Toumba and the city center, we attempt to investigate the extent to which the stereotyped assumption applies, according to which the settlement of the refugees of Toumba was socially and culturally marginalized compared to the city center. In parallel, we seek the significance of such assumption, which takes the form of symbolic capital for our informants (Ioannidou, 2008; Kokot, 1994).

The testimonies from the field can be classified into two main categories: those informants who recompose narratives of "poverty" and "marginalization" during the Nazi occupation and the first decade of the post-civil war state and those who recompose different narratives, which taxonomically should probably be placed at the polar opposite of "poor" others. More specifically, the social memory of refugeeism[7] is reproduced in both categories of narratives, recomposing a different sense of self for the subject that is linked or not linked to it based on the subject's family history.[8]

---

6   See Bakalaki (2003, pp. 218–219) on how the Greeks associate in general immigrants-foreigners with poverty, deprivation and backwardness to suppress their own similar past, managing thus to take some distance from it. The foreign others, hungry and poor, are jealous and covet the wealth painstakingly obtained within the context of growth in Greece and are led to criminal acts, such as burglary, aiming to put in danger the *noikokyri* and his/her ability to protect his/her property and family. By breaking into the prosperous houses (houses of *prokopi*), the immigrants-burglars unclothe the modern subjects leaving them socially and economically exposed.

7   Regarding the memory function in the establishment of the refugee identity intergenerationally in Greece, see Kyriakidou-Nestoros (1993b, pp. 227–290), Vergeti (2000, pp. 273–288), Voutira (1994, pp. 175–183, 1997, pp. 171–206), Collard (1993, pp. 357–389), Deltsou (2004, pp. 252–285), Hirschon-Filippaki (1993, pp. 327–356).

8   On the establishment of the identities of the refugees through the experience of their integration and adaptation to Greece, but also on the ways in which these are remod-

The new apartment as a result of post-war policies of cultural, economic and social reshaping of the country lifts progressively the borderline between Toumba and the city center and is translated by all informants, for different reasons, into a material proof of their successful participation in what is known in the public discourse as post-war modernization and Europeanization of the Greek society.[9]

3.1 The paradigm of Thessaloniki

In this specific study about the city of Thessaloniki, it is also interesting to focus on the residential policies implemented after 1912 and after the integration of the city into the Greek state, but also the subsequent population exchange as a result of signing the Treaty of Lausanne in 1923, which radically changed population sizes and the residential map of the city.[10] The choice of the state to plan almost exclusively settlements of refugees at the boundaries of the city had significant social and cultural consequences both on the city itself and on its inhabitants. The paradigm of Thessaloniki is different from that of Athens, mainly because of the history of the city as important urban center of the Ottoman empire.[11] Thessaloniki was "modernized" already by the mid-19th century as an important administrative Ottoman city, to respond to and integrate with the western modernity and meet the requirements of its pro-western urban classes threatening the cohesion and sovereignty of the empire (Anastasiadou, 2008; Colonas, 2005; Karadimou-Gerolympou, 1995, 1997, 2008, 2013; Mazower, 2006).

After the progressive fall of the walls in 1860 (Kyriakidou-Nestoros, 1993b, pp. 242–243), as it was the case also in other important metropoles of western empires, little by little and in particular towards the end of the 19th and the beginning of the 20th century, buildings that are representative of the specific era appear in Ottoman Thessaloniki. Following the model of the urban planning of Paris, Hamburg and

---

eled through the contact with other refugees or native populations, see: Karalidou (2008), Potiropoulos (2003), Voutira (1994, 1997, 2003) and Kyriakidou-Nestoros (1993a).

9   See Karalidou (2008), Deltsou (1995), on the resignifications of identity within the framework of political and social processes of modernization and development. More specifically, see Karalidou (2008), on the remodeling of cultural identities and their instrumentalization within the framework of European development programs.

10   See Voutira (1997, pp. 111–131) and Voutira and Harrell-Bond (2000, pp. 56–57).

11   Besides most studies that deal with the residential policy of the Greek state, family and residence use mainly the example of the capital city, a peripheral city of the Ottoman state that had to become the capital city of a newly established national state and an ambitious nationalism (see the review by Vanessa Martin (1997) about the ravaging and often exotic way in which cities of the Islamic world are grouped compared to the European example as a single constructed category).

other European metropoles, avenues are created, and big squares are designed, while the city expands to the east with the design of the luxurious district of Pyrgoi (Castles), current Faliro, with the aim of changing the social map of the city as well as the management of everyday life by introducing the concept of summer house. Upper-middle-class families leave their houses in the city center at Frangomacha-las[12] over the weekend, to travel by horse-drawn carriage to the countryside, to the seaside district of Faliro.

Buildings such as the administrative palace of the city, known as *konaki*, seat of the *wali*[13], important hospitals and vocational schools, charitable foundations and parks were built by important architects of the city, who were influenced mainly by the western style of eclecticism, for example Vitaliano Poselli and Pierro Arrigoni, but also of neoclassical architecture, for example Ernest Ziller and Xenophon Paion-idis. After the integration of Thessaloniki into the Greek state and the fire of 1917, an international architecture committee was established at the initiative of the government of the Liberals, which prepared a rational urban plan, on which the future remodeling of the destroyed city was to be based. This plan aimed to establish a modern European but mainly Greek big city, in the spirit of urban integration that characterized the governments of Eleftherios Venizelos and more specifically the then minister of transportation Alexandros Papanastasiou.

The developments following the fire changed drastically the population size of the city, making the housing problem one of the biggest problems of that period. From an important administrative Ottoman city with its mainland in the broader area of the Balkans, Thessaloniki is transformed into a small province city suffocating in the Greek national boundaries and the different economy. The arrival of thousand Christian refugees from Asia Minor (1923) requires leaving aside and readjusting the urban planning provisions of the city plan of 1921, leading necessarily to a residential development and expansion of a different logic (Chastaoglou, 2008, p. 54; Kyriakidou-Nestoros, 1993b, pp. 242–248).

---

12   It was a district of the city center where residents of western and central European origin lived.

13   Administrative title that was used in the Ottoman Empire to designate governors of administrative divisions.

3.2 About the material recognition of refugeeism: the first home [14]

In this subchapter, we will present the modalities in which the active subjects, by means of the material circumstance of the apartment, reconstruct their everyday life of the first home, where they were born and raised, to potentially understand the importance of the relationship with home, both as material reality and as an idea in shaping the individual's personality, but also to show the dynamics of this interaction. Moreover, highlighting the practices and conceptualizations around the first home will help understand the progressive transformation of the informants as a consequence of the changes in homes themselves but also of their moving into new homes, within the context of modernization characterizing them after the second half of the 1950s.

The materiality of the transition from the "old" to the "new and modern" confirms to the subjects the discourses of an efficient and successful policy of the post-war liberal urban state, which is directly linked with their personal *"prokopi"* (prosperity) (Bakalaki, 2003, pp. 214–217). The narration of this experience takes special dimensions in the specific circumstance of its recomposition during the long Greek crisis. The narrations of poverty and deprivation during the war but also during the first years of settlement in Thessaloniki give their place to narrations of a successful integration into the new way of living that characterizes the new middle strata after the war, to which the narrators feel they belong. At the level of everyday practices in the apartment and in the public sphere, the subjects feel they consume a unified way of living, within the context of a "common" and "national" culture (Williams, 1994), recomposing in their discourses the identity of the Greek *noikokyraios*. The concept of the "common culture", the way of living that is progressively perceived as normal, and its association with the ideological objectives of the western urban class to affirm itself at political and social level against a different way of living that characterized pre-industrial humans, is thoroughly developed by Norbert Elias in his book *"The Civilizing Process. The History of Manners"* (1997), which investigates in a clearly structural and functional way what we find also in other studies that try to analyze the emergence of the urban class and the prevalence of the capitalist way of produc-

---

14   The division and development of chapters follow the chronological order of the most important phases in the life and evolution of the study subjects, which appear in the changes of the materiality that characterizes houses and the whole built area that surrounds and finally shapes the identities of my informants. Therefore, the period 1928–1960 concerns women and men who were born at the end of the 1920s, lived in post-war Thessaloniki and experienced the change examined by this study as a research hypothesis. The chapters develop chronologically to reach this day, following the life of the subjects, involving also descendants of them, but also friends or other informants born at the end of the 1950s and the beginning of 1960s.

tion. Most studies[15] of this type, having an essentialist and rather holistic analytical point of view, eventually fail to show the importance of individualized action and the process of establishing the self through experiences of resistance, subordination and integration into different forms of power and hegemony.[16] On the other hand, they are of help, to the extent they provide a frame of reference, in order to perceive the discourses of the western hegemony, which are used also by the Greek state in the post-war era and can be identified in the ways in which my informants recompose the *noikokyraios* identity in their narration. [17]

3.2.1 Poverty, deprivation and strategies to recover a lost world

The "first home", often described by the inhabitants of refugee origin in Kato Toumba as the "old" or "low" house, is the one granted by the Greek state to the families of the informants after they became refugees in Greece. The informants from Toumba recall the "old home" by placing great importance on it, probably because socially it played a decisive part in shaping their own identity.[18]

The relationship of people with privately owned land or with the apartments they own in Greece is particularly useful to understand the importance of home owner-

---

15   On the Swedish urban class see Frykman and Löfgren (1987), on the English working class see Thompson (1991), on the English urban class in the Victorian era see Bailey (2013), on the respective French class in the years after Louis XIV the Sun King and the concept of "civilization" at the polar opposite of the German urban "culture [Kultur]" shaped vis-à-vis the way of living at the court of Frederick the Great and aiming at the emergence of a national culture based on and nurtured by the German language and education see Norbert Elias (2000), Habermas (1991) and Bourdieu (2008).

16   See Tsibiridou (2017), on alternative ways of resistance to space in modern neoliberal policies of transformation and refinement of the city.

17   Of particular interest for the Greek paradigm is the study by Greek folklorists of the conceptual differentiation in the Greek context between a popular and a scholarly urban culture. See Bada (2011) on the characteristics of residence and the everyday life of the Greeks in the pre-modern years but also in the first years of establishment of the Greek state; see Zografou-Korre (2007) on the everyday life of the Greeks from 1750 to 1950; see Selekou (2004) on the everyday life of the Greek upper-middle-class of the diaspora, mainly about the influence on decoration and everyday way of living of these families in a multi-ethnic and intercultural frame of reference; see Potamianos (2015) on the everyday life and practices of the Athenian *noikokyraioi* from 1880 to 1925.

18   See Potiropoulos (2003, pp. 71–104), on the first years of settlement and the survival strategies of the Refugees in Nea Michaniona in Thessaloniki; see also Karalidou (2008, pp. 125–168), about how the past of the communities in the sense of the established collective memory but also in the sense of tradition is reproduced intergenerationally and determines the cultural, economic and political relationships between active subjects within the framework of European and national policies of development and adaptation of the Greek countryside.

ship[19] in Greece and its dynamics in shaping identities (Vlachos, 1978). The practice of home ownership acquires a different dimension in the informants who are descendants of first-generation refugees, since the first home of the family in the host country works as a place of transition and maybe recovery of the lost domesticity, which is constantly reproduced through the narrations from generation to generation (Kyriakidou-Nestoros, 1993b, pp. 233–240; Potiropoulos, 2003, pp. 15–35; Karalidou, 2008, pp. 24–27). Moreover, few years after the exchange and the arrival of one million refugees, the Greek state with the legislative decree of 1927[20] provides for the first time for ownership of a floor or apartment, with the aim of maximizing the percentages of small properties in Greece, also paving the way for the construction of apartment buildings.[21]

The informants describe "old home" spaces, recall family members and neighbors, reconstructing in the present the lived experiences of their first years in Toumba until their adulthood. According to Passerini (1987), oral narrations are based on subjectivity and are not static memories of the past, but memories subject to a new processing based on the experiences and political positioning of the informant (Passerini, 1979, as cited in Abrams, 2014, p. 19). According to Abrams (2014, p. 19), the researcher must investigate how and why the specific narrations are produced. More specifically, one must be able to distinguish the environments of the narration facts, the cultural environment of the memory from that of remembrance. Kostis Kornetis (2015) refers to this particularity of oral interviews trying, as he characteristically mentions, to understand the facts that shaped the hegemonic narration about the Athens Polytechnic uprising. For this reason, he goes beyond the understanding of the facts, to the second life at collective and individual level (2015, p. 26). The important political and social changes that followed influence the narrations of the past of the protagonists of this generation in the present. Kornetis argues (2015, p. 26) that this distortion is not a product of the memory but is directly linked to the fact that the point of view of the protagonists of that time changed in the context of the historical circumstance in which the interviews are taking place (2015, p. 27). Thus, in this field survey, the place and moment in which

---

19   In the field of social sciences, there are very interesting studies focusing on the importance of home ownership and the objective of acquiring property, especially in the post-war context of reconstruction, see Tsoukalas (1977, 1981, 2005), Nikolaidou (1993), Maloutas (1990) and finally Giannoulopoulos (1992). In his ethnographic study on Voula, anthropologist Leonidas Oikonomou (2008) associates the post-war relationship with land and home with practices of the previous century and more specifically the conflicts around the land ownership and ottoman properties that characterized the post-revolutionary Greek society.

20   Official Government Gazette (of the H.R.), volume 1, serial number 46/LD 1/1927.

21   For more details see Gerolympou (1995); Chastaoglou (2008) on the concept of settlement of refugees with the aim of their successful social, cultural and economic integration in the host country after World War I, see Voutira and Harrell – Bond (2000, pp. 56–76).

the informants talk about the difficult years in the first homes of the settlement do matter. Their answers are reconstructed in the context of security of the modern apartment, but in a period when people in Greece feel particularly insecure about the future, due to the financial crises occurring in Greece already since 2008.

Through the Greek residential policy of establishing settlements composed entirely of refugees, especially from 1927 onwards, based on Miller's (2005) theory of materiality, the particular sense of self of the informants is objectified and placed at the polar opposite of the sense of self of the native inhabitants of the city. The spatial reality of the refugee settlement of Toumba as the experienced "outside world" according to the Hegelian consideration contributes, in cultural and material terms, to the establishment of the subject-refugee, who is obliged by the host country to live on the fringes of the developed historical center. The new material structures of the everyday life of Toumba seem to structure, according to Bourdieu (2008), the specific subjectivities of its inhabitants.[22]

Already from the beginning of the survey, I realized how important it was for the informants to narrate and describe the first forms of dwelling and in particular that house, which for most of them was the first home of their family in Greece and more specifically in the city of Thessaloniki.[23]

As we will see below from the ethnographic examples, the informants reconstruct in the setting of the modern apartment the everyday life and the practices of the "old home"[24], documenting through the materiality of their new spatial reality the successful personal fight to climb the social ladder, but also to integrate with the rest of the city. The old materiality is transferred through the objects-heirlooms, photographs, people and relationships of the past and present, by objectifying the continuity and evolution of their family identity and the substitution of an urban past, which was lost before they became refugees in Greece.[25] The identity of the cit-

---

22 In this way, Toumba becomes "the place of settlement", as Potiropoulos (2001, p. 264) characteristically calls Michaniona in his ethnography. Space is directly and decisively associated with the shaping of refugees' cultural identity and the specific history of their refugeeism (see Skouteri-Didaskalou, 1994, p. 84, as cited in Potiropoulos, 2001, p. 264).

23 In his ethnography on Nea Michaniona, Potiropoulos (2003, pp. 40–41) refers to the establishment of a collective memory, which concerns mainly the difficult experiences of the first setting-up and adaptation to the refugee settlements, but also to how this memory inflences and shapes intergenerationally the refugee identity of the residents of this specific settlement.

24 They use the term "old" to refer to the previous form of dwelling, the home where they were born and raised. The "old" is not always used to indicate oldness, but mainly to differentiate it from the apartment, which is the new home, in the sense of modern.

25 See the study by anthropologist Sophie Chevalier (1999) on the importance of the discursive practices, especially for objects that are not used.

izen-refugee or the refugee-poor/*tourkosporos*[26]/foreigner is transformed together with the transformation and the evolution of the *Pronoia* (welfare) home. From the "old *Pronoia* (welfare) home" initially hosting the families, we pass schematically to the narration of the proud person with Asia Minor origin, who manages, with the very few means at his/her disposal, to beautify the low *Pronoia* (welfare) home during the first post-war decades, while through the practice of *antiparochi* this same person finally achieves his/her successful integration into the projects of the domestic post-war way of living of the *noikokyraioi*.

3.2.2 Short personal and family stories about homes and belongings. Stories of extreme poverty and refugeeism

Using representative discourses from the field, the analysis will be structured around the above points, which in the discourse of my informants in Kato Toumba are crystallized through their own characteristic conceptualizations:

a) poverty, deprivation and survival strategies of the refugees
b) desire for upward social mobility, progress and integration into the social body of nation/state
c) adaptation to the development model of the modern Greek state

All the examples used here come from the refugee residential settlement of "NT"[27] of Kato Toumba; we will focus on its special characteristics now. The parents of my informants were forced to come to Thessaloniki as refugees during the period from

---

26   In Greek "Τουρκόσπορος" (lit. "Turkey seed"): offensive term to describe a Greek from Asia Minor (translator's note).

27   Initials NT are an acronym of the words "**N**ewly built [houses] of **T**oumba", which were built by the welfare fund in the settlement delimited by the following streets: Faiakon, Rodou, Chourmouzi, Chiou, Traianou, Apollonos and Tenedou. Contrary to other dwelling forms in Kato and Ano Toumba, these houses were built duplex houses with a tiled roof, consisting of one or two rooms, a living room, a kitchen and a bathroom. As it can be seen in the concessions, these houses were built in relatively big plots, which the residents transformed into beautiful gardens. The Social welfare service was exclusively in charge of the construction of the Newly built houses of Toumba; in addition to them, different authorities, such as the healthcare fund and the chamber of commerce, constructed for the same purpose different types of residence, such as the eight-sided shacks of Ano Toumba, one-floor duplex houses of the healthcare fund and chamber of commerce, German containers and *tôles* (metal hubs) in Ano Toumba, which much later housed the population "stricken by guerillas", and finally the wooden shacks, which were built in the current area of Klimataria, on An. Romylia, Faiakon, Pylaias and Dorylaiou streets. For more details, see Bountidou and Stergioudis (2002, 79–84).

1914 to 1923 and some of them initially had to stay in military wards and wooden shacks, before getting permanent houses from the state.[28]

Did all those people live in the same house?
"No, my uncle Christos received another house, because he had two children, so he received one room. He received one room. We received two."
Were those ready?
"[...] first my parents stayed at shacks..."
What kind of shacks were they?
"This is how they were called, shacks... They were made of wood... The state had built them so that refugees had a place to stay. A long time later the state built houses for them. And they owed money... They had not received a concession"
Was the house built where the shack was?
"No, the first house was a shack..."
Right, what about the house they gave them later?
"No, that was a built one..."
Does this mean there were built houses?
"Built houses, yes. Built, without a balcony... This how they were at that time, without balconies... I remember, our house then did not have any balconies... When my sister got married, then we built the balcony on the front side, you see? I remember this... And we painted the exterior side, so the wall was strikingly white"
Were there any other houses next to it?
"Yes, all houses were in a row, one after another."
Were they all refugees?
"They were all refugees; they gave them houses..."
And then you paid for these houses?
"We paid, so that my dad could get the concession. But he had not paid it off... He took it and assigned it to himself. But we also had rights, we were four children, that's why he got two rooms".[29]

It is interesting to note that these types of dwelling are never characterized as "homes"[30] mainly because of their transitional nature[31], but also because there was no ownership relationship, which was the case for the next type of dwelling.

---

28   On informants living in the military facilities of the Entente Cordiale allies and the Holy Union of Thessaloniki, see Bountidou and Stergioudis (2002, pp. 34–35) and Ioannidou (2008).

29   Translated Excerpt from the testimony of Maria from "NT".

30   On the "household" meaning of the term "home" in the Greek cultural context, see Papataxiarchis (2006a); Bakalaki (2003).

31   As characteristically mentioned by Voutira (1994, p. 177), refugees were initially in a "pending" situation, hoping that soon they would go back to their real homes.

"Not *tôles* (metal hubs), these were shacks. You know where there were *tôles* (metal hubs)? In Foinikas, in Ano Toumba. They gave us those when we came as refugees. Instead of giving us houses, this is what they gave us."[32]

As it can be seen also in the *Pronoia* (welfare) archives, the "NT" residential square was dwelled for the first time towards the end of the 1920s.[33] The settlement of Kato Toumba was the largest refugee settlement among 50 other refugee settlements in the city (Ioannidou, 2008; Kokot, 1994). As it results from the official decision of the General Administration of Macedonia, houses with the initials "NT" were distributed to 251 families.[34]

The ministerial decision of 1925 with number 16314 (About the expropriation of private lands located at the district of Kampoutzides of Thessaloniki)[35] provided for the mandatory expropriation of the private lands that belonged to the native inhabitants known as *kampoutzides*.[36]

With the above-mentioned decision the area of Toumba soon becomes a material reality (Lefebvre, 1991) and the houses or plots without a building are distributed to the refugees against an amount of money, which is regularly repaid to the state in the form of instalments.

The informants, to whom I will refer using fictitious names, already during the first minutes of the interview, point out that they were born in "NT", as if this was

---

32   Testimony of Koula from Klimataria.

33   It seems that the construction of houses in "NT" settlement started one year after the expropriation of the lands of *Kampoutzides* in this area (see Bountidou & Stergioudis, 2002, p. 82).

34   Prot. number 126027/Gen. Administration/Dept. of Antilipsi/Gr. L. of Residence/ 12/10/1934.

35   Number 16314/ Government Gazette (of the H.R.) 17/volume B/17.2.1925, (Welfare Archive).

36   The *kampoutzidianoi* or else *Pylaiotes* possessed in the broader area of current Kato Toumba lands where their animals browsed. According to testimonies, the *Kampoutzidianoi* owe their name to their quality of *kastrofylakes* (keepers of the castle) on the side of the gate of Kalamaria (see Bountidou & Stergioudis, 2002, p. 63). The *Kampoutzidianoi* were one of the biggest "enemies" of the refugees of Toumba, because the choice of the state to expropriate their lands in order to build the specific settlement led to big conflicts and retaliations between the refugees and the residents of current Pylaia. Even nowadays, a lot of informants from Toumba paint a grim picture of *Pylaiotes* as they reproduce the experiences of the first years of their parents' settlement in the area. The informants stress mainly their classist and ideological differentiation from *Pylaiotes*. The *Kampoutzidianoi* or *Pylaiotes* are described as "peasants and uncivilized", who dealt exclusively with okra cultivation. The subjects stress that until recently Pylaia was a village and its conversion into an expensive and luxurious suburb through the construction of housing complexes from 2000 onwards has not changed the manners of the native inhabitants, which differentiated it from Toumba. In the Album of the Municipality of Thessaloniki on Toumba (Bountidou & Stergioudis, 2002, p. 72), there are plenty of oral testimonies on Pylaiotes and their relationships with the first inhabitants of Kato Toumba.

something I should know from the beginning to understand the story they have to tell. The initials "NT" work for the inhabitants of this neighborhood like the number of their identity card. The establishment of this specific area by the state and *Pronoia* (welfare), dwelling in it and then its transformation through their individual efforts provides an element of identity and personal reference for them. [37]

When later on, towards the end of the field survey, I found the Toumba folder in the *Pronoia* (welfare) archives, where family files were kept for all those refugees who were eligible for urban settlement, the initials "NT" and the number that accompanied these two letters helped me identify the houses of the informants in the cadastral tables but also in the site plans of Toumba, which had been filed based on these initials.

In the Social Welfare archive, I found all visual and written documents that confirmed and complemented the informants' lives, covering a wide chronological range of development for them and their houses. My informants did not refer in detail to the "first house" from the beginning. The question "how do you remember your old house?" evokes memories of deprivation and family conflict.[38] It's not only poverty and adversities that a family of refugees experiences, especially during the first decade after the settlement; it is mainly the everyday life and practices that remove from these places the possibility to be experienced as a shelter, as a place where one can experience feelings of security and warmth.[39]

My informants describe very little the interior of the old houses. They only mention the number of rooms and the size of the plot.

> "It was eighty-eight square meters, consisting of two rooms, a kitchen and a living room"[40]. "It was 92 sq.m. with one room in a plot of 127.34 sq.m."[41]. "It was 92 sq.m. in a plot of 128.60 sq.m."[42]

The size of the plot but also the number of rooms constitute for the informants an element of distinction, not only because two rooms and more square meters of a plot rendered their life in these houses more comfortable and pleasant, but also because two or more rooms had a taxonomic function, as those who had more rooms enjoyed

---

37 On the importance of space in shaping a refugee identity, see Potiropoulos (2003, pp. 15–17).

38 The association of the first houses with negative refugeeism experiences and the first difficult years in Greece can be found also in other ethnographic studies which concern populations of refugees in Thessaloniki, see Potiropoulos (2003, p. 156).

39 On the association between social relationships and places we live in, see Chevalier (1999).

40 From the narration of Maria from Kato Toumba. All excerpts from the informant interviews have been translated from Greek to English.

41 From the narration of Soula from Kato Toumba.

42 Narration of Paraskevi from Kato Toumba. The numbers are accurate and confirmed by the concessions and property transfer deeds, which the resident acquired upon full payment of the property.

a better social position. Subsequently these same elements will constitute the object of claim and conflict within the context of the practice of *antiparochi*.[43] Constructors show a clear preference for big plots, as they provide an increased building surface.

The settlement of Toumba was built with the responsibility of Social Welfare and the assistance of *EAP* (Refugee Settlement Commission)[44]. The residences built there and in other refugee settlements followed a rather rational "modernist design", while they were built through contracting by private constructors: entire residential blocks of the settlement bore the initials of their names (Chastaoglou, 2008, pp. 70–71). According to the welfare archive in Kato Toumba, "German" prefabricated wooden houses, one-floor residences and arrays of two-floor residences were built.[45] In general, as it can be seen also on the topographic maps, the houses were built one right next to the other, following a "rectangular grid" with small yards along the street.

---

43   As mentioned also in the introduction, *antiparochi* is a mechanism of the market launched in the first post-war years, as a result of the Greek state policy for massive production of cheap residences. According to the study by Katsikas (2000) *antiparochi* goes hand in hand with the annulment of money functions. Instead of money, landholders choose an apartment as a plot equivalent. According to Katsikas (2000), this practice shows that landholders do not consider themselves owners of urban land, which they could sell out to get a considerable financial capital, which in the future they could invest with the best possible return and the best possible profit. They rather considered themselves as owners of a house, which they granted to the constructor to get a new one in replacement of the old one. Therefore, *antiparochi* was implemented to meet exclusively housing needs. Regardless of their financial status, my informants saw the apartment(s) resulting from *antiparochi* as profit, as a gift they received and for which they felt lucky (see also Athanasiou, 2001).

44   The Greek government, to provide care and settlement for the Christian refugees arriving from Asia Minor, asked the League of Nations for help. On the initiative of the League of Nations, in September 1923, an autonomous organization with full legal status, the Refugee Settlement Commission (*EAP*), was established in Athens. Its main mission was to provide refugees with productive employment and permanent housing.

45   It seems that Kato Toumba was built following a specific urban plan. Contrary to Ano Toumba, which was built without any plan, Kato Toumba followed a regular street planning (Bountidou & Stergioudis, 2002, pp. 34 and 85; Ioannidou, 2008; Kokot, 1994, 1996). Generally speaking, the example of Toumba and Charilaou contradicts the studies concerning big urban centers and post-war reconstruction. In these studies, an effort is made to differentiate Greece from Northern Europe, on the grounds that there is no policy of financial capital concentration, which would be invested in the reconstruction of the city with the exclusive control of the state itself. In the case of Thessaloniki, already in the Ottoman era, within the context of modernization of the empire, the city meets the same fate as many other European cities: following the fall of the wall, the city acquires new urban planning and modern infrastructure. After the fire of 1917, which destroyed a big part of the pre-modern and transitional phase of Thessaloniki of the last years of the 19th century, the Greek state formed a committee consisting of an equal number of Greek and foreign experts, who prepared a modern city plan aiming at the rationalization of the urban space in the spirit of similar modern reconstruction plans of European metropoles.

The residence was transferred by the state to the family head, in the name of whom the relevant folder has been kept up to this day. However, in the concession as well as in the sworn statement by which each refugee applied to the Greek state for urban settlement, all family members before and after their transfer to Greece were mentioned, and the right to live in the specific residence was recognized to the said family members.[46]

Quite often, while talking to the informants I had the impression I was reading again the official concession document, in which the state transferred the property in question, describing accurately its spaces and characteristics. This association of the quality of refugee with the material grant on behalf of the state, which is launched through these formal deeds, is quite interesting. Approximately one decade after their arrival in Greece, the state finally recognizes to these people the right to live in specific areas of the city, designing and implementing from above entire settlements in which refugees would live from that moment on their refugeeism, trying to reconstruct their lost previous life in the urban centers of the Ottoman Empire.[47]

My informants answer the questions about the "old house" by describing overall life and experience outside it; they remember the neighborhood and insufficient infrastructure that made everyday life difficult. They were all born, raised and some of them continued living in these houses for many years until they found their own personal pathway to follow; some of them never left, they simply moved to the apartment they acquired after the demolition of the old house and the construction of the multi-story apartment building. The lives of the residents of Kato Toumba are interwoven with one another, while the comparisons in relation to the material dimensions of the settlement of each family work taxonomically, creating the framework within which the present can be understood.

Maria is the last child of a family of nine members from the region of Istanbul. As it can be seen from the individual folder kept in the Welfare service, her family left for Greece in 1922 (Toumba Folder/ Department of Public Service). Initially the family lived in the "five wards of Toumba" and in 1930 got their own residence in "NT". Maria's "old" house in "NT" is associated with her parents' story, but also with the traumatic experiences of loss of people and belongings, which characterized the lives of the subjects of this study at least until the end of the 1950s.

---

46   See royal decree number 330 15 April/23 May 1960 (Official Government Gazette vol. A 69)/ Article 11 paragraph 3 of Article of royal decree dated 27–1/9.2.53.

47   According to Potiropoulos (2003, p. 15), the qualifying adjective 'new' usually used in the naming of neighborhoods consisting entirely of refugees has a dual function: on one hand, it reminds the place of origin; on the other hand, it promises the adaptation to the new place of settlement, which will become familiar.

"What can I remember, my son, poverty, problems, illnesses. When my parents came here, they were already married, my dad eloped with my mom and brought her here. My poor mom was an orphan, her mom had died young. In my mom's family, there were nine siblings [...]. My dad's family was richer than my mom's [...]. He also brought his own mom here; I remember my grandmother. I remember grandma Katina. Sure, she taught me how to knit and cook, she taught me so many things."

In Maria's narration, grandma Katina is a person associated with the "old house", since it is a person who takes care of her and teaches her things that will be useful in the future, when Maria becomes a *noikokyra* in the next phase of her life, when she leaves the "old house". At the beginning Maria refuses to talk about the everyday life in that home, which is probably associated with unpleasant experiences; thus, she reconstructs the narration of her grandma, who was the only positive element in the context of the old home of extreme poverty and unhappiness. In the narration of the "old house", grandma Katina is always a positive element for Maria. It is the woman who teaches her behaviors and manners that the informant will be able to capitalize in the coming years, when she moves as a daughter-in-law to the house of her in-laws. Katina comes back again and again to the narration concerning the "old house", as she represents the almost stereotyped role model of the good *noikokyra* from Asia Minor, who cooks well, is active, strict, diligent and clean (Hirschon, 2006, pp. 59–91; Kokot, 1994).[48] The "old house" will often provide the pretext for negative comments regarding Maria's origin. However, Maria chooses to identify with her grandmother, grandma Katina, considering the advice she received from her as the dowry she could not receive from her parents and in particular her father.

"Grandma worked in rich homes. She was a good cook. She was an old woman, maybe even sixty years old. In any case, she looked old. She used to wear only black clothes because she was a widow. She used to put her hair in a bun. She was very active, very smart, very good cook. She loved cleanliness, she came from Turkey and brought two young men here, my dad and my uncle. She spoke Greek and Turkish. My mom spoke Turkish, too. Grandma was very strict with everyone. I remember rich ladies showed a preference for her. There were a lot of rich ladies here then! The ones we found when we came here. They did not come after us, they were already here when we came."

The pattern of the widow in black clothes, who works in the "good" homes of the city center as a cook, loves cleanliness and is particularly strict, is repeated in many of

---

48   See also Dubisch (2019, pp. 10–11); du Boulay (1974) and Hirschon (1978, 1981), on the association of women with the domestic sphere and on how their lives are determined by the tasks and duties within the framework of the houselod, cited in Bakalaki (2003, pp. 215–216).

the interviews about the old and poor houses of Toumba, setting spatial boundaries, which separate the settlement of the refugees from the city center of the native population.[49] Grandma Katina in the ethnographic example of Maria, as well as other women in the descriptions of the informants, have cultural characteristics that allow for the association with the values of the city center.[50]

Paraskevi, Maria's neighbor from "NT", is the child of a four-member family of refugees from Hili (Sile) in Asia Minor. Paraskevi's mother is a widow and raises on her own her three children in the house of the refugee settlement. Paraskevi remembers her mother as a very young and beautiful woman, always in black because she was a widow. In the ethnographic example of Paraskevi, we see once again the cultural characteristics and specific value codes that some refugees bring with them and use them to build bridges with city residents outside the settlement and the common experience of extreme poverty and deprivation that refugees experience there (Potiropoulos, 2003, p. 108). Paraskevi's mother works in the house of an employee of the consulate of Great Britain. This differentiates her from the other women of the neighborhood, whom she avoided, *"because they were sharp-tongued and engaged in gossip"*; these features were often assigned also by other informants to neighbors who originated from Smyrna.[51]

Paraskevi's mother did not allow her daughter to spend time with the other children of the neighborhood, and in particular with the children that belonged to the Roma ethnic group and lived just across their house in shacks. Her mother even sent her to a private school to prevent her from socializing in the neighborhood. Until the end of the 1990s, that settlement was adjacent to slums, which are known to the informants as the "gipsy houses"[52]. These low houses were inhabited by Roma people, who most probably settled in the area before the refugees (Kokot, 1994). The informant's mother was for her, even when she was no longer alive, home itself; it was the

---

49   Regarding the structural, for the Greek society, distinction between refugees and native people, see Kyriakidou-Nestoros (1993b, p. 240), Potiropoulos (2003, pp. 106–108), Karalidou (2008, pp. 24–27).

50   As it can be seen in the official refugee population census of 1923 (source: Hellenic Statistical Authority – ELSTAT), the number of women who arrived in Greece was significantly higher than that of adult men. According to the population census of 1928 (source: Hellenic Statistical Authority – ELSTAT), widows who arrived in Greece with their children during that period accounted for a significant share of refugee adult women in total. It is worth noting that out of one hundred women 17.53 are widows, when 12.11 women are widows every 100 women of the total population (see also Hirschon, 2006, p. 95).

51   Regarding the cultural characteristics that were stereotypically attributed to refugees from various parts of the Ottoman Empire, see Kokot (1994, pp. 144–154), Hirschon (2006, pp. 59–91) and Potiropoulos (2003, pp. 109–114).

52   Such racist expressions were commonly used in the field. It seems that the white colour of the skin, the Orthodox Christian religion and the Greek language were the most important attributes of hierarchical classification in the city.

person who decided about everything at home, to such an extent that the informant was often left without any initiative at all. When I first met Paraskevi, she welcomed me and wished to offer me something, as it happened also in other houses, in a characteristic ritual way. She went to the display case of her living room where she kept all her good quality china and took a silver tray, and placed on it a crystal pitcher with liqueur, a crystal glass and a small plate with sweet cherry. As she pointed out, there was no doily on the tray,

> "not because I am not a good noikokyra as my friends say making fun of me", she said, "but because I am tired of knitting in my life, I have lots of those to show you, but I don't want them anymore, I am sick of them".

Her mother did not allow her to deal with housework, so that she could focus on embroidery, which offered an additional income to the family. When her mother died, Paraskevi said characteristically that she felt as if she was orphaned, as if she had lost her home, as she didn't know even where to find cutlery.

> "My mother had spoiled me, that's why the neighbors make fun of me, saying that I don't know how to cook. But my mother was one of the best cooks in the rich homes, what could I do?"

Paraskevi's identification of home with her mother shows the importance of social relationships when one experiences a place as familiar, as it is the case for our personal home (Chevalier, 1999).

The "diligent"[53] woman described above by the informants is a carrier of culture and good manners, while at the same time she is the communication channel who links the refugee house with the "civilized" and rich urban environment of the city center. At this point it is important to reflect on the terms "culture" and "civilized"[54], which are associated in this specific ethnographic context with words used in the field, such as *"noikokyremenos"* (tidy) and *"noikokyris"*, which almost always appear in the narration as polar opposites of concepts such as "peasant", "rebel", "hick", "desperado".[55]

A characteristic example is that of Katia, who is a neighbor of the three women. Katia, who was born in Kato Toumba in 1937, stresses her distinctness vis-à-vis the people originating from Greece, pointing out hospitality and cleanliness as the main

---

53   On the diligent refugee woman but also the inheritance that refugees brought with them, and which differentiated them from the native population, see Hirschon (2006, pp. 80–91 & 267–278; Kokot, 1994, p. 154; Potiropoulos, 2003, p. 108).

54   See 2.2 *"The analytical category of 'class' and its use in the post-war Greek context"* and also Norbert Elias (1978); Habermas (1991); Bourdieu (2008). Also, on the concept of "civilized" within the framework of Toumba and refugees, see Kokot (1994, pp. 159–160).

55   These differentiations have been pointed out in detail in other enthographic studies in Greece, see Hirschon (2006) and Kokot (1994, 1996).

characteristics of differentiation, which are presented as gender-based characteristics attributed to the women from Smyrna.[56] Katia was born in "NT" to a family of refugees from Smyrna.

> "It was impossible for a woman from Smyrna to see someone at her doorstep and not ask: 'would you like a coffee, a glass of water?' They were very hospitable and loved cleanliness."

According to the same person, these gender-based characteristics were a cause to create the image of a loose woman, who threatened the rest of society with her gossip and spells.

> "This is exactly what they misunderstood. [...] women from Smyrna used to take a bath. They called them clean, prostitutes, because they washed themselves".

Katia is conscious of reproducing in her narration the discourses of a constructed collective memory of Smyrna and its residents of that time, however, she feels the need to do so, because these stories were reproduced daily at her parental home, leading her to establishing a hybrid cultural identity.[57] *"I never lived in Smyrna, but even today I use words my grandmother used to use"*. Katia believes that most people in "NT" were from Smyrna, but this is not confirmed by the individual welfare folders, where it can be seen that even those who declared that were from Smyrna originated from the periphery of the city and not necessarily from the city itself.

It seems that the cosmopolitanism of Smyrna and the contacts of a big port with Western European countries provided a cultural advantage for refugees, especially against the backdrop of absolute poverty and misery in which they were forced to live during the first years of their settlement in Toumba (Hirschon, 2006; Salamone & Stanton, 2019). Refugees could use it as an antidote to the nationalism and racism of the native population. Greek nationalism and oriental racism have always been underpinned by the ideological construct of the West being better, in terms of "self-colonization", as this has been described by anthropologist Herzfeld (2002), and the East being "underdeveloped". Within this context, refugees used means of urban culture that could grant them an advantage in their fight to integrate with the Greek nation and could respond to the ideological construct of the Greek middle classes that were being shaped, known as class of the *Noikokyraioi*. Thus, the old house is associated with extreme material poverty, deprivation, poor hygiene, illness and death, but at the same time it is the place where the need for a better future is born, using behaviors and life values that these people learn in their everyday life in the poor houses of settlement in Toumba.

---

56   On the cosmopolitan heritage of the refugees, see Hirschon (2006); Kokot (1994, 1996).
57   See Potiropoulos (2003, pp. 109–110), about localism and the "special us" that various groups of refugees developed because of their specific origin.

Of interest are the portraits of women wearing black clothes in the pictures used by the refugees in the various applications but also in the identity card certificates that they presented to the Social Welfare service during the first years after their arrival, to be eligible for urban settlement. Such portraits are hanging in the private spaces of the apartment, acting as a bridge between the past and the present of the narration. The paper by Nafissa Naguib (2008, pp. 231–244) is quite enlightening about how pictures work in the narrations as proof of what happened, contributing to recalling the memory but also to establishing a unified memory without breaks and gaps. Picture as heirloom contributes to linking the individual memory with the continuum of collective memory, through which the individual/narrator is linked with his/her society of reference. The possibility to visualize the informants' description of people who are no longer alive but were playing a leading part in the narrations of "old houses" transferred, in terms of time and place, the narration of now at the *antiparochi* apartment, to the place and time of the picture, but also to the feelings of the pictured woman who was seeking a shelter, as living in the wards and slums was threatening her own and her family's integrity. These "diligent" women worked for the family and were taking care of their grandchildren and children. In many households, where the "head" was missing because he had passed away prior to the family's move or immediately after the family's arrival in Greece, the widowed mothers were taking over the role of family head and the house was transferred to them and their children.

In 1941, Maria's grandmother, Katina, died suddenly because of a flu. *"[...] she died in the old house; I can remember the room where she died! I often went to see her."* Not for a moment does Maria reminisce about the years in which she lived in the "old" house. For her, that house and "NT" are associated with moments of pain, social contempt and marginalization. "NT" and the "old" house spatialize the association of the social status of the informant with the history of refugees, which was linked to social and cultural contempt. Her older sister's death followed her grandmother's death, while in that same period Greece was under Nazi occupation and big cities suffered because of the Great Famine.

Maria remembers:

"My poor mom took me on her shoulders and brought me to Limodon [Hospital for Pestilential Diseases of Thessaloniki] on foot". According to Maria, those who had typhus were not easily accepted in hospital. Her sister Anna avoided contact with the informant but unfortunately, she didn't make it and died from the same disease while she was still very young. "A lot of people died then. People died also from hunger on the streets. In 1941, we saw dead people on the streets as we walked."

Death and war hardship, poor infrastructure, the absence of asphalt pavement, the lack of electricity and water supply created a gloomy situation, which intensified the experience of elementary, frugal and dangerous living in the first home in the refugee settlement of Kato Toumba (Kokot, 1994; Bountidou & Stergioudis, 2002; Potiropoulos, 2003, pp. 82–83). Several informants from "NT" referred to the diseases that threatened their life every day. Tuberculosis and typhus were common in the settlement.[58]

Another ethnographic example from "NT" and the experiences of deprivation and extreme poverty is that of Antigoni. In this narration, it is interesting to note the distance that the informant takes from the narrations of the neighbor about the difficult conditions in "NT" describing poverty as the outside world, a situation that prevailed in other households and in the public sphere, but not in her own household. However, her brother, as we will see later on, experienced quite differently the living in that household, and this had an impact also on the way in which he evaluates his current life in the apartment he managed to get through *antiparochi*. Antigoni was born in "NT" in 1938. She was the last child of a family of eight. Her father Nikolaos was born in 1897. He had a cart and sold fruit and vegetables in the city center. She distinguishes her own case from the conditions of hunger and poverty in which other people lived in "NT".

> "My dad was self-employed, and he was doing very well; unlike others, we were not deprived of anything, despite the hunger around. My mom and dad were merchants, this is how they provided for us. Day after day someone died here from hunger. Us, thank God [...], they managed to keep us alive. [...] And no one was hungry".

Antigoni remembers in detail and speaks about this house and everyday life at home already from the beginning of the interview.

> "We had NT 20 [...]. You see current Apollonos street? – Back then it was called NT – this was a low house [...]. Here there was a room, a little living room, a rectangular one, and a kitchen, when we were born. When we were little kids! All us kids slept in one room, bedding on the floor. Then they started from there! In front of us there was a road full of stones. There was a big plot here!"

My informant refuses to accept the association of her family home with hunger, as this would question the family head's efforts to meet the requirements of his role,

---

58   The phenomenon of the outbreak of various diseases in Toumba, such as typhoid fever, malaria, smallpox, tuberculosis, etc., started already in the first years of settlement of the refugees and it was due to a combination of various factors, including insufficient nourishment, small dwelling places, and lack of rudimentary infrastructure, etc. (see Bountidou & Stergioudis, 2002, p. 70; Potiropoulos, 2003, p. 82).

namely to "feed" the members of his family.[59] This narration is linked to the gender-based dimension of Antigoni's identity, who, as we will have the chance to see also later on, recognizes the role of head and protector of the family in men. She tried to also raise her son with the same values, and she still takes care of him, even though he is now an adult. On the contrary, Maria's relationship with her father has an impact on the narration and perception of the old home, especially when her role model, her grandmother, died suddenly because of the bad conditions that prevailed in that neighborhood.

Antigoni's description of the home and neighborhood is, however, particularly important. The house was "low" and "small", since six siblings had no other choice but bedding on the floor. However, the informant does not remember being hungry and this narration is important, as it is experienced as an achievement of her parents in the particularly difficult historical circumstance of the famine of 1941.

Her brother, who was born in 1935 describes in a different way the family home and the experiences from everyday life on Apollonos street during the difficult years of the 1940s.

> "Real poverty, bloody poverty. [...] here, if we happened to find a piece of watermelon rind on the soil, we would pick it up to take a bite. The Germans would throw – rotten – potatoes in the torrent and we would go pick them up. We would pick up bush branches to get warm. Here, this was a dirt road. There was only soil and one ditch here and another one there, and the little houses – on both sides – were low, very low and had a living room, a kitchen, a room, and a corridor".
>
> Was everyone poor or could some people be distinguished?
>
> "They were all refugees; they were all at the same level... Later, they managed to do things... We also did a kitchen, and everyone else did so... Until that moment, we were all on an equal footing"
>
> When did things change for the better? Meaning, when do you remember your parents buy furniture and other stuff?
>
> "For sure after the 1960s".

He had to start working at a very early age to help his family, but also to earn his own living. However, he recalls the first house with nostalgia and reminisces about it and the neighborhood of Toumba, as it was, with the "low little houses". He considers that the construction wave that followed changed their life drastically, isolated them in their apartments and in their problems and the social cohesion that characterized the neighborhood during the previous years was lost.

---

59   On the gender and symbolic roles inside and outside the household, see Hirschon (2006, pp. 267–298), but also the whole sixth chapter on home, see Hirschon (2006, pp. 204–298).

Was it a united neighborhood?

"Here? Very much! Especially this street[60], they all stood together. Meaning, if someone got sick, they would all stand together, they all used to eat and drink together, they stayed united in pain. They all painted their houses white together, at the same time."

There was no competition?

"No! At Easter time all houses had the same color, the same shutters – those wooden shutters. One day all neighbors together would paint one house, one neighbor would cook, and they would have lunch all together, on the day after this would happen at another neighbor's place, on the following day at yet another neighbor's place. We wish to make a dessert? Let's do it all together. The neighborhood was united, especially this street."

How was life in the apartment compared to the low house?

"There is nothing like the low house, my son."

Really?

"Of course! The low house was the best one. Even though the members of a family had to stay all together, even if they were married. Look, you had your little garden, your flowers, you had peace of mind. Not like now, for instance with the building fees – I don't pay – the roof broke up – I don't pay! It's hopeless! You know what I say? I'm putting a curse to the person who invented these buildings! Yes, this worked for a lot of people, it is convenient, but we got locked in!"

As it can be seen in the above ethnographic example, the informant associates nostalgically the low house with freedom, neighborhood, classless society, security and solidarity. Although he and his sister demolished the low house to acquire through *antiparochi* the apartments where they are currently living, as individuals they are linked to the values and way of living they experienced in the spaces of their old home. For the informant, his identity as a resident of Toumba is inextricably linked to the experience of living at the settlement houses. He reminisces about them because of the distress he feels about the way of living in modern apartment buildings. The apartment and the choice to demolish the house in which he was raised result from the need to provide for the family members, the children who get married and create their own families, while new needs emerge.

A different ethnographic example of the first houses and their association with memories of extreme poverty and deprivation in Kato Toumba is the case of Koula. This narration provides another dimension of the social and cultural differentiations of refugees in the same settlement. Koula was born in 1928. She is a very good friend of the other female informants and remembers with a lot of pain the years spent in the wooden shacks of Klimataria.[61] The *paragkiotes* [people living in the wooden

---

60   He means Apollonos street, one of the central streets of Kato Toumba.

61   "Klimataria" is the name of the whole area around the bus station with the same name, which is adjacent to the neighborhood of "NT". According to the narrations of my informants, the wooden shacks were located at the intersection of Apollonos, Vosporou and Ar-

shacks], as those who did not live in the houses of "NT" built by the Social Welfare were called, were, as mentioned also earlier, a special category of tenants in this specific area. The plan was that they would live there provisionally; some of them managed to move to built houses in the following years, but several of them continued living in the wooden shacks until the beginning of the 1960s (Bountidou & Stergioudis, 2002, p. 82).

The wooden shacks had only one room on the ground floor, while the tenants later dug the floor of the room to create a basement kitchen, which was used also as a living room. These wooden houses did not have a bathroom, so the tenants used the public toilets that had been built specifically for them. This specific fact rendered the refugees of this category inferior to those who managed to get access to the little houses built by the welfare service. Koula is known in the area as the *yaourtsou* [the yogurt girl], because both her father and her future husband were professional producers and sellers of fresh yogurt.[62] Koula lived in the wooden shack with her five siblings, her parents and her future husband until 1950, when she moved a bit further, to a little house in "NT", where her husband was born and raised and where her widowed mother-in-law used to live at that moment.

> "It was very hard, listen, we didn't have any water, we only had central taps and had to go there to collect water [...]. When it was raining, the place got covered with mud all over, we could not go out. I got married and was still living in the shack, my parents in the basement and us on the ground floor. There was so much unhappiness, we ate all together, it was awful for all of us. Starvation! There was no food, we spent two years eating corn. We sold my sister's sewing machine in the village, we went to Kallikratia on foot to earn a piece of bread."

According to the informant, although everyone more or less had to live in the military wards for a few years, the fact that some managed to move subsequently to the so-called "newly built" houses worked as an element of discrimination against those who lived in the wooden shacks. There were many cases in which relationships and marriages were prevented because of this difference in dwelling in "NT".

> "All the rich ladies lived in the shacks for some years! They now pretend to be rich, don't listen to them. They considered themselves better than us because they lived in built houses. As if the shacks belonged to us! We were lucky enough with the *antiparochi*, now these apartments are ours."

---

takis streets. Nowadays there is an elementary school, and the rest of the area is covered by central streets and sidewalks.

62   The use of predicates and qualifying adjectives indicating the profession or the origin or the appearance is a common phenomenon among the old inhabitants of Kato Toumba; this shows also the dynamics developed at neighborhood level among the refugees of this area.

This fact shows that already in the first years of settlement in the area, there were classist differentiations, which created associations, groupings and exclusions. This conclusion is useful to help us understand that refugeeism itself was not a sufficient quality automatically linked to the positive characteristics of the refugee cosmopolitan culture described also by Hirschon (2006) in her ethnography about Kokkinia. Dwelling, origin, overall behavior but also social contacts with the native population differentiated people within the same settlement.

For Koula, the first home was clearly a place of hunger, loss and social contempt. Her family and herself experienced in that specific home but also in the broader neighborhood not only poverty and deprivation, but also marginalization on behalf of other refugees who enjoyed a better settlement. This experience will have an impact also on the following years in the informant's life, while the choice to abandon eventually the country in the post-war era and become an immigrant in Germany will be her only opportunity to integrate much later into what Toumba had evolved into after the mid-1960s. Koula remembers that to survive the Nazi occupation, and especially the Great Famine, her parents were forced to sell her dowry to the surrounding villages in exchange for some corn.[63] The difficult living conditions did not change when Koula moved to the place of her mother-in-law. Even though it was one of the newly built houses in "NT", living with her husband's widowed mother and brother was very difficult. An element that was indicative of this negative experience was that the informant completely avoided to refer to the interior of that house where she also gave birth to her son. For her, home was only the apartment she got some years later through *antiparochi* in replacement of that house. The whole floor apartment on the fourth floor was the place that materially confirmed her social recognition and integration into the class of *noikokyraioi*. The demolition of those houses was for her the deletion of a hard past, memories of difficult social relationships and pressure experienced in those places.

On the occasion of the ethnographic example of Koula who reconstructs a negative narration of the old home, I go back at the end of this subchapter to the case of her friend Maria from "NT", who, as we saw earlier, avoided to refer to the "old home", as this was probably a negative memory. Maria feels sad, she says, about the fact that her parents did not take good care of her so that she could go to school and follow another life pathway. The lack of affection she experienced in that first

---

63   Similar description of the difficult years of the Nazi occupation in Kato Toumba can be found also in literature. There is a characteristic moment described in the autobiography book by well-known poet of Thessaloniki Dinos Christianopoulos "To Thessaloniki, where He sent me" about Toumba during the Nazi occupation: he walked together with his mother on snowy and full of dead bodies Botsari street in order to go to the city center. At a certain point, they were so hungry and tired that his mother decided "they should fall on the sidewalk and die there", since it was impossible to reach their destination (Christianopoulos, 2008).

home makes its memory unbearable. It reminds her of deaths, problems her parents had, poverty. All these things together made her feel insecure and lonely. In one of our many meetings, she disclosed that her father used to send her and her sisters to work as "maids" in "rich homes" to secure their livelihood.[64] As we saw also in the ethnographic examples of Antigoni and Paraskevi, child labor in the district of Toumba where refugees lived was rather common; all informants had to work at a very early age at the factories or small industries of the area. Female informants worked as maids or nurses. *"They didn't care about anything, son, I had a difficult life, I suffered a lot at my parents' place. Mom loved us a lot, our father didn't care"*. Maria at her current place, which she built with her husband, without benefiting from the practice of *antiparochi*, in a plot they bought themselves in Kato Toumba, believes that these experiences made her obstinate and stronger, preparing her adequately to follow a different pathway in life.

In this subchapter, we used ethnographic examples to highlight the modalities in which home as a material reality is linked to shaping experiences of the outside world of cultural production establishing identities (Miller, 2001) and determining individuals' social activity. In the following subchapter, we will focus on examples that differ from the narrations associating the experience of the initial refugee settlement with poverty and deprivation. On the opposite side of these negative experiences, these informants reconstruct positive experiences of strategies of integration and bridging of the cultural and social gap between the refugee settlement and the rest of the city. In the first post-war years and thanks to the better financial situation of themselves and the whole country, refugees beautify the settlement houses, make them bigger and develop in them a different sociability that will transform Toumba settlement into what my informants describe as a "beautiful garden city".

3.2.3 Efforts of integration and adaptation in the first post-war years

Chronologically the informants consider a general sense of improvement of their situation in Kato Toumba took place in the first two post-war decades.[65] They recompose the previous narration focusing on extreme poverty and loss by describing activities and initiatives aiming at improving their everyday life through the reconstruction of houses in "NT", especially after 1952 and after the rise of National Radical Union [in Greek: *Ethnikī Rizospastikī Énōsis* (ERE)] to power. Improving houses and

---

64   See Potiropoulos (2003, pp. 89–106), about the survival strategies of the refugees of Nea Michaniona during the first years of their settlement in this area.

65   Such a distinction between before and after the war is confirmed also by other ethnographic studies in Thessaloniki, see Potiropoulos (2003, p. 123).

purchasing new furniture with the aim of creating a "nice place"[66] are associated mainly with the better financial situation achieved by the informants in the post-war era after the end of the 1950s, which is confirmed also by the ethnography of Kokot (1994) in Kato Toumba in the 1980s.[67] Greater social activity and other family social events, such as the informants' weddings, render necessary the improvement of the image of the houses.

This is depicted also in the Social Welfare archives, as in all family folders there are applications to the service, in order to be granted the definitive title deed for the properties in "NT", the majority of which seem to be paid off during that period.[68] In addition, in the folders there are applications by which the subjects seek to proceed to works of expansion or repair of their old house.

These initiatives play a central part in their narrations, as they gave rise to great conflicts between family members, who, due to their individual need of self-housing claim a part of the family house. The practice of building an additional room in the same plot in order to house a family member who got married or the parents so that the newlywed couple can live in the "old house" is also common.[69] These practices do not seem to occur only in Toumba, but constitute what Bourdieu characteristically calls "taste of necessity" (Bourdieu, 2008, p. 374), because of the difficult circumstances and economic hardship, but also because of the need for the family to stay together in the same place. There are some characteristic descriptions by Renée Hirschon in her field survey conducted in the 1970s in the "German houses" of Kokkinia and the methods of dowry provision, which represent the exact same logic (Hirschon, 2006, pp. 228–233). In addition, Thomas Maloutas in his book "Athens, Residence, Family" stresses the family-centered character of social reproduction in the Greek society, mainly because of the limited development of a welfare state, which could work as a safety net for people, and financial autonomy which is not based on salary but on the mutual help taking place within a broader family environment (Maloutas, 1990, p. 22).

By using excerpts from the ethnographic example of Maria that we saw also in the previous subchapter, I will show how informants by changing and improving

---

66   "Nice" as a translation of the Greek work "καλό" (good) refers to the Romanian houses of dignity described by Vintila Mihailescu (2014, pp. 83–107) in his ethnography on the post-socialist era.

67   Potiropoulos (2003, p. 156) ascertains also the association of practices of reconstruction of the settlement houses with the experience and the feeling of informants of "financial and social progress" in relation to the previous lived experience of poverty, deprivation and in general "social and financial decline" within the context of the first years of living in Greece.

68   According to Potiropoulos (2003, p. 121), in the post-war years the "ideology of economic development" prevailed; more specifically, the refugee populations focused on their recovery and their financial and social integration into the Greek society.

69   About similar housing practices, see Potiropoulos (2003, p. 158).

the settlement houses adopt and progressively reproduce social characteristics that make them feel that they also change and improve as human beings, while they actually adapt to the principles and ideals of the Greek middle classes. The improvement that the informants see in their lives and homes, especially during the first two post-war decades is linked to the fact they no longer feel they are significantly different at social level in the city. Therefore, as Kokot (1994, pp. 31–35) also puts it, in this way the cultural and spatial boundaries of distinction between the settlement and the historical city center is progressively lifted.

> *"I remember the house. Our house had stairs, it was plain, not even walls around, four stairs, a door and a little window next to the door on this side and another window on that side. The sides of the house were white and in the middle it was yellow. I used to paint it. We painted the lower part and sides white and used yellow paint for the yellow parts."*
> *How many rooms were there in the house?*
> *"Two rooms and a small living room; as you entered there was a corridor and a little kitchen."*
> *And where did you sleep?*
> *"We all slept in one room. My brother slept in the living room. I remember we had a bed with an iron frame, I remember it... Once I saw that this frame had a metal part and my dad had placed bullets in there[70], it was a round part. Once my brother took it out to beat me, when he found out I had been to Pate with Stavros."[71]*

The iron bed became the reason for Maria to tell me the story of Kilkis, which finally led to her marriage with Stavros, who would gradually liberate her from the environment of the "old home" and the neighborhood of "NT". A friend of her brother disclosed that Maria had not gone to aunt Sophia that afternoon, as she had told her parents, but to the movies with a young man from another neighborhood of Kato Toumba. Her brother then beat her and sent her to relatives in Kilkis for some days to punish her before the fact could be forgotten.

> "[...] Fanis told me, if my older sister does not get engaged first, I will not allow this for you, can you hear me? And so, there was a whole fight to come back from Kilkis. Then guerillas did not allow trains to pass, something could happen to me on the trip [...]! When I got engaged, my son, I helped my dad enter the foundation where my father-in-law and my husband worked."

---

70   According to the informant, her father was a communist and had been imprisoned several times in the post-war years. This fact has always been for her a negative one, of which she was ashamed, as it stigmatized herself and her siblings in their subsequent development.

71   Well-known cinema in Faliro.

Maria always associates the improvement of her family home with her marriage. She considers that her effort to enter a "good home",[72] to behave in a "tidy" and "proper" way,[73] as she characteristically describes it, contributed not only to her personal social progress but also to that of her family, especially her father. She remembers how happy she was when from the window of her family house she saw her father-in-law coming to ask for her hand.

> "He was tall, noble, a true *noikokyris*, I felt so proud. My mother-in-law had asked around in the neighborhood about our family and a neighbor disclosed to her that my father was a communist and had been in jail."

Both her father-in-law and her husband were carpenters and worked in an orphanage in the area, where they taught the craft to the orphans. However, they were also a family of refugees from the settlement of Kato Toumba. For this family, the ideological conviction of her father was an obstacle to her smooth integration into the city.[74] Maria, on one hand, quite often praised the craftmanship of her father, who was a skillful blacksmith and made wonderful banisters and fences, but also elaborate lamps, which had been placed even in public buildings of the city. On the other hand, her father-in-law was the opposite of her father's personality. Maria admired the studiousness of her father-in-law, who knew how to discuss in a "calm and civilized" way with his informants. In addition, her father-in-law used to read translated works of ancient writers in his free time, just like her husband. *"My in-laws were not involved in politics, they were democratic people, they were probably supporters of Venizelos."*

It's not so much poverty itself but the stigma of differentiation of this family in an urban neighborhood of refugees that makes my informant integrate and finally

---

72   I use at this point the term "good home" mainly referring to the dual concept of the old home and good homes of the city center, to explain that the informant conceptualizes the good home as the home of *noikokyraioi*, politically moderate in-laws. In addition, Maria's remark that her father-in-law was a churchwarden in the local parish is very interesting; this is directly linked in this political and historical context with the political moderation of her husband's family.

73   See the interesting ethnography by Bakalaki (2003, p. 216) about the importance of "tidy" as an opposite to the old-fashioned and outdated way of living, especially within the framework of modernization of Greek life.

74   At this point, it is important for the analysis of the ethnographic examples to remember the characteristics but also the consequences caused to the subject by his/her genic relationship with what Panourgia (2013, p. 35) calls a "dangerous citizen", at least as this has been progressively shaped in Europe since the beginning of the 19th century and in Greece since the 1920s. What is interesting in this study is to understand the term *noikokyraios*, always associated in the informants' narrations with the western and Greek normality, as an opposite of the "dangerous citizen" that threatens this condition and must, as Panourgia (2013, p. 35) characteristically mentions, be expelled from the political body and be spatially limited.

reproduce the hegemonic discourses of that era, which, as we saw also in the introduction, not only demonized such a political conviction but also tried to suppress it with any possible means and in any possible way.[75] This of course created fear and guilt to a young child who was not in a position to perceive the issue. Besides Maria wanted very much to become a good *noikokyra* and family head like her grandmother Katina, who worked as a cook in middle class homes in the city center, outside the settlement. Since Maria got married, her father-in-law made sure that her father would also work at the foundation. Thus, her family managed to have a stable income, which soon allowed them to make modifications at the refugee house.

From the family folder of the Social Welfare, it results that Maria's father applied to the Social Welfare in 1953, to proceed with the construction of an additional room at the initial house. It also mentions that this fact is linked to the immediate need to create space, because of his daughter's marriage. Following a discussion I had on this issue, the informant initially denied that her father built the room for her. She considered that because of her brother's marriage and because of her sister there was a space problem and thus her father built the room for himself. Maria in general always feels she was treated unfairly in relation to the house; the fact that neither her father nor her siblings wanted to help her with the dwelling issue during the first years of her marriage still hurts her. The "leftist" father always appears "egocentric and heartless", especially as opposed to her "civilized" father-in-law. It is important here to remember the material world theories (Miller, 2005) and that the material world eventually shapes the personality of the person who lives in and possesses it. In the case of Maria, the "old house" is clearly the materiality in which specific social relations, reflections and emotions take place and evolve. Maria claims spaces of her parental property, because she still claims the love she was missing in that home. She seeks to be treated in a "right and fair" way, as she says. She complains because her father did not take care to give her dowry, and this could have put her marriage with Stavros and her personal development in danger.[76]

The room that Maria claims was for years an object of conflict,[77] as my informant holds that she fought a lot so that her brother could get married, and her sister could come back and live with them in "NT". She explains, therefore, that part of the

---

75   See Panourgia (2013).

76   See Hirschon (2006, pp. 221–239). As mentioned by the author, the provision of dowry was a state law at least until 1983. Due to financial hardship, a lot of informants in the German houses followed the same practice as the inhabitants of Kato Toumba. About the issue of dowry and the women issue in the Greek society, see also Skouteri-Didaskalou (1984, pp. 155–258).

77   See Bakalaki (2003, p. 215), about the houses that objectify conflicts or even friendly relationships between family members or with other relatives from whom these houses have been given as dowry or heritage.

house belongs to her, as her practices contributed to the reunification of home-family. On the contrary, the others tried to kick her out and completely appropriate it. Her father even called the police to declare that his daughter was illegally living at his house, asking her to leave the house and seek for another place to live in. The adventure of finding a place in combination with the economic difficulties she had to deal with during the first years of her marriage leads her to providing a detailed description of her adventures but also of the practices of *noikokyrema* (tidying up),[78] as she characteristically says, referring mainly to the ways and methods she used to save money, in order to build her own house in Kato Toumba towards the end of the 1950s and set herself free, at least materially, from the "old house". It is worth noting that, like other informants as well, she had to stay for some years at her in-laws' place, where she participated in household expenses by paying an amount as rent money. Her father later transferred to Maria this room, which was located in the plot of the house but outside the main house, together with the lights, the iron fence and the Singer sewing machine, which he gave her as dowry. This specific space would still be an issue of conflict between herself and her siblings in the context of *antiparochi* of the house in the following years.

As most informants in Toumba, Maria considers that the practice of renting an apartment is a very negative one, because she believes that one loses money that could have been invested to buy a property.[79] It is interesting to note that also in the ethnography performed by Hirschon (2006, pp. 225–226) in the "German houses" of Kokkinia, the refugees' negative attitude towards renting a house had emerged. Hirschon mentions characteristically that the "repulsion caused by the idea of renting was linked to the particular emphasis placed on the independence of each family-centered household in the "German houses" (2004, p. 225). The status of renting seems to have a negative connotation in the post-war context and be directly linked with the ideal of home ownership promoted also by the Greek state in the post-war era (Maloutas, 1990).

Precisely for this reason already from the first years of her marriage Maria sought at all costs to avoid renting. Because of this logic, she had to live for some years at the place of her husband's parents, in order to save some money and build her own house. *"I have always dreamt of this round balcony and myself in a silk robe going out to take care of my flowers."* Maria does not simply want to build a house; it is

---

78   Maria is the counterexample of what Skouteri-Didaskalou (1984, pp. 216–258) describes as "richly endowered daughter-in-law", as the person who has to deal with the consequences [translation of the Greek idiomatic expression "pay for the daughter-in-law"] cannot fulfill this role of the Greek patriarchy, leading thus the informant to practices of making up for this weakness.

79   This is confirmed also by studies conducted by EKKE (Greek National Center of Social Research) showing high percentages of home ownership in Greece. See Maloutas (1990, p. 50).

obvious she seeks to live a better life than her parents, following the general spirit of progress and modernization that prevailed in society.

The new house, in which Maria eventually settled in 1956 with her husband, was built under an architect's supervision; it was one of the first houses of the area and everyone would stop to observe it, as other informants from "NT" characteristically told me. It is interesting to mention that the house was built only a heartbeat away from Maria's old neighborhood. Maria is particularly proud of this house, which symbolizes her own evolution and progress within the settlement.

Finally, the improvement of the dwelling spaces in Kato Toumba and the memories of a better life should be considered also within the context of a general change and improvement of everyday life, which takes place in the settlement and is linked to improvements in infrastructure, electrification of the area with alternating current, water supply to houses and connection of the district of Toumba to the central sewage system of the city; these improvements seem to influence progressively the social and cultural integration of the residents of Toumba into the single body of the city. [80]

3.2.4 *Antiparochi* as miraculous adaptation

I met almost all informants in Toumba in apartments they acquired through purchase or as a result of the practice of *antiparochi* mainly after 1970, when this district started becoming attractive for contractors. I would therefore say that this way of *home ownership* is an element that culturally and socially connects informants among them, regardless of a deeper class or other social differentiation. During the whole field work, all informants I met were owners of not only one, but even more apartments and properties; this fact led me from the outset to an intense reflection about the importance of the apartment in establishing a specific dwelling culture in post-war Thessaloniki, which clearly seems to influence the everyday life of subjects in this city and progressively shape a new type of "modern" and "tidy" way of living that culturally and socially influences the broad middle classes both upwards and downwards.

This dwelling culture is particularly important if we consider that the ethnography takes place in the place and neighborhood where the informant once lived with his/her family in very different dwelling conditions, better or worse depending on the way the informant sees the above comparison, as we saw in the previous subchapters.

The apartment they acquire through purchase or through the practice of *antiparochi* replaces the family house with a garden and is overall perceived as a cultural and social progress, while at the same time it is lived as the most modern and ideal

---

80   This specific change is described in detail in the fifth chapter of this study.

way of urban dwelling. In this way, their integration into the middle class seems to definitively take place, while at a symbolic level the class distance from the "good homes" seems to be reduced, as it is documented based on the memories with the negative connotation of "refugee" and "refugee-*tourkosporos* [Turkey seed]", hetero-determinations that placed them on the margins of society.

The change of houses seems to be a synonym of the change that took place in shaping the subject's personality. This transition from one house to another, from a house to an apartment, triggered important changes in terms of everyday life and way of living. Demolition, destruction and complete disappearance of every trace of material existence of the previous dwelling form leads us to a second level of analysis of the transition to the new-modern as absence emerging from the necessity of the modernizing project of a process of violent urbanization.

Born in 1932, Maria is currently eighty-seven years old and lives with her children and grandchildren in a three-floor apartment building in Kato Toumba she built in 1956 with her husband. Her apartment is very close to the old neighborhood of "NT". She points out the fact that she was among the first women in the neighborhood to buy electrical domestic appliances and to have her own bathtub and bathroom inside the house already at the end of the 1950s. These material conquests were clearly very important for her and the size of social change achieved during this period was huge. This fact becomes even more important if we consider the past of this informant, who, as we saw in the previous subchapters, had to deal with experiences of extreme poverty as a child due to the refugeeism of her family but also due to the ideological convictions of her father, who was placed by the official state and the social entourage in the group of rather "dangerous citizens" mentioned by Panourgia (2013). In the place of Maria's parental house, in 2000 and following intense family conflicts, a seven-floor luxurious apartment building has been built, in which the informant possesses the whole third floor, which she rents to a couple. Maria points out that this apartment is the most modern apartment one could find, as it has verandas, three large balconies with barbecue and a luxurious fireplace in the living room.[81] The apartment has two bedrooms and two bathrooms. My informant complains about the low rent that her tenants pay. *"500 euros do not match,* she says, *the value of the property and maintenance expenses."* However, she is happy that the "old house" was eventually demolished and even at an old age and after her husband's death she managed to get the dowry her father owed her. Both her siblings also received an apartment in the seven-floor apartment building, which they subsequently sold. Maria does not miss the "old house" and old neighborhood at all. *"Living*

---

81   These elements are underlined by the informants as they raise the value of the property in the market and justify their description as super modern luxurious properties. In the current context of crisis, there is no longer high demand for such apartments, as it was the case until 2010, when they were rented for very high amounts of money.

in that environment was stressful," she says. The *antiparochi* was the only way for her to get something from this house, which was given to them, as she says, by the Social Welfare.

As both Maria and her neighbors point out, the *antiparochi* reached 50%, mainly during the last years, which at least until the crisis was a big percentage compared to the past and especially the first years when this practice was implemented in Kato Toumba. As a result, precisely because Maria had the most meters over the plot, she took the biggest apartment in the apartment building that was constructed. Because of the financial crisis that started in the country in 2008–9 and deepened in 2010, Maria was forced to reduce the rent by at least 30% of its initial value because she feared that the tenants would leave and the apartment would be left empty, like the shop she has on Vassilissis Olgas avenue. As she said, her husband was self-employed, and he had to do three different jobs to create all these "things" that the state now wants to take back. The informant seems to now be a member of a middle-class threatened by the current crisis. Through successive tax reforms but also reductions in retirees' incomes, crisis policies seek, as she specifically mentions, to "destroy" everything that Maria built in the post-war years. *"They are targeting us noikokyraioi my son, us who were running things well."*[82] Specifically Maria is afraid that her children and grandchildren will not manage to maintain what she built through hard practices of saving money in an era that investment in buying properties could bring financial benefits. Therefore, many of my informants are afraid that their own model of progress and "way of living as *noikokyraioi*", as this was shaped and promoted in the post-war era, is not likely to be reproduced in the future.

Next, with Maria's help I met her beloved friends Soula and Paraskevi. These two women, during the whole period in which Maria was in conflict with her sister and sister-in-law as they did not agree with the informant's wish to give the "old house" in "NT" as *antiparochi*, tried to convince Maria's relatives of the benefits of the apartment building, but also of the injustice their friend suffered because she had not yet received the part from the family house that corresponded to her. *"I am bitter blooded",* Maria says *"and although I did so much good to them, they were envious of me because they thought I had become rich, and I didn't need anything anymore."* In 2000, Maria's siblings were still living in the "old house" and didn't see why they had to demolish it, since everyone had a place to live in.

> "My father had converted it into a two-floor little villa, with beautiful rails and balusters, my sister-in-law and my sister lived there. But if it weren't for me, who helped my father enter the foundation and manage to make his way."

---

82   See Papataxiarchis (2006a); Bakalaki (2003, pp. 215–216) about running the household as a business, aiming at increasing the financial and social profit.

Maria of course insisted that part of the plot belonged to her, and she had to find a way to get even now the part from the family house in "NT" that was hers. Soula was born in 1926. She has two married children and four grandchildren. Her son lives on the last floor of an apartment building, in an apartment that Soula has conceded to him. Her daughter lives in an apartment in an adjacent apartment building that her mother bought for her. As the informant says, she made sure that both her children would have a place to live in, in order not to spend money to pay rent. This choice is also linked to the fact that Soula, as well as the other informants, arranged in this way to receive their children's care now that they need it more than ever. Therefore, the practice of *antiparochi* and the logic of living together in the modern apartment building have also practical dimensions in terms of family relationships of mutual support and care. The apartment building in which Soula and her son live was also built with the practice of *antiparochi*, when the informant eventually managed to convince Paraskevi and her mother, as we saw in the previous chapters, that the demolition of the old house and the acquisition of a modern apartment would change their life.

> "I kept telling Paraskevi, why do you wish to keep this piece of junk, when you can immediately get a new bathroom, new doors and windows, installations, without paying anything?"

Paraskevi was born in 1925. At the time of the field work, she lived in an apartment next to Soula's, in the apartment building that resulted from the *antiparochi* of the 1970s. The old houses of the two women were one next to another in the same plot, as it can be seen also in their concession documents. Their plot was rather small; therefore, its division would not allow the construction of an apartment building. Soula lived there with her mother, her husband and their two children, while Paraskevi lived with her husband and mother. Already at the beginning of the 1950s, when she got married, Soula moved to a newly built apartment on Agiou Dimitriou street in the city center, as she was concerned about her children's future if she continued living in Toumba. *"I wanted them to go to university, to study, there all private schools were nearby."* The informant perceives the challenges of the times and chooses to abandon the neighborhood district. Living in a modern apartment in the city center seems to meet my informant's need for a "more modern everyday life" and at the same time it provides the possibility of better socialization and progress for her children, far from the dangers of the less "developed" Toumba.

Due to her mother's widowhood, Soula started working at a very young age at the textile factories of Toumba and felt the social stigma very early because of her family history and living in "NT". Her relationship with a young boy who lived right opposite "NT" but did not belong to the big family of refugees made her realize the limits that still separated Toumba from the rest of the city and its other inhabitants:

"When I passed in front of their house to go to the factory to work, his mother used to curse me because I had seduced her son, she wished I would burn alive, but as luck would have it, this was her own death."

Giorgos is 59 years old and lives with his family in an apartment building close to Soula's, which was built in 1990 in a plot of his family. Giorgos is a nephew of Manos, Soula's greatest love, which stigmatized her life and is constantly discussed among the three friends and other informants in "NT". He explained that his grandfather's relationship with the royal family and the city authorities, police and the Metropolitan[83], who regularly visited his family, was an important fact for the residents of Toumba which distinguished them from the rest of the settlement. According to him, Toumba was a poor neighborhood, so it was normal for all these people to be leftist. His grandfather was right-wing but not a royalist, despite the good relationships he had with the royal family.

I cite at this point one letter from the unpublished archive of correspondence of Giorgos' grandfather with the family of king George II of Greece. My informant's family name has been removed from the letter, to preserve his anonymity.

"Grandfather was born in 1880 in Kifissia, in Athens, and happened to live close to a garden city with very nice people back then – upper-middle-class – elite society, but who did not diminish others; when you socialize with people of a higher level, you also cultivate habits and manners even if you don't have the education, you cultivate sociability and knowledge, and for sure when you are with upper strata you have something to gain."

---

83   Orthodox bishop (translator's note).

Figure 1: Thank you letter of the Royal Family to the informant's family.

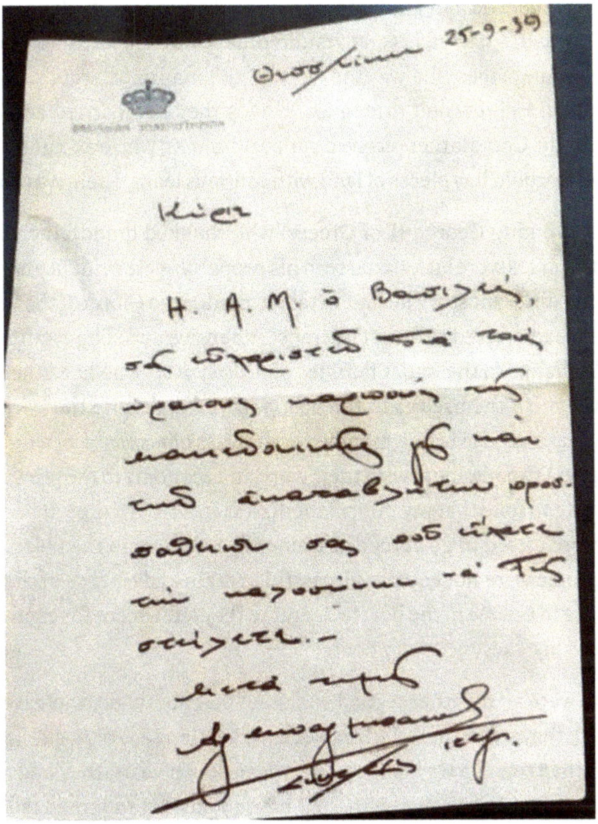

Source: Family's personal archive.

However, according to him, their social supremacy never prevented him from making friends with the children living in his neighborhood.

> "No, we didn't have any problem, we played, our group of friends were here; we did have also some "gipsies" but without being racist. They were so kind. Hospitable, generous. Their houses were so clean one was ashamed to enter."

According to him, his grandfather had settled in the area before the refugees, by buying pieces of land, which then created a big plot of 44 stremmas where his family lived and worked.

"Grandfather had a recommendation from Athens and started working for X..., he came to work for X... Grandfather lived in the mansion of X... on Vasilissis Olgas avenue and there he met grandmother. He worked as head gardener there, thanks to the knowledge he had [...] and grandmother from Kolindros was a woman who spoke four languages, she was the heart of the mansion because she spoke German, Italian, Hebrew and Armenian. In 1905 they got married and in 1915 they had my uncle. Grandfather received support from X., who was a guarantor so that grandfather could buy pieces of land with usurious loans. There was nothing here."

The letters from king George II of Greece, who thanked grandfather for the good fruit that princesses were lucky to taste in his property, were evidence of his different origin and the different story he had to tell. According to Giorgos, the settlement of Kato Toumba had evolved to one of the most expensive and sought-after suburbs of Thessaloniki thanks to the "quiet families of *noikokyraioi*" who lived there and managed to distinguish themselves in the post-war years, despite the initial problems they had to deal with. He feels a member of the class of *noikokyraioi* who managed in the post-war era to contribute with their work and economy to the growth of Greece. It is interesting to note that my informant dissociates from the group of *noikokyraioi* those who were forced to go abroad as economic migrants in the 1960s. He believes that these people were not equally successful in taking advantage of the opportunities there were in Greece in the post-war era, so they left Greece for central European countries because they were very poor.

"Here we were all together, a good and quiet neighborhood, there were no criminals. Since they stayed here and did not leave for Germany or Australia, this means that they had found a way to survive in the post-war years, they had a profession, [...] they were all *noikokyraioi* with their households. [...] You could tell people who ran a household efficiently apart, they were *noikokyraioi*, they had no bad habits."

In his discourse, as in the narrations of Maria and other informants, we notice the expression "running a household", which means control life itself, adversity but also good moments. "Running a household" as a basic ability of *noikokyraioi* is not limited to financial management only but concerns also the possibility or the talent of self-control and suffering management.

Giorgos' mother sent him to school in the city center, both in primary and secondary education; this was something that bothered him a lot, not only because the school was far away and he had to go there on foot every day, but also because this was something that separated him from the rest of the children in the neighborhood.

"So that you understand the habits of my family, I used to go to the primary school down there, you see the church of Sotiras? Miaouli street, if you know ..."
Was it a private school?
"No, it was a public one!"

Were schools in the city center better?
"No, they were not better, nonsense! I should have gone to school here in Toumba, as everyone else did! (...) This happened in primary education. In secondary education, new mad-
ness. I had to go to the 5th gymnasium, far away, on Antheon street."

Like Paraskevi's mother and like Soula for her children, Giorgos' mother wished to
avoid her child's socialization in this neighborhood. The choice of school, group of
friends, clothing were common ways in which families sought to improve their social status. This disciplining of bodies and behaviors described also by Foucault is a
characteristic way in which the urban way of living and urban ethics was productively adopted and reproduced by a large part of society (Foucault, 1987, pp.11–37).

Financial problems and eventually the passing of Giorgos' grandfather at the end
of the 1940s would lead to the progressive fragmentation of the plot into smaller
plots, which would be sold in the post-war years to private citizens and refugee families from "NT". Through the practice of *antiparochi*, numerous apartments will be
built and distributed to Giorgos' large family. Initially the area had no particular
value and plots were sold at a very low price.

"No, the *antiparochi* was not worth it yet, I even remember a case in which my
grandmother had sold a corner plot of 220 square meters to only receive a small
shop of 54 square meters [...]. At the beginning it was 20%. After the 1970s it was
worth it, because it was more than 40%, back then the current plot ratio did not
apply."

The fragmentation of and building on this big plot will radically change the aspect
of the settlement of Kato Toumba, since a large part of the green space that sur-
rounded the neighborhood will be lost and replaced by multi-story apartment buildings. These will be among the first apartment buildings in the area, which will be
dwelled also by new residents in addition to the families of refugees.

As it results from Paraskevi's and Soula's family folder, in 1965 they submitted
an application to the Social Welfare center to receive copies of the concession documents, to be used for issuing a construction permit for an apartment building. Soula
wanted very much to go back to her old neighborhood, as she told me. She had really missed it and, contrary to what she initially believed, she now thinks that her
children lost their way and got caught up in groups of friends from the city center in
which they shouldn't have been involved. She used to work long hours in the cinema
that had opened in the city center and there was no one to take care of the children.
"In Toumba, things were different, there was a neighborhood, people were helping one another."
The possibility to acquire a modern apartment where she could live and one more she
could rent was very attractive and enabled her to take the decision to go back to her
old neighborhood.

On the other hand, Paraskevi, who lived with her mother and her husband and had no children, as she mentioned during the interviews, did not find Soula's suggestion to demolish the house attractive, as she had already invested, like other informants as well, in the renovation of the old house, which was in a very good condition since then. *"If it wasn't for Soula and if I was not afraid of a misunderstanding, I would have never given the old house for an* antiparochi." Her mother, who is a central character in Paraskevi's narration, disagreed with this choice, as she was planning to build a second floor and rent the first one to ensure an income, as it happened often with the little houses of the area mainly after 1955 (Kokot, 1994).

All three ethnographic examples showcase the importance of the change that the demolition of the "old house" entailed for these people, but also the world and the way of living that this symbolized. As we saw in the above examples, this decision was never an easy one and had to do with the progress, needs and requirements created by the new way of living in the city of Thessaloniki. People did not change only their way of dwelling in order to acquire a new consumer good, as the modern apartment was seen by many of them, but also because through this decision they improved their financial status and living conditions and also because they gave more people the possibility to live in the place where previously they lived alone. Therefore, there were financial but also social reasons. The *antiparochi* and construction in Kato Toumba changed radically its neighborhoods and shaped a way of living which was similar to that of the rest of the city.

3.3 The distinction: the "good homes" of the city center

In the middle of the fieldwork in 2013–2014 I moved to an apartment in a block of apartments in the city center, to continue my research and perceive the dynamics of the relationships developed among the tenants of an apartment building in this area of the city. This moving to a building located across the new city hall and other important public buildings hosting administrative authorities of Thessaloniki and built mostly in the post-war years gave me the opportunity to get in touch with the *noikokyraioi* from the "good old homes" in the city center.

This block of apartments was built in 1955 without an *antiparochi*, but through the purchase of the already built plot by the architect, as it results from the contract of purchase of the apartment of Aglaia, who lived on the fourth floor and was, thanks also to her role as building administrator, one of my main informants. Aglaia was the daughter of a member of the parliament of the political party of National Radical Union [in Greek: *Ethnikī Rizospastikī Énōsis* (ERE)] from Macedonia, who was also fond of ancient Greece and follower of strong antisemitic views. As all informants told me, the apartment building was particularly modern for its era, with balconies, projections and interesting sculpture. Aglaia was very proud to live in this apartment building, which was called "the tower" after the White Tower of Thessaloniki, due also to the fact that between these two buildings there was no other higher building. The block of apartments was designed and built by the well-known architect of the city Konstantinos Philippou, while a picture of the building is included in the collective volume on the 100 years of architecture history of the city by Vasilis Kolonas, professor of Social History of Architecture at the University of Thessaly: *Architecture of a century: Thessaloniki 1912–2012* (2012). Like most apartment buildings on this avenue, known also as "avenue of the countryside", it was built on a plot where there was a mansion built already at the end of the 19th century, which belonged to a Jewish family of the city:

> "[...] an old three-floor house with the plot, courtyard and remaining parts, annexes and appurtenances [...]. This property became owned by the sellers according to the above percentages for each one of them by inheritance ab indiviso from their aunt Riketta wife of [...] killed in Auschwitz, Poland, by the Germans on 30 May 1943."[84]

As it can be seen also in the above excerpt of the purchase contract of the apartment of Aglaia, the apartment building represented precisely what in the public discourse was described as "destruction". It was a modern post-war building; to build it, another building had to be demolished. The latter was associated with the Ottoman multi-community Thessaloniki of the era of Tanzimat reforms, industrialization and a multicultural ruling class and according to the logic of the law of 1985 had to be "preserved". It is interesting to note that the majority of the first tenants of the apartment building – some of whom became my housemates and informants in the next year and a half – had moved to Thessaloniki from other cities or towns of Macedonia and Thrace due to a transfer and held high level offices in the Greek post-war state.

On the day I moved to the block of apartments, I had to use the lift to bring my personal belongings to the 6th floor. To my surprise, while I was trying to keep the entrance door open with my father's help, at the entrance there was a tall lady in black clothes, who was feverishly cleaning the stairs, rendering any moving at least dangerous. At a certain point I asked her to stop, and I promised I would personally clean the entrance once the moving would be finished. She answered shortly there was no problem, as she was finishing and besides this was something she was doing every day. Then she followed me in the lift and asked me not to use it, because, as she told me, it was new and made by a German company, cost a lot of money and she was afraid that using it to transport heavy objects could cause problems. I reassured her and she then asked me what exactly I was and what I did for a living,

---

84   Contract of sale of property on credit for Drachmas 180,000/Number 24724, from the informant's personal archive.

stressing emphatically that *"noikokyraioi* and family heads" lived in this building. In addition, she highlighted that a large part of the tenants were university professors, while students lived across on narrow streets. I spontaneously asked her what exactly her own status was, assuming that the imposing lady with the black clothes and the tight chignon was a university professor. She was taken by surprise and told me she was head of library at a department of the Aristotle University of Thessaloniki. When I replied that I was working on my doctoral thesis at the University of Macedonia, Anthi showed, at least at that moment, that she was very pleased, welcomed me and wished that the quiet apartment of the sixth floor would give me the chance to become one day a university professor, like her other *noikokyraioi* housemates. As it was indicated on the door of her apartment, Anthi was the daughter of a general of the Greek army and she had inherited the apartment from her parents. After many difficult moments during my one-and-a-half year stay at the apartment, Anthi towards the end of my stay would become one of my supporters and one of my main informants in the building. As I was trying to satisfy my curiosity, already from the outset I would find out that she had been placed by her father and had indeed signed a contract to work at the library of a department, and during that period, due to measures taken by the government of Samaras[85], she would be suspended; this caused huge stress and uncertainty to her, according also to the narrations of the other tenants of the apartment building, who were trying to justify her strange behavior.

Informants from the city center always stress how different they are from the other residents of the city, using discourses and practices to play the special role of the old resident of the city center. Reference to numerous historical events and personalities of the city, and their participation in various social networks of power, political and cultural representation, responded to the need of these subjects to associate and identify themselves with the core of the urban life of the city as part of its history. The centrality of their dwelling locations in relation to the centers of power was even used as proof of their relationship with the "old" and "authentic" Thessaloniki.

Most of the time during our meetings informants mentioned names of families, for whom I would find out in the long-term that they had a special activity in the city in the previous years, while their presence and their social role had been repeatedly reported by the society pages of the newspapers of that era. These names and their activity were mentioned also in online discussions about old Thessaloniki and in general they provided me with an easy way of approaching informants in the city center, since making reference to specific people and events from Thessaloniki of the first post-war years helped the research subjects feel comfortable and reconstruct in the present the complex network of people and things that determined their own

---

85   Prime Minister of Greece from 20 June 2012 to 26 January 2015.

progress and life in the city. A series of books by local authors, who tried to safeguard this lost era of a "cosmopolitan urban" Thessaloniki, were shown by the informants who were interested in the modern past of the city, of which they felt part. A characteristic album among the many that reached me through the informants is entitled *Ladies of Thessaloniki* by Stratos Simitzis and was published in 2011. I use the example of this specific album, to start my analysis in this subchapter, since the description "ladies" used by the author in the title is a native definition of the hostesses of "good homes". The definition "lady" is often used in Greece in the public discourse, in order to describe a woman who rose to the occasion, handled issues with humility, altruism and selflessness.[86] It is mainly attributed to women of public life who have never provoked with their private life and became famous by letting their work speak for them.

The "good homes" that usually "know how to act" are also those that, according to the informants, contributed historically to "tidying up" the Greek state, especially in the post-war years after the liberation. More specifically, reference is made to 1944, the win over the communists during the civil war and the reconstruction of the Greek state while it was governed by the parties of *Synagermos*, *ERE* and the Greek junta until *PASOK* came to power in 1981. This latter period is for most of the informants a completely different one, which is usually distinguished by what is described as "economic miracle" and "tidying up" of the first post-war years.

Using again as main analytical tool the home in which the informants reconstruct the past and describe the first years of their life, I will refer to practices and experiences of informants who were born and raised in the historical city center. The description of these homes as "good homes" is a native one and originates from informants at Kato Toumba as well as from informants of the city center, who feel they represent them.

"Good homes" are usually dwelled by rich families whose practices and public image corresponded already before the war to the ideal social type of a *noikokyraios*. This social type that concerns the *noikokyraioi* of the "good homes" has different qualities from the type of *noikokyraios* that was thoroughly described in the previous chapters. More specifically, the *noikokyraios* of the informants from the center is usually linked to the contribution and devotion to the state, usually through patriotic acts. For example, participation in the civil war, in the *EAM* groups, does not fall within the usual practices of this specific type of *noikokyraios*, as it puts in danger the existence and security of the household, as we characteristically saw earlier in the case of Maria and her father.[87] Even in the discourses of some informants from Toumba whose parents or relatives participated in the armed struggle or were

---

86   The use of the term "lady" is characteristic in metonymic references to people of culture with a moral and qualitative contribution, e.g. The great lady of the Greek music stage, etc.

87   See also Panourgia (2013).

blamed and expelled from the country for similar acts, the two concepts, namely "*noikokyraios* and communist", are rather used in contrast to each other, asking the informant to make a relevant decision. Regarding the informants from the city center and mainly those originated from the broader area of Macedonia, the term *noikokyraios* is associated with important people of the city with intense voluntary and charitable activity, whose ancestors fought and were active in the Macedonian Struggle (1904–1908), and therefore contributed practically to the integration of a part of Macedonia into Greece.

I am citing as an example the below excerpt of an interview, in order to showcase the way in which my informant Aglaia establishes her discourse, her narration and eventually through the interview herself as part of the *noikokyraioi*: a modern gender-based social subject, a resident of the co-capital, a citizen with "right-wing political ideas".

3.3.1 Speaking with a main informant on the fringes of the city center

"Anyway, so the daughter got married to the military officer, and they supposedly were not happy because he was Greek, but luckily he was Greek and they survived as well. So, let's see. My aunt lived in the adjacent one, precisely the one adjacent to Ilysia."

Do you mean your father's sister?

"Yes, she was my aunt, her husband was a lawyer, specialized in tax law; he was quite wealthy, but a communist. Urban class but leftist. He was also an atheist; my aunt argued a lot with my father. Unfortunately, she had become a communist as well. So, she lived in this house, in the top-floor apartment, when this was built; the political gatherings usually took place here, above Ilysia. That of Papandreou took place once, I remember I saw old Papandreou, and that of EDA also took place once."

I see, that of Iliou?

"I don't remember, it could be Iliou, in any case I remember the red flags."

I can imagine your father was contrary to EDA?

"Yes! Of course, however, when he was a Prefect. Because it was... it was a good party, let's say."

EDA?

"No, wait, let me tell you! Eh... The truth stands somewhere in the middle. Eh, when my father was a Prefect, whoever was leftist or a relative of a leftist, they expelled him from the country. My father was ordered to expel everyone from Veroia, so informers came to see him and indicated such and such person, so he had a list. So, my father called them to his office to check and of them some he would expel from the country and for some others he would investigate if they really were dangerous or not, because they had some kind of involvement or could simply be his brother or father. He could, therefore, not expel him as well from the country, if a person was a noikokyraios, had a family, he could not expel him for no reason. This attitude of course was not likeable, this aggravated his position."

Of your father?

"Of my father! Although he was a man of the party, he was fair, they have gathered a lot against him and slandered him, they set it up for him and did him harm."

The leftists?

"No, people from his own party! Despite all this, he remained a right-wing person, because there was Ch..., who misappropriated money. A member of the parliament of New Democracy, M..., Minister of Northern Greece and a patriot, noikokyraios, son of Makedonomachos[88] M..., who was a really avaricious person. Of course... He was involved also in the properties of the Jewish people with Karamanlis. But my dad was an incorruptible one."

All these people were politicians in Veroia, so did they have anything to do with the right-wing party here?

"I am telling you, minister of Northern Greece?!"

M...?

"Sure. To avoid messing up, first they had sent him to Kilkis, then Veroia rose up in protest, because they had never seen such a prefect before, and they thought that my father had made a big fortune in Thessaloniki. My father had no fortune, he lived thanks to a rent and when he received his lump sum payment, we bought this house. 'The Tower after the White Tower', one of the first modern apartment buildings on Vasileos Georgiou street. But we bought it thanks to our savings, you see what I mean? This was the huge fortune of the Prefect! They said we had 4 apartments!"

How did the aunt, who was also a leftist person, react to this?

"Ah, she was such a cranky person! Anyway, let's talk about EDA now. We had this secret, this was a bad secret, that my aunt was a communist!"

Was it bad for the family?

"Yes, it was bad for the family, everyone in the family was right-wing."

Also, your mother was right-wing?

"My mother didn't care... Wherever my father belonged to."

And your mother's family? Although they were refugees? Because usually refugees were...

"Refugees were with Venizelos, but all those who were informed about the developments, the most intelligent amongst them stopped supporting Venizelos, you know it, because Venizelos actually fooled them, no matter what the most ingenuous believed, the most intelligent ones came back immediately; anyway, as we were watching downstairs from the balcony, my aunt had the brilliant idea to applaud, those from downstairs turned their head up and started gesturing (that they would cut our heads off): – We will cut off your heads –, I was scared to death, I asked, but, aunt, why should they cut off our heads? – Go in to be on the safe side –. They didn't know she was a communist. What could we say? That aunt was a communist so that they cut off her head? My aunt stopped applauding. I asked, aunt, why are the flags red? – Of blood –, she said. Whose blood,

---

88   *Makedonomachoi* were the Greek fighters of the Macedonian Struggle (translator's note).

*aunt? – Everyone's..., stop asking about everything. I said: we will go, aunt! Then I told
my mom, don't go. If they kill aunt, at least they didn't know where our place was. There
was this fear to hide it... But how did they do it? They did it shamelessly! This is what I
remember from my childhood and since then..."*

Obviously because they knew your father?

"No."

Then why did they do it?

*"They did it against the allegedly rich people from the "good homes" who lived in the
luxurious apartment buildings, that the poor ones would go upstairs to slaughter them
and take their houses. You see what I mean? They didn't care about the fact that she
was a communist, but then what kind of communist? Don't think that she ever helped a
poor person! Not even her own sister. This was the kind of communist she was. While my
father, the right-wing one, was giving to everyone."*

Did she have a luxurious house? The aunt, I mean.

*"She had a normal house! But she wouldn't miss any trip, theater, going out, whatever...
Only for herself! No cats, no dogs, no... Anyway, so, that's all. Very rich families lived in
the house where my aunt lived. Down there, in that corner apartment building, where
Philippou schools were built later. Entire floor apartments, with servants, everything!
She had a parterre..."*

*Since those people had money, why didn't they build houses with gardens and bought
apartments instead?*

*"Eh, this is how they lived, honey! This was more modern those years. The apartments
were luxurious, the city center was very nice."*

I mean, why didn't they buy a villa?

*"There was no smog, maybe they already had one! How can one know? Panorama was
there all along, maybe they already had one. So, these apartments were of huge dimensions, they also had servants, the lower floor apartment had three doors at the entrance,
so they could use whatever door they liked to enter, from the middle door they entered
the living room, from the other door they entered the kitchen, from the other door I don't
know what room they entered, and they also had a huge parterre with windows all
around, a parterre and an air shaft let's call it. Very big and it had wooden bridges the
servants used to go from one end of the house to the other."*

I see, so these floor apartments were that big?

*"Yes, they were! They had those bridges they used as a shortcut without having to go
through the house making a whole circle."*

So, your aunt's house was like that but she didn't have any servants, correct?

*"My aunt's house was a top-floor apartment, it formed a corner, and you could see the
parterres from there, this air shaft, it was a penthouse so it was small, it could not
surround the whole..."*

Was it maybe the Eratira palace, which is located a bit further?

"I don't know the palace you have named, it has not changed, it is the old mansion, downstairs there were carpets in the past. There were Philippou schools, Ilysia, on one corner you have Ilysia, on the other corner you have this one, there are some corridor carpets nowadays."

Was it Fokas, do you mean this building? On Mitropoleos street?

"No, honey"

Nowadays this is Konstantinidis' patisserie!

"This surrounds a huge parterre, an air shaft with wooden bridges to go from one end of the apartment to the other and the women met there for gossiping. Laughter and small talk with each other, the servants had a chat, that's it. Behind us there was a very big one, a big parterre with a big tree, full of jackdaws. Those days there was a bounty of 5 drachmas per jackdaw because they stole things and I was counting them and calculating a lot of money, to buy a lot of Mickey Mouse volumes."[89]

Figure 2: Little Aglaia at her Father's home.

Source: Inoformant's Personal Family archive.

---

89   Excerpt from the narration of Aglaia from the center of Thessaloniki 2014.

3.3.2 "Good homes" and architectural heritage of the city: conflicting public discourses

The discourses of the informants from the city center and their individual memory about the "good homes" of Thessaloniki, as it can be seen also from the above indicative excerpt of Aglaia's interview, are associated with a respective public discourse and a collective memory of contempt of the workers' movement and the national Greek Resistance during the post-war years. The public discourse[90] about the "good old Thessaloniki" during the fieldwork became pluralistic and was multiplied due to the internet as well as due to the different approach of the new administration of the city regarding its interest in highlighting also other aspects of its long history focusing on the Ottoman years and the activity of the Jews of the city.

More specifically, during the fieldwork (2012–2015), groups had been established on certain social media aiming at showcasing the "great past" of the urban development of Thessaloniki.[91] These discourses developed already earlier, culminating in the period of the European Cultural Capital in 1997, as it can be proved by the numerous albums that were published regarding the social and cultural activity of urban families of Thessaloniki.[92]

More specifically, during the period of the fieldwork, the public discourse of the city started to progressively change, and a need was being shaped to protect what was considered to have been saved in the urban public space, which had to be showcased and appreciated by broader groups of citizens. Free online newspapers and other brochures of the city, Giannis Boutaris, businessman and well-known member of a rich family of wine producers from Macedonia, who was elected mayor in the municipal elections in 2010, leading the party "Initiative for Thessaloniki", the publication of the book *Salonica, city of ghosts* by historian Mark Mazower in 2006, as well as experimental initiatives aiming at the greatest possible use of public space, such as "Thessaloniki in a different way" in 2010, were occasions for discussing more the unknown, but for them precious, past of the city.

The public discussion focused on conversations around the "multicultural" past of Thessaloniki, culminating in the events organized by the Municipality of Thessa-

---

90   By public discourse about old Thessaloniki I mean the discourse articulated on the city in a series of literature and history books, biographies of old residents of Thessaloniki and oral discourses of public personalities of the city, as well as pages dedicated to the city that have been created on the internet in recent years.

91   A characteristic one is the group "Unknown Thessaloniki" on Facebook, which currently counts more than 100 000 members.

92   See for example Valagianni Alumni Association 1996; Asylo tou Paidiou [Children's Asylum] 1994; Megas and Chorbos 2002, etc.

loniki on the occasion of the 100 years from its liberation.[93] The content of the events
for the celebration of the 100 years led to a conflict between the new administration
of the city with the then Prefect, Panagiotis Psomiadis, who represented a different Thessaloniki, mainly that of the era of the "European Cultural Capital" and of
the previous administrations of the city, and wished, as in the past, to showcase in
the celebrations the history of the Greek identity, honoring those who "liberated" it
from the "Turks" in 1912. The Mayor of the city Giannis Boutaris and his party wished
a celebration that would showcase the long history of the city, from the moment it
was founded by Cassander, king of Macedonia, focusing mainly on its Jewish and ottoman past, which had not been showcased sufficiently in the previous years, stressing its difference from other Greek cities as to its long-standing urban character and
its financial importance before its integration into the Greek state in 1912.

It is worth noting that American historian Mark Mazower, who contributed
with his 2006 study on Thessaloniki to showcasing the Ottoman history and multi-
community character of the city prior to its integration into the Greek state in 1912,
opened the events of the Municipality for the celebration of 2012 with a speech at
the Thessaloniki Concert Hall.[94]

In this online groups,[95] which multiplied during the three years of fieldwork,
members voluntarily post pictures of the city and discuss about the families and

---

93 "On the occasion of the centenary anniversary of the liberation of Thessaloniki in 1912, as a major
festivity, the Municipality of Thessaloniki organizes an international scientific conference on the following subject: "Thessaloniki: a city in transition, 1912–2012". The conference will take place from 18
to 21 October 2012 at the Conference and Science Center of the Thessaloniki Concert Hall. The aim of
the conference is to provide a meeting point for modern historiographical movements and all relevant
social sciences, such as history, social anthropology, economy, law, international relations and arts.
Participants will include: **Edhem Eldem** (Bogazici University), **Khaled Fahmy** (New York University), **Eyal Ginio** (Hebrew University of Jerusalem), **Charles King** (Georgetown University), **Paschalis
Kitromilidis** (University of Athens), **Yura Konstantinova** (Bulgarian Academy of Sciences), **Nora
Lafi** (Zentrum Moderner Orient). Mayor Giannis Boutaris will open the conference. Opening speeches
will be given by **Mark Mazower** (Columbia University) and **Konstantinos Svolopoulos** (Academy of
Athens). The conference will be structured around three thematic axes:
a) Friday 19/10/2012: Seeking for an identity
b) Saturday 20/10/2012: A city in transition
c) Sunday 21/10/2012: Mapping the future of Thessaloniki
The scientific committee is composed of Professor emeritus at the University of Athens and academic, Mr Konstantinos Svolopoulos, professors at the Aristotle University of Thessaloniki, Mr Vasilis
Gounaris and Mr Giannis Stefanidis, assistant professor Mr Dimitris Lyvanios, and Professor at
Columbia University of New York, Mr Mark Mazower. The organization committee is headed by Associate Professor at Panteion University, Mr Dimitris Kairidis." (see http://www.thessaloniki2012
.gr/.)
94 Op.cit.
95 For example, "Unknown Thessaloniki" https://www.facebook.com/groups/agnosti.thessalo
niki/?ref=bookmarks, accessed October 22, 2022. Project "Conservation buildings of Thes-

stories that are linked to the pictures. Some of them are nostalgic of the multi-community composition of Thessaloniki, which, as they point out, was marked by the loss of the "real" urban class of the city. This past is mainly linked with the urban interventions that took place in the city, at the end of the Ottoman empire (eastern railways, central avenues and demolition of the marine and eastern walls of the city) as a result of the Tanzimat reforms, industrialization and general economic growth as well as with the transition of the city from the empire to the Greek national state (Anastasiadou, 2008; Kyriakidou-Nestoros, 1993b, pp. 241–243).

Architecture, which usually becomes a subject for commenting, concerns what is described as "mansions", countryside residences on the then avenue of the towers, current Vassilissis Olgas avenue, public buildings and apartment buildings, which were built under architectural supervision by the end of the 1950s in Thessaloniki and are linked with western and modern architecture movements, such as that of Modernism in the interwar period and Eclecticism in the previous years (Colonas, 2005).

The remaining buildings of this era, which are known as "conservation buildings" due to the relevant law of 1985, which has been protecting them since then, are associated with the missed opportunity of an integrated and rational urbanization in the spirit of western Europe. What was experienced as "destruction" of the cultural and mainly of the architectural heritage of the city is largely attributed by these websites, but also by the public discourse, to the "enlarged" lower middle class of the post-war years, the class of *noikokyraioi* modern Greeks, who with the *antiparochi* and the uncontrollable and improvised reconstruction of the country destroyed an important part of its cultural heritage, which had to be protected and preserved.[96]

On the opposite side of those who define themselves in relation to the "good homes" we find the *noikokyraioi*. The latter ones manage, through their sociability and their intentional social activity, to secure their individual interests, which coincide with their household interests (Papataxiarchis, 2006a; Salamone & Stanton, 2019). Finally, *noikokyraioi* are associated with the manners and characteristics that correspond to the ideal of the European urban and at the same time Greek orthodox tradition, which the subjects present at the opposite of a non-urban ideal of culture

saloniki" https://www.facebook.com/groups/504888489524433/, accessed October 22, 2022, and, finally, "Memories of Thessaloniki-Link with the present".

96   The term enlarged middle strata development is used by geographer Th. Maloutas in his book *Athens, Residence, Family* (1990). In general, as it can be seen also in the introduction, many Greek sociologists, philosophers and historians talk about the problematic urban development of the Greek state, especially during the first post-war years, which is attributed to the inability to establish a Greek urban class similar to western examples of central and western Europe, as a result of the great ideological movements in modern urban national states, see Tsoukalas (1977, 1981, 2005), Charalampis (1985, 1989), Kondylis (1991, 1995) and Axelos (2010).

that is linked, on one hand, to the Greek countryside and, on the other hand, to the "oriental culture" and left wing.

The fact that the informants in Kato Toumba as well as in the city center make a frequent use of the term *noikokyraios* with a positive connotation, in order to describe their social and cultural contribution to the life of the city, but also the achievement of their personal and family objectives within the post-war framework of development led me to shifting my research field also to the heart of the center of Thessaloniki, with the aim of delving into the understanding of the bourgeoisie mentality.

3.3.3 Living in the center: life history

When Lydia was asked to participate with her biography in the publication of an Album with the title "Ladies of Thessaloniki", she refused, because, as she told me, she didn't like the title:

> "What does 'Ladies of Thessaloniki' mean? Ms Valagianni[97] told us "I want you to be 'your own women'", but this concept was misunderstood, and I no longer like it."

I met Lydia for the first time within the framework of a guided tour of an important foundation with long-standing charitable activity in the city, of which she was the chairwoman for many years. There I asked her directly if she knew anything about all these things I was reading on the society pages of the newspapers 'Makedonia' and 'Ellenikos Vorras' regarding glamorous bals in which all "high society" of Thessaloniki participated.

Taken by surprise, my informant asked: *"how do you know about all these things?"* She encouraged me to look for her, in order to discuss about this "great era" of the city. Two months later and while my research in the city center was moving on, an informant, Tzeni, proposed to meet a "real Lady" that, in her opinion, represented old urban Thessaloniki and had nothing to do with "refugees", a term that she used with contempt. I immediately perceived that the informant felt a lot of respect and awe for this person, while she stressed emphatically that this acquaintance is very important, because Ms Lydia originates from one of the "good homes" of the city and it wouldn't be easy to approach her differently without her intermediation and the relationship that linked them.

Born in 1951, Tzeni originates from a family of textile workers and merchants of Macedonia: *"I am a real child of the city center."* She currently lives in a privately-owned apartment on Aristotelous square.

---

97   The principal of the private school attended by several of my informants in the city center. The name used is not the real one, in order to protect the informant's personal data.

Figure 3: Tzeni's window on Aristotelous square.

Source: Image by Miltiadis Zermpoulis.

During our last meeting, Tzeni called Lydia and talked to her about me, opening thus the way to call her in person and meet her again, this time in her personal space. Lydia received me in the apartment she acquired in 1964 through *antiparochi* in the area of Agia Sophia in the city center.

> "They started constructing apartment buildings everywhere, all of them through *antiparochi*. They all say we received the greatest *antiparochi*. We received four floors. At the beginning, they didn't give anything. A plot and I will tell you who, Ch., have you ever heard of him? His sister is a friend of mine, we were classmates. Well, Ch. together with doctor P. had a plot on Ippodromiou street and received one apartment each through *antiparochi*. Exactly! One apartment each! People didn't know. I remember the discussion about this, that they received one apartment each thanks to the plot they had on Ippodromiou street. Eh, how would constructors become so rich otherwise?"

She had prepared hand-made truffles and first thing she asked was what I would like to drink. As I entered the apartment, there was a reception space, while the apartment had two doors. Later, I realized that the second door led to the rest of the house, the most private part. The door from which she received me led to the living room, which had a view to the central street. The living room had one more door, which led to the servant's room, which she now used as a storage room. The first time I paid her a visit at the dining room, she had gathered some bags with magazines and newspapers from the "golden era", in order to sort them and give them to someone that would find them useful, before she dies and her children throw them away, as they will not be aware of their value.

> "You met me in a period in which I have taken bags down from my attic, to clean up my memories, because my children will not know where to throw them and maybe some of them will be useful to someone."

The living room was divided with furniture into smaller spaces, which gave the possibility to host more than one visitor, less visitors, only two visitors, face-to-face meetings or even small corners for the owner's exclusive use, like the writing desk and the piano.

> "When my husband was alive, we used to put some music on our stereo system and sit in the living room, can you believe that I have never used the stereo system since then? This year I have switched it off, I haven't even removed the covers, I don't use it, I set up my home, it hurts me, I have a little face there, this is how I call a smaller stereo system, I sit back there, I put a CD and listen to my music in a different place, let alone there is also television."

We sat on two armchairs on the back side of the main living room, consisting of a sofa, two armchairs and a small table between them. The armchairs were of classic baroque style, while the small table between them evoked the oriental tradition. This little living room created at the back of the main living room included a classic Biedermeier credenza at the opposite wall, on which there was a painting by Asprogerakas[98] from the family of my informant's stepfather, well-known tobacco merchant of the city.

---

98   Nikolaos Asprogerakas (1874–1942) was a Greek painter and university professor.

Figure 4: The two armchairs and the small table; Figure 5 Lydia's Saloni.

Source: Photo by Miltiadis Zermpoulis.; Source: Photo by Miltiadis Zermpoulis.

On the credenza there were two Chinese vases of her Italian grandfather. Next to them, there was a writing desk, on which she keeps the household accounts with the help of a small lamp, which, as she pointed out, was a "galet" from an old "vaporisateur" of her mother that she converted into a lamp.

Figure 6: Lydia's Secrétaire.

Source: Photo by Miltiadis Zermpoulis

At the central door and next to the writing desk, there was an old black television, for which Lydia felt somehow uncomfortable because of the disorder it created. On many occasions during our meeting she tried to justify herself about the presence of this television, associating it with three things: the love of her beloved ones, her tidiness, which is linked to her dear habit of saving up, including by utilizing old things, and finally the progressive abandonment of this semi-private space, which, especially after her husband's passing and her retirement from the social life of the city, remains closed.

> "[...] For as long as it gets the job done, I don't have any problem at all! There was a great fight about the television. But why did you bring this to me? I said – *But you have no such television, grandma!* – So, what, it gets the job done, it's fine, it's a big television, I don't wish to give it away now, I will take it to Gerakini[99], where I have a smaller one, I will install it over there and I will have a second one in Gerakini."

On the table between the armchairs where we were sitting when we met, there was a round metal object with three letters carved on it. Lydia showed this to me from the beginning, as it was the emblem of the private school she attended during her whole school life, which, as I would understand later, played an important part in her upbringing and education as well as in her social life in the following years and up to this day.

From the outset, I was impressed by her appearance and her way of pronouncing foreign words. Lydia wore a pair of gradient glasses, which prevented the person sitting opposite her from looking into her eyes. In our discussion, her knowledge of the French language became immediately obvious and was an important part in our communication. Lydia grew up as a bilingual person: at home they spoke mainly French and outside home they spoke Greek. However, due also to the special story of her parents, at home they spoke also other languages, such as Turkish and Italian.[100]

> "When we recruited a cook of Turkish origin, my parents spoke Turkish and I also started to understand what my poor dad was saying: – now what language do we have to speak so that she doesn't understand?" Her mother was Italian, but she had attended a French school and, therefore, the language she used most was French."

Lydia has fragmentary memories from her mother's narrations about the past of the family in Italy.

> "My mother was blonde, but she used to also dye her eyes, like young ladies do today, and I used to tell her, but, mother, how do you do this? When I was in Italy,

---

99   A common holiday destination for the people of Thessaloniki in Chalkidiki.

100   Her mother originated from a family of Italian engineers who settled at the end of the 19th century in the Ottoman Empire, taking part in the development plans for the reconstruction and modernization of the Empire.

there was an English lady, she told me 'come here and I'll show you how I also dye my eyes, so that I may look like as if I had blond eyelashes'. Such things occurred." She had narrated many times – because I have a little box – a silver little box that small, which has a crown on it and there it is written jamais à une autre, 'never to another one'. Umberto gave her this box in a bal, which took place in a hotel, they were there dancing, etc. They danced and when he left, he gave her the box. And she told me: – I sit, my kid, at my table, and next to me there was the daughter of Marshal Galean, I told her look what the prince gave me, I didn't even get to take the box out of the bag, and she took out her own. – He was giving the same box to every woman! (laughs)."

Her grandfather's family did business in Istanbul and subsequently in Thessaloniki during the period of great infrastructure works within the framework of modernization of the empire.

"My grandfather was an engineer of the water company Katikioy-Skoutari. Turkey was a place where, if you were a foreigner and you had acquaintances, you could do a lot of things. He had a factory and a foundry, he did cocoons, he was taking over contract works, he built buildings and bridges. He had built a bridge here at Sidirokastro. There was still the Turkish rule when he was here. Imagine, when I went to Italy in 1982 and my mom's brother was there, he asked me: -On the beach at Thessaloniki, are there still guitars? – But I said, how do you know about Thessaloniki? – What a question! When we did the railways, I spent some time in Thessaloniki!- Therefore... My mom knew he had done the 'bendia' of Thessaloniki, the 'bendia' were the water supply installations. And the subsequent manager of the water company, R., whose place is a privately-owned!!! house at the corner of Agias Sophias and Georgiou Stavrou streets, a conservation house [...]."
Regarding R. – was it his wife's or his own property?
"I'm not sure about this, indeed his wife was also from Konstantinoupoli. In any case, he was a subordinate of my grandfather in Konstantinoupoli. So, when my grandfather did this business, after the fire he saw that land was profitable. He sent his son-in-law, his older daughter's husband, who was also an engineer, to start buying plots and he brought all household goods. Very sociable people, my aunt was extremely sociable until her very last moment, she opened her home and started receiving people. There were some engineers who had come from abroad, there was engineer Theodosiadis, subsequent minister [...], Proikos, who was a university professor, and his privately-owned house was located at the corner of Aristotelous and Ermou streets, now there is Xyni there."
Who?
"That corner building, which was Proikos' house. Among them there was also my dad. Eh, not much was needed, love affairs of that period got started. My mom used to play the piano, she wrote some amour word, my father would underline it and so on. This led to Souvenir de Salonique, Souvenir de Costantinople...."

All members in Lydia's family were engineers. As she told me, this stopped at the grandchildren of her mother's brother, whom they found through Facebook in Venezuela[101] and they are all doctors.

"My great-grandfather was an interior designer and some Mustafa, a sultan had invited him, because my mother used to say that decoration – how can we call it – the medals that the sultan offered to him were full of pearls, brilliants and rubies [...]. Regarding my grandmother, her father used to work at the French consulate but when I asked her: *but mom, was he a consul or a clerk?* She replied: – *A, Je ne sais pas!-.*"

For Lydia, the "old home" in the area of Agia Sophia is associated with the history of her grandfathers in the Ottoman empire and more specifically in its two important cities. The detailed description of its interior delimits the specifics of her own family in a pre-war Thessaloniki looking for its pace within the framework of a modern national state after the events that followed the collapse of the empire and the birth of the Turkish national state. The descriptions of the interior of this two-floor mansion that the family bought in 1926 are very similar to the urban house of the 19th and beginning of 20th century that characterized the new way of domestic life launched by the European urban class, in order to differentiate itself from nobility and working class (Frykman & Löfgren, 1987, p. 142; Tebbe, 2008; Habermas, 1991, p. 10). The urban home, which is warm, has private and public spaces, but differs from mansions and palaces, and from the "scenery" living rooms of the aristocracy of the era of Louis XIV the Sun King, plays a leading part in the informant's descriptions.

"I had the old house until 1964. At the front, there were two rooms, a living room and a dining room. When I was a child, this front room was the living room, but also the office of my father, who was also a keen collector of stamps. I still have the collection, which stops at 1940, but a lot of stamps must have been stolen from my mother, allegedly they wanted to see them. The dining room was in the middle, namely there were the two rooms at the front, then there was the dining room – a big room – then my mother's bedroom, here there was another room, and my own bedroom was on this side. In the morning, when we did housework in the kitchen, we kept the living room closed, in the evening and when my father came home, he opened the living room and worked in his office. You entered an entré and then you would find the dining room and then the kitchen, separate bathroom and toilet. On the left there was the bathroom and a separate WC, a servant's room, and a kitchen. In those days houses had no bathrooms [...]."

The existence of a bathroom is a feature that, according to the informant, differentiates her from other families in Thessaloniki.

---

101   Lydia was also a member of these Facebook groups dealing with the past of Thessaloniki.

"I remember before 1940, there was an empty apartment below ours and our servant came and told my mother: – Madam, they also brought their bathtub – It was a fact! We rented an apartment after 1942 to a rather wealthy family, their bathroom was a storage room, although we had a built sink, well yes, they used the sink, but in there they placed their fridge and ice bucket."

They didn't place a bathtub, they probably went to the baths, right?

"No, they didn't go to the baths, they used a tub, a basin (laughs)."

You upstairs, did you have a bathtub?

"Of course, we had a bathtub, I beg your pardon! We have always had a bathtub, since I remember myself! And you don't know the good thing about me... When we first went to Versailles in 1949, to an international camp where I went with the guides and I knew there was no bathroom, but – what a scandal!–, as I was a child, I asked the guide: and the queen's bathroom, where was it?. And she replied: There was no bathroom, they were dirty (French accent). Yes, she told me this, straightforward: j´etais sale!. Yes, the only bathroom was at the petit Trianon, which was a thing like this, the exterior part seems a piece of furniture and above it is closed, you see this and wonder what this can be and how this can have a bathtub."

The bathroom is the part of the house on which Lydia insisted, mentioning specific memories from the pre-war era. The existence of a bathtub and meeting hygiene needs inside the house was associated with another quality that differentiated her from other "good homes" of the city, but linked her to another group, that of the refugees. When at a certain point I asked Lydia about Toumba and the refugees, she remembered a story, in which cleanliness was linked to the habits of the refugees of the 1922 exchange and their "civilized" way of living, in spite of their poverty. The refugeeism of her father, who died before the war, became the occasion for a "lady" of Thessaloniki to refer to this fact with contempt.

"Although I didn't live this... – Tourkosporoi, they call them!- Like when PAOK[102] plays in Athens, they call us Bulgarians, those days they did not accept the refugees. I remember I met a "lady", and her name also appears in the Album, who was also a member of the board of A., very active in the foundation of L.E.. I was a child, a young girl, and I was at Tzeni's uncle's place and she said: -They were refugees, my child!-my father's family- Refugees- And I say, they were refugees but they knew how to wash themselves and they also spoke three languages, when they came."

What about her? Was she native, from Macedonia?

"She must have been from Macedonia, because the name was from Chalkidiki, a well-known family of Chalkidiki, landowners. (...) There was one lady, as we went up Agia Marina street. I used to go to a lady. She used to sew – she was (...) in Ano Toumba, going up after the church her house was on the left, it was something like a tôle, this is what it was,

---

102   One of the main local sports teams of the city of Thessaloniki (translator's note).

and she was from a very good family from Smyrna. My mom knew them, she knew they were a good family from Smyrna. Whatever they were, they were noikokyraioi at their place, on both sides. The same thing happened with the Turks who went there, this up-rooting of people is terrible. How did they distinguish houses? There was a cousin of my husband, my husband was from Anchialos of Eastern Rumelia, there was the grandfather there who made wine and had salt pans. His cousin was an agronomist, director of Agrotiki Bank[103], and travelled in the villages. He told me:-do you know that I can tell a refugee village from far away? The first thing you see is a pot with basil."

Lydia associates the Nazi occupation years with the food distribution station of the Italians, fish in Salamina, green card and confinement in the old house because of her mother's widowhood, which rendered almost impossible her movement in public areas.

"This is where we were during the Nazi occupation, opposite there was P. who brought Germans with newspaper 'Nea Europe'. We had of course here all the time a lot of friends, close friends, for instance I., was then director in a Bank, and A. In addition, there was a couple of Italians, no, five couples that were my mother's friends. We had a green card, with which we could have fish from Salamina or from the Italians' station, you would go out and no one would ask for your identity card to know who you were. And one day, an Italian who was in Salamina told her: – Ms Ch., you are taking a lot of fish! – The child has to eat fish, my mother told him. My mother took fish, which then she gave also to her friends. There was a station at the "Bosporan Palace", which is called Lepenki, the whole basement, that's why I didn't miss them, although I didn't have the right to take chocolate, they always gave me some when I went shopping. It was either me or the servant who went there... At the end I told her: you have to get married, so that I can have some rest."

According to Lydia, the social mores of the era rendered particularly difficult the position of a widow, especially when she had to go outside in a public area.

"She used to wear a black veil, the georgette that started in the front and went behind reaching the floor. There were days she had to go to the tax services with that thing and she was a beautiful woman. We used to go to Flokaki[104] on Agiou Mina street, there the tram would turn and go back [...]. We used to go there, and she would offer me truffle chocolate that I liked a lot. I would eat a truffle standing and the rest to take away. We went back home, we couldn't sit there, because what people would say about a widow sitting there. And I told her, this situation cannot

---

103   The Agricultural Bank of Greece.
104   Well-known patisserie of the city, owned by Floka family.

go on, me being the widow's daughter. I was in second grade then. When I turned 14, I managed to convince her to get married."

Lydia remembers intensely how hard it was to abandon the new building hosting the private school she was attending, as this was commandeered by the Nazis. She also remembers the bombing that destroyed the dome of Agia Sophia church, but also the trams where they were forced to sit in the back seats, as the front part could be used only by the Germans.

When I pointed out that her experiences from the Nazi occupation do not contain the usual references to poverty and famine of the times and that her neighborhood seemed to be different because of the good financial standing of the residents, Lydia stopped me and said: *"We had Jews. I have written something…"* Contrary to most informants, by recomposing the experiences of the Nazi occupation and the first years of her life, Lydia cannot omit referring to the loss of so many classmates and friends, whom she unexpectedly lost in 1943. It is important for her to find and read to me a text she had written recently within the context of a commemoration organized by the Jewish community where she was asked to give a speech. Lydia stresses that she wrote some things, to express what she was feeling at the moment of writing this text. The text she gives me is not the formal one, as some notes and corrections can still be seen at various points of the speech.

"We had Jewish children here, it is terrible!" But she wants to read the text to me, as she fears she will not describe her feelings correctly about what had happened to her fellow citizens.

She wears her glasses and reads:

"The Nazi occupation came, gloom atmosphere in the city, only the SS boots could be heard in the night's silence. Why did they separate my friends from me putting that awful star on their chest? Before you know it, I lost them, they took them to another neighborhood, where, why, why? Weren't they also children like us, why did they separate them from us? And then one morning, murmuring was heard on Egnatia street, us children ran to the corner of the street, and we saw a silent, gloomy caravan dragging their feet. I stood there frozen and motionless, trying to distinguish my friends. I stayed there, until the caravan was lost in the dust of Egnatia street. Unforgettable scene, which after all these years still lives in my memory. The neighborhood was silent, no children's voices could be heard and nearby, in the market of Kapani, most shops were closed. You could not hear any merchants hawk their wares with their singing voices. How was this living element of our city, distinguished in commerce, science, letters, culture, which had given so many signs of love to fellow beings, how was this lost? Don't we owe the beautiful conservation buildings of our city to them? How many of them were lost in the fury of reconstruction? There is a long list of benefactors who, thanks to their legacy, have contributed and still contribute to the improvement of our standard of living, Baron Hirsch, etc. They made a special contribution to the history of Thessaloniki, tradesmen, distinguished scientists, people of the letters, bankers. The Israelites of our city of that era published newspapers in French. Rich lords but also breadwinners set the tone in the events of the city. How was a whole population deceived, how could an unwise man deceive a whole population and slaughter humanity? Today let's shout all together, never again, never again bloodshed, never again a genocide, never again a holocaust in history!"

My informant, during the whole duration of our discussion, was conscious of the different social position of her parents, at least during the period before the war, belonging to the minority of the city. According to her, Greece was not able to have a "western type" urban class because of "clientelism relationships" and the "unorthodox non-western way of running the Greek state."

> "There was no urban class in Greece; I will tell you stories from the pre-war era about my father and mother who were among the most – how can I name them – well-known people in the society of Thessaloniki. One man, head of the technical service of the refugee bank – yes, there was a refugee bank, in interchangeable goods –and how come he didn't make a fortune? (laughs). Why? Since then I found out that some of the interchangeable goods – there was a lady who had a garden behind and intended to build another apartment building there – I asked: where did he work? She said: at the interchangeable goods. I said: I see, because our man was a head and with the exception of this house he didn't leave anything else and I can say that even this house we bought it with my mother's money."

With this example, Lydia associates directly the national urban class with quick enrichment through illegal practices, but also its dependence on the public sector and the state, which the urban class took advantage of to the benefit of their individual interests.

Lydia's "old house" was one of the many buildings of eclecticist architectural style, particularly popular in the Ottoman cities at the end of the 19th century, but also in the great European capitals, in which traditional medieval architecture and neoclassical buildings of the beginning of the 19th century are replaced by massive historicism governing the architecture of the 19th and beginning of the 20th century (Kalogirou, 1992).[105]

---

105   The architectural differentiation of Thessaloniki is a quite characteristic one, as it adopts eclecticism in relation to Neoclassical Athens that strives to support also materially the constructed national origin of modern Greeks from ancient Greeks. It is not by chance that the neoclassical buildings of Thessaloniki, as described also in the introduction, are related to the small Greek community of the city and architect Paionidis, who designs buildings mainly in the name of the Greek community of the imperial city, like for instance Papafion foundation, in order to differentiate it from other communities, such as the Armenian and the

"In my neighborhood, we had trees on both sides, they were very beautiful, while we were waiting for the Italians to bomb, we were playing corners. This house across the street is the only mansion that has been left on this street and had also the function of a shelter. We went down there to protect ourselves. All these are pre-war houses and the two corner houses must have been built in 1926 and in 1928, because also our house was built then. My house was like the house of Ms B. on Philippou street, almost the same. The only thing it didn't have was the little balcony on the first floor; the cement tiles at the entrance were the same, black checked tiles. I tell her sometimes, because she comes down here to receive us, so that we don't have to go up there. Well done K., I tell her when I enter, I have the feeling I enter my own place, it's exactly the same, there was also a second door to enter the garden. The house had what we called a salamander, which worked with anthracite, and in the back part we also had a heater. I also lived in this place as a married woman, on the first floor."

The destruction suffered because of the war, the various state policies after the Nazi occupation to support the weaker strata but also their financial weakness in the post-war years, which did not allow them to maintain such a big house, mainly because her husband was self-employed, led them to demolishing it to acquire through *antiparochi* that coveted modern apartment.

"Let alone the rent control, we could not receive a higher rate. In these circumstances, we didn't have the financial possibility to maintain it. All that side had been destroyed by bombs, who would give me the money? It's the second time except for *ENFIA*[106] that the owners take on the weight and the rent control didn't teach them anything. The Greeks want their own house. That's it, and an apartment meets that requirement."

Nowadays, Lydia lives in the apartment with her daughter and her two dogs, while she owns 47% of the apartment building.[107] Until recently she was the building administrator and this role allowed her to have full control over the whole building.

Jewish ones, which opt for architectural tendencies that are contemporary to their era of construction, e.g. the projects by Pierro Arrigoni, Vitaliano Poselli, etc. More specifically, at the end of the 19th century, the only neoclassical buildings of the city are the current Metropolis and the ex consulate of the Greek Kingdom, current Museum of the Macedonian Struggle, both built by German architect Ernst Ziller, who belonged to a group of German architects already before the years of the Bavarian administration of the small Greek Kingdom, who undertook the project of material representation of the national ideology of the Greek State vis-à-vis the "Ottoman brutality" (see Kolonas, 2012).

106   Unified Property Tax (translator's note).

107   This is due to the fact that she managed to claim a large percentage of *antiparochi* from the construction company that demolished the old house and built the new multi-storey building.

4. Things in post-war home: modernity, innovation and becoming a *noikokyra/noikokyris*

In this chapter, I discuss the concept of "modern" as a sociological and analytical category[1] within the context of the post-war state and internalization process of this "civilizing" hegemonic imperative by my informants in the field. It is the result of their relationship with the "modern"[2] material world that surrounds them in the apartments where they live.[3]

As we saw also in the second chapter,[4] anthropologist Daniel Miller (2005) referred to the ability of objects to go unnoticed, which allows them to have a more drastic impact on humans. According to him, this is an analysis of the context itself, as this was shaped and lived by people. According to Miller, humans' behavior and action is a result of the expectations created by their context of action (Miller, 2005, pp. 4–5). Drawing on art historian Gombrich's book *The sense of Order: A Study in the psychology of Decorate Art* (1979) on the importance of the frame, Miller (2005, p. 5) gives the example of an art painting, which suddenly becomes visible, when it is framed up with an appropriate frame, in the sense that the context of a gallery and the appropriate way of promoting and presenting art makes it special and defines the way in which people approach it, by investing money and time. In addition, according to Miller (2005, p. 6–7), Pierre Bourdieu's theory of practice is a unique milestone in cultural theories, as it shows that people socialize through repeated practices concerning a person's relationship with specific cultural objects in a specific cultural and

---

1   See in introductory chapter 2.4 *"Modernization, urbanization and ideological civilizing: an anthropological reading"* the modernization policies and the importance of "modern" in the post-war "civilizing" of the post-civil war society.

2   It is important to understand the transition, as we saw in the third chapter, from the context of total lack to the post-war context of ability to consume. The change of the material relationships and the new post-war context of development and modernization shape different subjectivities and material worlds.

3   See Bakalaki (2003, p. 214), on the "traditional ideal" of "becoming modern", especially within the context of the autonomous units that households have been over time.

4   See subchapter 2.4 *"Modernization, urbanization and ideological civilizing: an anthropological reading"*.

social frame of reference. The cultural material world is imposed on us, as Miller put it, in an almost normative way, in terms of habitus (2005, p. 5).

The analysis takes also into account the debate developed by Hicks and Beaudry in their collective volume published in 2010 advocating for an interdisciplinary approach of the material world, which will take some distance from the impact of a purely cultural and sociological Durkheimian approach characterizing the writings on material culture mainly in Great Britain (Gialouri, 2012, pp. 25–31; Hicks & Beaudry, 2010, pp. 25–99). By attempting a historical overview of the forms in which the relationship between subject and object was approached since the end of the 19th century and the material-centered view of things in terms of cultural diffusion both in Anthropology and in Archaeology, as well as the establishment of material culture studies in Great Britain and America, they criticize a more human-centered vision of the material world, which is usually studied only when it plays a part in the social relationships of people. The material action of objects in these studies seems to be only "social" and static, without a substantial effort to equally investigate also the physical materiality and its consequences on the life of objects and subjects. Thus, by criticizing Daniel Miller, Tim Ingold suggests focusing on "material" rather than on "materiality" (Ingold, 2007b, pp. 1–16, 2008).

However, an ethnography that aims at showcasing social changes and the different stages of establishing cultural identities in the post-war Greek society cannot really focus only on the physical materiality of things and changes in their substance. What can be better followed is the role of things, their different stories and uses in informants' everyday life and finally the meaning produced by this use. This approach can disclose interesting aspects of their common history, which could be revealing for the objects and their use as well as for the establishment of subjectivities through "objectifications"[5] in the Greek post-war context of westernization and expansion of middle classes.

Thus, the analysis seeks to understand the informants' relationships with the objects decorating the interior of their houses, as well as with those that no longer exist or are hidden in closets and attics[6], but participate through discursive practices in their biographical narrations, associating them with people and situations that no longer exist.[7]

The objects acquired after the war within the context of modernizing everyday life help us understand how informants perceive and experience the social and cultural change in their personal life. In parallel, we are given the possibility to follow

---

5   On the term "objectification" see Miller (2005, pp. 7–10) and Gialouri (2012, pp. 25–30).

6   I refer mainly to objects that are no longer used but continue to act efficiently in the everyday life of people who possess them, see Thompson (2017) on the practices concerning objects that have lost their emotional and economic value).

7   See relevant ethnographies in Chevalier (1999) and Hecht (2001).

the development of this relationship and changes in their use and conceptualization in the social and cultural context of decoration of the post-war house. In other words, through these material things we seek meaning in the establishment of the identity of the "modernized" and "civilized" subject.[8]

In this chapter, together with the analytical categories of material culture, class and space, it is necessary to focus on the gender point of view and more specifically the conceptual approach of "becoming a man or a woman" (Papataxiarchis, 2006a; Salamone & Stanton, 2019; Bakalaki, 1994; Gkefou-Madianou, 2006), but this time within the context of post-war Greek urban society of a metropolitan Greek city and in the specific context of the imperative for modernization and further westernization of the Greek society.[9] The aim is to study further the gender-based dimension in the strategies followed by the informants in order to consume what is modern and through this possibility become an integral part of the class of *noikokyraioi*.

This specific analytical category was not mentioned for many years, neither in the first ethnographies conducted in Greece during the first post-war decades nor in anthropology in general before 1970. It appears only later, mainly because of the impact that the feminist criticism had on anthropology and other social sciences and humanities (Bakalaki, 1994, 2003; Dubisch, 2019; Gkefou-Madianou, 2006). The gender viewpoint and the institution of *noikokyrio* as a frame of reference, as this has been already analyzed in the ethnography concerning housework and gender in the Greek world (Papataxiarchis, 2006a, Salamone & Stanton, 2019; Bakalaki, 2013), will significantly help us gain a better understanding of the specific gender-based identities established in the post-war era within the context of mass urbanization, as well as the general social, political and cultural transformation taking place in Greece during the first three post-war decades.

In this study, female informants are approached as active subjects that focus, in cooperation with their husbands within the context of the *noikokyrio* policy (see Papataxiarchis, 2006a), on the modernization of their life, but also on their full integration into an "imaginary" European lifestyle.[10] According to Bakalaki (2003, pp.

---

8   Both terms are translations of the expressions used by informants in the field to describe their post-war subjectivity in the framework of a *noikokyremeni* life.

9   These identities were analyzed mainly for rural Greece but also for the islands of the Aegean Sea, see Dubisch (2019); Gkefou-Madianou (2006).

10   At this point it is important to repeat what we commented in the introduction, which has been aptly identified by both Herzfeld (2019) and Bakalaki (2008, p. 548, 2003), regarding Greece's relationship with Europe and the paradoxical ambiguity of the cultural identities shaped in different contexts. According to the above-mentioned authors, there are two different systems within the context of which people negotiate their identity. On one hand, there is the Greek model in History and in whatever concerns the cultural identity, which identifies with the nationalistic ideology and aims at acknowledging Greece as a part of the European world. On the other hand, there is a *"Rhōmaíikos"* subjectification model, which

3–4), women as subjects were restored in Anthropology mainly after the 1970s, when they were approached not only as subjects submitted to man's domination in the authoritative dual culture/nature, but as action subjects. The exoticization of the Greek rural society in the first ethnographies of the Greek world had to do, according to Gkefou-Madianou (2006, pp. 111–181), also with the fact that the first anthropologists who studied Greece as well as most of their informants were men. In the introduction of her very important book on gender and power in the Greek ethnography, Dubisch (2019) refers to this one-dimensional approach of the first ethnographies, which even insisted in the strict spatial distinction in the processes of establishment and reproduction of gender-based identities in Greece. Both Dubisch (2019) and Herzfeld (2019) propose to go beyond the dichotomies of public/private sphere, inside/outside, closed/open, which finally reproduce ethnocentric and rather androcentric concepts. More specifically, Herzfeld (2019; Gkefou-Madianou, 2006, p. 145) believes that these classifications are symbolic and therefore particularly fluid, and individuals use them to define themselves depending on the social circumstances. Both Dubisch (2019), in particular in her study on Tinos (2000), and Gkefou-Madianou (2006) through their own ethnographic experience focus more on the interrelation of the public and private sphere, in particular regarding the distribution of work and social action in the Greek society at gender level. Gkefou-Madianou, based on her ethnography on Mesogeia, characteristically stresses the existence of multiple models and discourses, but also the fluidity that characterizes the establishment of gender-based subjects:

> "[…] it is difficult to consider that the separation of genders in space is a vertical one and includes all sectors and that this is the only element determining the establishment of gender-based identities. Regarding western-origin idioms overstressing a separation of "public"/"domestic" based on a perfectly established internal and external orientation, it would be wrong to accept that they apply to the community, because such an admission would mean that social values of family

---

materializes in local contexts and contrasts with the first one. As we will see also in the ethnographic examples, the Greeks have internalized and reproduce a rather western European self, while at the same time some voices in Greece and in Europe classify Greece as a specific example, a "different other" in relation to a substance represented by "Europe" and "western culture". Bakalaki (2008) showcases this paradoxical ambiguity in a very insightful way, by presenting consonance and similarities in the discourses of the ethnographers of the Greek case as otherness with the official discourses about the education of women produced in the 19th century. The cultural representations of the ethnographers of the 1960s and 1970s, which are classified as otherness of the Mediterranean other, are identified 100 years earlier in the discourses of a local elite, which, by following the European model, lays the foundations of the household space and gender-based household identity of urban Greek women, having a significant impact on a large part of the Greek society through education.

are in constant contrast and opposition with those of the world outside the house-hold."[11] (Gkefou-Madianou, 2006, pp. 159–160)

Also, Salamone and Stanton (2019), based on the example of the island of Ammou-liani as land of refugees, stress the complementarity of the individuals' gender-based roles within the context of the institution of *noikokyrio*. A man's social prestige and value as a *noikokyris* depend on the action taken by the *noikokyra* woman, who complements him. According to Salamone and Stanton (2019), prior to getting married, a man is not considered as an adult. The gender-based identity of a *noikokyris* man is shaped through the process of *noikokyrema* (tidying up), meaning through living together with a "competent better half", which, within the context of the in-stitution of *noikokyrio* as a primarily, according to Papataxiarchis (2006a, pp. 7–11), economic field, means shaping gender-based subjects with specific characteristics. Gkefou-Madianou (2006) as well as Papataxiarchis (2006b) stress the interrelation and complementarity in establishing the self and the other, where the other is not always the woman. The establishment of gender-based subjects is rather character-ized by a certain fluidity, is not natural and should not always be taken for granted or expected.

Going back to the material culture viewpoint, it is important to stress the mate-rial dimension of *noikokyrio*, which, in post-war Greece, is expected to play a "civiliz-ing" part, providing a context of activity; it is therefore expected to change a big part of the population, integrating them into the specific, according to Papataxiarchis (2006a), cosmology in which individuals act as "economic human beings" aiming at profit. Salamone and Stanton (2019, pp. 97–121) believe that the institution of *noikokyrio* and in particular its economic dimension as "business" has survived from an older institution established in the Ottoman empire, which was not related to the respective institutions of the old rural and continental Greece. It was rather linked to the modernization itself and the adoption of capitalist and European characteristics of the Ottoman empire of the late 19th century.

This study associates the institution of *noikokyrio* and the gender-based dimen-sions of the complementary action of the subjects within its context with the pro-gressive establishment of a Greek national urban class at the end of the 19th cen-tury and in particular the expansion of the class of *noikokyraioi* during the Venize-los era (Potamianos, 2015). The characteristics of this institution are not necessarily adopted from the West and are not necessarily far from the logic of acting of the peo-ple of rural Greece. Besides, Bakalaki (2008, pp. 557–571) in her interesting study on women education in Greece stresses the crypto-colonialist[12] nature of such analyses associating the modern with city and Europe and the "savage" or "non-civilized" and

---

11   Translation of the original written in Greek.
12   The term belongs to Herzfeld, see Herzfeld (2002, pp. 899–926).

peculiar with the Greek provinces, as this was approached by American and British anthropologists during the first post-war decades. More specifically, she mentions:

> "I believe that the analysis of the "European" orientation of the educated elite of the 19th century can offer an interesting point of view about the re-examination of modern cultural constructions concerning the distinction between self/other or the concepts of particularity. As I mentioned earlier, ethnographers of Greece placed a special focus on the cultural particularity of the countries of their field work and the "diversity" of the people they studied (Herzfeld, 1987, p. 92). Moreover, they attributed to them clear and absolute distinctions of self/other."[13] (as quoted in Bakalaki, 2008, p. 564)

As it can be inferred from the study of archives and the interviews of informants, the gender-based and intensely political identity of *noikokyraioi* seems to be the one that prevails and is reproduced in everyday public and private practices of the individuals in the post-war era. The production and reproduction of this specific lifestyle within the context of the model of an urban *noikokyrio* is associated with policies seeking the biggest possible urbanization of the until then mainly rural society and the avoidance of an ideological shift, which would threaten the European and capitalist progress of the country.

4.1 From acting subjects to the interaction of subjects-objects

As it results from the fieldwork material, the changes taking place in post-war Greece of constant reconstruction and modernization both in the public and in the private field are decisive for the "material things" as well as for the people that use them and live with them. People change and with them objects also change in terms of form, materiality and role in the various social networks in which they participate. Ethnographies focusing on practices concerning the use of specific decorative objects at home are particularly helpful towards this direction. These ethnographies describe the multiple ways in which objects or home itself as a place influence people, but also how social relationships are intermediated by the action of material things.[14]

The material of the field work in Thessaloniki shows that the materiality of these objects (Miller, 2005), which accompany and delimit the everyday life of informants

---

13   Translation of the original written in Greek.

14   See in the very interesting volume about home and material culture by Daniel Miller (2001) *Home Possessions. Material Culture behind closed Doors.* The study by Vlachoutsikou about the arrangements of the limits of gender-based subjectivity through consumption practices is also very interesting (Vlachoutsikou, 1999, pp. 169–194).

in the field, is constantly negotiated and redetermined by them at the different phases of their life. The informants talk about the changes in their life, and the material world surrounding them participates in this narration, not only as a setting that helps document past experiences, but also as an element of "interaction" (Gialouri, 2012, pp. 35–42) and "intermediation" among informants and researchers.[15] Quite often the informants rephrase their narration on the occasion of a domestic object, which acts upon them at the moment of the interview dictating something different or facilitating the evocation of a specific memory that the subject has in the meantime repelled.

On the other hand, the researcher overcomes the initial tendency of classification of objects in aesthetic and social terms (Gell, 1998) perceiving "the thread and life lines", as these were characteristically described by Ingold (2007a), associating the stories of people with the objects that exist and participate when the researcher meets them. The interaction between the researcher and his/her informant is different when the narration takes place at the personal space of the latter, precisely because of the action of the material world that participates actively in this contact and exchange.

It is interesting to note the fact that the questions about material things initially confuse the informants, who are rather surprised by the researcher's interest in the carpet on which they both step at the moment of the interview.[16] Quite often informants expect to be asked questions about the history of the place and they are taken by surprise by the kind of questions asked by an "expert" working on "culture" and "history". The focus on things is rather personal and changes the context of the discussion, converting it from "formal" into "informal". In parallel, some informants tried to bring the conversation back to the facts that were "important" for them following the Asia Minor Catastrophe, reproducing the stories narrated by their parents, associating the reason of my visit with this special past of their family of refugees.

The importance of the materiality of objects and its change over time corresponds to the course of the object in the owner's life. The informants participate in the discussion mainly using specific objects; however, this is not a conscious action, but rather a set of everyday practices related to the way each individual socializes and is culturally shaped. My visit motivates a series of practices that

---

15   See in Zermpoulis (2017) about the impact of heirlooms and in particular old pictures on the establishment of a uniform narration of family continuity. Through old pictures and family pictures that she uses in the present, the informant heals the wounds of the past by recomposing narrations of a uniform and imperturbable family life. These objects are used by the informant in the present, to activate and justify the choices and plans of their possessor.

16   See Miller (1987, 2005) on the ability of the objects to go unnoticed and the action of the material world as a framework.

can take place through specific objects and specific paths in space defined by their position. Serving on a silver-plated tray covered with or without needlecraft and the subject's movements in space, which in that instance plays a series of roles related to the subject's gender, nationality, social status, etc., occur in a complementary way. It is difficult to see the subject separately from the acting objects that play a leading role in these performances.

Quite often objects were revealed to my informants also through my own questions, while the individual, despite his/her initial awkwardness, was trying to re-compose the story linking him/her to the possession of the object in question. As Banks's and Zeitlyn's (2015, p. 26) put it, "seeing is not a physical quality like all sensorial experiences. The interpretation of what one sees is culturally and historically intermediated". The objects, as we will see also in the analysis, participated and continue to participate in multiple networks of relationships and carry this dynamic, which in turn defines the relationship with them (Banks & Zeitlyn, 2015; Edwards, 2012; Miller, 1998). Nothing has been placed by chance in a setting. All objects and home itself speak to one another and quite often designate to the subject their position in the setting.

In this chapter, the objects that my informants use in their narration to document the change in their family life are usually mass production objects. By buying them, my informants seek to either consume the modern and participate in the westernization of the Greek urban society or meet practical needs, which emerge in the new cultural and political context of this circumstance.

The "novelty items" and consumption of the modern, despite their mass production and the dynamics of advertisement proposing them, seem to become part of the informants' lives, completing social processes and cultural needs of earlier years. These objects complete or replace other objects, while quite often, when they are no longer useful, they are thrown away, hidden in storage rooms, converted in something else or kept in their initial form participating in multi-factor networks of bidirectional agency (Gell, 1998; Latour, 2005). For example, all these uses and the changes they present, as we will see from the ethnographic examples below, are related to their establishment as subjects through the way in which they perceive their own position in the world to which they feel they belong, but also to the changes that have occurred in their identity.

Thus, regardless of the criticism exerted on the approach of anthropologists like Daniel Miller regarding the importance of consumption of mass production products in the establishment of subjectivity through objectifications within the context of everyday life, it seems that it is probably a stratagem, to avoid essentialist approaches of the material world, resorting only to semiotic interpretations and symbolisms. Objects can indeed be purchased precisely because they objectify cultural values and often serve subjects' social convenience purposes, but, as many ethnographies of material culture have shown in recent years, [17] the study of their everyday use and their relationship with the people possessing them can be revealing in relation to the different actions they fulfill.

To conclude, electrification and water supply of Kato Toumpa and the improvement of the city infrastructure, as a synonym of the change and improvement of its space in the after-war period, is almost always linked in the narrations with those objects that constitute for the informants the material documentation of their own participation in modernity (Bakalaki, 2003). The first fridge, the first cooker, the first *Stromatex* mattress that the informants acquire in the field works in the narration as the starting point for the description of a different life, which seeks modernity, to meet the conditions of the best possible *"noikokyremeni* (tidy) life", which was not possible in the previous stage of the narration. The *"noikokyremeni* (tidy) life", which is often lost due to political circumstances, [18] is compensated in the post-civil-war state or is updated through objects representing modernity. The year of acquisition of these objects always works as proof of faster achievement of the pursued goal and of a person who did better compared to others, shaping thus, and reproducing the modern subject in the redeveloped spatiality of Toumba. Almost all my informants, who were deprived of the privileges of a *"noikokyremeni* (tidy) life" during and before the war, experience a top-ranking sense regarding their relationship with modernity. The neighborhood, described always as the "others", is there to assess the transition to the next stage of people's materiality.

4.1.1   Strategies and practices of integration into a *"noikokyremeno"* lifestyle. The case of Maria from Toumba

The important social distinction between the informants of the city center and those of Kato Toumpa described in the third chapter, in particular during the Nazi occupation and civil war, seems to be progressively lifted as of the end of 1950s onwards. Several informants from Kato Toumpa, being the children of refugees from Asia Minor, identify in the period launched by the premiership of Konstantinos Karamanlis and the creation of the party of *ERE* the first signs of this change.

As we saw also in the previous chapter, the previous years were experienced as years of general loss and deprivation, in particular because of the complete lack of goods required for survival. [19] The houses in the lost homelands, the objects they car-

---

17   On this see Attfield (2006), Miller (2008), Navaro-Yashin (2009), Bourdieu (2006, 2008), Chevalier (1999), McCracken (1989) and Gullestad (1984).

18   On this see chapter 3.2.2 *"Short personal and family stories about homes and belongings. Stories of extreme poverty and refugeeism"*, for example due to refugeeism, famine of 1940, exile of parents due to ideological convictions.

19   See narrations about the experience of the famine of 1941 in chapter 3.2.2 *"Short personal and family stories about homes and belongings. Stories of extreme poverty and refugeeism"*.

ried with them but also new objects are sold and constantly lost anew, so that people can survive an uneven battle in a hostile environment that seems to question their self-evident right to an equal coexistence with native people. The questioning that refugee families probably experience in Greece from native inhabitants is internalized and becomes a pretext for discrimination and differentiation among them within the post-war context. When Katia[20] says that the neighbors "blabbed" about her father and "sent" him to exile *"because he managed to get electricity and water"*, it is precisely this internalization of a rather hegemonic stereotype, according to which refugees are not *noikokyraioi* and when they become so and slowly integrate into the social imperative, they have to face the envy of those still living in different, "non-*noikokyremenes*" material conditions, reproducing the same discourses. Here the internal competition of refugee families, as this results from their discourses, becomes important. Informants seem to have internalized the stereotype of poverty being a synonym of refugeeism. This concerns many such cases of subaltern social groups, like for instance minority groups in Thrace, the Roma, etc. [21]

On the contrary, Lydia's memory[22] of the existence of a bathtub at her parental home and the stories she narrates, in order to integrate the materiality of the bathtub into the social and cultural context of the interwar period, aim at documenting her various experiences, which led her since a very early age to finding "her own way", that same way that was sought much later also by other informants through practices facilitating such strategies. The bathtub reminds her of the different lifestyle she could have during that period, when some other fellow citizens did not even have a bathroom inside their house. The physical experience and the lifestyle linked to this household object subjectifies in terms of "habitus" (Bourdieu, 2006, 2008) Lydia, steering the way she decorates and uses her place today in Thessaloniki.

In this subchapter, we will benefit from the ethnographic example of Maria from Toumba of "NT" to showcase how the stories about the acquisition and use of the "first" modern objects and the memory of the importance they get at the different stages of the informants' life are useful, in order to take stock of the processes of establishment of the imaginary, which concern the emerging collective and gender-based identity of Greek men and women *noikokyraioi*. This cultural identity is of course not static; it is constantly redefined and reshaped by the active subjects them-

---

20   See ethnographic example in chapter 3.2.2 *"Short personal and family stories about homes and belongings. Stories of extreme poverty and refugeeism"*.

21   On these internal competitions there are interesting ethnographies like the ones concerning the internal competitions between the religious minority of Thrace, see for example: Tsibiridou (2006a, pp. 131–161, 2006b) and Ioannidou (2004).

22   See an ethnographic example about the narrations on "good homes" in the third chapter, more specifically in 3.3.3 *"Living in the center: life history"*.

selves. It is therefore characterized by fluidity and contingency (Vlachoutsikou, 1999; Gkefou-Madianou, 2006).

Overall, the ethnographic examples I use in the fourth chapter concern mainly the discourses of widowed women; however, I wish to stress that this choice has to do with the fact that they were my main informants in the field, with whom I held most meetings. When men are alive, they actively participate in the narrations about things and home and, for sure, even when they are no longer present, they are still visible through their personal belongings and their personal space, showcasing probably in the best possible way the complementarity that characterizes the Greek household (Papataxiarchis, 2006a) regarding the activities taking place inside and outside it.

Nevertheless, as it was stressed also at the beginning of the chapter, the aim is to also highlight the role of the gender of informants in this transition to the "new" and "modern". In Toumba, I spoke with both men and women, and I had the chance to see that both genders within the context of *noikokyrio* fulfill[23] a clearly complementary, though of a different type[24], gender-based identity, which follows strategies of "upgrading" the *noikokyrio*, with the aim of integrating it into the "modern" and "western" world with which they wish to dialogue. The gender-based subject of *noikokyra* woman and *noikokyris* man[25] who opts for an apartment, purchases "modern" furniture, dresses in a "modern way" and undertakes new roles in the social life of the neighborhood and city, takes a critical stance with regard to the traditional gender-based roles, which he/she links to an old-fashioned and "non-western provincialism" that is not consistent with life in the city.[26] Informants in Toumba that originate

---

23   On the formative dimension of occurrence according to Butler see Giannakopoulos (2006, p. 51) and the study by Salamone and Stanton (2019) about the refugee society of Ammouliani.

24   See Papataxiarchis (2006a).

25   Informants in the field use alternatively as self-determination the categories of *noikokyris* man and *noikokyra* woman; however, when they refer to their political and social status in Thessaloniki they use plural form and the category *noikokyraioi*, e.g. we were *noikokyraioi*, without making a gender-based distinction. In this study, all three categories are used alternatively, depending on the context they refer to.

26   Here it is important to refer to the study by Salamone and Stanton (2019), mainly because it concerned, like the ethnography by Hirschon (2006), refugees from Asia Minor. Salamone and Stanton (2019, p. 101) point out the significant difference among the refugee populations of Greece compared to the local rural ones. Asia Minor communities, being in the sphere of economic and cultural influence of Istanbul, which already at the end of the 19th century was going through social and cultural reforms within the context of modernization of the Ottoman empire, are very different from the local communities of continental Greece, which will experience such changes and transformations only after World War II. I cite a characteristic excerpt from the ethnographic narrations of Ammouliani: *"Peasants! Peasants! Because their clothes were the cheapest ones. Greek wool, few silver florins hanging on their clothes. Old-fashioned clothes and manners. But we were progressive 'intellectual pioneers'. We breathed dif-*

from refugee families speak about the cosmopolitanism and openness that characterized their ancestors' lives before coming to Greece.

Most of my female informants in Toumba, like Maria in this subchapter, have as their role model female relatives who did not limit themselves to the private space[27] of refugee houses but crossed the limit that separated poor Toumba from the city center.[28] Working as cooks or maids in the city center they managed to survive, becoming, in addition, carriers and channels of the modern and urban lifestyle in the refugee and then poor Toumba. In this chapter, their daughters and sons constitute gender-based identities that are representatively modern and fully integrated into the post-war imperative of westernization and modernization.

If we reflect in terms of political economy and in particular in terms of expansion and maximization of the fundamental accumulation that the worldwide capitalism attempts after the end of World War II, useful conclusions can be drawn about the violent way in which the Greek province is called to change. As we will see, internal and external migration obliges some of my informants to abandon their lifestyle, but also eventually to redetermine the gender-based roles they played in the social context of the Greek province or even refugee Toumba. Mothers leave their children with grandparents and become workers at mass industrialization factories. When these women and men come back to Greece to invest their savings in the newly built apartments of Toumba, they also bring with them new customs and lifestyles that "trouble", to use the words of Butler (2009), the customs and lifestyle of the *noikokyraioi* of Toumba.[29]

The shift from the "anthropology of women to the gender anthropology", as mentioned by Bakalaki (1994, p. 34), precisely shows this tendency to turn to a non-hierarchical and dual establishment of subjects, which, according to the author, is sought by patriarchy as well as a more macho perception of the hierarchy of people. According to Bakalaki, gender-based subjects are established socially in specific contexts and therefore "share the image of the world of the other, from whom they strive to separate"; she also holds that "the others of feminism are not separated and

---

ferent air!!! We wore latest fashion items. Whatever was fashionable in the city became fashionable also on our island. On our island we were keen on Russian style."

27   See categorizations/dichotomies in the Mediterranean ethnography of the 1960s "domesticity-woman"/"public sphere-man" in Gkefou-Madianou (2006) and in Skouteri-Didaskalou (1984, pp. 77–110).

28   See chapter three *"Poverty, refugeeism and material adaptation. Houses and people in a dynamic relationship"*.

29   The study by Silvia Federici (2011) *Kaliban and the Witch. Women, body and primary accumulation* is of particular interest and helps understand the important consequences of the expansion of capitalist relations of production on people's lives. More specifically, it helps understand how capitalism as an economic system of production hinders social reproduction by radically transforming people's lives.

distinguished from a feminine us" (pp. 39–40). In the case of Toumba, "the others" are usually the local inhabitants of the city center, whose hegemonic imperatives seem to be internalized by the inhabitants of Toumba or even, as we will see in the last subchapter of this chapter, the "peasants" and "*lazogermanoi*"[30] [31] that settle in Toumba after the war.

Maria provides a characteristic description of the neighborhood's reaction to the material changes occurring in her life. When for example she purchases the first domestic appliances and these are transported to her apartment in Toumba, she describes scenes of neighbors watching and being impressed by seeing something "new" and "modern". "Modern" is mainly associated with modern technology brought also by the electrification in Toumba. The neighborhood is the social context and setting where hegemonic discourses determining the gender-based subjectivities of my informants are produced and reproduced. The subject converses in her narrations with the imaginary of the era of modernization and post-war change, recalls memories concerning the objects of her everyday life, recomposing a narration of her life and her personal "fight" aiming for something better, for the constant progress sought for herself and her family. [32]

All objects are positioned and related among them, providing an everyday life setting, in ways that only their owner can explain to the visitor. The user and possessor of the objects is the creator of a life setting known only to himself/herself. The inspirer and protagonist of this life can recompose stories concerning the decoration choices as well as the ways of and reasons for acquiring and using the objects. The researcher's initial focus on them leads to interesting realizations and helps recall stories from the past which make the individual reflect on his/her choices. The collection of objects at home is a gathering of things, like a "museum collection", as Hecht pointed out, which is fully linked to the person living there (Hecht, 2001, pp. 123–148).

I will never forget the experience of disintegration and dissolution I personally lived when during the fieldwork, one week after the passing of one of my informants, I accidentally found, in front of the waste container of her neighborhood, pieces of that collectivity I was able to mentally reassemble following the ways and choices of this specific person. Ekavi's personal belongings, which she took care of every day, cherished, and linked to her personal course in life had turned into a simple pile

---

30   These terms are native, see subchapter 4.2 *"The counterexample: 'peasants' and 'migrants from Germany' in Toumba of 'eastern suburbs'"*.

31   "Lazogermanos" is a scornful characterization of Greek immigrants in Germany (translator's note).

32   On the syndrome for constant progress that characterizes the Greeks see Dertilis (2015, p. 3).

of materials, screws, pieces of furniture, bags with clothes, all piled up in the side-walk public area. These materials had an impact on me because of their biography, which associated them with the informant in the field, the home in which they used to be placed and finally the use and meaning attributed to them by Ekavi during our meetings. Their fate was of course declaratory of the social relationships in which she participated when she was alive but also of the heirs' inability to emotionally connect to these objects. The need to quickly empty the apartment to sell it was al-ready establishing the new setting of a "post-era" within the context of the crisis. The era of establishing the "identity of a *noikokyraios*", to which the objects of this woman were linked, had irrevocably passed.

Through life narrations, uses and behaviors occasioned by everyday life objects, I will now try to show how the memories of acquiring what in the setting of post-war Thessaloniki was considered "rare" or "unique" are associated with the emergence of a "modern subject" and his/her "progressive" cultural integration into the impera-tives of a "*noikokyremeno* lifestyle".

Every time I met Maria we sat in her kitchen, on the back side of the house; this was the place she has been using most in recent years while living on her own. Maria's house has two entrance doors; one of them is at the kitchen.[33] Her friends, Paraskevi and Soula, often gathered in the kitchen as well, to play cards or watch together their favorite Turkish series on television. Maria's kitchen is an informal place, in which she used to spend most of her time. On the contrary, Maria's living room, as we will see later, was used very little. Maria has a specific schedule, to which she has been sticking for years; for this reason, she preferred to meet me in the evening, when the TV series had finished, and she had free time for a chat. At lunch time it was always impossible, because she had to cook, and after lunch she absolutely had to take a nap. Over the weekend she met her friends to "play cards", as she said, or to have coffee and ice-cream in the city center.

Maria constantly stressed that she has always been the "first" one to do every-thing. In the context of establishing the identity of a *noikokyraios*, being original is very important. My informants feel that they are the first ones to discover whatever is innovative and particularly modern. In most sociological studies on *petty bourgeoi-sism*, reference is made to the tendency of the petty bourgeois to imitate, though in a wrong way because of the absence of the respective cultural capital, the con-sumption habits of urban people (Bourdieu, 2008).[34] The *noikokyraios's* originality sometimes lies in his/her ability to accurately imitate the original, which is also com-bined with the best and most convenient purchase price. Besides, as Salamone and

---

33   Kitchens in Toumba were usually on the back side of the apartment, contrary to the living rooms, which were always on the front side towards the street, to meet different practical needs and purposes.

34   This usually concerns domestic appliances.

Stanton (2019) also mention, the main aim of the "complementary" relationship of the spouses within the context of a *noikokyrio* is the maximization of profit. In my opinion, this profit can be both financial and social. The originality concerns the social context of each neighborhood that until then ignored what the *noikokyraios* brings and proposes as fully innovative. *"I had everything; I was lacking in nothing. The first fridge, the first television, the most impressive living room in the neighborhood."* All new things in the informants' life became particularly important when compared to life in the refugee houses of Toumba, and the milestone dates that marked an early or late progress were always highlighted.

My informant got engaged to Stavros in 1947 and started saving the money he sent her when he was in the army and occasionally worked as a photographer. Maria opens the escritoire[35] in the casual room[36] and shows me her husband's camera. *"I was frugal, my boy, that's why I progressed; my husband was naïve and spent all his money."*[37] Most of my informants in Toumba and in the city center were charged with the correct management of money with the aim of investing it in a prosperous way in consumption goals in the future. In most cases, they were not allowed to take over paid employment outside home, as this would mean that their husband was not able to ensure the best possible living for them.[38] As we will see later, this does not mean that my female informants did not eventually take over paid employment over their whole lifetime. This happened in a lot of cases when hard conditions and circum-

---

35   The escritoire belonged to Stavros, who passed away in 2000. The escritoire is still full of bills, notes of Stavros, his glasses and other personal belongings of Stavros.

36   The "*procheiro* [casual room]" is a semi-formal space next to the "*saloni* [main living room]" that Maria used on a daily basis together with the kitchen. The existence of a television in this room is usually an indication of its non-formal character.

37   The characterization "naïve" reminds us of the interesting study by Salamone and Stanton (2019) on the island society of Ammouliani. According to Salamone, no man is considered an adult until he gets married and enjoys the protection of his wife, who was educated since a very early age to be a good *noikokyra*. More specifically, Salamone and Stanton mention that women have great power in taking decisions that concern the household, while the prestige of the family and the man himself depend on the woman. According to the authors, the two are partners in the maintenance and success of their household. Salamone considers that the model of complementary co-existence of the household as a family business with the main aim of making profit is associated with the socioeconomic organization and lifestyle in Asia Minor (2019, p. 99).

38   As Maria explained to me, her husband's trust was because Maria through her actions soon proved her ability to handle the household money. On the contrary, her father never entrusted his money to her mother, which was indicative of the general contempt of her mother within the context of their marriage.

stances led them to this choice, to maintain their economic and social prestige. For this reason, this choice was often kept secret.[39]

Through the ethnographic example of Maria, we can see the characteristic element of gender complementarity within the context of a *noikokyrio*, as described by Papataxiarchis (2006a), and, in addition, the gender-based establishment of "masculinity" of Stavros through a powerful and centralist woman and wife identity, on which the first one seems indeed to depend.

In her ethnographic study in Mesogeia in Athens, Gkefou-Madianou (2006) tries to lift the separation line between the private and public sphere and in particular their identification with the gender-based identities established in these spheres. The anthropologist shows the interrelation and mutual way in which the spheres are shaped by both genders. According to Gkefou-Madianou, their discourses and finally their gender-based identities are rather a result of the dynamic relationship between the two genders (2006, pp. 111–181). More specifically, the example of Maria reveals how the public sphere in which she takes action and manages her household, e.g. contact with banks, purchase and sale of real estate, etc., is the one that complements the multi-dimensional[40] *noikokyrio* sphere to subjectify Maria as a handler and good *noikokyra*.

In 1953, and while Maria is preparing to get married to Stavors, Minister of Coordination Markezinis announces the devaluation of the drachma[41]. This fact destroys her plans, and she automatically loses half of her savings.[42] Her father proposes they live at the family's house in "NT", so that Maria does not "lose" her money paying a rent. It is known from the ethnographies in Greece that the practice of renting property is linked to a negative consumerism, not corresponding to the main goal of a household, which is, as we saw earlier, to make profit (Vlachoutsikou, 1999, pp. 169–194).

As we saw also in the third chapter, renting is for all informants something very negative, which they try in any possible way to avoid over their lifetime. Renting becomes positive only when they manage to rent their own properties to others, complementing thus their income. To avoid renting a house, Maria accepts her father's proposal and lives with him for a short period. This is a reasonable choice within

---

39   On the position of women regarding reproduction relationships within the context of family as a "reserve of a special type", see Skouteri-Didaskalou (1984, pp. 97–110).

40   By the term "multi-dimensional" I mean the polysemy of the private sphere that includes public-formal, informal-semi-formal and totally private spaces.

41   The drachma was Greece's national currency from 1833 to 1 January 2002, when it was replaced by the euro.

42   This relationship that Maria has with money is interesting. Although she never had to work outside home during her marriage, it is always her that makes and not the man who struggles to bring money to the household (on the concepts of "making" and "eating" see Vlachoutsikou, 1999).

the context of the *noikokyrio* code, as in this way money can be saved and invested in more productive choices in the future (Vlachoutsikou, 1999; Papataxiarchis, 2006a).

Her choice to introduce her brother to a girl from the neighborhood, so that he gets married as well since he was much older than her, will soon threaten the possibility of further staying at the parental home, which will be claimed following the same rationale also by her brother. As she characteristically says, my informant was, since a very early age, conscious of her role to take care of other people's but also her own issues, aiming at the biggest possible profit for the people involved. She was aware of the social and cultural codes of "good homes" and made sure to adopt behaviors that would provide social benefits but also teach others about these.

> "My brother was not married, but he had a girlfriend whom I didn't like. Of course, among my siblings I was more like this[43] than all others; although I was the youngest, I was the wisest one. My mind worked like that of an older person, that's why I progressed [...].[44] In the meantime, the uncle from America, the brother of my mother-in-law came and said: "I will take care of their wedding!" I didn't want to get married, I wished to have a house first and then get married [...]. [45] Meanwhile I arranged matchmaking for my brother, I told him he should not marry this girl because she was a fisherman's daughter, her brother only had a *tavla* [plank][46]. The girl was nice, later I got to know her better, she bought this plot on the back and got her act together."

At this point, it is important to note how the femininity of Maria, who was not married yet, occurs: as a younger sister, she decides on her brother's future wife. This wife must be a girl who will have a social profile that will be different from that of a worker, in a profession that, according to Maria, is a men's one. Her goal is the social upgrade of her family, which will potentially contribute also to the achievement of

---

43   With the demonstrative pronoun "this", the informant stresses the extroverted and efficient character she had, which distinguished her from her siblings and other family members. As we saw in the previous chapter, Maria's role model was her grandmother, who used to work as a cook at the "good" homes of the city center. Since then, Maria has been progressively materializing (Butler, 2009), mainly through the self-formative nature of this performing process, the gender-based identity of a wife that will be able to meet the requirements of such upward mobility through marriage.

44   In many ethnographies of Greece and Greek household, we find the power and influence exercised by the establishment of an efficient and managing femininity beyond the private sphere (see Dubisch, 2019, pp. 3–42).

45   According to Papataxiarchis (2006a), the *noikokyrio* is a native theory of action. The *noikokyrio* constitutes a process through which women and men fulfill their respective "nature". The subjects act on a daily basis driven by the interest of the "family" (see Papataxiarchis, 2006a, pp. 9–10).

46   Means the table he used to sell fish on the street.

her own goal to move upwards through marriage. The humanization of the "fisherman's daughter" candidate bride occurs only when in the future she manages thanks to her savings to buy a plot, which of course in the context of post-war Thessaloniki of *antiparochi* made her the possessor of an important capital.

> "And I invited Aphroditi, whom I met through the sister-in-law of my mother-in-law. Aunt Marika, the sister of my father-in-law, was a proper lady, she was involved in the Guiding Association, in the Red Cross, in the circle of Anatolia College. When I went there, she used to praise Aphroditi a lot. She was an orphan from her neighborhood [...]. I therefore invited her to my wedding. I also have pictures of her, she came like a poor thing. Poor girl, she lived with a stranger woman, her sister kicked her out, because they promised the house to the sister who was a bit handicapped [...]. Thus, Katina, a neighbor took her, because Aphroditi was a dressmaker with golden hands, and she felt sorry for the kid and took her [...]. My brother saw her and he liked her [...]. They got engaged and then she revolted against him. My father encouraged her, he thought she was a nice girl and he wanted to put the house in order so that they could get married. We promised to give her the house, so that she could stay there. Eh, she could stay for as long as she wished, we did not intend to stay there. I asked her to wait for a while so that I could wrap it up and then I would leave and they would get married. But she would not accept. Her brother came from America, and wanted to take care of their wedding before he could go back [...]. They wanted to kick me away [...]!"

Aphroditi was, according to Maria, the best choice for her brother, as the fact that she was an orphan[47] rendered her a person with limited possibility of influence within the context of managing the *noikokyrio* of Maria's father. Moreover, the recommendations from aunt Marika, who had a superior social status, regarding Aphroditi's qualities as a "beautiful young lady with golden hands" made her the right choice within the context of the financial dimension of the *noikokyrio* (Papataxiarchis, 2006a; Salamone & Stanton, 2019; Skouteri-Didaskalou, 1984).

As Papataxiarchis (2006a) mentions, within the context of a *noikokyrio*, the co-existence of two spouse units is undesirable and considered as an indication of low social status and failure. Thus, my informant, who is aware of this condition, seeks very soon, with the money she manages to save from Stavros' seasonal employment as photographer and thanks to her provisional stay at the parental home and later at her mother-in-law's place, to buy finally a house, which "was unfinished". This detail allowed Maria to buy it at a lower price, but achievieng for the time being the

---

47   Aphroditi's orphanhood as a characteristic that plays a restrictive role, according to Maria, in her equal activity within the context of the household, must be analyzed within the context of establishment of female passivity versus an active femininity, like that of Maria (see Giannakopoulos, 2001).

goal of home ownership, which was very important for her. Besides, as it can be seen also from studies about housing practices in post-war Greece (Maloutas, 1990), home ownership is the most common practice within the context of mass construction.

> "And I went to live on Papafi street when my child was three months old. In the meantime, I had been saving money for about one year and I had bought the building plot in Toumba, because this is where we used to go out. This is where we really wished to have a plot. This plot created a lot of problems to us, because it was pledged to the bank and the state would not give us a building permit."

Maria claims a better life in Toumba, following different strategies of saving money in cooperation with her husband but also with Stavros' parents, who support these choices without creating obstacles to their implementation. As she characteristically repeats to me, these were plans she had been making since she was very young and now, with the help of her husband, who is hard-working and supportive, she can materialize, objectifying through these practices the gender-based identity of a successful *noikokyra* within the social context of middle strata lifestyle of the *noikokyraioi*.

Just next to the refugee settlement, as mentioned also in the third chapter, there was a huge field, where fruit and vegetables were cultivated and used by the family that owned the field to supply the market of Thessaloniki. However, the Nazi occupation and the founder's premature death leads to the progressive financial collapse of the company, which starts selling out pieces of the big field that used to be the absolute border between the refugees and the family members of the landowner, who had the honor, according to his grandson's testimony, to receive from time to time even the royal family. The big land of 44 stremmas[48] is being divided and sold, to pay off the rest of the loan to the bank. Thus, Maria is one of the first inhabitants to buy a plot from the big land of Giorgos's grandfather and in this way, she feels that she achieves the transition from the life of poor refugees to the life of a successful middle-strata family.[49] This experience is lived as a personal success of a "long-standing fight" for a better life, as she meant it. This spatial transition, through its class dimension, differentiates her from that moment on from the other members

---

48   The stremma is a unit of area measurement, used mainly in Greece to measure areas of land for sale, especially parcels of land. A stremma is equivalent to 1 000 square metres.

49   The spatial dimension (Low & Lawrence-Zúñiga, 2007; Giannakopoulos & Giannitsiotis, 2010) of this plot, which was inaccessible to the refugee families and directly associated with the life and lifestyle of the good homes of the city center (see third chapter) plays an establishing role in the subjectification of my informant, through the possibility of its symbolic and real appropriation.

of her family and makes her the "object of envy" and at the same time "an example to follow" in her old neighborhood.

> "In the meantime, I kept saving, I have always been saving, my boy. We didn't know the plot was pledged; his notary cheated us. We had signed a preliminary agreement, but we had to issue a normal permit to be able to build [...]. And then Stavros went to his shop in the city center – in the meantime, he had opened a bakery – and told him: 'I will kill you; I risk going to jail, my wife will divorce me!' And he grabbed a thing to beat him and then he was frightened, he realized he was really angry, and he could no longer lie to him, because Manos kept lying to him – and he went to his notary and asked him to lift the pledge and put it to the adjacent plot, and this is how we received the permit. In the meantime, on the day we laid the foundations here in 1956, I was trying to sell the other house, too, but it was unfinished, and I was not successful. Then my uncle, aunt Olga's husband, former military officer, who became a real estate agent, managed to sell the house for me. On that day, when I slaughtered the cock, I sold it to two different people. In the morning, I sold it to a lady with her husband, we even received an advance payment. After a while, and while I had already sold the house, an old man came and wished to buy the house as well; he was willing to pay more money for it, 45 000 drachmas. I said, now I have to give back the advance payment, what a shame! The old man told me: "I have a brother on Mount Athos, he will not need the house, I am willing to buy it, but if you wish to have an alternative solution, keep me here to look after me, how many more years will I live?" I did not accept such a proposal, bring home an old man only to sell the house, I was a newlywed girl, I was young. He gave us the money, and one week later he was killed in a car accident. Meaning, if I was lucky, I would still have the house and would give it for *antiparochi*, this is what they did, they gave it for *antiparochi* and a lot of luxurious houses were built there."

This narration of Maria reproduces, within the context of representation, her active femininity, which was founded on her ability to handle the money from her husband's work. Maria is still proud of her ability to handle and save money. The description "frugal" is a synonym of her gender-based identity as a *noikokyra*. On the opposite side of this identity there is always the weak masculinity of her communist and womanizer father who spent all his money, but also the passive femininity of her sister, who had no "control", as she characteristically says. In addition, she uses the savings as a means of pressure to achieve her goals, especially concerning her children. Maria and Stavros were not ready at that time to make any possible sacrifice driven by profit. The old man's proposal was rejected, as it was the case also for Maria's further stay in a rented house or at her mother-in-law's place, since all the above choices would jeopardize the couple's social upward mobility, which was symbolized by the purchase of the plot in the old field opposite the refugee settlement and the establishment of an independent *noikokyrio*.

However, my informant does not forget about the fact that her sister-in-law and her brother led her to leaving prematurely her parental home, threatening thus the smooth establishment of her own *noikokyrio*.

"Then they realized their mistake and my sister-in-law invited me to the wedding, if you see the pictures, you'll see that I am next to her with my nice clothes. I put on a black lace dress, my sweetheart, and Stavros was still a soldier. I participated in everything she organized, I also went to see her dowry and everything, although she had kicked me out of my parental home. It was her fault! Then my father bought me a *Singer* sewing machine.[50] I still have it. He also bought me a lamp and this clock. He bought the same clocks for everyone, but in my case, he included this in his testament, that he gave me a clock and he made the iron parts of my house, and he bought me also the sewing machine. What he would have given me for the rent, he gave me as gifts, to flatter me, because I was the reason why he and my brother had a good life. It was thanks to me that he could work at the foundation and become rich. Hadn't I been involved, how would he have entered the foundation?[51] My dad was a craftsman, but he had not found a good position yet. I kindly asked my father-in-law, and he started working there, he established a partnership with the foundation and did projects also outside

50   This sewing machine, which Maria keeps in her bedroom, is directly associated with the representative performance of beautiful and modern Maria that everyone wishes to have next to them in social events, as it was mentioned earlier. Maria always makes and mends her clothes on her own at home. No-one can be present during this process, as she always wishes to be seen only when she is ready. Maria always uses various solutions to adapt the clothes to the characteristics of her own body (for example, pads at the chest and shoulders, special belts inside to show her waist, etc.). Stavros, her husband, had paid the sewing course in exchange for a promise that she would not go out to work as a hairdresser or a seamstress, which would have undermined the social status of the couple. Maria wished to work as a hairdresser or a seamstress. She is passionate about hairstyle even now that she is an older woman. She keeps lots of albums with all the buns and hairstyling that she did for formal events or for the regular annual reception she organized at home on Stavros's name day. She copied the clothes and hairstyling from foreign and Greek magazines that she bought to this end. Her goal was to be modern and elegant: *"I didn't have any special clothes, no! Just a suit, like this – but it suited me well. It was red – when I put it on and with the right hairstyle – when I walked I was like a butterfly! Once the propeller guy, this is how we used to call him, told me: "I will never forget you, Maria, when you passed outside the coffee shop and we went out just to look at you, you were so beautiful" – I mean I wore a simple thing but it suited me really well."* (excerpt from the conversations with Maria)

51   By the term "foundation" she means the orphanage, where both her husband's family and her father taught their crafts to the orphans.

the foundation and he also did the rails at the metropolitan church of Kalamaria. If you see the windows, you will understand, he was a good craftsman."

In the above excerpt of the narration, we understand what many anthropologists have pointed out about running the *noikokyrio* like a business (Papataxiarchis, 2006a). Maria takes it for granted that she should receive a dowry[52] or at least her father's support during the first years of her marriage, as this was the case in the refugee families in urban areas, as we know from the ethnography of Hirschon (2006) in Kokkinia, but also in the Greek province (Salamone & Stanton, 2019). Maria perceives the wedding gifts, namely the rails of her house fence, the chandelier in the living room, the clock and the *Singer* sewing machine, as dowry but also in return for her arrangement to restitute the social prestige of her father, who, after coming back from exile as communist, was placed in a permanent employment position thanks to her intervention.[53] Through her marriage, Maria does not secure only her own future but also that of her father and mother. Already Vlachoutsikou (1999), in her very interesting study on a village of Voiotia, refers to the importance of setting limits and to the importance of limits in the readaptation and renegotiation of gender-based identities and cultural classifications. The "device" of Vlachoutsikou's informant in Voiotia to compensate her choice for a rented house, which is classified as something she "eats", with her work in the fields, which is classified as something she "makes", allows her to free herself from the control of her mother-in-law and renegotiate the possibilities and choices that were not allowed until that moment according to her gender-based identity. Gkefou-Madianou (2006, pp. 148–157) claims that women experience social change early and adapt to it more easily. According to the anthropologist, both women and men in Mesogeia are between the traditional and the modern. By means of everyday practices and instances, they expand, move and constantly redetermine their cultural classifications. Thus, the anthropologist (2006, p.157), following the tendencies of the post-modern and feminist post-structuralist theory about the establishment of identities, proposes to focus on the practices themselves, through which finally gender manifests, being fluid and open to change, far from universal gender-based classifications and biologisms (Bakalaki, 1994, pp. 13–74; Giannakopoulos, 2006, pp. 17–102; Skouteri-Didaskalou, 1984, pp. 136–7).

Maria's relationship with her father is always crucial in the way the informant lives her parental home, but also the various phases in her personal life. The "old house" in "NT" becomes bigger and more beautiful. Maria progresses in life and

---

52   Regarding dowry and its importance in relation to women's inferior position in the Greek society, see Skouteri-Didaskalou (1984, pp. 155–215).

53   See about the conceptualization of exchange at the coffee shop, on the opposite side of which Papataxiarchis (1992) places the competitive and hierarchical relationships of relatives.

acquires her own house, and all this is somehow connected to her father and the course of their relationship, which is eventually decisive also for the evolution of the material world surrounding them. The experience of the new materiality of the house and the successful outcome of the strategies of the informant for social ascent are determining for the subjectivity shaped in the post-war era through them. Her marriage with Stavros's *noikokyremeni* family progressively contributes to tidying up not only her own life, but also the life of her "communist" and "womanizer" father. Therefore, Maria through her active femininity, which she progressively establishes through the above-mentioned practices, reshapes and redetermines her father's passive masculinity. Besides, according to Foucault, the individual is not shaped by a power outside and beyond him/her being fully submissive to it. Individuals are subjectified by the power exercised in their everyday life; it is a bio-power producing bodies as fields for exercising power relations (Giannakopoulos, 2006, pp. 30–31). Maria has clearly internalized the hegemonic normative model of a *noikokyremeni* family life, as this has been shaped historically, and adopts practices of disciplining the capitalist ethics[54] to tame her father, who with his lifestyle threatens her own smooth integration into the normality of the *noikokyraioi* represented by her husband's family. *"My father fixed the house, little by little, we had a gate, my son, it was all carved, then my niece took it, anyway. The refugee house was turned into a palace!"*

The lack of support from her father and Maria's strategy to save money aiming at becoming independent and establishing her own *noikokyrio* leads her, as we have already mentioned, to living with her in-laws for a certain period.

> "And I became a servant for my mother-in-law, and she was astounded by my *noikokyrosyni* (tidiness). We also paid a weekly rent for living there. I stayed there for four months, until the kitchen was finished. When I came, these were all unplastered. Then all rooms were fixed, the house was done, but we left the living room as it was."

Maria, thus, does not enter her husband's household as an equal member; she is figuratively transformed into a "servant", wishing in this way to show her mother-in-law her ability, regardless of the social status of her family, to become a worthy and equal member, by performing the gender-based identity of a *noikokyra*, initially inferior or hierarchically submitted within the context of the *noikokyrio* of her *noikokyraioi* in-laws. At the level of symbolisms, an equivalent role was played, as it results from the interesting study of Hantzaroula (2002, 2012), by young girls from the province, who worked as "stepchildren" in urban houses of Athens to build up their dowry.

---

54   See the relationship with money and subjectification established based on achieving the largest possible profit and productivity.

Maria's dream of a privately owned house with an "oval" terrace, where she will be able to walk in the morning in a silk robe and water the pergolas in the built-in flower beds of the terrace, came true. The representative performance of this gender-based identity in Butler's terms (2009) starts in my informant's case as a constantly repeated dream, energized with truth segments by the grandmother's experience at the city center homes. With various strategies, devices, exchanges, concessions, and resistance, she manages to truly live it. The house is not entirely built. This progressive completion of the family buildings is typical in the context of housing practices and target setting for home ownership in post-war Greece (Maloutas, 1990). The living room was initially used as workplace by her father-in-law, brother-in-law, and husband. Thus, for many years it was used as a carpenter's workplace and my informant served the three men who used the common parts of her newly built house.

> "My brother-in-law, Stavros and my father-in-law came and worked here. I had also a bedroom of course, on that side; on this side, I had a small living room. Beautiful things, some of them I gave to a Russian-Pontic cleaning lady. The living room was still unplastered as well."

4.1.2   Gender-based performances of the modern. The case of Vasiliki from the second generation of women from Toumba

As it can be seen also from the narration of Maria, to achieve their goal, which is obviously home ownership and acquisition of what was considered necessary in the cultural context and for the social needs of the post-war modernization of everyday life in Thessaloniki, the inhabitants of the area followed different and often difficult pathways in each generation.

The example of Vasiliki is a characteristic one. Vasiliki represents the generation following the one of the main informants of the survey. [55] She was born in 1952 in Kato Toumba in a refugee house of "NT". Vasiliki lived similar experiences as Maria and Katia, who are her mother's age, since her father was also exiled to Makronisos for nine months due to his ideological convictions. Vasiliki was very much ashamed of her neighborhood and often complained to her father about people's standard of living and poverty. He used to comfort her and kept telling her that everything will change one day and Toumba will become a "nice suburb". The informant believes that her dad was particularly "wise", since indeed Toumba after the 1970s started turning into one of the sought-after suburbs of the city, "in particular thanks to the good climate and modern buildings", which were massively constructed during that period,

---

55   The first generation of informants includes men and women born in Thessaloniki at the end of the 1920s and beginning of the 1930s.

as she also points out. My informant now feels privileged to live in Kato Toumba of the "eastern suburbs" of the city, as she characteristically mentions to me.

Vasiliki's fight to reach her current standard of living, threatened by the recent financial crisis that broke out in 2010, was not an easy one. In 1973, to marry her husband, the family decided to demolish the old refugee house and build two smaller ones on the ground floor, so that she could have her own apartment. As mentioned above, home ownership is a main component of the successful establishment of a *noikokyrio*. In Toumba and in Thessaloniki in general, there is the phenomenon of dowry, observed in the form of provision of an apartment or money, which is mainly given by the bride's family; this is a way, according to the informants, to compensate for the fact that the woman does not work in the context of her marriage.[56] The *antiparochi* was perfectly responding to this practice, as it gave many families the possibility to take care of the immediate "settlement" of their children, providing them with separate apartments, based on the hegemonic standards of a *"noikokyremenos way of living"*.

In the case of Vasiliki, the practice of *antiparochi* had just started in Toumba and its percentage could not fulfill the target of "settlement" of both daughters of Vasiliki's father. But they also had little money and their decision to eventually demolish their only house raised a lot of difficulties for them. Vasiliki's father, who was a shoemaker, managed thanks to his savings to lay the foundations and build the two apartments, but there was no additional money and Vasiliki could not get all those things she thought the new apartment should have. She could not afford to equip it and live in there.[57] Her husband was a radio operator and she worked as an employee at a crystal shop in the city center. Her monthly salary of two thousand drachmas did not allow her to materialize her plans and thus she decided to embark with her husband for 18 months, [58] to quickly earn the money she needed to set up a *noikokyrio*, as she characteristically mentioned to me. During that period, her husband earned

---

56 On this, see Skouteri-Didaskalou (1984, pp. 216–258).

57 Several informants explained that they postponed the wedding because they were not able to get some furniture, for example the (mixed) display cabinet in the living room, the dining table, etc., which was considered necessary to "open" the home one week before the wedding and receive the guests' gifts. Particularly the second generation used to "show" the new house before the wedding; in this way they communicated the beginning of their household to their social entourage. The guests used to offer gifts that complemented the household objects.

58 Vasiliki did not work on the ship, but accompanied her husband during this big journey, because she was afraid of putting her marriage in danger by leaving her husband alone for so many months. At this point, it would be interesting to refer to the interesting study by Giannakopoulos (2001, pp. 242–268) about the establishment of masculinity in Greece and the direct association of establishment of a gender-based identity with a physical sexual behavior based on the male genitals. In deprivation circumstances, the sexual behavior and physical instincts of a man cannot be restricted and manifest in a direct way within the

30 000 drachmas, and very quickly they managed to save a considerable amount of money, which would help them make their dreams come true. According to Papataxiarchis (2006a), all choices and strategies opted for are "legitimized" within the context of the *noikokyrio*. The subject as member of the *noikokyrio* team acts in the interest of the family, is therefore "on duty". As we saw also in the example of Maria, the activity of the *noikokyra* who associates the present with the future subjecting the former to the latter constitutes the prototype of calculated reasoned action (Papataxiarchis, 2006a, pp. 1–17).

> "In 1973, we demolished the old one, I left, we finished the ground floor, and my mom came. We paid for this! Because we didn't have money! We were cleaned out, we didn't have enough money to build two houses back in 1973. Later everyone gave their old houses for *antiparochi* and received three apartments each, while we did it ourselves. [...] We therefore embarked because we didn't have enough money to furnish it. This is what my father could do. How would I do afterwards – working as a seller at a crystal shop for a monthly salary of only two thousand drachmas?!"

Vasiliki's father was a "moralist", as she says, and was very sad with her daughter's decision to embark on a ship with so many men around her. To save her marriage by setting up an independent *noikokyrio*, Vasiliki "negotiates the "limits and delimitations" of her gender-based identity" (Vlachoutsikou, 1999, p. 170) and remodels them through a new performance of her gender-based self, as a woman that will spend eight months facing the masculinity of her husband's colleagues on a ship. Finally, this choice is not without consequences, as it threatens the honor and prestige of her parental home in Toumba. She believes that this choice of hers in combination with the fact that her sister got pregnant at the age of 16 and therefore had to get married immediately to her current husband caused a huge distress to her father, who finally got sick and passed away five years later, without being able to see their progress. Thus, the resistance, in Foucault's terms, of my informant to the cultural classifications of Toumba but also her sister's choices that go beyond the "limits" and renegotiate the gender-based roles have an impact on her father's physical condition and at least figuratively, at discourse level, kill him. Moreover, the capitalism needs in post-war Greece that seek the biggest possible expansion of the middle class change drastically the conditions in people's lives in Toumba, readjusting and arranging anew settings, materials, and people in this small society. Vasiliki and her husband transform the delimitations of their gender-based identity, to be able in the future, in the reshaped area of Toumba, to perform a different type of gender-based subjectivity within the context of middle-class life in the newly built apartment.

---

context of heterosexual or even homosexual sexual encounters, which are considered as a natural consequence of male sexuality.

Figure 7: The Rosenthal dinnerware set.

Source: Photo by Miltiadis Zermpoulis.

Vasiliki performs vividly in our meeting the gender-based identity of *noikokyra*. She brings to the table and shows me a set of *Rosenthal* dinnerware, which is part of a rich collection that she created over time; she is afraid that the next generation and more specifically her daughter will not appreciate it. The dinnerware is shown within the context of the discussion about the change and transformation of life in Toumba. It is directly linked to modern everyday life and the imperatives of this life within the new context of modernization of European urban life.

> "Look at the house as a building, this dinnerware, all stuff will pass, will be given to other individuals, maybe not even my children, other generations, which means I should enjoy them for as long as I am alive, then they will move elsewhere, all things and houses. My children don't want them. I have a very beautiful crystal display cabinet full of crystals that I wish to give her, she doesn't want them, because she has no time to clean them, all this takes love, care, and work. All this it's me... That display cabinet, twice a year all this stuff needs to be taken out and washed in the dishwasher, they need to be dusted. I don't regret. Imagine if I didn't have this piece of furniture... How would the wall look like? Empty? Nowadays homes are simple, they fill them with stuff from IKEA, I see how my daughter does, she has her fireplace, her plasma TV, two couches and that's it."

The new material reality is the framework, the canvas, as Daniel Miller (2005) put it, in which my informant perceives and eventually delimits her gender-based self at the moment of the narration. She is no longer the shoemaker's daughter. She is the wife of a former radio operator and current insurer, the daughter of a communist and low-paid employee at Zoura shop, who is forced to immigrate for a certain period, to respond to the new imperatives of capitalism but also to her personal need for a "different, more developed Toumba". Since she came back to Greece, she did not have to work outside home. Besides, her new financial and class status were characterized by new gender-based delimitations and compromises.

Within ten years after her return to Thessaloniki in 1975, by saving money and living in the small ground floor apartment that her father had built for her, she managed to gather enough money to build the first-floor apartment where she currently lives.[59]

The big display cabinet against the central wall of the living room, which reached the ceiling, caught my attention immediately. It was one of the biggest ones I had seen, compared to the other apartments I had visited. This piece of furniture was the most precious thing at Vasiliki's home, as it took her a lot of years and money to fill it.

> "2 000 drachmas were 700 euros of today; so, we were paid 30 000 for eighteen months and we managed to buy all the furniture, we did the kitchen cupboards, we bought a *Zastava* car. [...] I bought this display cabinet you see there. I still have it and I will not give it away".

When I asked her what exactly the purpose of this specific piece of furniture was, Vasiliki explained that it was a kind of display case, something like the old "china cabinet" one could find in older houses, to keep and display porcelain. "It used to be fashionable – I also liked porcelain – now things have become simpler. Then there was the *Akron Ilion Crystal* shop on Tsimiski street and further on there was *Zoura* shop, where I worked; this used to sell crystal items; it was a seven-floor shop. These shops opened after 1967 and were very fashionable; Bohemia crystals, these rows you see there, silver-plated, silver items, all of these were very fashionable! Chinese embroidery... People started progressing, they started organizing dinners and wished to show their *noikokyrosyni* with crystal glasses. I had to have crystal glasses and the Chinese piece of embroidery that I am now keeping in the drawers, which have now become antiques (laughs) and are no longer used. This is German dinnerware, *Rosenthal* porcelain, my dear, very expensive, I bought it from *Akron Ilion Krystal* shop, it cost me one month's salary."

---

59   Vasiliki's three-floor apartment building is a common example of construction in Toumba and a common example of exclusively family settlement. The informants describe this way of dwelling as "upstairs-downstairs", describing thus the dwelling of the core family members of middle-class strata by floor.

Vasiliki takes me to the "display cabinet"[60] and shows me the whole collection, which she bought little by little, to fill the huge display cabinet in the living room, of which she is proud, even though she does not use most of these objects.

Figure 8: Vasiliki's China Cabinet.

Source: Photo by Miltiadis Zermpoulis.

In the evenings she switches on the internal lights, and they shine and beautify her living room, giving it a "noble and aristocratic elegance", as she says. Vasiliki explains that, as she travelled a lot with her husband, she liked to buy beautiful things, which would make the difference in the neighborhood. Quite often she admired the homes of the wives of businessmen, on whose ships her husband worked.

---

60   The term "(mixed) display cabinet" is obviously related to the logic of this piece of furniture, which is assembled to combine different possibilities and uses. Usually this type of furniture had a little cocktail cabinet covered with a mirror, shelves where the Encyclopedia or other similar sets of books, such as cookbooks, were placed. The display cabinet also had a part for placing dinnerware, which was protected with glass doors and had hidden lighting.

Figure 9: Vasiliki's Chandelier.

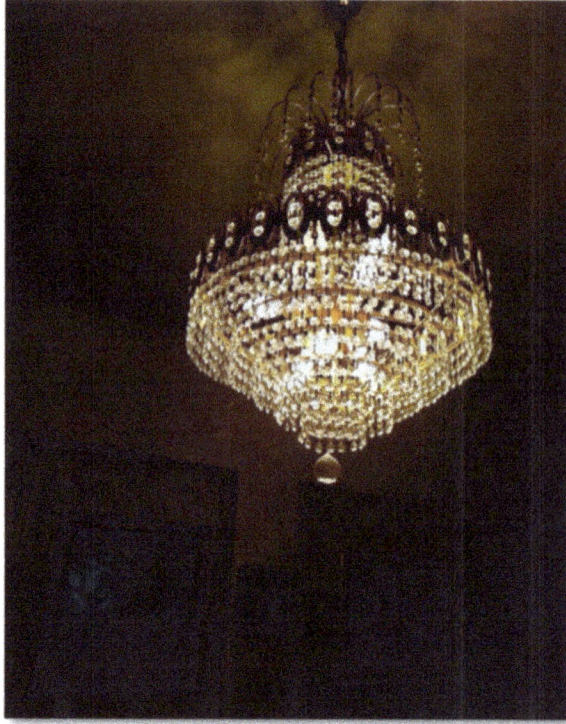

Source: Photo by Miltiadis Zermpoulis.

"Look, I worked for this stuff; I paid one month's salary for the crystals and one month's salary for the tablecloths and embroidery; I worked one month for these lights; this is *Bohemia* stuff, for these lamps, one more month for these curtains, namely in total I worked for three years for this stuff. [...] These lights are *Bohemia* little crystals; the curtains are French, imported; this is *Solingen* cutlery. Cutlery in a case, crystal, porcelain, this was all basic stuff. But I enjoyed them, I organized lots of dinners. I had to wash them by hand, I didn't have a dishwasher yet, I stayed up until three o'clock in the morning to dry them without leaving any fingerprints. We saw these things at one another's place. I saw them at a friend's place who lived in Chicago, in America, and she saw them at the place of an American friend of hers who was an aristocrat. [...] Of course, I speak about families that were tidy and could afford it [...]. He worked to earn our living and I worked to have what I wished, the luxury stuff.[61] When I managed to do what I wished I stopped working. The truth is that these things require a lot of work, I need an entire day to clean these two lamps, I need two hours and a half for each one of them, because I clean by hand all the little crystals one by one. But they are so beautiful, when the sun shines on them and I can see this red, green, yellow color of the rainbow, I like it so much.[62] Look at this crystal ball, from wherever you look at it you will see reflections. All this was done with painful and hard work."

In this specific ethnographic example, the establishment of the gender-based identity of the informant as a *noikokyra* and her social class status[63] is directly associated with the everyday practices she performs in relation to the material things that decorate her place. Vasiliki works and consumes European luxurious objects to upgrade and transform her everyday life at home and give it the style of urban luxury. It's not only about some objects she chose to have at her place. Through the possession, use and careful handling of these objects, she perceives her gender-based role as a woman with European taste, who sought to create a beautiful environment for her family and friends. She dedicates a lot of man-hours to the maintenance of these objects, to preserve them also for the next generations.[64] This hardwork justifies and is a synonym of her staying at home (Skouteri-Didaskalou, 1984, pp. 77–110). On the contrary, her daughter has chosen a different, simpler decoration style, and therefore she can work outside home, and "she doesn't need this stuff", "she doesn't even want it".[65] Taking care of this place and the correct use of objects, when the need arises, is under her full responsibility. Quite often she refers to the weekly visits of her friends, who, as she says, know the necessity of possessing these objects and can

---

61   In a complementary way, through this type of consumption, and because she is well aware of the subject-matter because she works in a relevant shop, Vasiliki undertakes to shape the social image of her household. By the phrase "I worked for the luxury stuff" she meant that she was working in parallel with her husband, serving their common goal of upward social mobility within the context of post-war change prevailing in Toumba.

62   Here we can see the dimension of activity of the objects mentioned by Gell (1998) in his study about the objects. The deflection of light through the little crystals of the chandelier fills my informant with joy.

63   The upper social class status lies with the fact that she has the possibility to not work and can, contrary to other women, take care of her home and raise her children. This type of establishment of a gender-based identity can be understood within the context of discipline of the female body, the woman's restriction at home, aiming at the silenced domestic work and basic contribution to social reproduction (see Federici, 2011, & Skouteri-Didaskalou, 1984, pp. 77–110).

64   Characteristic feature of urban ethics aiming at the intergenerational multiplication of capital.

65   Vasiliki is very concerned about her daughter. According to Vasiliki, her inability to keep her marriage is linked to the modern lifestyle of total individualization of the way of living in big cities. "My daughter lives only for herself."

appreciate her efforts. These objects remind her of the past and her successful strategy to change and improve her lifestyle in Kato Toumba.

4.1.3   Homes of "*prokopi*" and "dignity". Social relations intermediated by material things

Going back to the ethnographic example of Maria, we attempt to showcase how the efforts in the informants' narrations are not always associated with paid work and goods resulting from it. Material things can result also from a complex network of social and family relationships and its successful management. Social relations allow or quite often create the context within which the informants prepare the setting of a *noikokyremenos* lifestyle in Toumba. Maria shows me the solid railing of her house and explains that her father did all this, in return for the excellent relationships they had developed, as thanks to her intermediation he managed to get a stable job. Maria, therefore, contributes to the improvement of her father's life and in return for this she gets the impressive fence of solid rails for her house in Toumba. Her father translates this exchange into a wedding gift and Maria perceives it as a sign of recognition and reconciliation with her father.

In the competitive context of *antiparochi*, which upgrades the paternal inheritance, as it replaces an old refugee house with a modern apartment building, these objects get a new meaning. The railing was mentioned also in the testament of Maria's father, argument used by her siblings to prove that Maria was not entitled to the legal share of her paternal house in "NT", which, as we saw in the third chapter, in 2000 would become an apartment building through the practice of *antiparochi*.

> "For my siblings I was the rich one, I was the intelligent one, the one who had a good marriage, even though things were not as they thought. Well, my father did all these things and then my sister-in-law was feeling guilty for kicking me out. She came with me afterwards, when I went into labor she came with me to the clinic, to the asylum where I gave birth. She was the first one to see my son, and she told me she wanted to be his godmother, to make amends for what she had done. Meanwhile, she was backbiting about my mother. Well, daughter-in-law and mother-in-law did not get along well, and I swear to you I was telling my mother: 'mommy, don't mind, she is a young girl with three children'. My mother had an issue, she used to do housework and leave everything upside down. I used to tidy up and I kept advising her and she thought I was backbiting [...]. Because my mother chose me, my son, because I did housework as I should, cleaning under the beds and everything. Because they had a preference for me and my mother-in-law was praising me, 'Maria sews clothes for herself, she takes care of her hairstyle by herself, she saves money, she did this, she did that', she kicked me out. I used to pick up

my mother and my mother-in-law and take them to Agia Triada and Perea,[66] with my husband. We offered lunch to both; we went for a swim and came back. Nobody did this. We used to take both to the beach, to make them feel happy. And my mother-in-law used to say: 'I didn't know anything about Charilaou[67], Maria showed me and then I learnt how to go there by myself'. And when you are praised, other people hate you, they start competing with you [...]."

Maria and several other informants have the feeling that *noikokyrosyni* and thoroughly taking care of their home and family contributed to their social and financial progress, but at the same time caused competition and isolation,[68] both within their close family environment and in the broader neighborhood environment. Maria's "active femininity" and successful integration into the post-war imperative for modernization and urbanization was an obstacle to her relationships with other family members. Maria believes that the neighborhood and her relatives envied her and up to this day they don't pay a visit to her, because she was the first one to do certain things and she was a pioneer for her era.

"We were the first ones to get a TV, a telephone, water. We bought the TV in Pylaia, it was a black-and-white TV, nobody had a TV here yet. I was the only one to have a TV – and a telephone – and they were making fun of me. You see? We also brought water here. Stavros used to carry water – because I was pregnant – from Koula, the fountain was there, and used to carry it upstairs taking the stairs that my father had made and put it into the water tank. They used to say about the telephone that it was luxury. Can you imagine? This neighbor next to me! And then when the time came, he asked for favors, and also Toula came from across the street, because she had a boyfriend and talked with him on the phone for hours, while Stavros needed the telephone to get updates on his son, if he was sick. He was at work and wanted to know how he was, meaning we got a telephone mainly for our children. When they came to see my home, how I did it, especially after I finished my living room, they were astonished! The whole neighborhood was talking about it, especially Giorgaki's mother, the newsagent, everyone, my son, honestly! When I came here, there was only Kostas next to me, the son of Ms Aliki; they were the only people I knew, because on Papafi street, where I had bought the house back then, people were very sad [...]. Stavros had made a fridge for me, an ice bucket. I

---

66   Seaside towns near Thessaloniki with many holiday homes that, especially in the 1960s, gathered many people from Thessaloniki who used to spend their summer holidays there.

67   According to the testimonies of many informants, there were several leisure centers on Charilaou which attracted many young refugees, especially during the weekend.

68   See Veikou (1998, cited in Bakalaki, 2003, p. 216), on the feelings of hostility that success may cause, but also on the concept of "evil eye", which can have a negative impact on the evolution of a situation.

was the first one to get an ice bucket. Stavros did it, on his own, and I had ice. They were all... One of them was divorced and had her new boyfriend at home. Misery... I used to tell Stavros, poor girl, pay the electricity bill for her and she was courting Stavros. My husband told me that as soon as I left, she opened her shirt to show her breasts. People were not nice there, and I was afraid of going outside. Every time I went out something happened to me. I used to go out in Toumba; instead of going to the city center, silly us; we used to come here, we were attracted by this place, because we were raised here, that's why we bought a plot here [...]. No house had been built here back then, only Ms Aliki's. Of course, across there was the house of Amalia, the house of Ms Ekavi, the coffee shop. Opposite us, there was a marble shop. This was a sandlot here; when the earthquake occurred, we set up the tents outside. All these houses across the street on this side were of Giorgos's mother. Her brother Manos gave them to her, and all these houses were built after ours, all of them through the practice of *antiparochi*!!! When I built my house, there was no *antiparochi* yet. Had we known, we would have bought many more building plots."

Through these objects and through the lifestyle she managed quite early to have in Toumba, Maria materializes the cultural identity of a modern and sparing woman. However, the consciousness of this difference compared to others and the fear of going back to experiences of poverty like the ones she had when she lived at her father's place in "NT" creates a paradoxical behavior. Maria constantly stresses that she has always been and still is a "secret" person, meaning that she never reveals her plans before they are fulfilled, because she is afraid of the negative energy of others, which can, in her opinion, have a negative impact on the outcome of her endeavors. At the same time, she is eventually concerned and worried by her social isolation, which is caused, in her opinion, by her success. According to several informants, a *noikokyraios* must not communicate problems but achievements. The negative outcome, which is a synonym of failure, is a proof of bad design and non-informed home economics, which is eventually a synonym of low social class status and inability to handle social relations with the aim of maintaining the prestige of the family. In Toumba, I was often impressed by the refusal of my informants to communicate their or their husbands' illness, while several of them avoided going out during that period, because they were afraid of the questions people would ask. Even today, Maria makes sure she goes to church on Sunday, in order not to raise doubts or comments. She never uses a cane, even if she must stop halfway on her way back home because she can no longer breathe, calling a taxi to take her home.

One day I paid Ms Ekavi a visit. As other informants in the neighborhood explained, she originated from a "good"[69] family, mainly thanks to the coffee shop

---

69   By the term "good" the informants from Thessaloniki mean good financial standing but also correct household management, according to the social and value norms of the *noikokyraioi*.

that her father had in Toumba and the successful laundry business her husband ran subsequently. Ekavi got married in 1953 and in the following year they built, together with her husband, one more house on the back side of the refugee house of her mother-in-law, precisely opposite Maria's house.[70] During the fieldwork, Ekavi lived in a small apartment in the apartment building that was built in 1980s with *antiparochi* where the old house initially was. When Ekavi hears the word "old", she laughs and explains that it was not old at all, it was simply too cold and costly because it was on the back side and the sun could never reach it.

> "Look, our house was rather good; it was very nice; we also had a pine forest; on the front side there was a little living room with a little table, little curtains for protection from the sun. It was a noble house! It was built in 1954, so it was not really an old one, but Violeta next to us wanted to move on, Giorgos as well, and we were in the middle, so we decided to give it together with Giorgos who was next to us."

As other informants mentioned in the third chapter, *antiparochi* was not always the solution that would give them something better or more "modern" than what they already had, but there were also social reasons and pressure from the neighborhood that led people to take the decision to demolish a house they had built or renovated investing money a few years ago.

In the case of Ekavi, the house was only twenty years old when the family decided to demolish it within the context of *antiparochi*, together with the refugee house of her mother-in-law and the neighbor's house next to them.

> "I was forced to do so, my boy; they kept building apartment buildings; and then, the house was really cold, I had three heaters and still it was not warm; it was on the back side and the sun did not reach it; this humidity was harming us; there was a heater in the living room, another one in the kitchen and a third one for the children, I used to consume a lot of heating oil and still it was cold; so I decided to give it away and I warmed my bones, so to say!"

Initially Ekavi lived on the second floor, in a bigger apartment, but she gave it to her son and she – being a widow – moved to the apartment of the third floor. Throughout the interview Ekavi was overwhelmed with stress, as she was concerned by the recording because she didn't wish the neighborhood to know anything. At the beginning I could not understand what exactly it was that scared her most, as usually all other informants never objected to the recording of our conversation. Soon her

---

70   As we also know from Hirschon's ethnography (2006), such practices of settling in refugee houses with the aim of social and economic integration of the newlyweds were also common in Kokkinia.

grandson came in and stayed with us for the rest of the interview of that first meeting. Her grandson has been a drug addict and the whole family has been fighting, as Ekavi says, for many years, to help him recover. She even had to sell a whole apartment once, so that he could be admitted in a special rehabilitation clinic.[71] Ekavi is constantly embarrassed and stresses that she has never had difficulties in her life. She belonged to one of the best families in Toumba and this fact now makes her feel ashamed. Being conscious of her social status and the cultural classifications that delimit the *noikokyrio* model in Toumba, she feels uncomfortable with the presence of her grandson, who, because of his flaw, puts at risk her efforts to build, as she says, this reputation in the neighborhood. This situation threatens to destroy her *noikokyrio* as well as her gender-based identity of *noikokyra*-mother-widow-grand-mother.

> "It is painful", she says. "I don't want him to come here, I don't want the neighborhood to see him. His parents would wish he died,[72] they don't know how to handle this issue, they don't know what to say. They have lost a lot of money."

Ekavi is afraid that her grandson's issue may threaten the family's good reputation in the neighborhood. Contrary to all other refugees, her own family never faced difficulties. As it can be seen also in the Social Welfare folders for her family, Ekavi's family possessed already immovable and movable property when they became refugees in Greece, while they paid off the amount required by the state already before the end of the 1940s, which reinforced the prestige of this specific family.[73] This was in full contrast with all other informants from Toumba, who managed to receive the coveted concession after the war, towards the end of the 1950s.

> "For us things were fine, we were the first ones in Toumba, we didn't face any difficulties, we were already noikokyraioi. We were the best ones in Toumba and whoever you ask, even today, if you say the name of E. they will say 'they were the best!'"

This fact embarrasses her during our meeting, especially when her grandson is present. As she mentioned, her son left the neighborhood and now lives in another area, as he could not withstand other people's comments.

---

71   The symbolism of capitalization of the apartment of *antiparochi*, so that the family can achieve the restoration of social prestige through the funding of the grandson's drug treatment and return to normality, is important.

72   At this point we see once again the consequences of the physical discipline technologies (Foucault, 1991). In this case, only death can bring this family back to a "tidy" normal status.

73   This detail associates again the "tidy way" with the correct money management and the category of "making" as this is described in several ethnographies of the Greek territory (Papataxiarchis, 2006a; Vlachoutsikou, 1991; Salamone & Stanton, 2019).

Ekavi remembers the first years, when she had to live with her mother-in-law, while her husband would be doing his military service, in an effort, as we said, to save as much money as possible, and aiming at successfully establishing an independent *noikokyrio* (Papataxiarchis, 2006a). The first thing she bought was furniture for her bedroom. As Sophie Chevalier (1999, pp. 83–94) observes in her very insightful paper on giving meaning to home in post-war France, furniture embodies family life and home. According to Putnam (1999), the experience of dwelling is at the center of the world where people place themselves. Through the physical experience of dwelling and personal evolution stages, one can perceive the different stages of evolution of the individual who lives in it in relation to himself/herself and others. The materiality of the bedroom is associated by several fieldwork informants with the establishment of an independent *noikokyrio* and the beginning of the effort for a better life. Their bedroom is the first stone for establishing their *noikokyrio*, as they have dreamt of it. I was impressed by the fact that the informants very rarely change this first furniture. The bedroom furniture had not been replaced in almost any of the houses I visited. Even though Ekavi has been a widow for many years, she still uses her bridal bed, above which she has placed her wedding crowns.

During our meetings, Ekavi always came back to her relationship with her home paintings and the big display cabinet she acquired subsequently, to place there all her precious silverware and crystals. The paintings were essentially embroidery items she had prepared herself and then framed them, to be able to see and enjoy them. She told me that these embroidery items and the lamp next to the armchair where she sat were the most important things in her home. Their materiality was associated with a difficult moment for Ekavi: the loss of her husband.[74] Hanging on the wall, they seemed like degrees confirming the efforts to maintain her family's good reputation in the neighborhood.

"I went blind embroidering under this lamp.[75] I can no longer move my hands; I was even operated. This embroidery hobby was intensified after my husband's death at a relatively young age, fifty-four years old. I used to embroider the whole day until late at night, and this took the form of professional occupation. I took advantage of the fact that some friends felt sorry for me because I became a widow at such a young age, and they did not have the heart not to buy [...]."

---

74   The household model based on the two spouses' complementarity is threatened when one of the two passes aways (see Papataxiarchis, 2006a).

75   It is worth noting the references to the consequences of work and in general the strategies adopted by the informants in order to achieve their goals in the post-war context of expanded middle-strata society. These consequences mainly concern the body and are negative. If we think in Foucault's (1991) terms, within the context of power relationships, to survive, integrate and fulfill the imperatives of the new era, the subjects experience figuratively the consequences of bio-power exercised on them.

The new reality gives a new meaning and redetermines, as we saw also in the other ethnographic examples, the delimitations in relation to the use of objects within the context of social relations and the gender-based identity of *noikokyra* and widow. To maintain her social status and the *noikokyrio* she created with her husband, she uses an occupation, which until that moment was related to her gender-based identity of *noikokyra* – good and sparing wife and mother who does not work and can take care of the *noikokyrio*. What was a domestic occupation until then – embroidery – was transformed into paid employment outside home. According to Bakalaki (2008), in the 19th century, embroidery and in general production of needlework was part of the education programs for women in Greece. Needlework is not a native occupation; it can be found already in the 16th century in Europe as an occupation of merchants' wives. According to Bakalaki, female education in the 19th century concerned mainly the native elite, who tried to align it with the imperatives of their "civilizing" and europeanizing work. Therefore, embroidery was associated with a European way of living of upper-class women who do not work and within the context of domesticity they make good use of their everyday time productively. Bakalaki referred also to teaching embroidery to lower class women, since it was a profitable occupation, especially within the context of dowry (Bakalaki, 2008, pp. 538–546).

Thus, Ekavi uses widowhood to maximize the probabilities of work success, taking advantage of the social relations she had as a married woman. Her acquaintances and potential clients know about her *noikokyrosyni* but also Ekavi's need within the new context of widowhood, qualities that Ekavi tries to capitalize through this choice of hers. As she explained, her new employment kept her alive, as she woke up very early in the morning to buy pieces of embroidery and then go to various areas where she had acquaintances to sell them. This is how she managed to save some money, which she needed within the context of a correct and productive management of her *noikokyrio* and the performance of her gender-based identity of a mother and *noikokyra*.

4.1.4 The concept of "noble" and "aristocratic" as a normative decoration standard in the homes of *noikokyraioi*

Going back to Maria's narration, I will focus – based on this specific ethnographic example – on the meaning assigned by the informants to the words "noble" or "aristocratic", mainly when they wish to describe the decoration choices for the *saloni* (main living room) of the apartment, which is also the place where most of them receive me.

In Maria's imposing *saloni*, all furniture is handmade by her husband. The dining table for six follows the post-war modern design of furniture, combining plain geometrical lines with few classical elements. The dining table is at the center of the big living room, which is divided in two by a big arch in plaster coating, which points to neoclassical architecture. It is a high ceiling house with a quite imposing living room with a lot of lamps, with wall light fixtures above the sideboard and the small chest of drawers, where various crystal glasses, silverware and porcelain dinnerware are placed. In the living room, all paintings were made on demand by painters of Thessaloniki and usually represent dark natural landscapes. The big Persian carpets on the floor are so thick that one sinks while walking on them. According to Maria, her living room is a "noble" one.

Figure 10: Maria's noble saloni; Figure 11 Maria's China Cabinet

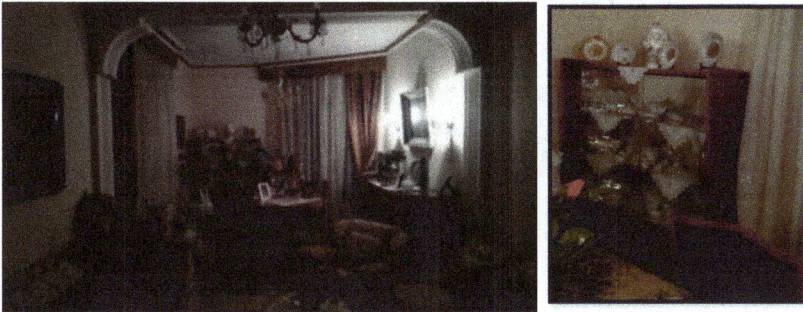

Source: Photo by Miltiadis Zermpoulis; Source: Photo by Miltiadis Zermpoulis.

As we saw also in the case of Vasiliki, most informants use the adjective "noble" or "aristocratic" to describe their homes and especially their living rooms. Several anthropologists, who studied the respective interior decoration practices in houses of Northern and Western Europe and North America, stress the importance of a "warm" place, translating the English term "homey" and the German term "gemütlich", which describes the interior and especially the living room of middle-class homes (Tebbe, 2008, pp. 195–215; McCracken, 1989). This term is conceptually in full contrast with the goal setting and the feeling my informants have about their homes and especially the living room, as it results from the above examples.

My informants usually receive me in their living room by switching on their six-light chandeliers, even in daylight, always stressing their intention as they wish their home to emit "nobility" and "aristocratic" elegance. It is a place that is not used daily, but mainly on important occasions, when they receive guests at home.

Figure 12: China Cabinet of an Informant in Toumba.

Source: Photo by Miltiadis Zermpoulis.

This feeling of an intensely lighted place is clearly associated with the formality of the occasion but also with the need to shed as much light as possible to the material world that the subject managed to collect. Living rooms are always on the front side towards the street, and what occurs in them gets special visibility when they are used.[76] The lamps, wall fixtures, lights, well-polished silverware, and colorful crystals make visible the *prokopi* of their owners within the context of *noikokyrio* as a financial business with the ultimate goal of profit (Papataxiarchis, 2006a; Salamone & Stanton, 2019). Moreover, as far as the woman is concerned, they provide clear evidence of the correct performance of her role as a *noikokyra* and hostess. Very often the homes remind of the interior of Greek orthodox churches and refer to the byzantine tradition, as they have features that can be found also in mansions of Macedonia.

As described above, the aim of the *saloni* is not to serve people in their everyday life; it mainly seeks to impress, requiring careful use and constant care from the subject for the few festive occasions. In many living rooms, I saw objects that were

---

76   In Toumba, when the living room was prepared and "opened" for friends on the name day of the owners, the exterior lighting of the front balcony where the living room was located signaled the beginning of the celebration. The light was on when everything was ready, so that the first neighbors could start visiting. Switching off the lights and closing the shutters signaled the end of the celebration and the departure of the last guest, which allowed the hosts to open the gifts.

covered and protected, like silverware covered with transparent film in Lydia's living room – as it can be seen in the below picture.

Figure 13: Lydia's silverware covered with transparent film.

Source: Photo by Miltiadis Zermpoulis.

The *saloni* and objects are not used always and by everyone. *Noikokyraioi* have the luxury to have this additional space and dedicated equipment they use only if needs arise.[77] What is particularly interesting in the case of Toumba is that many informants invested the money they earned in the context of post-war development to get this space that was eventually "useless" for their everyday life, while they did not invest money to offer their children separate bedrooms with children's furniture. My informants' children used to sleep and study on improvised pieces of furniture with multiple uses, which could be found in common spaces, deprived of the privacy that a personal space can offer. This is interesting because it is not due to limited space, but to space arrangement and family's priorities.

At this point, it is interesting to cite the following excerpt from my discussions with Katia from Toumba, in which she describes the practices of maintenance of the living room objects:

---

77   This urban practice has been clearly known since the 19th century; urban people give a different dimension to this space, wishing to differentiate themselves from the aristocrats (see Frykman & Löfgren, 1987, p. 142; Tebbe, 2008; Habermas, 1991, p. 10).

Katia: "Even for covering stuff there were specific instructions! The late Thanasis had told me: 'you will first place a soft blanket, then a nylon layer and on top you will put the cover.' And this is how I kept it. When relatives came from Athens, we ate there. When we were on our own, we ate in the kitchen.

Why weren't you entitled to eat at the dining room? Why didn't people eventually use their living room? (researcher's question).

Katia: "Look, we don't use it, because we have been working all our life and we wish to be comfortable, but we needed some space for guests. We needed some tidy space, with doilies[78] [...]. Our way of thinking was, here is the table, here is the sink, let's clean up and go to work."

What is characteristic in Katia's living room is a classic – huge for that space – dining table of dark wood, which has been placed at the center of the living room. As her husband explains, the dining table is new, and he has chosen it. Manolis doesn't like old stuff. *"[...] I wish to change. Repressed feelings!"* In 1993, Katia and her husband built this apartment building on their own, in the place of the "old house," and settled on the fourth floor. It was the first time they managed to get their own living room after so many years. A lot of the old furniture that Katia had bought in the 1960s she left initially at the place of her parents, who settled on the first floor, in order not to lose contact with the old neighborhood. The new dining table is a subject of controversy between the two spouses, as Katia does not acknowledge its quality.

Manolis: "[...]I don't know if she liked it, I said I liked it, and it was over."

Katia: "In 1960, with my first salary, I bought a display cabinet, two small tables and the dining table, which could be unfolded and become a big one, and I said: '-Manoli! Let's take it back from mom!' 'No, leave it there!' And he bought this crappy stuff! [...]We could see how formica could be cleaned so well and we didn't wonder how formica was made. We removed the good quality wooden doors and put plastic ones instead and now I think to myself: how stupid were we?"

---

78   See Bakalaki (2008, p. 557) on the European influence regarding the practices of using needlework on the popular families of Thessaloniki. According to the anthropologist, embroidery with Greek influence is associated with the practices of an intellectual urban class aiming at promoting the Greek tradition. I cite a characteristic excerpt from her testimony: *"I have vivid childhood memories of women and young girls embroidering such patterns in my neighborhood, in Thessaloniki, at the end of the 1950s and later. I remember the pride they took in showing their work, the pleasure to pronounce the foreign names of materials, techniques and patterns, the admiration when they looked at the magazine pictures with decorative handmade pieces of work that decorated the modern furniture of living rooms or the nicely prepared tables at the dining rooms. I also admired all this as a child, and the disapproval of my parents and their educated friends, who found all this of a rather "peasant taste" seemed inexplicable and most of all unfair."*

Katia believes that the first custom-made dining table she bought in 1960 was of different quality and she regrets leaving it in her deceased parents' apartment, which has been rented for some years to a family of migrants from Albania.

> "I had never lived in a house with my own living room, things changed here. I was very happy for this, everything I added, everything I touched, I used to say: how beautiful this is."[79]

For Katia, the moment of change and the best years for herself and her family are linked to the job she managed to find through an uncle of hers and the investment of her first salary in three important objects. Because of her father's exile, she could not get a certificate of social convictions from the police station of Toumba, to be able to study at the department of Archaeology, which was the dream of her life:

> "K[80] knew us, because every single week, and I wish him all the best or may God forgive him if he has passed away, he sent us a police officer and asked us to go to the police station. My mother told him: 'Mr. K. my daughter finished high school and she wishes to sit an exam to enter university, she needs a certificate of social convictions.' K: 'Don't worry, what applies to a mother does not necessarily apply to a daughter as well. You will have the certificate on time.' But the certificate never reached the department of Archaeology."

The informant, and while her father returns from exile, struggles to find a job, to help her mother who had been working all this time as a seamstress,[81] to contribute to their *noikokyrio* and support her father who was trying little by little to reintegrate into normal life:

---

79   The word "happy" relates to the fact that this living room was built in the 1990s, when the fashion of the time imposed the American single space in which kitchen and living room coexist (see Fehérváry, 2002). The other informants who still have the "noble" living rooms are not "happy" for these spaces, because they remain closed and are used selectively. When I paid a visit, they would bring a cleaning lady, they would switch on the radiators one day earlier to keep the place warm, and they would uncover the objects in that place. When I was at their place, they would naturally ask if I wished to "pass to the living room", as if this was an everyday normal thing that had nothing to do with the formality of my presence there. Of course, the term "pass" had a figurative function of a transition to a formal world, in which I had to be accompanied by the host.

80   This was a high-ranking police officer in Kato Toumba who was responsible for issuing social certificates that citizens needed to communicate with the public services. The aim was to fight the alleged communist danger.

81   Many women from Toumba worked from home during that period as seamstresses. It is worth noting that even those that did not work made sure they would apprentice to a seamstress and a sewing machine at home to meet the domestic needs. As it was mentioned also earlier, sewing, embroidery, etc. were associated with the gender-based identity of a *noikokyra*, within the context of household goal setting, meaning profit.

"[...] towards the end of 1959 I started looking for a job, since I could not study. Closed doors everywhere, just like now; an uncle of mine helped me get a job at the political office of an *ERE* parliamentarian [...]. There were no jobs! It worked like this: I know something, I'll introduce you to someone. I took an examination to enter *OTE* [82] and we went to see a very close friend – because he was a doctor in *OTE* – he loved us a lot (!) – and told her that the posts were taken, and the competition was conducted to make them permanent."

The informant precisely associates this first big change to the better in her life with a second fact, which is a characteristic element to understand how social transformation requires and presupposes a change of the framework in which the new social class subjectivity will be progressively established. With the first salary she earned as a secretary at the political office of *ERE*, Katia bought porcelain dinnerware, a classic handmade dining table and a Greek flag. These three objects are indicative of the progressive social class transformation of Katia and her progressive integration into the habits and values of the urban way of living that her new salaried employment at the office of an *ERE* politician allows her to have. The Greek flag and classic dining table with porcelain dinnerware, symbols and necessary accessories of a noble living room, and therefore Greek urban lifestyle,[83] can be understood very well within the context of the aspirations of middle class, to which Katia and her husband feel they belong:

Katia knows the context in which she must move and acts. At the office where she works, she has a first-hand experience of clientelism and its importance in the post-war society of Thessaloniki.

"Politicians have always taken care of their acquaintances, so that they could be elected again and again. I worked there for seven years, and they appreciated me! Probably my boss knew that my father had been exiled, but he never mentioned anything."

Now that Katia has moved to a small apartment, she has taken the habit of changing the arrangement of the living room furniture, so that the place looks bigger.[84] She

---

82   Hellenic Telecommunications Organisation.

83   In the 1960s, in most newly built apartments there was a special base on the balcony railing where the Greek flag could be placed. According to some informants, these were used afterwards after the end of the dictatorship, when the flag with a flagpole with a cross was obligatory only on national celebrations. The years of the economic crisis and the rise of far-right forces in Greece saw a massive re-use of these bases. The flags slept on every balcony for the whole year.

84   Similar practices have been described also in other ethnographies focusing on the interaction of subjects and objects and the impact of objects on the emotional world of subjects. More specifically, in the ethnography by Pauline Garvey (2001, pp. 47–69) on the material

was forced to move here a few years ago, as she gave the big apartment to her son who has become a doctor and "needed something better".[85]

Figure 14: Katia's Favorite armchair, placed next to her bed.

Source: Photo by Miltiadis Zermpoulis.

The furniture that had been bought for that apartment takes a lot of space and does not really fit in the smaller new apartment. However, her most treasured objects continue to be some pieces of furniture from the old house that Katia now reassesses in the new context, in which "old", "tradition" and "refugee" life have acquired a positive connotation. These include an armchair and an old sideboard that their parents acquired at the beginning of their marriage. This armchair is the only

dimension of apartments in Norway, it was pointed out that moving furniture to rearrange a space creates feelings of joy and satisfaction in the subject.

85   The classic model of caring for children by ensuring a home for them is reproduced here. In this case, Katia goes out of the new apartment she struggled to make, in which she eventually stayed for a very short period because she passed it on to her son. Katia and Manolis ensure and support further upward social mobility at intergenerational level by granting to the Doctor the biggest apartment of the apartment building they built.

one she uses to rest, as it has a beneficial impact on Katia's back problem: because of its shape, it embraces her whole body.[86]

The old sideboard is in a small room, which she calls *procheiro* (casual room), but I had the feeling that this room was the only place of the house that represents the continuation of the family tradition from Smyrna, providing a connection with the family's life and difficulties in the refugee house in "NT", in replacement of which the modern apartment building was built.[87] Objects with special symbolism have been placed on the sideboard. More specifically, Katia has placed pictures of her parents precisely in the center of the sideboard and behind them a big picture from Asia Minor depicting her grandfather with the characteristic fez, little old cups, a censer, and a small icon of the Virgin with a red little light that shines at night and keeps inextinguishable the memory of the past. As Katia told me, she substantially saved this sideboard and armchair from oblivion and destruction, when these pieces of furniture lost both their economic and emotional value in Thompson's (1979) terms, and were placed outside in the courtyard, where her father placed them on two bricks and started using them as a toolbox. Old furniture was then replaced, within the context of modernization, with new curved solid "noble" furniture and the old refugee furniture was thrown away or was used for other purposes. In the new apartment, Katia saved the old sideboard, despite the disagreement of her husband, who wished to equip the modern apartment with modern and new stuff, by placing it in this little room, just behind the main living room.

In Katia's apartment, the living room forms a single room with the kitchen, while there is no corridor to separate this part of the house from the entrance door; as a result, as you enter the apartment you face the big dining table. This is the case for most of the informants who live in quite new apartments, while those who moved earlier, during the 1960s and 1970s made sure to keep the logic of the closed living room. Several informants tried in various ways to use some objects of this kind to create separate spaces, by cutting the single space imposed by the new design of apartments.

Contrary to that of Katia, Maria's living room is usually closed with closed shutters; it is a space often used also as a storage room of the rest of the house. At a certain point approximately 20 years ago, when all her friends moved to the apartments they acquired through *antiparochi*, she decided to remove the two "glass doors" that separated the big living room from the small entrance corridor, while she considered demolishing the wall that separated the living room from the casual room. However, due to the oldness of the building and the additions that followed and to accommodate also her two children, she eventually decided to avoid any change in

---

86   See Gell (1998) on the impact of objects on subjects' emotional world.

87   On the intergenerational integration of the refugees into the Greek state, see Kyriakidou-Nestoros (1993b, p. 233).

the wall structure of the house: *"They all had single spaces, so I took them to the basement[88] where they wear out, my sweetheart."* In recent years, the informant placed an air conditioner, and it was easier to keep the place warm, as in the past the heaters that looked like small fireplaces required wood fuel, which Maria had to carry from the laundry room, which was located at the backyard of the house. According to Maria, there was no reason to keep this place warm, since she had a smaller living room, which she calls *procheiro* [casual room], and in which she spends, as we have already mentioned, more than half of her day, since there is also a big television there and furniture – the "Danish" furniture, as she calls it – is more comfortable, protected with top covers that created a warmer and friendlier atmosphere, on the opposite side of the "aristocratic/noble" *saloni* [main living room].

Five years ago, she proceeded to the installation of natural gas radiators, which allowed Maria to make more use of the "intact" *saloni* [main living room]. Of course, the recent crisis had led her once again to choices she had made in the past, closing the living room doors again, using the kitchen door mainly as entrance door.

Maria is particularly careful with the furniture and much of it is covered, as, according to her, it is her husband's artefact. Even crystal chandeliers had been made by her father, in a period that mass production of such objects had not started yet. Despite her 83 years of age, Maria takes care of all these spaces on her own and knows the objects one by one. With almost religious devotion, she cleans the crystals of the chandelier once a week. She explains that once, in a reception she arranged for the forty years of marriage with her husband, a cousin of hers accidentally poured some ouzo on the dining table and ruined the polish. *"This furniture is too heavy to move. Stavros brought it home. Even when we had to paint the walls of the living room, it was very difficult to move it inside the house."* She is concerned about their future when she dies.

Eventually, home looks like a theatre stage and all things have their own role in subjects' everyday life. Their stories are parallel to the ones of the subjects, while they are never static and cannot be explained in semiotics or symbolism terms. We see how the various practices and choices of my informants in the field regarding the material world that surrounds them were altogether shaped as a result of their needs and the social relationships within which objects and subjects are in constant interdependence. The daily use of objects but also the changes in their use over the course of time are revealing as to their importance in shaping the various subjectivities, depending always on the cultural and social frame of reference in which they participate.

---

88   The living room doors.

4.2 The counterexample: "peasants" and "migrants from Germany" in Toumba of "eastern suburbs"[89]

At the beginning of the 1960s, the mass immigration of the Greeks to Northern Europe countries (Germany, Belgium, etc.) started after the signature of bilateral agreements. During this same period, several Greeks abandoned the Greek province to massively settle in the urban centers of Greece, which promised the possibility of consumption of modern lifestyles.[90]

Regarding the immigration to Germany[91], it officially started on 30 March 1960 after the signature of a bilateral agreement between the two countries, aiming at the recruitment of unspecialized workers, who would be employed for a certain period in the industry of Western Germany and then would return to their country (Voukelatos, 2003; Nikolaidis, 2008).

In the case of Kato Toumba, the immigration to Germany has a different dynamic but also a special symbolism, which was clearly expressed, both by those who moved to Germany to work and those who observed the phenomenon. At the beginning, some of the informants had a negative attitude towards introducing to me an informant who had immigrated to Germany. They considered that the story he/she would have to tell was not necessarily linked to the history of their area.[92] When Maria presented me to a friend of hers who had been living in Toumba for the last 40 years and we went to her place together, so that I could meet her in person and do a first interview, she asked her if she should present me also to another common friend of theirs, so that I can do an interview also with her; then she reacted, and this was the interesting dialogue that followed:

> *Maria: "Anyway, she is not the right person to involve in anything?!"*
>
> *Georgia: "No, she reads a lot, but she hasn't even completed primary education, she is not*

---

89 The expression "eastern suburbs" is placed in quotation marks because this chapter deals with its problematization, particularly in relation to the reproduction of contemptuous discourses developed by some informants about the most recent inhabitants of Toumba within the context of its post-war quality upgrade. In the context of Thessaloniki, "eastern suburbs" are on the opposite side of the "western suburbs", which are regarded as "degraded" because they are close to the industrial area of the city and are inhabited by repatriated immigrants and citizens with a migratory background, on this see Angelopoulos (2003, pp. 35–43).

90 On the policies of mass urbanization and the policy promoting immigration to countries of Central and Northern Europe, see Chapter Two "'Transformation' and 'Petty bourgeoisism'. The Greek class distinctiveness and the theories of 'underdevelopment'".

91 I refer specifically to Germany, since all informants that had a similar story to tell had immigrated to this country.

92 As we saw also earlier, several informants associated Toumba only with its refugee history. The subsequent evolution of Toumba, which is largely associated also with the immigration of lots of inhabitants to Germany, is not mentioned.

the right person for this! You see? She was younger."
Maria: *"But alright, she will speak about her life!"*
Georgia: *"That she left for Germany?!"*
Maria: *"Did she go to Germany?!"*
Georgia: *"Is this what she wants to talk about?!"*
Maria: *"Ah, did she go to Germany as well?"*

Cultural representations for Toumba follow a linear evolution. Stigmatized refugees who experienced eradication and social contempt in the new country find little by little their pace in the big city and become an integral part of its history, especially towards the end of the 1960s.[93] This period is presented by the informants, who are the second generation of Asia Minor refugees, as we saw earlier in this chapter, as a period of "progress" and "change" that has an impact also on their everyday life, through which "modern" subjectivities are established. These subjectivities result from tangible and objectified, according to Miller (2005), identifications with the hegemonic imperative of modernization, successful integration into the cultural values of the Greek middle-class society. However, as we will see in this subchapter, some subjectifications follow alternative pathways of participation in "modernity".

As we saw earlier, the old refugee houses in Toumba are renovated little by little or even demolished to build something more "modern" in their place. The informants seek and consume a lot of "soft furnishings"[94] of which they imagine they form an integral part of a modern life. The materiality of the new houses and interaction with modern mass consumption objects are, as we have already mentioned, particularly formative, shaping subjects of the "modern" *noikokyremeno* lifestyle (Miller, 1987, 2005; Gialouri, 2012). According to Bourdieu (2006), the structuring structures of the new condition of a new or modernized apartment or even the improved public space as spatiality are normatively imposed and shape the social subject of *noikokyraios* in post-war Thessaloniki.

The inhabitants of Toumba seem to progressively internalize and successfully reproduce the hegemonic standards of the "good homes" and thus remove through these "identifying" performances the marginal character of Toumba.[95] The "soft fur-

---

93 This linear evolution that I encounter in most biographies led me also to the structure of the chapters of the thesis. The chapters of the thesis follow this historical succession of facts in Toumba, but also its transformation phases as a spatial reality. Besides, what is interesting about this thesis, as it is highlighted also in the introductory chapters, is the showcase of concepts and meanings that this historical change establishes and produces around material, space and human-being.

94 According to the informants in Thessaloniki, there were shops that used this term, as there were shops selling "European" or colonial items.

95 On the importance of the margins and the cultural identities produced in such contexts, see Ioannidou (2004, unpublished thesis).

nishings", modern objects with which they equip their homes in a neighborhood that used to consist entirely of refugees in the past, and the housing structures work as carriers of the cultural and social expectations of the social group in which my informants are raised. The fact that the country was soon governed by a non-democratic regime is sometimes reluctantly described as the reason for this improved everyday life. The infrastructure works that the informants remember taking place in the public space of the neighborhood during this period provide tangible evidence of the progressive integration of their area into the city map. The city was "smartened up", as they characteristically mention, and the "conservatism" of post-war regimes is justified based on this condition. The city and life in it *noikokyreuetai*, just like the lives of the inhabitants of Toumba. From being a refugee neighborhood, Toumba is progressively transformed, as we have mentioned earlied, into one of the most sought-after middle-class suburbs in the eastern part of the city.[96]

According to Kokot (1994, pp. 30–31), the change in Toumba took place between the 1960s and 1970s. The anthropologist associates the return of some immigrants from Germany, and the mass migration of the surrounding province to Thessaloniki, with the change that took place in the area. According to the same author, 30% to 40% of the old houses in Toumba are no longer inhabited by refugee families.

The purchase of the old houses but also of the first newly built apartments by the new residents of the area creates new dynamics and reshapes the until then negative conceptualization of this settlement as a bastion of communism. According to the anthropologist (1994), in 1983, during her field research only on small and secondary streets there were "old houses", while on the important streets, multi-story and modern apartment buildings had already been built (Kokot, 1994, p. 30).

The population of Toumba progressively increases to reach 150 000 inhabitants, and according to Kokot, only one third of these inhabitants originate from families of the first refugees of the area. This specific area, stigmatized for many years as the "red Toumba" or "little Stalingrad", because of the ideological convictions of its inhabitants during the Nazi occupation and civil war, will be excluded, according to the German anthropologist (1994, p. 30), for many years from the policies of development and improvement of the infrastructure and public space already taking place in the rest of the city since the previous decade.

Kokot highlights also the conflicts taking place between the old and the new inhabitants of Toumba, those who return from Germany and those who settle in the area abandoning the province.

Immigration demonstrates for some of my informants, as we saw earlier in the dialogue between Maria and her friend, the inability of some people to keep

---

96   On the importance and social dimension of space as built environment but also its impact on subjectification see Low and Lawrence-Zúñiga (2007) and Giannakopoulos and Giannitsiotis (2010).

pace with what the others experienced as change and development in relation to the fights and experiences of refugeeism, Nazi occupation and civil war. Native people, either as immigrants in Germany or internal migrants, cannot share with the refugees' children the experiences of spatiality and materiality that changes, is transformed, and finally shapes through repeated practices the specific subjectivities of Toumba (Low & Lawrence- Zúñiga, 2007; Miller, 2005).

Moreover, immigration to Germany was largely associated with the image of a farmer abandoning his/her village. The informants who were children of refugees were all born in Thessaloniki, and their parents originated from urban areas of the Ottoman empire,[97] therefore the immigration being connected with the Greek province and stereotyped image of the "native peasant" (Salamone & Stanton, 2019, p. 151) created unwanted associations within the context of 'urbanization' and 'westernization'. Even for the native populations, immigration becomes an indicator of social failure and non-integration into the context of post-war development of the country.

When my informants referred to immigration and those people, they used degrading expressions aiming at presenting this phenomenon as extraneous to the history of the inhabitants of Toumba. Several informants from the field referred scornfully to the inhabitants of Toumba who immigrated to Germany as *Lazogermanoi*[98]. In the album that the Municipality of Thessaloniki published in cooperation with the Thessaloniki History Centre (2002) on Kato Toumba, its history is reconstructed only through the narrations of the refugees' descendants, supressing the presence of other groups that played an equally important part in the evolution of this suburb.

Toumba was associated with specific "self-awareness" instances,[99] such as civil war, fights between rebels and *tagmatasfalites* (Security Battalions) on its "red" territory, refugeeism, poverty, marginalization, but not with immigration abroad,

---

97   On the urban origin and western influence of people from Asia Minor see Bakalaki (2008, p. 551), Hirschon (2006, pp. 59–91) and Salamone and Stanton (2019, p. 151).

98   A term often used negatively to describe Greeks who worked in Germany after the war. The word etymologically consists of two words, the adjective Lazos and the adjective Germanos. According to informants, the word indicates the origin of many immigrants to Germany from what is now eastern Turkey and the Black Sea coast. That is to say, they were exchanged Christians from the wider Black Sea region who were forced to emigrate to Germany after the war due to economic difficulties. For more information about Lazistan and the ethnic groups, among them Greek Pontians, who seem to have lived in the region since ancient times, see Merten (2014).

99   Here I use the pertinent term of Herzfeld within the context of the ambiguity that characterizes the Greek model of social establishment, according to which Greek people perform self-presentation or self-awareness depending on their frame of reference (1998, as cited in Ioannidou, 2004, p. 66).

which, in the context of "self-presentation" (Herzfeld, 2008), was, as we mentioned earlier, a negative condition.

Several informants mentioned the Greek repatriated immigrants from Germany mainly when they wished to refer to the change that took place in Toumba at the beginning of the 1970s because of the reconstruction, since lots of apartments in their neighborhood were purchased by Greeks who lived in Germany or people from Toumba who invested the capital they had created in Germany. The below excerpt from my conversation with a couple of informants from Toumba in 2013 is a characteristic one:

When do you think Toumba started changing and for what reason?
Kostis:"Hmm I will tell you when this changed... From 1976 onwards, when the construction started. The buildings were the reason, because everyone was trying to give it [the old house] and receive an apartment for their children[100]. On top, so many strangers gathered. Everyone came from the villages, from Germany... They left their villages, went to Germany. They made money and then came here, as our neighbors did, to buy a house."
Were there differences with those people, did they have other habits?
Kostis:"They pretended to be different, they became Europeans.[101] But people from Toumba had a different style. I mean, they were generous, their houses were tidy. People from the villages were starving, that's why they went abroad. Cut off without a penny, they went to Germany, they came back with two drachmas [cents] and they thought they were different. They started wearing hats with feathers. They looked down on us, you see what I mean? And then us, especially the women of my family, quarreled with the neighbors."

In summer 2013, I met through other informants a couple who lived on Karanou street, behind the church of Agiou Therapontos. Waltraud Kokot had conducted her field work on this specific street from 1983 to 1985.[102] The informants referred often to the German anthropologist who lived precisely next to them during the years of her research. The truth is that their descriptions and narrations about the anthropologist but also their efforts to have news from her put me in a difficult position ini-

---

100   The informant refers to the practice of *antiparochi*.

101   Once again, this ambiguity to which Herzfeld refers about the two models, within the context of which the national cultural identities of the Greeks are established, is observed here. On one hand, there is the completely local, "Romaic" model, and on the other hand there is the "Greek model for History and cultural identity, which is identified with nationalistic ideology and aims at the recognition of the Greeks by the Europeans", on this see Bakalaki (2008, p. 522).

102   This random event was a fortunate coincidence for me and helped my research a lot. At this point, I wish to thank Professor Emerita Waltraud Kokot once again for the hospitality in Hamburg, the discussions about Karanou street in the 1980s, and for the fieldwork notes she shared with me.

tially, as at that time I hadn't managed yet to find the unpublished paper of her post-doctoral thesis *Kognition und soziale Identität in einem Flüchtlingsviertel: Kato Toumpa, Thessaloniki*, and I hadn't met her yet, as she had already retired from the University of Hamburg when I joined in 2015. This couple was used by Kokot as an ethnographic example to document the conflictual reasons that were formed in the field between the "civilized" refugees and the "dangerous peasants" or those who returned from Germany, the "*Lazogermanoi* immigrants".

I met Georgia and Kostas thirty years later, at the apartment they acquired through *antiparochi* of their old house in Toumba, where Kokot met them in 1983. My informants, with the only difference that they were older and lived in an apartment building that had been built through *antiparochi* on the plot of the "old house" of the family, restructured the same narration that also Waltraud Kokot reproduces in her post-doctoral thesis, experiencing in the same way everyday life in the neighborhood, the conflicts between old and new inhabitants, and also their interpersonal relationship as a couple that started their common life in Kato Toumba.

The researcher's choice to live in an "old house" and have Georgia and Kostas as her first informants prevented her initially from getting in touch with other inhabitants of the neighborhood, who were part of the "native inhabitants of Toumba". More specifically, the researcher soon got the reputation of a "flighty woman", of which she managed to free herself when her mother paid her a visit during Christmas time; after that she "moved to the category of good girl and student" (Kokot, 1994, pp. 262–268).[103]

The testimony of Kostas and Georgia is an indicative example of people who chose to live in Toumba when the district started having a different status in the anthropogeography of the city. They even feel that through their practices they have contributed to the change that took place in Toumba of the refugees, transforming the refugee little house into a "little villa":

---

103   Here it is interesting to reflect on the gender-based identities of the female informants of Toumba but also the trouble, in Butler's (2009) terms, created by a "foreign" woman who chooses to stay at an "old" house, although she is European and therefore "advanced". The inhabitants of Toumba believe that during those years, by consuming the modern, they perform their European and western identity, wishing to keep an ideological distance from the life they imagine that prevails on the other side of the wall that separates Europe. Waltraud hosts colleagues with a different skin color, has a cat and is not married, she therefore has no household, and this is untidy and exotic within the context of the gender-based relationships of the *noikokyraioi* of Toumba. This transforms her into a free woman, without commitments – "whore". Here of course, we have to take into account also the analyses by Giannakopoulos (2001, pp. 171–183) in relation to the cultural perceptions of sexuality and sexual behavior in Greece, and also biologism in relation to the conceptual establishment of gender-based identities.

"There's nothing left now, only a few little houses. Those on which heirs cannot reach an agreement! Antiparochi wiped everything out!"

Georgia feels that people from Toumba were jealous because they had the possibility to buy the "old house" and transform it very quickly into a "modern" one:

"Yes, we bought it and made it look like a little villa. At the front, there was a living room and a second room, there was no corridor at that time – and at the back one more room. In any case, it was much bigger than this one. There was no kitchen. On this side, where the staircase was, we built a kitchen and a bathroom outside. This is how those houses were, with one room – the refugee houses as they used to call them."

As Georgia will explain later, she detested this area, and her dream was to buy a modern apartment in the city center.[104]

"When I participated in the examinations for the Academy at the Ministry of Northern Greece, I was dreaming of living in a modern apartment in the center of Thessaloniki. But I did not pass the exams because of social convictions. When my husband and I got engaged and bought the house, we wished to live here, close to his sister and his aunt! Unmade road!"

However, the financial status of the young couple and the fact that Georgia did not manage to study, as she planned, at the Academy led them to this area, in which they knew mainly "leftist refugees" lived. The fact that her husband had rightist ideological convictions and was of Arvanite origin would create difficulties from the outset regarding their integration into this neighborhood.[105] Here we notice that it's not only the origin that leads to conflicts, but also the competition at the level of performances of "self-awareness" of leftist refugees versus the "self-awareness" of the rightist Arvanite (Herzfeld, 1998).

From the beginning the informants state the difference between the terms of material living of the refugees and those of the village where they were raised, even though, as we will see in the excerpt below, they are two different versions of the same "self-presentation" (Herzfeld, 1998), which is dictated by the hegemonic normative standard of westernization and the moral values of capitalism.

"Look, at the village we were leading a rich life. Our village was a very rich one, because there was running water, there were authorizations available to cultivate tobacco, because there was the right type of land for this cultivation, and when the merchants came to pay us for the tobacco, a suitcase was not enough for the

---

104   On the hegemonic imperative of urbanization see chapter two.
105   On the establishment of the cultural other in the Greek society see Papataxiarchis (2006b).

money, and everyone was so well-dressed; it was the only village that had running water and hard-working people, we could wear and eat everything, meaning
I used to take the bus to come here and shop my festive coat and suit!"

With the financial capital they had, they managed after their wedding to perform
in Toumba the dream of urbanization that many young people had in the Greek
province:

"Houses were so old and horrible. How was I going to say that I got married and I
would now live in Thessaloniki! How could I invite them to come here! Because in
the city center there were apartments. People did not buy houses and things like
that, people bought apartments!"

But in Toumba very soon they experienced non-acceptance, which hindered their
socialization in the district: *"They called us peasants here!"* According to Kokot's notes,
Georgia's origin from a village close to "Slavic-speaking Yugoslavian Macedonia" in
combination with the fact that she was married to a rightist Arvanite created problems in the environment of Toumba. The concept of "civilized" that refugees often
used to describe their lifestyle in their cities of origin was associated to characteristics that contrasted the new inhabitants of Toumba, who were natives from villages
in the region of Thessaloniki.[106] "Civilization" was linked to the urban lifestyle and
cosmopolitanism of the urban centers of the Ottoman empire, which the families of
Toumba were forced to leave.[107]

In the following meetings, Georgia was trying to isolate me from Kostas, who
was always sitting at the balcony, performing a different gender-based identity from
the one she performed when we were at the balcony with him. The husband's presence had a drastic impact on the performance of Georgia's gender-based identity.
In our private discussions, the quiet and acquiescent Georgia was transformed into
a dynamic and decisive woman, who consciously directed her husband to the fulfilment of her own goal setting. Georgia had substantially internalized the negative
attitude of the neighborhood for Kostas, believing indeed that her husband was a
"peasant" and an "old-fashioned" person, who even hindered her in her interpersonal relationships with the rest of the neighborhood.

Georgia thinks that everything that she managed to create is due to her own
noikokyrosyni,[108] perseverance and work, reproducing in this way the hegemonic narration of this specific field (Papataxiarchis, 2006a; Salamone & Stanton, 2019). It is

---

106 See also Bakalaki (2008, p. 551), Hirschon (2006, pp. 59–91) and Salamone and Stanton (2019,
      p. 151).
107 Op. cit..
108 It is interesting to note that Georgia reproduces a different type of a gender-based version
      of tidiness, as it is not established complementarily to the role of Kostas within the context
      of the household.

not by chance that she feels she has the best relationships with her neighbors from Toumba, contrary to her husband who never managed to integrate and still constantly fights with the neighbors, performing a man's identity that blatantly resists to the "self-presentations" of the "civilized" refugees. As Georgia revealed to me during our private conversations in the kitchen, so that her husband could not listen to us, her husband's family, although they lived in the city for years, they never managed to purchase their own house. The absence of this goal setting and the associative version of a masculinity who "eats"[109] and does not "make" provided Georgia with a reason to take action to establish her *noikokyrio* in Toumba.

According to Georgia, just like for my other informants, [110] paying a rent was a "waste" of money, and this is why she insisted so much on giving the house as *antiparochi* and pushed Kostas to buy apartments for his two daughters and endower them as it was his duty to do like a "proper *noikokyraios*"[111], since he had two girls. These goals of Georgia would provide a permanent reason of conflict between them.

Regarding the interior decoration of the apartment, Georgia does not reproduce in her narration the reasoning of an "aristocratic" or "noble" living room. The interior of her house was very different from the houses of the families of native inhabitants of Toumba and inhabitants of the city center. It was very simple and there were no decorative elements or other solemn furniture. Being functional and clean were Georgia's main aspirations for her home, which made her insist against her husband and opt for the demolition of the old house, which she considered a "wreck", "dirty" and "non-functional" because of its oldness.

> "Look, this house was of the settlement era – do you know how much trouble it was? – I had a readymade railing and then the gutter clogged, and water started running in the living room and the bedroom from the ceiling light, these houses were too old, my son, too old".

Her *noikokyrosyni* was mainly associated with her ability to keep her house clean, but also with her ability to act as a mediator between her children and her husband, making sure their needs would be met and ensuring the best possible future for them, including funding for their studies and dowry in the form of granting an apartment in the district of Toumba.[112] Georgia seems to agree with the neighborhood that Kostas

---

109   On the concepts of "eat" and "make" see Vlachoutsikou (1999).

110   On the conceptualization of renting an apartment within the context of a "household", see above subchapter 4.1.2 *"Gender-based performances of the modern. The case of Vasiliki from the second generation of women from Toumba"*.

111   It is interesting to note that Kostas never used the term *noikokyris* or *noikokyraios* in our discussions, while he constantly repeated the term "peasant", which he didn't seem to perceive as a contemptuous one, contrary to Georgia.

112   This differentiation regarding home decoration and devotion to more practical and functional aspects of the household reminds us of female role models that, according to Bakalaki

was a "peasant", "stubborn" and "uncivilized" person, stressing that these characteristics prevented for many years her unhindered communication with the neighbors. Kostas and Georgia believe that Toumba changed because of the investment of money by people like them, who sought for a cheap housing solution near the city center, as well as by repatriated immigrants, who bought, as we saw also in the Introduction, the newly built apartments, contributing to the expansion of the phenomenon of *antiparochi* and overall reconstruction of the settlement. Such an example is the case of Marika, who managed to buy apartments in Toumba, and live there, with the money she saved by working in various cities of Germany. Marika is a very interesting case, as she combines both the experience of internal immigration from the village to the city and the experience of immigration to Germany. The example of Marika is indicative of the dynamic character she showed by resisting the hegemonic cultural classifications regarding her gender (Dubisch, 2019; Gkefou-Madianou, 2006; Vlachoutsikou, 1999). Marika resisted to the constraints and delimitations of patriarchy that put her existence, but also the future of her two children, in danger. Besides, Butler[113] claimed that precisely this constant repetition of "performativity" can sometimes lead to incomplete "identifications" or performances that are not fully adapted to the normative standards. In these "gaps" and "deficiencies" the individual may proceed to alternative performances, from which a transformed subject will emerge.

(2008, p. 530), were showcased within the context of the discussion about the education of women in Greece in the 19th century. Luxury and showing off, in particular regarding needlecraft and embroidery were associated, according to the anthropologist (2008, pp. 538–546), with the negative stereotype of a superficially educated and vain graduate of a girls' school, which eventually was against the moral values of the capitalist spirit that was promoted by a part of the intellectual people of that era.

113   (Butler, 1997, 1999 as cited in Ioannidou, 2004, pp. 59–60).

Figure 15: Ashtray to the bottom of which Marika had sticked a piece of a postcard representing an evyone and two peasant girls. Marika always carried this object from her village to remember her country while in Germany.

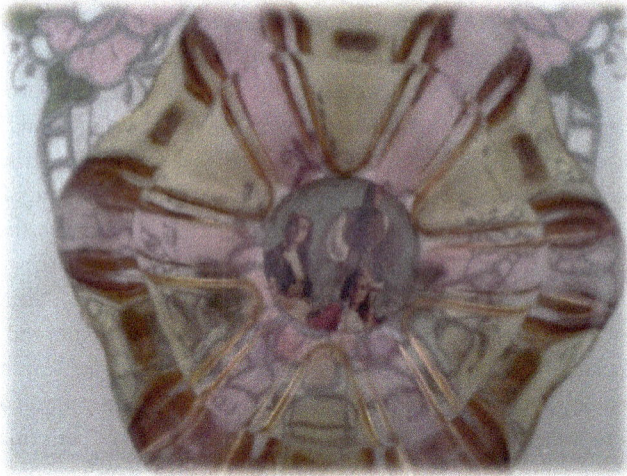

Source: Photo by Miltiadis Zermpoulis.

Marika from the village of Cherso got married at the age of fifteen to a much older man. According to Marika, there was no other choice for her widowed mother, who, in view of a new marriage and setting up of a new *noikokyrio* had to take care of the pending issues of the previous one. Therefore, this choice was made by her mother, who personally knew the family of her future husband. The first years were very tough due to Marika's moving to her husband's home, and because of the big distance that separated my informant from her mother and siblings. After six years of marriage and at the age of 21, Marika became a widow and two years later she left the village to go to Thessaloniki because of the difficult family relationships. The relationship with her brother-in-law who tried to impose himself on her and undertake entirely the management of the family property led the two individuals to a great conflict. Marika struggled for two years to meet the new requirements of her role, working in her husband's fields, and creating the necessary privacy at home. Her resistance to the expansionary practices of her brother-in-law led her to abandon the village and rent the fields and the house.

"My younger brother went to the [pedagogical] academy. We had the same mother, and he was here in Kato Toumba, he lived here. I took care of everything, I rented the fields, how did I do? I rented them all, I took my children, it was

October! I loaded my stuff! What kind of stuff could I have?! A room – and I came here – and you know where I rented an apartment? On Botsari street!!! Toumba was full of fields. When I came, the house of Ms Domna had three floors, she was the only one to have an apartment building, and everything else was gipsy stuff, and the streets were small and narrow, water was flowing from the channels, the gipsies played the davuls and zurnas, the revelry, can you imagine?"

Marika found it hard to survive as a young woman and widow in the male-dominated environment of Toumba, and particularly that of its factories. Cultural perceptions about masculinity, sexuality and premarital sex formed a hostile and rather dangerous working environment for a young widowed female worker. The gender category in Greece is associated with the nature of the man or woman (in terms of anatomy) and is independent of the sexual behavior of the subject that finally determines his/her gender-based identity. According to Giannakopoulos (2001), every sexual relationship in Greece is a "hierarchical" one and concerns strictly the relationship of two "partners, whose sexual roles are strictly distinguished in 'male', namely 'active', and 'female', namely 'passive'. The active partner is a man who 'acts', dominates, while the passive one is a woman or a queer/homo who 'suffers', 'endures'" (Giannakopoulos, 2001, pp. 171–172). Thus, when Marika started working in Thessaloniki, she faced sexual harassment a lot of times, and this forced her to constantly change jobs.

At this point, it is useful to cite an excerpt from my discussion with Marika, which is indicative of the gender-based establishments within the context of the factories and life in the public sphere of Thessaloniki:

"Initially I started working at PAIK".
What is PAIK?
"PAIK was a military service located in Ilioupoli. They did the screening of clothes there, how can I say, they selected jackets, trousers, shirts, shoes, all this we had to screen, I worked there for five or six months, I don't remember exactly."
Didn't you like the job there?
"I liked it, but I was fired. It was a seasonal job. I was then wondering where to go, what to do, in our village we had a police officer, and we had the police in our courtyard, my dad was a communist, they had charged him with a lot of things!"
Was he a rightist person?
"Yes, he was, but he was human! Likewise, my dad was a communist, but he was a nice person and they had good relationship, his children grew up with my mother's milk."
Didn't he inform on him?
"No, he threw out everything, he tore all the documents. 'You are so good people, such a good family, how can they keep these papers against you, what kind of story is this?' Then he said to my mom: 'Don't worry Ms Alexandra, I will take care of your daughter', and he even wanted to marry his daughter with my younger brother, the teacher; this did not

happen at the end, but we got along so well, he loved our family so much that he wanted to become related by marriage. So, this person got me a job. Then it was called Tourbal. Yes, this is how it was called, Tourbal; now it is called YFANET!"

This factory? In Agios Fanourios?

"Yes, I went to work on foot. I started with the engine, the cotton. I had to feed it, and it would make a thread. You know, at that time widows were very easy to recognize, because at that time only widows were dressed in black; nowadays no-one is dressed in black, nowadays even young women wear black clothes. He helped me enter Tourbal, Yfanet, and I worked, he spoke about me, you know at that time the Police controlled everything."

Even these private factories?

"Yes, they could even close them!!! A policeman would close them!"

Could a police officer close them?

"Yes, he could shut them down! He spoke to the boss and told him 'I will send a girl that I know, be careful', he told him, 'alright police officer'; you know, my boss also in the office had some bastards, pardon my French, there were bastards in there. No, the supervisor and the manager were upstairs, I was inside, do you know where the torrent is? Back there I was feeding the engine, the windows were back there, I remember it so well, as if I could see it now. And at the front other people worked and operated the cotton mill, I was at the back, a short old man used to come 'little widow, come here, little widow', and I had to leave from there, I went on the other side, 'what are you afraid of? Do you think I am going to eat you, and you leave here, and you leave there?' Excuse me for the expression, but these were his words, I replied that 'I went to work, I didn't go to fondle'".

I see.

"Do you know what he told me? 'She pretends to be a moral girl, you come from a village, you peasant girl', he said, 'and you pretend to be moral, who knows how many...'"

As it can be seen from the above excerpt, the environment in which my informant acts, is entirely male dominated. All those people who determine her movements, either with a good or with an evil intention, are men. Very often in the field I heard from my informants that "the man had to 'fondle' and in general satisfy his sexual instinct, since this was the way to perform his virility". Marika would even justify infidelity and frequent visits of men to brothels, believing that these practices are natural and are associated with male sexuality. On the contrary, she believed that women due to menstruation did not have similar "impulses". According to Giannakopoulos (2001, p. 176), "male sexual desire is not a simple physical desire but rather an uncontrolled and pressing 'need' of the male organ", which, in the context of the above narration, justifies the sexual aggressivity that my informant experienced as a widow (without a husband – non-virgin).

But Marika, loyal to the reflective consideration of her identity and in a more active performance of femininity within the context of the patriarchy of *noikokyraioi*, continues to perform identities of resistance to violence, which is exercised on her working and female body:

> "And what did I do? I spitted on his face with saliva when he mentioned this word! Shame on you! How dare you call me a whore! I stained him with saliva, and we started fighting. [...] Do you know what they told me? 'We have left no-one alone here, widows, divorcees, married women, we fondled everyone, and you think you will go away intact?'."

The situation in that factory was not sustainable, so she addressed a request to another man, who had more power than her colleagues, to change working environment and be able to continue working:

> "After this, you know, the police officer, my mother's acquaintance from Cherso, made sure I would work at a hospital – it is now called *Gennimatas* – at that time it was called *Kentrikon (Central)*. At the central hospital I worked as a cleaning lady. I cleaned the offices, and you know, I was very good at cleaning. The director came once —do you know how the director's furniture looks like? Everything in leather, I took everything out to the corridor, when the director came – it was on Saint Dimitrios day – he came to check and saw all his stuff outside and asked: 'What happened? What does this mean?' I said 'Sir, it's me, I am cleaning.' 'What an exceptional cleaning! You take the furniture out to clean?' the director, Tryfon, said – how did I remember this?!"

Despite her efforts to work in the best possible way, she faced anew the same "male aggressivity" at this workplace, too:

> "The supervisor did everything to fondle me. One day I was taking a shower, poor me, I was cleaning but also taking a shower there, I did not have a bathroom at home – we were renting an apartment – he was knocking on the door to get in. I told him 'go away because I will turn you in to the TV channels, I will put you up for auction', that's what I told him (laughter), I didn't really know where to turn him in. 'Where will you put me up for Ms Marika?' 'For auction!' I did not open the door, I took my shower, I got dressed, I came out of the bathroom. 'I'll show you', he was after me everywhere. Ilias the cashier, this supervisor and Galanis – how did this come to mind? – from whom I took the material to clean – I went to the basement – Ilias would tell me: 'little widow, I'll pay you last'".

What is interesting is that Marika thought that it was the black clothes and the fact that they knew she was a widow that caused this type of behavior. On the other hand, within the specific patriarchy system, the unprotected widow dressed in black performs this specific identity, which, however, is contradictory, at least during that period of time, with my informant's desire to move in the public sphere. However, her social class does not allow her to remain protected in the domestic sphere, safeguarding through isolation from public life the cultural value of an honest widow. In this dystopian context that threatens her social reproduction, Marika decided to immigrate to Germany: *"In 1962, I left for Germany, I could not stand it any longer!"*

As the above excerpt shows, the informant made several efforts to survive in the new environment of a big city, after she abandoned her village. However, her gender and social class made it impossible to survive in the environment of the socially ascending *noikokyraioi* of the area. Especially the fact that this woman was a young poor mother from a village, who had to work to maintain her children, rendered her automatically inferior at a social and moral level in comparison to a married *noikokyra* who enjoyed the protection of a *noikokyraios* husband.

Marika, like many other informants, had no other choice; to be part of the development and change that was taking place during that era in the district of Toumba and city of Thessaloniki, she had to work for a certain period in industrialized Western Germany, to acquire the financial and social capital that would allow her to return to the neighborhood under different terms. Marika was soon forced to take her children to an orphanage to be able to go to Germany. Even though she made several efforts to bring them to Germany, the children's different lifestyle and their inability to speak the language always created a very different context, which forced Marika to come back to Greece, trying to make up for the gap that had been created between them.

My informant lost a lot of money because she was unable to stabilize her way of living in Germany. Love and marriage with a younger man, four dramatic miscarriages and constant conflicts with the children often made her stay in Germany impossible. Despite these problems, she managed to buy, as she told me, a few apartments in Toumba with promissory contracts and live in the district thanks to the pension she is entitled to due to her work in Germany.

Although Marika is now 85 years old, she considers she did not have the chance to live her childhood because of all the difficult circumstances she faced. She got married at a very young age and she had to work, to be able to fulfill her obligations. At her apartment in Toumba there are many objects creating the feeling of a child's room. Marika chooses to decorate the apartment and the common spaces of the apartment building where she lives with stickers representing child's toys in pink shades. Her friend Maria comments in a negative way these practices of Marika, reproducing in this way the aesthetic classifications establishing the model of a "noble" and "aristocratic living room" that we saw earlier. Marika does not comply with these aesthetic suggestions of her friend, as noble living rooms are too "solemn" and "dark", as she explains, reminding her of the solemn atmosphere of Germany.

Marika's decoration practices result from a reflective mood towards the experiences of constant spatial movements, impoverishment, female passivity, and work experience in the factories of late capitalism.[114] All over the place, there were a lot of toys, teddy bears and all types of stuffed dolls, placed in such a way so as to create a "trouble"[115] within the context of the hegemonic decoration practices in the field. Alfred Gell (1998, as cited in Gialouri, 2012, p. 37) proposes to focus on the activity of the objects outside our aesthetic classifications and cultural codifications.

Figure 16: Marika's Chandelier; Figure 17 Marika's Living room.

Source: Photo by Miltiadis Zermpoulis; Source: Photo by Miltiadis Zermpoulis.

Objects are "active" not because we, as human beings, see them as such, but because they have an impact on us, causing feelings of joy, fear, sorrow, affecting our social life (Gell, 1998, as cited in Gialouri, 2001, p. 38). Marika loves colors and this is why she chose to paint the apartment in joyful colors. This apartment cheers her up and "protects" her against the aggressive masculinity of the public space.

During the period of fieldwork, my informant used to cover the metal railing of the balcony with a non-transparent plastic membrane. Initially I thought that Marika's intention was to protect the railing of her new apartment against the wear that can be caused by rain. But this was again a culturally intermediated interpretation influenced by the hegemonic representations in the field about *noikokyrosyni* and the cultural values associated with it. This practice is associated with the gender-based performance of female honesty that protects the "passive body" against the eyes of "virile masculinity" watching her:

"I don't wish to provoke, my son. A young man at the age of my daughter works across the street. In this way I can move around without thinking about it."

---

114   See Tsibiridou (2013) on the establishment of gender-based identities through "experiences of precariousness, compliance and undermining" of normative hegemonic standards.

115   Here I use the pertinent term of Bultler "trouble" (2009) about the alternative performances of gender in a figurative way for objects, when these are reframed and causing reversals and alternative subjectifications.

This is precisely the reason why she covers the railing of the apartment with a plastic cover, so that no-one can watch her when she goes out to the balcony.

Figure 18: Stickers on the lift at Marika's apartment building.

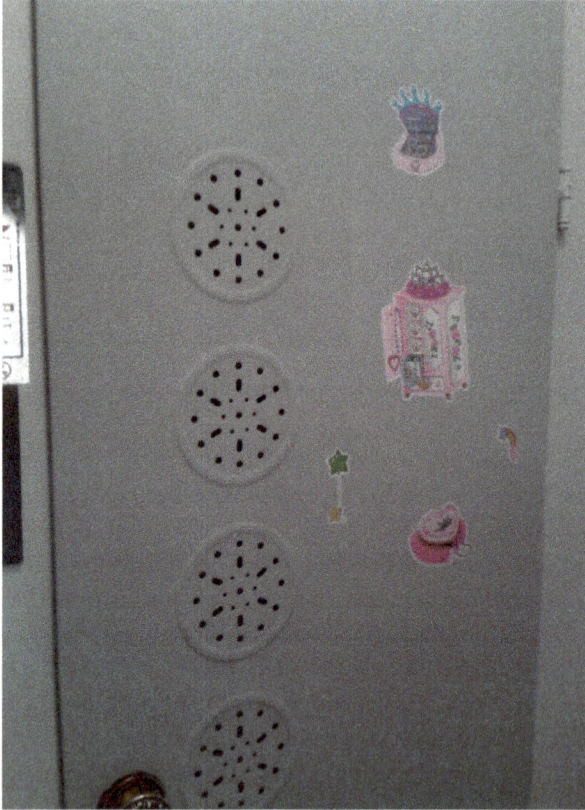

Source: Photo by Miltiadis Zermpoulis.

As a conclusion, we could say that both ethnographic examples show that the multiple spatial movements and the different biographies of these informants lead to different performances of "modern". Their practices converse and are often influenced by hegemonic standards; however, their experiences in contexts of different cultural values lead to alternative subjectifications and a "trouble" in the field. The "peasants" from Toumba and *Lazogermanoi* – "immigrants" contributed in an equally decisive way, as the above examples show, to the transformation and development of this district.

Figure 19: The metal railing of the balcony covered with non-transparent plastic membrance.

Source: Photo by Miltiadis Zermpoulis.

5. "Modern" state, "*noikokyraioi*" citizens and local shades of "corruption"

In this chapter, an attempt is made to investigate the dynamic of the social concept of "state" in relation to its hegemonic power on citizens (Gramsci, 2006; Althusser, 2006; Abrams, 1988; Steinmetz, 1999; Sharma & Gupta, 2006). The adjectives used in the title of chapter five to describe the nouns "state" (modern) and "citizens" (*noikokyraioi*/tidy) pertain to the Greek ethnographic paradigm and are terms that informants largely used in the field, being always perfectly connected and identified among them.[1]

The "modern" Greek post-war state cannot be understood, as we saw also in the third and fourth chapters, without the hegemonic cultural constructions regarding *noikokyraioi* citizens and their practices in this specific normative context of fulfilling the national – collective goal of reconstruction of Greece that had been destroyed by the war. "Modern" describes the contemporary state emerging from reconstruction, modernization of Greek administration, extended electrification of the country[2], construction of modern infrastructure, but also in terms of customary and procedural law[3], and everyday life (Avdela, 2002, pp. 212–224). *Noikokyraioi* citizens – usually heads of families with a conservative political ideology – manage in the post-war era to achieve the upward social mobility that consists in a successful professional course, mainly through self-employment, the construction of a privately owned, furnished and decorated house,[4] not only to meet the private needs of the family, but also to promote their social life and mainly their image to the neighborhood and the broader social community they targeted.

---

1   See third and fourth chapter.

2   "*As it has been stressed, electricity is a capital factor of social and economic life. And DEI, as economic organization managing electrical energy, must follow the whole economic and social evolution of the country, with which its activity is directly or indirectly linked.*" (Excerpt from the activity report of Public Power Corporation for financial years 1950–1951 and 1951–1952, p. 11, *DEI* Historical Archive)

3   For more details see second chapter: "*'Transformation' and 'petty bourgeoisism'. The Greek class distinctiveness and theories of 'underdevelopment'*".

4   See third and fourth chapter.

Taking into account the theories of anthropology of the state (Steinmetz, 1999; Sharma & Gupta, 2006) as well as other ethnographies (Oikonomou, 1999, 2008; Vla-choutsikou, 1999; Papataxiarchis & Paradellis, 1992) dealing with the modernization and urbanization of the Greek society, we will attempt a historical ethnography for the material[5] from post-war Thessaloniki. Through this specific ethnographic example of post-war Thessaloniki and the archival research we will show that eventually the modern Greek state is not the one that creates the *noikokyraioi* citizens, being a single and powerful apparatus able to determine citizens' lifestyle top down and affect the ideological establishment of the different social groups (Steinmetz, 1999; Sharma & Gupta, 2006). As it will be shown from the analysis of the ethnographic material and the historical sources, the *noikokyraioi* and the "modern" post-war state are rather produced and reproduced in an interactive way within a capitalist development system, which in the Greek case includes different everyday experiences and practices of dependence of simple citizens in their contact with the state apparatus and employees representing it.

5.1 *DEI* civilization

The informants from Toumba often refer to "before" and "after". The first years of settlement, the difficult years of the war, famine and struggle for survival. Unmade roads, mud, life in a shack or refugee house and experiences of everyday struggle for survival give their place in the after-war era to narrations of successful transition to a different everyday life made of paved roads, sidewalks, modern apartments with modern amenities, such as bathroom with a bathtub, boiler, washing machine and kitchen and the establishment of a new lifestyle that allows for consumption, not only for survival, but mainly for the fulfillment of further social needs. The tendency to a better life and the need to conquer any possible summit in any field of social life that has characterized the average Greek family since then is associated with the everyday experience of the "modern states", which provides electricity, makes roads, reconstructs and promotes industrialization, which will bring the coveted transformation of the country.

Being a place with a negative connotation because of refugeeism and the attitude of many inhabitants during the civil war, Toumba is transformed and progressively integrated into the rest of the city (Kokot, 1994). At least until the period when the latest financial crisis started in Greece[6] Toumba was one of the most sought-after

---

5   As we saw also in the first chapter, the material concerns the fieldwork and archive research in the historical archive of *DEI* and the archive of Social Welfare in the department of Public Property of Thessaloniki.

6   Financial crisis of 2010.

dwelling places of the lower middle class Greek family, forming part of the "eastern suburbs" of the city, on the opposite side of the "western" ones.[7] Through the practice of *antiparochi*, refugee Toumba was constantly and intensely reconstructed, responding to the high demand for newly built apartments, which characterized mainly the last decades before the crisis.

The completion of the electrification project, which was funded by the American Economic Recovery Act – known as Marshall Plan (Stathakis, 1993; Giannoulopoulos, 1992; Chatziiosif, 1993) – changed the domestic everyday life and life in public space. *DEI*'s campaign aiming to "bring civilization" in people's lives seems to have progressively shaped new realities for them. The constantly muddy and dark poor neighborhood is illuminated and acquires a new image during the first post-war decades. The "progress" and *"prokopi"* must now be the goal of every "sound" citizen, establishing the conceptual concept of a seemingly "programming" "civilization". The new power corporation, enjoying the state monopoly, strives to bring electricity to every household, making it necessary and obvious for the simple citizen, by promising a change in the lifestyle of the social groups that can participate in this different "culture" of modern life.

Figure 20: From the advertising campaign of the Press office of the corporation.

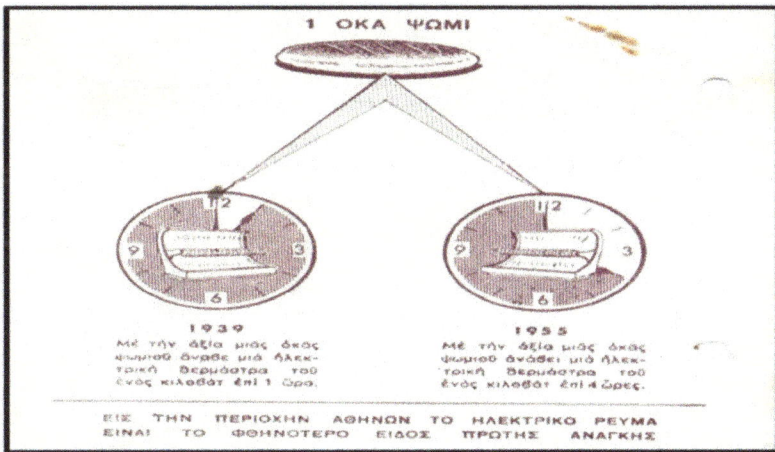

Source: *DEI* Historical Archive Thessaloniki / Folder: Campaign Press office.

---

7   On the different conceptualization of the two districts of the city, see fourth chapter *"Things in post-war home: modernity, innovation and becoming a noikokyra/ noikokyris".*

The campaigns for the promotion of household appliances and bigger consumption of electricity multiply, trying to make modern life products attractive to a public that initially seems indifferent.

As we can observe in the above brochure promoting *DEI* products, four hours of electricity consumption, to keep the bathroom or the spaces where family gathers warm cost as much as an oke of bread. Electricity is therefore offered at a low price to as many people as possible and symbolically becomes equally important as bread, which for many was a luxury item during the Nazi occupation, as mentioned also in Chapter three.

DEI creates manual computers, as it can be seen on the below picture, calculating the proportion between kilowatt-hour and drachma, to intensify its argument that greater consumption is a bargain. Electricity and the modern and efficient way of living that it guarantees must, according to the formal discourses of the corporation, reach every "household" seeking first *"prokopi"* and "progress" for the family and second *"prokopi"* for the Greek nation.[8]

Electricity is offered at a low price, to allow for the highest possible participation in the consumption of modern amenities, aiming to transform the Greek way of living, but also the everyday domestic practices of a large share of the Greek population.

The slogan "the more, the better" indicated above on the *DEI* brochures aims to dramatically change the consumption habits of the Greeks, creating a new generation of consumers who will buy and participate without a high cost in the "modern" way of living. *DEI* has the monopoly of energy and constitutes one of the biggest projects of post-war industrial Greece (Pantelakis, 1991; Tsotsoros, 1995). Many Greek companies rely for their survival on these campaigns, to increase consumption in a market that has not been shaped yet. The Greek *noikokyraioi*, as we saw also in the fourth chapter, will make sure, by saving the necessary amount of money, to equip their households with the new appliances that respond to the new ideal of a modern, organized and efficient family – domestic life. It is interesting to compare these practices with the respective objectifications taking place within the context of modernization[9] and westernization of the domestic life in the former socialist republics.[10]

---

8   On the importance of the Greek *noikokyrio* and Greek mother in the broader development of the Greek nation, see Bakalaki (2008, pp. 527–532).

9   On everyday practices and cultural representations, which can be conceptualized in the context of biopolitical technologies aiming at transformation within the context of the "Europeanization" logic, see Borneman and Fowler (1997, as cited in Papataxiarchis, 2006b, p. 40, citation 79).

10   See relevant ethnographies in second chapter 2.5 *"Space and objects in the discourses and practices of the noikokyraioi from Thessaloniki".*

At this point, it is interesting to cite excerpts from the speech[11] of the director of
the Prefecture of Macedonia-Thrace of *DEI* entitled: *"the five-year program of electrification and the Greek market of domestic appliances"*, which was presented at the second
conference of *Izola* company. This archive was found in the folder with the speeches
of the Director of Public Power Corporation of the Prefecture of Macedonia-Thrace.
In this specific excerpt, it is interesting to notice the type of produced formal discourse regarding the image of the Greek economy but also that of the state itself
before and after the war. The "obsolete ways of thinking" and "old pace" of the Greek
economy will change only through the cooperation of "problematic" Greece with a
"modern" and "progressive" "West" represented in the name of the newly established
state. What is required for this perspective is a change in the Greeks' way of living
and its full adaptation to the cultural values of capitalist consumption of massively
produced modernization products. It is a type of marketing discourse of that era
aiming at the increase of the consumption needs of the customers of a Greek industry of domestic appliances. The text shows the possibilities of the market discourse
to create consumption needs for users, who eventually through their use become,
as we saw also in the third and fourth chapter, bourgeois and petty bourgeois subjects[12].

> "[...] a lot is being said lately about the connection of our country with the Eu-
> ropean Economic Community, the Economic Community of the Six (France, Italy,
> Western Germany, Belgium, the Netherlands and Luxembourg), which is known
> to all of us as Common European market. However, in very general terms we can
> say that the common European market and our connection with it will constitute
> a milestone in the evolution of the course of our economy. [...] Let's not think now
> that thanks to the C.E.M. all our problems will be automatically solved. This has
> never been and can never be the question. Of course, our connection with the
> C.E.M. will be a milestone for us, provided that we also change our way of think-
> ing, the ways of our production efforts, our trade policy and lots of other obsolete
> ways of doing, which are totally irrelevant to modern life. Because we will have to
> admit, that although we insisted for so many years to follow an old pace, namely
> although we dealt with things with an unforgivable blissfulness, implementing
> methods that the post-war world does not accept even for museums, although –
> I repeat – for so many years we have been able to enjoy this luxury of blissfulness,
> today we no longer have this possibility.
> [...] The conditions to make good use of these two important things are not many.
> There is only one condition: create for Izola a strong domestic market. [...] Thus,

---

11   See *DEI* Historical Archive ΙΑΔΗΜ-Θ/ΔΕΗ/Folder15/1, 15/2 speeches 1958.

12   On how within the context of neoliberal capitalist development and globalization a new
      type of Islamist lifestyle is established in Muslim countries see Tsibiridou (2015, pp. 60–81).

our first conclusion, positive and certain, is only one: create, at this very moment, a strong market for Izola within Greece. We, each one of us, in our region and in our own quality, have this duty. Izola on its side has the duty to help with all its forces each one of us. Sparing no effort. [...] Which means, study the good numbers, and say: "IZOLA has sold up to this day 175 000 appliances. This is enough. We have stuffed the market. There is nothing else to be done." [...] The Greek market is a pristine territory.

But let's come to the good numbers. The census of the country, which took place a few months ago, showed that the population of the country has reached approximately eight and a half million people. This means that we have approximately 2 100 000 households. Now pay attention. If each one of these households bought a heater, we would have to admit that we could sell 2 100 000 heaters. Yes, but theory is as far from practice as is the earth from the moon (even if Gagarin and Shepard jump into the universe). Of all households, we have to remove I don't know how many of them that are rural and thanks to their fireplace they don't need our heater. Also, those who need our heater but have no money to buy it. [...] Take again the 2 100 000 and remove first of all those who have not yet got electricity [...]. Overall, based on *DEI*'s population movement statement for domestic use, 462 thousand 711 households out of a total of two million households are supplied with electricity. Let's add to them also all households of the capital to find that currently households with electricity are approximately one million. [...] Of them, let's remove one third, who cannot buy appliances yet for financial reasons. We are left with 800 000 households. This number is amazing. And it becomes even more dramatic if we consider the fact that today we have made available to the market four types of IZOLA appliances: cooker, fridge, boiler, heater. If we assume, (don't rush to tell me it's an erroneous assumption, I know this) if we assume that each one of these 800 thousand households buys all four of our appliances, only then we will be able to say that we have stuffed the Greek market of domestic appliances. [...]

What is the approximate number of domestic appliances that operate all over the country today? [...] Sirs, this number does not exceed 300 thousand [...]. [...] a remainder of two million nine hundred thousand appliances can still be made available to the Greek market. [...] Of course, there are many conditions. However, let's not forget that together with the new families that are created, thousands of new houses are built. Just think that of the building activity we observe around us, approximately 50% is destined for houses. [...] If grandmother and mother were attached to the brazier, the daughter in the new house will surely escape from this anachronism. She will look for something new. And this new she will seek for, we have to offer this to her. [...] IZOLA gives us a lot of advantages. It basically gives us the right appliance. The appliance that is designed and studied for the Greek household. The oven of our cooker is as big as required by our own giouvetsi[13] and our baking sheet. Or the cooling mechanism of our fridge has been studied to fit our own climate. This means that the appliance is not destined for consumption at the tropical equator or in Lapland."[14]

There is some consonance between the discourses produced and reproduced by officials during that period and my observations in relation to the practices and cultural representations in the field. The 1960s and in particular the apartment are directly associated in the informants' interviews with the first domestic appliances they managed to buy through practices of saving money. What is particularly interesting is the fact that this experience is lived as an individual success within the context of the progressive establishment of the *noikokyraios* identity. The sentence "we were the first ones to bring..." has a distinctive function compared to other people, while it also states the degree and rate of integration into the new hegemonic cultural frame of reference that is being shaped in the post-war era. The acquisition of these first amenities is, on one hand, an indicator of social and cultural superiority but, on the other hand, states the ability to align with what seems to be normal for that era.

Through painful savings, the *noikokyraioi* will buy a fridge, a cooker, a heater and a fan and some time later a washing machine and a television, showing their neighbors but also themselves the results of their "hard-working and diligent way of living". The consumption of electricity and the use of domestic appliances inaugurate this new way of living at home and found the new lifestyle of a rather "low middle class" living "in a modern and proper way" in the cities. Within the context of recovery of the Greek economy, the plans established from 1948 onwards, as it can be seen in the below text, give priority to the creation of an integrated national electricity supply network, which would also allow for the transformation of the Greek economy from purely rural to industrial. The alternating current provides new possibilities and transforms everyday life in the city. As we saw above, the goal of the corporation is not only high production of current, but also its consumption by the largest possible share of population. *DEI*'s advertising campaigns aim at promoting a different family life standard from the one that prevails in the 1950s and 1960s in Greece, focusing though considerably on the gender-based division of tasks in the domestic sphere, showcasing emphatically, as we will see below, the Greek middle-class *noikokyra* as the exclusive competent handler of the modern machines that will contribute to the improvement of her family's living conditions. Therefore, in these

---

13   Traditional Greek meat and pasta dish (translator's note).

14   Translated exerpt from the Folder *"speeches of the Director of Public Power Corporation of the Prefecture of Macedonia-Thrace"*, see *DEI* Historical Archive IAΔHM-Θ/ΔEH/Folder15/1, 15/2 speeches 1958.

DEI campaigns of the corporation department of public relations, women are represented as the primarily "modern" subject, whose main mission is the adaptation of her family to the new lifestyle that, as we saw earlier, will lead to the overall development of the country. The consonance observed between the ethnographic examples and the analysis of the previous chapters with *DEI*'s archive material are quite interesting and rather indicative within the specific context of post-war Greece. The discourses of *DEI*'s advertising campaign, being particularly gender-based, use powerful images, not only to shape the cultural identities of the Greek female *noikokyra* and Greek male *noikokyris* of modern everyday life in the city apartment, but also to achieve the highest possible consumption through the reproduction of values and a cultural code, with which the potential consumers are rather familiar within the context of the Greek household, as this has been shaped over time (Bakalaki, 2008; Papataxiarchis, 2006a). The Greek *noikokyra* must change her habits and modernize the way she cooks and washes by saving time and energy, but the cultural values of saving, efficient time management and optimal fulfilment of the family's needs constitute elements of the already established subjectivities of "tidiness" (Papataxiarchis, 2006a; Salamone & Stanton, 2019).

Figure 21: "Comfort is a right".

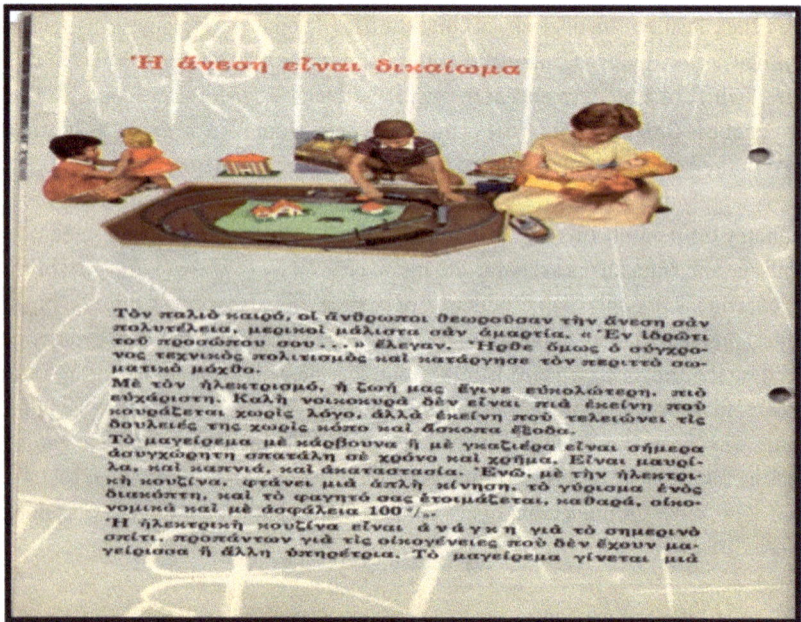

Source: ΙΑΔΗΜ-Θ/ΔΕΗ (DEI Historical Archive Thessaloniki) / Folder "Press office".

In this campaign, "modern" is identified to functional, immediate and economical, since the "modern" Greek mother is the person who *"does not get tired without a reason but finishes her housework effortlessly and without unnecessary expenses"*[15]; therefore, she is efficient, fast and sparing. Minimization of "effort" and "time required" is the purpose of a capitalist society that aims at the productive employment of all its members in view of multiplying productive efficiency and expanding profit. Precisely this logic finds its best expression in the Greek household model as a business aiming at increasing profit (Papataxiarchis, 2006a). Besides, these cultural values are reproduced, as we saw also in the fourth chapter, in the informants' discourses, responding to the financial goals of the Greek household (Papataxiarchis, 2006a).

The "modern" Greek *noikokyra*, as she is represented in *DEI*'s advertising campaigns, is well-groomed during the whole day, even when she cooks or washes at home.[16] "Comfort is a right" is the title of the above advertisement of the corporation (see Figure 21), which pictures a well-dressed mother and her children playing with modern and luxurious toys. Often at the *DEI* exhibitions at the corporation's exhibition venue – 10, Tsimiski street – popular women of that era were recruited and invited to cook and recommend to the public the modern lifestyle, as this was represented in the cinema and magazines of that era (Mylonaki, 2012).

---

15   Translated excerpt from the advertising campaign, see *DEI* Historical Archive/ Folder Press office.

16   During the study of *DEI Historical* Archive, I was impressed by the degree of similarity between the gender-based picture reproduced by this campaign and the cultural representations in the field. Both the discourses and actions of several women informants of middle classes in Thessaloniki, and in particular those who had a better financial standing in the post-war period, responded to the cultural imperatives of this way of living. More specifically, the picture of the stylish *noikokyra* reminds us of the representations of Maria from Toumba (see chapters 3 and 4).

Figure 22: "A relaxing occupation, the noikokyra does not get angry, does not lose her fresh-ness and beaty. So, the electric cooker is also a guarantee of family harmony."; Figure 23 The "modern" noikokyra.

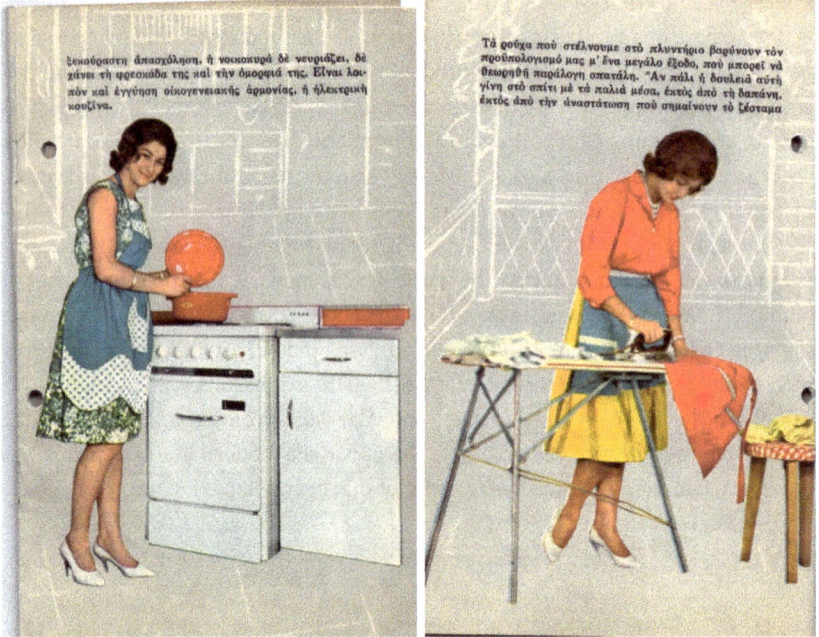

Source: ΙΑΔΗΜ-Θ/ΔΕΗ (DEI Historical Archive Thessaloniki) / Folder "Press office"; Source: ΙΑΔΗΜ-Θ/ΔΕΗ (DEI Historical Archive Thessaloniki) / Folder "Press office".

The "modern" *noikokyra* must think in a practical and economical way. The wash-ing machine and electric iron promise her energy, money and time saving. In addi-tion, the new electronic appliances render superfluous the employment of personnel for the laundry.

The time that the *noikokyra* spent on housework can now be creatively dedicated to the family. The modern wife and mother is a relaxed and smiling woman who can work well-groomed at home, next to the living room, while she speaks with her husband or plays with her children. As it becomes obvious from the above archival material, *DEI* places the woman at the center of this modernization challenge, task-ing her with the responsibility of its implementation within the context of the Greek family. "Becoming modern" concerns first and foremost the biopolitical technology (Foucault, 1987, 1991; Giannakopoulos, 2006, pp. 29–37) of the familiarization of the *noikokyra* with the domestic appliances.[17] It is worth noting the analysis by Tim Putnam (1999, p. 146) about the modern home in America: it is likened to a sort of technical station, which serves and supports the life of a modern subject, ensuring a healthy and safe living, and contributing substantially to time and energy saving. By means of its appliances, this home objectifies, in Miller's (2005) terms, the modern domestic life, as we saw also in the second chapter.

Within the context of *DEI's* advertising campaign and the domestic life it proposes, "modern" women should get rid of their old appliances and change their everyday way of living by modernizing it. Gas cookers, ice buckets and lamps, which, as we saw in the third chapter, were still used in the 1950s and 1960s by the informants from Thessaloniki, can and must be replaced by modern appliances that will bring "civilization" to their home and will contribute to the objective of "national *prokopi*" within the context of westernization.[18]

Finally, electricity and its expanded supply is used as a gear of transformation of a society that is being "civilized" in the spirit of the modern western world.[19] "Civilization" is of course not limited to the extent to which a company advertises massively its products to the public, but comprises organized efforts of education and nurturing of unsuspecting masses, calling on personalities of the state and public life, such as military officers, unions and traditional associations, priests and popular actors, in order to create the necessary atmosphere and frame of trust that is imposed by such structural transformation.

The corporation and its people appear both on the brochures and at the formal events as a unified, although gender-based, group of people, aiming at the nation's progress and at making people's everyday life easier. *DEI*, thus, becomes a symbol of modernization and development of capitalist Greece (Pantelakis, 1991; Stathakis, 2000; Tsotsoros, 1995).

---

17   On how the globalized market within the context of a neoliberal agenda uses mainly Muslim women for the establishment of a modern Islamist lifestyle, see Tsibiridou (2015).

18   See Attfield (1999), Chevalier (1999), Dimova (2006), Donner (2015), Fehervary (2002), Haralovich (1988), Mihailescu (2014), Putnam (1999) for respective ethnographies concerning policies and efforts of modernization of the home space in the post-war period in America, Europe and post-socialist societies.

19   On the objective of the then rising Greek elite to "civilize" women through education by adopting western standards, which in practice though often seemed distorted and combined with traditional ways of thinking see Bakalaki (2008, p. 526).

Figure 24: DEI's pavilion at the Thessaloniki International Trade Fair / Current Macedonian Museum of Contemporary Art of Thessaloniki; Figure 25 Christmas at the Exhibition Center of DEI, Koffa- Tsanidou Palace.

Source: ΙΑΔΗΜ-Θ/ΔΕΗ (DEI Historical Archive Thessaloniki) / Folder "Press office"; Source: ΙΑΔΗΜ-Θ/ΔΕΗ (DEI Historical Archive Thessaloniki) / Folder "Press office".

In this spirit, *DEI* organizes exhibitions to present the new appliances that promise to change their users' everyday life. It is interesting to see how the commercial service of the corporation promotes these exhibitions to the local directorates that will take over their organization. As it can be seen from the above office memorandum[20], the purpose of these exhibitions is primarily "cultural" and "social":

"Office Memorandum"
To: Regional Directorates and Offices
From: Regional Commercial Service
Object: Conduct of exhibitions of electricity applications
The exhibitions of electric appliances of domestic and other use at the Regions of our Corporation constitute a serious activity; its main purpose is the development and promotion of sale of electrical energy and the consequent increase of the Corporation's income. But in addition to this main purpose of a strictly commercial nature, these exhibitions provide the opportunity to promote our corporation and to establish good relationships between our corporation and its customers and society in general, as well as to serve its cultural and social purposes." (ΙΑΔΗΜ-Θ/ΔΕΗ [*DEI* Historical Archive Thessaloniki] / Folder "Press office")

---

20   ΙΑΔΗΜ-Θ/ΔΕΗ (*DEI* Historical Archive Thessaloniki / Folder "Press office".

Figure 26: Exhibitions of electric appliances and promotion of the campaign for the fast adoption of new ways of living offered by electricity.

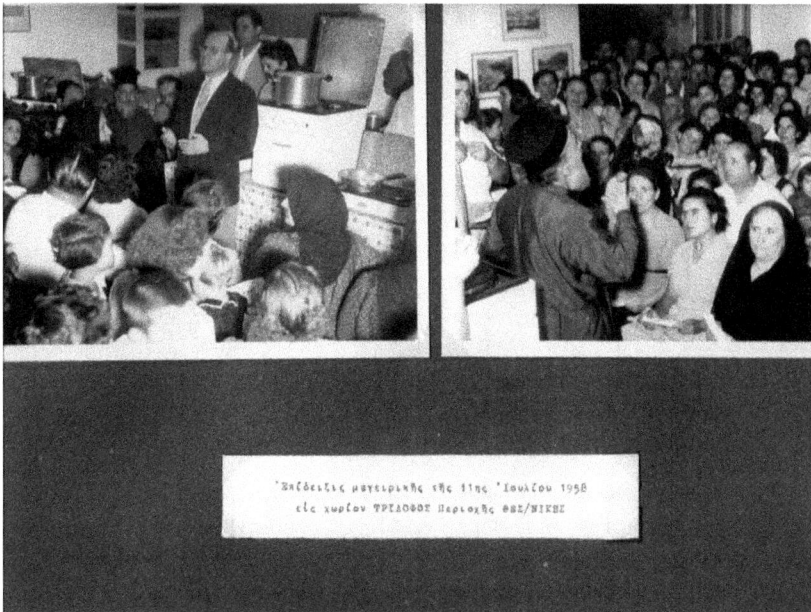

Source: ΙΑΔΗΜ-Θ/ΔΕΗ [DEI Historical Archive Thessaloniki] / Folder "Press office")

Kitchens and bathrooms must be integrated into the modern apartment and no longer be placed in the yards. Besides, *Izola* and *Pitsos* electric appliances will have the appearance of modern luxurious furniture, aiming at forming part of the public image of the home. From that moment on, the kitchen will become a habitable place and much later, based on American dwelling standards, the *antiparochi* will impose the "open kitchen" system, the well-known *"salokouzina"* (living room-kitchen) that will prevail in Greece mainly after 1980.[21]

5.1.1 "In the 1960s, I already had a dishwasher and a mixer, my sweetheart". Objectifications of the "modern" in the example of Antigoni

In this subchapter, we attempt to show the way in which the cultural political program of the post-war state is associated with the needs of those classes that were seeking upward social mobility already before the war. These classes are in favor of

---

21   See ethnography by Ferhevary (2002) on the conceptualization of "normal" in relation to the prevalence of the Americal type of unified kitchen and living room in Hungary.

and support the country's westernization within the context of capitalist development, being often themselves the ambassadors of this distinctness that needs to be transmitted and touch a larger share of the post-war society.

Antigoni, daughter of refugees from Caesarea in Cappadocia asks her daughter while I am present if in this case she is allowed to openly share with me the way in which they lived as a family in the 1960s, mainly in contrast to the poverty that prevailed in neighboring households. Antigoni is cautious with me, because her daughter reprimands her, when, in summer during their holidays in Chalkidiki, she describes her lifestyle to people that, in her daughter's opinion, come from very different social groups and cannot understand her.

Antigoni was raised in the center of Thessaloniki, in the surroundings of Ptolemaiou street. Her father, a small grocer of the city center, and her mother, a *noikokyra*, struggle to make sure that Antigoni will enjoy privileges that the neighbors' children did not have. The private schools she had the chance to attend gave her the possibility of upward mobility, because she had the chance to make friends, as she characteristically says, with the "elite" of the post-war Greek city.

The appointment with her had been scheduled well in advance and, therefore, Antigoni was aware of the topic of my thesis. Her daughter, who is a teacher and lived in the period of the fieldwork a bit further in a privately owned house, accompanied me to Antigoni's apartment that was built in the 1990s through *antiparochi* in Kato Toumba.

When she was sixteen years old, she met Socratis, who originated from a family of small merchants in the field of production and sale of shirts. This acquaintance allowed her to acquire, with the help also of her parents, a newly built apartment in one of the first apartment buildings of Toumba, at the end of the 1960s.[22] This apartment and especially its low selling price compared to the respective newly built apartments that were being built during that period within the context of reconstruction of the center, and more specifically the area of *"exoches"* (countryside) in the east of the city, is the reason why the informant started her relationship with the area of Toumba, which she detested until that moment. According to my informant, the apartment was cheaper than those at Depo[23], where friends and relatives of hers were moving from the old center.

In this ethnographic example, home ownership is a necessary condition within the context of a lifestyle that sets as a priority the progress and safe living of the family (Papataxiarchis, 2006a). Both Antigoni and her parents opted for buying the

---

22   The apartment where she lives today is not the same as the apartment of the 1960s. To ensure the possibility of home ownership to her older daughter when she got married, in 1990, Antigoni moved to the new apartment, where our meeting took place.

23   An area of Thessaloniki.

houses where they lived, while they use other properties to top up their basic in-come. Saving money is the only way to achieve this goal and, according to Antigoni, it is a practice implemented mainly by women.[24] A *noikokyra* has the possibility to use her "dynamic personality" and her "providence" to connect the public and domestic sphere of her family life. According to Antigoni, her husband can be generous, mainly because she was "frugal" when managing household incomes in transactions outside it.[25] Savings are usually invested exclusively in the home and children's education. The need to fulfill the social imperatives of the social stratum of *noikokyraioi* leads my informants to a particularly suffocating and austere way of living that can ensure the saving of the required capital. Opening the home on "national holidays and anniversaries", as Antigoni characteristically mentions, preserves and reproduces the social status of the family vis-à-vis her familiar people. Maintaining the family in the most modern version of the current fashion and showing off new belongings is the primary practice and reason for opening the home, and especially those rooms that remain closed during the rest of the time, to third people.[26] The comparative mirror action in the process of becoming a subject ends up being competition in the capitalist culture of individual prosperity. The others are usually poor because they do not struggle and do not manage to meet the requirements of the new life in the city. As we saw also in the third chapter, this usually reflects a "right-wing" rhetoric, according to which who works prospers, while who is poor is necessarily a "lazy" person.[27] The differentiation that the *noikokyraioi* achieve through their consumption behaviors, which are cultivated and encouraged by the state that aims at the reconstruction and rapid development, cannot be understood without the extended stratum of the poor people of the cities, who cannot live in the same way. This differentiation is primarily hierarchical, and it is the only way to establish a complementary and contrasting subjectivity of *noikokyraios*.[28] Besides, as Herzfeld (1987) reminds us, binary oppositions reproduce power inequalities.

This cultural representation can be analyzed through the very useful analytical categories that Herzfeld (1998) introduced for the Greek example regarding practices of "self-presentation" or "self-awareness". The case of successful *noikokyraios* is clearly a representation in the public space that can be analyzed within the context

---

24   On the establishment of the gender-based identity of *noikokyra* in the Greek territory, see Salamone and Stanton (2019); Gkefou-Madianou (2006); Vlachoutsikou (1999).

25   See the interesting consonance with the ethnographic example of Maria in relation to the cultural values of the gender-based identities of *noikokyraioi* in the "apartments of development".

26   On the conceptualizations of "closed living room" see fourth chapter.

27   On the conceptual association communist-lazy see the analysis of the ethnographic example of Maria in the third chapter.

28   On the function of such hierarchical dichotomies in the Greek ethnographic example see Gkefou-Madianou (2006); Bakalaki (1994).

of the point of view of self-presentation, since it is assessed on the basis of the western example as an intrinsic element and is characterized by a need for competition and individuality.

Already since our first meetings, Antigoni has tried to differentiate herself from the fate of "poor refugees". On the opposite side of refugees' bad luck, she provides arguments to differentiate her family from the life of the other refugees. She originates from a family of oil merchants, who are forced to abandon Cappadocia but migrate to Greece on their own expenses. This allows her from the outset to have a different position in the anthropogeography of post-war Thessaloniki. As Antigoni stresses, this happens mainly through the purchase of a house at the limits of the city center. Her mother is presented as a woman who is "different" from the conservative circle of *noikokyraioi* and the city to which she migrates.

The characteristics that compose this specificity are her independence, dynamic personality, progressive character and "non-tidiness". Antigoni's mother is the counterexample[29] of the Greek *noikokyra*, as both Antigoni, and her daughter, who is a teacher, characteristically stress. This woman follows her own fate, distinguishing her position from the family of oil merchants who strive to fully integrate into the Greek middle class, by choosing a very poor man, whom she imposes to her family, making him initially a "bag boy" at her father's "grocery store". However, things seem to not serve her purposes and thus, she helps her husband open a grocery store himself, at which she makes pickled vegetables, a beloved eating habit of the poor Jews of the city, according to the testimony of Antigoni. The small grocery store and the selling of pickled vegetables will soon allow for the purchase of the "old house" behind Ptolemaion street, to respond essentially, as we will see, through alternative gender-based performances of modernity, the main purposes of integration into the normative standards of the Greek society.

Mother Eri seeks to emancipate her daughter in the most sought-after sector of that time, the industry of Greek cinema. The daughter must become a new Vougiouklaki[30], and early on a different school is chosen, to allow her to get the knowledge and make the acquaintances that will open new paths for her in adult life. Antigoni feels bad among her very rich classmates, since she is the grocer's daughter. On the other hand, school gives her the chance to meet all the girls of the "good homes" of Thessaloniki, who, thanks to their financial position, distinguish themselves from the poor and miserable mass of the city living under the Nazi occupation.

---

29   See alternative performances of the modern in the fourth chapter.

30   Popular actress of commercial cinema and theatre, who was known in the public discourse as "national star".

Antigoni can now speak freely about what embarrasses her leftist daughter, who was a member of *KKE*[31] youth during her student years. On the contrary, Antigoni's parents and Antigoni herself were eager followers of the royal family of Greece:

> "My mother, sweetheart, spent the night on Areopagitou street, outside the current presidential palace, to attend the crowning of the new King Constantine II of Greece."

Eri did no housework. She had a maid in the "old house" at Vardari neighborhood, a young girl from a village, a stepchild who had the role of a servant.[32] The servant and Antigoni, Eri's adopted daughter, used to sleep "feet to feet" on the "combination couch-chest" of the living room,[33] as there were no more bedrooms on their ground floor apartment of a two-floor building. The other parts of the building were rented and contributed significantly to the income of this household. As a young student at Valagianni school, Antigoni is invited to homes of bourgeois doctors and lawyers, impressed by the rich decoration of these houses in the city center. In parallel, the daughter attends ballet classes and enrolls at a very young age at Triantafyllidis theater school. As Antigoni's daughter characteristically says, Eri "destined her to become a Karezi, a Vougiouklaki, a Zoe Laskari"[34], but since a very young age she wished to become a *noikokyra* and mother.

Before finishing school, Antigoni got pregnant by Socratis and even though this was a scandal in that era, her mother supported her. But life at the home of her mother-in-law is not easy for the "spoiled"[35] only daughter of Eri. Her mother-in-law needed some help with the hard daily work of taking care of a house and three men, who needed clean clothes and meals on time. The regular bath at the thermal baths soon becomes the object of negative criticism while washing and ironing shirts and underwear are considered self-evident tasks. Within the context of the "Greek household" code (Papataxiarchis, 2006a), the young woman had to integrate into the gender-based distribution of housework aiming at increasing the family profit. Antigoni complies with the biopolitical technology of discipline exercised by her mother-in-law, finding in this way of living her subsequent role of mother and wife, which, as we will see later, she plays through the performance of modernity

---

31   Communist Party of Greece (translator's note).

32   On stepchildren and the role of young girls from the provinces see the interesting study of Pothiti Hantzaroula (2002, 2012).

33   On the absence of children's rooms in the apartments of Toumba and the use of multi-use furniture for this purpose see fourth chapter.

34   Popular actresses of commercial Greek cinema.

35   This term is used by Antigoni's husband in his letters to her. He associates this term with his anxiety about the future of their relationship and his ability to meet Antigoni's requirements within the context of married life.

in the post-war context of getting a modern apartment and establishing a separate household.

Antigoni made another pause and hesitated before telling me about the way in which she lived in the 1960s. Her daughter encourages her to proceed:

"Now you can tell this person, what I told you is not to tell the poor women in the village. You know, she used to go to the village and tell these women, who are oddball".

Antigoni: "Yes, my sweetheart. But you know why? Because it was the 1960s, when we had no light. In the 1960s, I already had a dishwasher and a mixer, my sweetheart. Look, here is my mixer. I bought it for three thousand drachmas then, and when we came here to Toumba, they told my husband: 'but what can you expect from a woman who is willing to pay three thousand drachmas for a mixer?' There you go!!!" (contemptuous gesture with the hands)

Figure 27: Antigoni's favourite cookbooks.

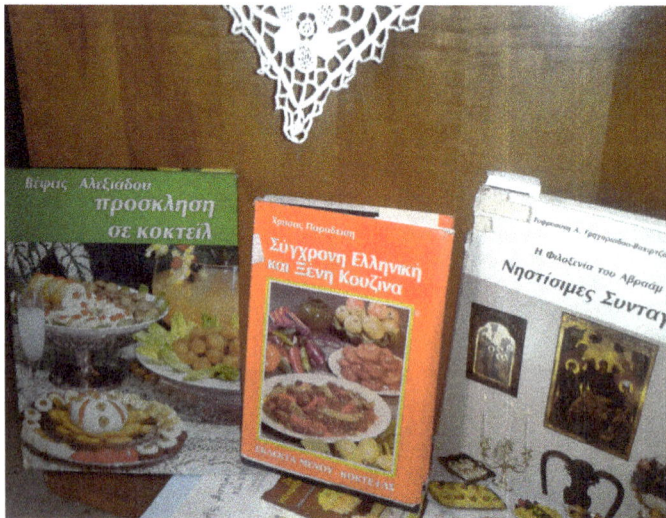

Source: Photo by Miltiadis Zermpoulis.

What based on typical sociological analyses looks like a showy consumption could be seen through the materiality of the mixer and the action of the object (Miller, 2005; Gell, 1998) within the context of establishing the modern subject of *noikokyra* through indicated practices. From the point of view of "self-presentation" (Herzfeld, 1998), Antigoni reproduces discursively on the beach, in her conflicts with the oddball women of the village, but also in a performing way at home, through the use and decoration of these things, her identification with the subjectifications of "making" (Vlachoutsikou, 1999), not only within the context of the individual household, but overall in relation to the challenge of integrating the country into the western way of living.[36]

An indication of this intention is that she places three cooking books, one of them by Vefa Alexiadou[37] (see Figure 27), on the shelf that connects the official space of the living room with the space of the kitchen in the informant's apartment, as it can be seen on the above pictures. Sutton and Vornelis (2009) in their very interesting ethnography on the conceptualizations on TV cooking shows of Vefa Alexiadou and Ilias Mamalakis within the cultural context of the provincial society of Kalymnos and urban life in Thessaloniki reach the very interesting conclusion that the dislike of some people from Thessaloniki for the product that Alexiadou suggests is linked to the romantic attitude of an urban society that seeks what has been lost and is still considered traditional, opting for the "nationalist romanticism" that Mamalakis reproduces in his shows. On the contrary, people from Kalymnos prefer the shows of Vefa, as she manages to transform – according to people from Thessaloniki she "blurs" – the limits of what is authentically Greek with what is considered foreign-European. Within the context of my own ethnography, which concerns the establishment of subjectivities in the first post-war decades, "fanciful"[38] Vefa Alexiadou of the above ethnography (2009), who "blurs the cultural limits", remaining, however, stable in the gender-based dimension of space, performs in a performing way in her kitchen, just like Antigoni in the field, the subjectivity of modern *noikokyra* within the context of post-war urbanization and westernization. This performing act (Bultler, 2009) consists in the appearance of an always well-groomed woman, wearing expensive and gold jewels, hairstyle at the hairdresser's, expensive clothes, loyal to the orthodox tradition, and finally westernized *noikokyra*, who has a duty to take care of her husband, children and grandchildren through her domestic and public[39] work.

Things for Antigoni have not always been easy. In 1955, her father-in-law had borrowed money and after the revaluation of the British pound his debt doubled.

---

36   On *DEI's* "civilizing" program and formal speeches about westernization and development see the above subchapter.

37   Vefa Alexiadou is known as a luminary of Greek cuisine. She is a best-selling author, has published many cookbooks in Greece, regularly writes articles for various magazines and used to have her own TV show for many years.

38   This characterization belongs to an informant from Thessaloniki in the ethnography by Sutton and Vornelis (2009).

39   I am referring to dealing with all financial and social tasks, such as grocery shopping, transactions with banks, communication with school teachers or university professors, etc. The *noikokyra* of the *noikokyraioi* moves inside and outside home, always stylish, aiming at the achievement of family objectives.

The affluence of the family of her in-laws was threatened. Her mother-in-law was a particularly proud person, and this led her to locking herself in the house for a long period:

> "She used to spend time with the 'inferior' ladies of the neighborhood, so that she could feel better. At a certain point, her sister invited her home for dinner. [40] She asked her over the phone to put on her good coat, which was in the closet covered with sheets. She refused to pay that visit. It was going to be a dinner with head-masters, teachers, etc., and because her sister asked her to put on her good coat she was offended."

Antigoni got married to Socratis when she was only seventeen years old. In the hundreds of letters she showed me, young Socratis was worried because he didn't know if he would manage to satisfy the "spoiled" girl. At the beginning, as the couple could not afford a house, they lived with Socratis's parents at their home. As we saw also in the ethnographic examples of Toumba, they initially bought only the bedroom: *"We had to save some money to be able to make 'prokopi' (prosper)."*

Figure 28: The suitcase with the letters from Socratis.

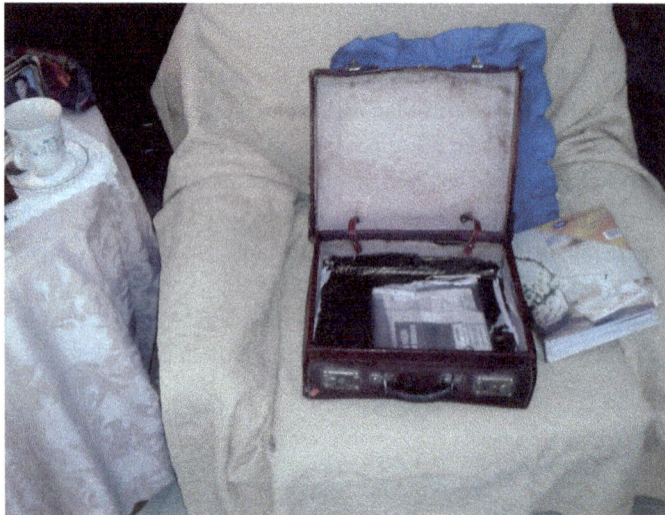

Source: Photo by Miltiadis Zermpoulis.

---

40   At this point she means the sister of her mother-in-law, who belonged, according to the informant's narration, to the class of "good homes", see third chapter.

Her mother-in-law gave her a room behind, with a view to the kitchens and toilets of the hotels on Ptolemaion street. Outside their door she placed a couch, where Socratis's older brother, still unmarried, would sleep.[41] A particularly descriptive and characteristic scene was when the new *Stromatex* mattress was delivered to the house of Socratis's family. The neighbors came out on the balconies, ecstatic to see a king-size modern mattress. The goal of Antigoni is to create her own "tidy" and "noble" home, just like the one her friends and relatives had. Soon, when she had her second child, she moved to one of the small apartments that her father rented at her parents' house. Antigoni tells me the story of a classmate of hers from the Valagianni private school, who was the daughter of a well-known textile businessman, about when she went to Antigoni's home to pay a visit. This narration is indicative of the way in which the informant adopts and progressively shapes specific consumption behaviors, imitating the cultural style of the "good homes" of the city:

> "Imagine, her first apartment was above the restaurant of "Stratis".[42] When she got married, she moved to an apartment across Mitropoli. This is where I saw cretonne for the first time – guys, what a home she had – what furniture – I was so amazed! The dining table was like this and above there was a... It was summer, she had patterned cretonne, because below she had silk fabric!!! My sweetheart, when I had my own home, with an iron bed and carpet, I also wanted to have cretonne there. I made a cretonne drape and on top of it I also placed the carpet not to spot the cretonne fabric; Varvara, a friend, used to come, we were also relatives, her father was a doctor. Yes, it was like this, I have so many stories to tell! There, on Ptolemaion street, there is her home. I put another one on top, not to spot the cretonne fabric."[43]

During the reconstruction period, the informant moved to a new neighborhood, where it was said that the apartments were cheap. With her father's help and by means of bills of exchange, in 1964, she bought a newly built apartment of 110 square meters in Toumba: *"It must have been one of the first apartment buildings, because all around there were low houses and fields."*

The house was very cheap compared to those of her friends who moved mostly to the area of Faliro. Antigoni was hugely stressed because of this fact; for this rea-

---

41   Here we notice the control of the sexuality of the young couple through the spatial arrangement of the bed of the unmarried brother of Socratis, see Giannakopoulos (2001).

42   Well-known high-society restaurant on Nikis avenue, which was mentioned also by other informants of the city center. It usually attracted the urban families of the city on Sundays. Restaurant "Stratis" and patisserie "Flokas" were two landmarks of Thessaloniki of the 1960s mentioned by most informants.

43   At this point we see what other studies have pointed out about the practices of imitation and wrong, due to ignorance and fear, use of urban taste by the petty bourgeois, see Bourdieu (2006).

son, at least the decoration of the apartment had to meet the standards of her circle of acquaintances. I will cite at this point a big excerpt from Antigoni's narration
regarding the features of the new apartment in Toumba, which is indicative of the
type of subjectification that takes place through the interaction of the subject with
the material world of the apartment:

> Antigoni: "[...] we gave one hundred thousand more for bathroom floors, because the san-
> itary articles were too simple. The bathtub, the sink, the bidet, they were all combined,
> with little pink flowers, with the tiles."
>
> Where could you buy these items?
>
> Antigoni: "A person named Iakovos sold these items, – I remember his name, Iakovos–, he
> sold expensive sanitary articles."
>
> Did you have a bathtub at the old house?
>
> Antigoni: "Of course not, my sweetheart, we used to go to the baths of Foinikas. It was
> called "fasina". So, when I moved there as a daughter-in-law, I knew that every week I
> had to go to the baths, and when I got married, my mother gave me a bathrobe, a bath
> cup and all these things, so the first week I prepared this little suitcase. I went there, then
> next week (how was I going to take a bath?) They asked me "Are you going again to the
> baths? Use the bathroom." It is true that their bathroom was quite big; they used to heat
> up the water and this is where they took their bath. At my parental home we had a laun-
> dry room, which also had a cauldron, and therefore, in-between I could also take a bath
> there, so as not to go to the baths all the time. The first thing I bought after the fridge was
> a washing machine."
>
> This must have been too much in that era, is this correct?
>
> Antigoni: "Yes, too much! But other women had it, I had already seen it, look, I saw that
> the Jewish lady had it. The other ladies used to hire a woman. Ms Eleni, an unforgettable
> lady – also at my parental home we used to have a woman, who was doing the laundry.
> And then my mother bought me a Service – I cannot forget it – this is how it was called. It
> was composed of two bins. You had to place the laundry in the first bin – cla cloucla clou
> – it was like a washtub."
>
> Was there an advertisement for this one? Did anyone go to people's houses to show it?
>
> Antigoni: "Yes, of course, they came here to show us. And there was an advertisement as
> well. Few people bought it at that time. And you had to take the wet laundry from one
> bin, you could leave it for as long as you wished, and you could stop the washing when you
> wished – and put it into the other bin – and you had to turn it and it would squeeze the
> laundry. It was like a washtub, it was very practical.[44] There was no need to throw the
> water away, you could take the clean laundry from the back side, then you could wash the
> dark laundry and then the dusters, to give just an example, like you did with a washtub,

---

44   It is worth noting the consonance of this ethnographic example with the formal speeches
of *DEI* "civilizing" program, presented in the previous subchapter.

you took out the white laundry and added the dark clothes, you see what I mean? This was the way... Then we came to Toumba, with our washing machines and everything. We had wooden mosaic parquet flooring, it still exists. And the bedrooms had wooden floors of course, the kitchen had tiles, not a mosaic, and the corridor outside had a mosaic parquet floor. The funny thing was with the bathroom, where the plumbers didn't know what the bidet was for, so they didn't place it. I come and go, watching them, the bidet was not placed. They assembled the sinks, and all the rest. I asked them, guys, why did you leave this out? "Eh, what is this for, lady?" What could I tell him? I said: look, we are going to use this to wash our feet. "Your feet?, he asked" I said: Look, put it here, where there is empty space and leave it there; then, when he placed it and sat on it, they got mad. They wondered... What is it going on here? This is how people were! Then, when the kitchen was delivered, it was a Formica kitchen, but what Formica? I ordered it at a carpenter, who made this for me, in this color, Formica; my daughter had it until recently. The kitchen measured four by three meters, it was very big. This is where I kept my fridge, my cooker, my washing machine. The neighboors came to see, they were curious, they had never seen such things before. In the kitchen, I also had a couch. It was a habitable kitchen with an oil stove. I had three stoves; the only room where there was no stove was the bedroom. Let me tell you another thing now. This house was built from the foundations. We get to the third floor, we took two apartments, and it became 110 meters, a small and a smaller one. And I come here, my son, and what do I see? Can you see this beam? The living room was six meters, huge living room, six by four meters. And then, there was one more room with sliding doors for the casual room, this how we used to call it. There a was a stove there and a casual living room and inside the dining room and the main living room. But this beam would go across, and I got mad when I realized this. Meanwhile, Z... is a well-known architect, who started working in that period. I asked him: what is this? Ah, he told me, "it will be closed here". Meaning, from five meters, my living room will be three meters wide and six meters long and here in the corridor, there will be a door, with a second bathroom, because there was already a main bathroom. Here the corridor, and here the door. I said, but what door are you talking about? This is crazy!!! Two doors, sweetheart!!! Here, you would enter the corridor and bathroom and here you would enter the living room. And they had started laying the bricks. I stepped with my foot and the bricks started falling. He said "you have to pay double for this!" I will even pay it four times, I said. May I ask, sir, I said. The landowner, to build a robust house he placed... And indeed, it was a robust house, when there was the earthquake, it resulted green. He said "here". I said: alright, leave it there, you will not build this part. And I went to the contractor. And Z... came as well, and I told them: look, this house will not receive people from Toumba, we will receive people from the city center, who already have houses on Vasilissis Olgas avenue, as you may understand Mr Z..., it's not in your interest, and I don't know how we can deal with this. And he gives me, my sweetheart, ten thousand drachmas. Ten thousand drachmas, why? To bring an interior designer, who would close it. The interior designer came, and he took the amount of ten thousand. Mr Aristeidis, absent! A certain Miltiadis came, supposedly to close it. Meanwhile they asked for an additional amount of three thousand to paint it, for extra painting. We had already bought the house for 150 000 drachmas, and we had spent another 100 000. It was two hundred fifty thousand for the plot, as it was, with his own works, let's say, then I paid another hundred thousand, and we paid a bill of exchange, alright, but enough is enough. My dad gave me another 10 000 for the floors, they requested an additional amount of money for the materials. So... I didn't have the right to bring my own painter, if he didn't do it; although we had agreed on the amount of two thousand, he asked for three thousand. No, I told him, you will not do it. So, I stayed, for approximately one year, my son, with the beam hanging, and the walls as they had been painted initially when the building was constructed. Nothing! I only placed the floors because there were no floors, but only the floors. It was not possible. And then I got in touch with Miltiadis, who was the best painter in Thessaloniki; I can no longer remember who recommended him to me, anyway. So, this young man came, he had come from Germany, and you know what he did, son? This part you see here, he repaired it with a plasterboard. I want you one day to go to my daughter's place to see it, so, he did it with a plasterboard, and he placed hidden lights in there, and this space from here to there is so beautiful. And he repaired this, and he painted, Miltiadis, he did a great job, coated with stucco! But the amount of money he took; ten thousand went to this. We spent most of the time in the casual living room because we had the stove there. When I asked my daughter to bring something from the living room, she got angry, it was freezing cold. And the frames were of really bad quality. When it was windy, they opened by themselves. We bought it because we wanted to have a big house. And then we needed stoves to keep it warm, the living room remained closed. We spent our time in the kitchen, we didn't even have a television, and in the children's room only where there was a stove. And we used to read, and eat, and do everything there. Then in the evening, we used to light up the stove in the casual living room, there was a sliding door there."

So, you kept the main living room closed?

Antigoni: "I told her: please go to the living room, please do this, please bring me..."

Daughter: "Are you crazy? Better if you send me across the street... (Laughter)" It was that cold! Really cold. Freezing cold."

And you opened the main living room only for celebrations?

Antigoni: "National holidays and anniversaries! Yes, meaning, it did not exist... When I had guests, on Saturdays, etc. [...]."

As it can be seen from the above example, Antigoni wishes to be part of a social group of people characterized by a specific way of living. The informant's consumption practices are indicative of the way these take place in a country that seeks to transform and modernize. Antigoni tries many different things and looks for solutions, to meet the requirements and hegemonic expectations of the society, to which she seeks to belong. It is interesting to note the progressive way of imitating practices that the subject wishes to become familiar with and copy. The result is never identical to the original, but it is close to it. Usually, the imitation effort is positive for the subject: the effort to achieve goals can potentially transform and improve the subject. Besides, the goal within the specific post-war social and political context is something better and higher, mainly through policies of deprivation and targeted investment of the accumulated capital.

Her choice to mention specific experiences from her life, knowing that my study focuses on *petty bourgeoisism* and the establishment of a lifestyle within the context of post-war policies for the financial and political reconstruction of the country shows the conscious way in which she materializes these choices, dealing critically with the term I bring to the field. What I and others describe as "petty bourgeois", she reverses, presenting the version of the proud *noikokyraioi* of the city, who supported and helped the country to develop through their savings and investments in the country's economy. People like Antigoni managed to make their childhood dreams come true and move to the last stage of their life having laid the foundations for the generations to come. Finally, I cite as an example the below excerpt from the narration of the informant and her reflective attitude towards the formal discourses about *petty bourgeoisism*. [45] Her opinion about the characteristics of the *noikokyraioi* presents interesting repetitions and consonance with the way in which Potamianos (2015)[46], defined the *noikokyraioi* in his social history about the establishment of this particular class in Athens at the end of the 19th century:

> "[...] We were, allow me to say, the good class... The middle class! Private schools for me, colleges for children. All members of this middle class – the good class – had their own businesses, they were professionals. Civil servants were poor, my darling. I'll give you an example, so you understand how underestimated public positions were. What really counted was market networks, the networks of the *noikokyraioi* who had a good face in society and pulled the strings [...]."

---

45   On the formal discourse about *petty bourgeoisism* and conceptualization of the Greek class specifics, see second chapter.

46   At this point, it is useful to mention that Professor Voutira, member of the jury of my thesis, pointed out on several occasions the differentiation of this class that Venizelos established in Northern Greece through successful programs of integration of refugees. According to Prof. Voutira, most of the sociological studies dealing with the Greek *petty bourgeoisism* as class specifics concern the example of old Greece; therefore, in the example of Thessaloniki it is important to understand the importance of northern borders and the threat they present in shaping this social formation.

5.2 Employees versus employees: daily stories of bureaucratic disobedience in post-war *DEI*

The reconstruction and rationalization of electricity production and distribution at the beginning of the 1950s with the foundation of Public Power Corporation (*DEI*) were among the main objectives of the American plans for the recovery of the Greek economy that had been destroyed by the war (Pantelakis, 1991; Tsotsoros, 1995). As we saw also in the previous chapter, *DEI* was the precursor company for the Greek post-war development and *DEI* employees were charged with the "sacred objective" of this difficult venture of "modernization" of the Greek economy.

At this point, I would like to cite an indicative excerpt from the speech[47] of the *DEI* Director of the Prefecture of Macedonia-Thrace from the corporate archives, which defines precisely the content of those duties and responsibilities that every civil servant that works in the most important post-war service of Greece takes up due to his/her role:

> "I think you will all agree with me that we should not consider ourselves as simple employees having the obligations of a diligent salaried worker. We were entrusted with the challenging but also beautiful task to offer something more than the simple duties of each worker. We were chosen to offer as much as possible to ensure better living conditions for all residents of our country, and especially for the residents of the countryside. This mission, which I am sure that will fill your hearts, as it fills mine, with joy, must make us proud and inspire us to take the decision not to save efforts to justify the hopes we were entrusted with." (*DEI* Historical Archive/ ΙΑΔΗΜ-Θ/ΔΕΗ Folder 15/1,15/2)[48]

The funding provided for by the Marshall Plan (1948) and the American know-how provided the guarantee and the safe foundations on which this state service would be set up and operate. I cite as an example one more excerpt from the speech[49] of the *DEI* Director of the Prefecture of Macedonia – Thrace dated 1958, which is enlightening about the precise role of the American Government and the Organisation for European Economic Cooperation in shaping this energy program promising the modernization of the country and equal development within the context of post-war capitalism. The participation of Americans and Europeans in the establishment of this service would provide a guarantee for its perfect operation according to the standards of an imaginary constructed, as we will see below, "western bureaucracy":

---

47   Speech of Head of *DEI*, Prefecture of Macedonia-Thrace 30/01/1957 in the 2nd Panhellenic Conference of *DEI* executives, see ΙΑΔΗΜ-Θ/ΔΕΗ, folder 15/1,15/2.

48   Translation into English of the original speech written in Greek.

49   See ΙΑΔΗΜ-Θ/ΔΕΗ Folder Speeches 1958/ Excerpt of the speech of Director of Prefecture of Macedonia-Thrace *DEI*.

"[...] This perfectly rational reflection and perfectly radical plan resulted from the funding provided by the Marshall plan to financially support Europe in general and our country in particular; as a result a Greek energy plan was established, which was approved first by the Organisation for European Economic Cooperation and then by the American Economic Cooperation Administration, E.C.A. [...] *DEI* organization was a project of American specialist consultants. In 1950, the then Greek Government signed a contract with the American company EBASCO SER-VICES INC., which was called to execute the works that constitute the First Energy program of the country studied by EBASCO: it initially included works of 220 million dollar value, but later the budget was reduced to finally include works of 125 million dollars. The cut was due to the review of the aid plan, which was provided by the American Government to the European countries, and was the result of new reflections of the then American Government."

This specific "rhetoric" of *DEI*, as it results from the formal speeches of the company, establishes an "imaginary us", which can be understood within the context of "cultural intimacy", as this is specified by Herzfeld (1992, p. 80) in his study on bureaucracy. These corporate speeches are not addressed only to the corporate staff, but also to all these people that would address them from that moment on. Staff and citizens confront every day in the simple transactions with the imperative of this dominant "rhetoric", establishing and re-establishing identities that distinguish the personal from the public and collective self of the *DEI* employee.

Some anthropologists have stressed the non-existence of such distinction, which though, at the level of everyday practices and performance of the role of state representative or citizen respectively, may influence the outcome of any case towards one or the other direction (Nujiten & Anders, 2007, p. 10; Haller & Shore, 2005, p. 4). To prove this argument, I cite an example from the correspondence folder of the *DEI* Director of the Prefecture of Macedonia – Thrace, which concerns a dispute between service employees and professionals cooperating with the service. It is interesting to focus on the arguments but also on the representations of self, through which interesting cultural constructions are established creatively and actively. The concept of social poetics proposed by Herzfeld (1997, 2008) is particularly useful for our analysis at this point, to understand the different discourses and subjectivities dynamically established in the below dispute:

"We cannot describe the indignation we contractors electricians feel. While until now F... was torturing us to issue the orders and if we didn't bribe him he would delay the payment, now with the submission of the plans you cannot imagine what is going on, we submitted the plans 15 days ago and they have not been checked yet, whoever bribes him finishes his job easily, it is a pity and a shame, but what happens here is also unfair, we are determined to denounce this to the press, we have children, we cannot accept that a mischievous and immoral employee like F.... tortures us."[50]

The discourses of the electricians cooperating with *DEI* establish another reality, which does not comply with the dominant discourses of *DEI*, which, as we have already mentioned, construct culturally the exemplary employee of western bureaucracy (Weber, 1946, 2006), who must fulfil his/her duties and diligently serve the imperative of modernization of the country.

The distinction made in the above example between a state apparatus, for which there is the requirement to be impartial and fair for the simple citizen, whose interests have priority and who should be immediately served, is directly linked with the imaginary character of establishment of a western national state, which defends and takes care of the civil society that is distant from it, maintaining and reproducing through different "statism" languages, such as institutional symbolisms, texts and discourses, images, and also everyday performances, its indisputable existence and unified substance (Hansen & Stepputat, 2001, pp. 1–8). There is a characteristic style in the answer of the service, which reconstructs, through its representative, and eventually defends the dominant social construction for it:

"In no case has there been or is there an intentional delay in the completion of the statements of installations to check the internal electrical installations. [...] In our opinion, the whole trouble created was caused by some extremist elements of the Association of Contractors Electricians, who for purely self-serving purposes and to create an effect push their colleagues to inappropriate actions, with the pretext of issuing support materials. Regarding the latest and most important accusation of bribery against Mr F...,[51] we have neither a proof nor a simple indication that something like this is taking or has taken place."[52]

The employees of this specific post-war state service serving the imperative of modernization and capitalist development of the country must be educated and disciplined, in order to serve in the most efficient and persuasive way the national purpose, under which the state and civil society are linked to form a unified entity. The national purpose of the Greek reconstruction and salvation, intermediated by American, as we saw above, technologies of development, state reorganization and ratio-

---

50   15.5.59/ Letter of electrician engineers of Thessaloniki to the Management of *DEI* / Folder Management Correspondence.

51   In the whole thesis, informants' real names have been replaced by fictitious names. The same practice is followed for the names appearing in *DEI* archives, in order to protect the anonymity of these people.

52   See ΙΑΔΗΜ-Θ/ΔΕΗ (*DEI* Historical Archive Thessaloniki) /Folder "Confidential letter of the Management of Region of Thessaloniki to the Management of Prefecture of Macedonia – Thrace".

nalization within the context of cold-war demonization of the leftist danger[53], is not diffused to society only at the flowing and easily convertible level of politics and public discourses, as described by Laclau and Mouffe (2001), but on the contrary, as it results from the investigation of the *DEI* archive, it is the result of daily practices of assimilation and implementation of the ideas among numerous active people who interact on the occasion of the energy and development activity of the company. I cite the following example:

> "Internal Correspondence Confidential
> To: Directorate of Region of Macedonia-Thrace
> From: S... I...
> Subject: Disobedience of employee
> We would like to inform you that the employee of the General Warehouses of the Region (Slaughterhouses) D... A... visited the above-mentioned Warehouse during inappropriate and non-working hours (in the afternoon and evening), often accompanied by women of suspicious morality. To the remarks of the guards, he answered that he suffered from insomnia and carried out raids to check if they were sleeping." (*DEI* Historical Archive /Folder ΙΑΔΗΜ-Θ/ΔΕΗ) [54]

Within the context of post-war "governmentality" in Foucault's (2006, pp. 131–143) terms, the Greek post-civil-war society had to be "transformed" through the implementation of drastic biopolitical technologies that would change its everyday life and activity, so that the state as a whole could respond to the ideal "western development standards". Besides, *DEI*, as it results from the archives of the speeches of the CEO and those of the disciplinary proceedings and sentences, aimed at communicating the state narrative, which consisted in modernizing citizens' everyday life and making it easier. At the same time, being the largest public corporation, it had to contribute to the almost obsessed pursuit of post-civil-war governments for modernization and full integration into the capitalist economies of Europe and America. I cite three indicative examples from the disciplinary proceedings folders[55], to show the type of behaviors that create a problem in the corporate functioning, and also the biopolitical technologies of discipline and reinstatement of employees to serving the public interest, as this is performed in the official corporate discourses:

---

53   See in detail second chapter: *"'Transformation' and 'petty bourgeoisism'. The Greek class distinctiveness and theories of 'underdevelopment'"*.

54   See ΙΑΔΗΜ-Θ/ΔΕΗ (Historical Archive *DEI* Thessaloniki) Folder 7. Disciplinary proceedings.

55   op. cit.

Example 1[56]

Directorate of Region Macedonia-Thrace

Office of legal affairs

Undisciplined behavior of pump operator P... M....

Confidential

27 September 1960

From the interrogation conducted on the incident between I... and M... the following was concluded:

Pump operator M... needed to go to the bathroom and kindly asked engineer S... to replace him. A risk of fall of the water was observed and upon observations from employees who noticed this, M... went immediately to open the hydrants. [...] It seems that during the relevant discussion M... blamed Mr I... for the risk of fall of the water. This frustrated Mr I..., and when M... was having lunch, he ordered him to leave the service and as he was late in doing so he dragged him. [...] M... in his defence claimed that he had been hit by Mr I..., but this was not testified by anyone else. Only engineer S... testifies that Mr I... attacked and dragged M.... The allegation in the report of Mr I... that M... attacked him with a plank is denied by the witnesses.

Example 2

Subject: Written reprimand

Further to our document number E/344/28-5-60 addressed to you, by which you were called to answer why during the execution of your service on 5.4.1960 you climbed on a pole of the network to perform the connection to the supply without using the special flexible gloves and, as a result, you suffered a light electric shock [...]

Example 3

Defence of Ms E. P.

Indeed, I left my office only for five minutes, after having received the relevant authorization to do so from Mr M., who stated that he was replacing Mr O. in his absence. When I came back Mr O. was there and reprimanded me because I was not in my office. I replied that, following authorization, I left my office for a serious family reason and specifically to collect money due to my family from the Office located in Building D and that for this reason I was absent for only 5 minutes. Mr O. continued reprimanding me and stated that I should no longer be absent for any reason. I replied that I cannot guarantee this because if there is force majeure and

---

56   This is an exact translation of the reports into English by removing the real names of the civil servants, see ΙΑΔΗΜ-Θ/ΔΕΗ (*DEI* Historical Archive Thessaloniki) / Folder 7 "Disciplinary proceedings".

need to be absent, I will ask for authorization again and I will be absent. [...] Mr O.'s reply was "Stop being disrespectful. Do you understand you are being disrespectful? Do you want me to fire you from the Office?" I was astounded to hear this and I replied that if you fire me there will be another office to hire me, because I sweat to earn this money...

As it can be seen from the above three examples, the service through its disciplinary body and CEO, is called to deal with such simple daily cases of "disobedience" and "rearrangement" of the prescriptive corporate discourses, prior to a disruption of its prevailing image of a "healthy" member of the unified national entity aiming at serving the collective purpose of development (Herzfeld, 1992, pp. 23–40). The employees controlled and perceived by the supervision governors as threatening the image of the single and top-down centralized administration are sentenced, moved, or banished from the single entity because they are seen as a foreign body.

Herzfeld (1992) describes the modalities in which bureaucratic "indifference" is produced as a stereotype in citizens' discourses and expectations, as well as in the practices of civil servants that are charged with its reproduction because of their role. Indifference and lack of interest in the human problem and weakness coexist most of the time with political entities and schemes representing democratic and isonomic ideals (Herzfeld, 1992, p. 1). *DEI's* aim is to bring "civilization" and "light" to people's homes by penalizing and sentencing the personal attitude and singularity of its employees. Late arrival to the workplace, wrong appearance, inappropriate behavior towards clients, anything that eventually reveals the human side of the indifferent, incorruptible, and impartial representative of the state must be eradicated.

DEI's archive in Thessaloniki with the individual folders of the corporate employees, the various cases in which they are involved and for which they are punished, the archives of *DEI's* office of public relations and in particular the archives that concern the corporate policy and administration from 1940 to 1974 give the possibility of a historic ethnographic representation of the everyday life and functioning of a state corporation, as well as of its relationship and impact on the simple citizens of the region of Macedonia.

Before I close this subchapter, I would like to use a short story of the dispute of a lower employee with a former parliamentarian of *ERE* to refer to a different hegemonic dimension of the cultural construction that is diffused through the official speeches of the corporation. This dominant cultural construction is directly associated with the hegemonic ideology of the Greek state that defends the "national pride" versus the potential prevalence of "Communism" already since the era of its governance by Eleftherios Venizelos, but particularly also as a result of the civil war during the first post-war decades.[57] This threat concerns particularly Northern Greece and is related to the nationalist ideology of the state and the expectation of annexation of additional territories of the former Ottoman empire.[58]

This dispute between the lower *DEI* employee and the former member of the parliament of *ERE* showcases maybe in the best possible way the extent of the political and social division that characterized post-war society, but also the role of the state and that of people in its development and establishment. The case of employee P… and his dispute with the lawyer and former parliamentarian of *ERE* K. G… is probably one of the most indicative ones regarding the function and dynamic use of discourses through which the state of "nationalist development" is reproduced in the everyday relationships of citizens with the administration; as it can be seen from this example, this state is threatened by this employee, who, with his actions, tries to put in danger the honor and reputation of the citizen who fights for the good of the country.

This short story shows in the most comprehensible way how the post-war state is associated, at least at discursive level, with the conservative party of *ERE*, which pursues, with the help of western powers, the reconstruction of Greece in the way of other capitalist states.

A simple *DEI* operator is accused by a former parliamentarian of *ERE* of cutting of the electricity supply in the home of this "special" citizen and more specifically at the dental surgery of the politician's daughter, creating problems of a "moral and practical nature" to him and his daughter. As we can read in the replying telegram dated 24 October 1960 of the CEO of *DEI* to the former politician, the latter neglected to sign the relevant contract, on which he had been informed by the special form distributed by the service to the interested parties, in order to change the direct current of his property into alternating.[59] According to the directors of the state service, because of the politician's negligence, there is no liability for the employee for the decision to proceed to the cut-off, but specifically for the time at which this took place, because it excluded the possibility of arrangement and agreement.

In his letter to the director, the former politician analyses the reasons for his indignation, also expressing his concern about the commitment of this employee to the national ambitious project of the government. G… stresses already at the beginning of his letter, which he also sent to the prosecutor of the magistrate's court of Edessa, that, in his opinion, this employee is classified among those who forget "their obligations towards the *DEI* clients and their high mission". We therefore see that the citizen – former political representative of the state – reproduces the idea

---

57   See second chapter: "'Transformation' and 'petty bourgeoisism'. The Greek class distinctiveness and theories of 'underdevelopment'".

58   Op. cit.

59   ΙΑΔΗΜ-Θ/ΔΕΗ (Historical Archive *DEI* Thessaloniki) / Folder 14.4.

of the unified state and common mission of the employees, addressing top executives of public services. He even underlines that nevertheless he fulfills his obligations and commitment to the state, since he has not chosen to disclose this case to the press, creating thus a problem to the image that the State is trying to convey to the civil society. According to him, such an action could become the object of political exploitation from "anarchist elements" threatening this governance. Referring also to other cases of "arbitrariness" of civil employees against famous fellow citizens, he wonders if the service employs "cryptocommunists", who, in particular in the case of power cutoff at *ERE* premises in Edessa, wish to defame the political party. The citizen closes his letter, signing with the socially and culturally important quality of former member of the parliament, pointing out that the act of power cutoff damaged him mainly at moral level, since his social circle in Edessa and particularly his political opponents make fun of him, considering this treatment is an oxymoron, since the service should treat him differently as a friend of the governing party. In the discourses of the politician, a rather normative bipolar contrast is reproduced, which we have identified also in the discourses of the informant of Toumba,[60] among citizens that because of their communist ideological conviction threaten law-abiding citizens (*noikokyraioi*) [61] who respect and seek the successful outcome of the imperative of post-war development, which in this specific case is expressed through the correct running of *DEI*.[62] As we have seen also in the Introduction[63], the party of conservative rightism has been traditionally linked with the class of *noikokyraioi*. Herzfeld (2008, p. 498) points out that such contrasts concern a rather symbolic polarization since any interested party "invokes the contrasts of the formal discourse to serve personal interests". And he continues by saying that "the ontology of these contrasts does not lie in any "existence" or not of relevant values, but in the extent to which the ability of the interested parties to invoke them with some apparent success – meaning some direct and observed impact on the consequences – covers them temporarily with the clothing of such existence" (2008, p. 499).

At this point, I would like to cite an excerpt of the letter from the member of the parliament to the Director of the Region of Macedonia-Thrace of *DEI*, sent on 21 August 1960:

---

60   See ethnographic examples in third chapter and conceptualization of Red Toumba as opposed to the rightist center.

61   The use of this category is mine, in an effort to understand the consonance between the cultural values of identities reproduced in the field and those reproduced in the *DEI* Historical Archive in Thessaloniki.

62   On the establishment of Communist / Leftist as a "dangerous citizen" see Panourgia (2013).

63   See second chapter: "'Transformation' and 'petty bourgeoisism'. The Greek class distinctiveness and theories of 'underdevelopment'".

"[...] I have the honor (...) at your discretion copy of my telegram report, to the Pros-
ecutor of Magistrates of Edessa to proceed to the legal actions against one of the
DEI employees in Edessa, who neglected their obligations towards the clients of
DEI and their high mission.

I have not contacted the press and I contact you because I do not wish to contribute
to the demagogy of anarchist elements (...) who make sure to take political advantage even of the most trivial incident.

In addition, I wish to inform you of some of the many cases of arbitrariness that
(...) some *DEI* employees commit against the *DEI* clients from Edessa.

They cut off the power at the place of G... F... on the grounds that he had not paid
for the value of electricity consumed. This was not true because he presented the
receipt of full payment. For the same reason, they cut off the power at the premises
of *ERE* at the prefecture of Pella as Secretary-General Mr N... M... informed me, and
I am wondering if *DEI* employs cryptocommunists who wish to defame *ERE* with
such actions. [...] The power cutoff of my own property was immediately taken care
of by your service on the day following the arbitrary cutoff, by reconnecting the
electricity without asking [...]. Dear Director, I was forced to give such extent to
this small incident because it had a great impact on the circles of Edessa, including my political opponents, [...] who laughed at me for the treatment I received
from the agents of your service." (ΙΑΔΗΜ-Θ/ΔΕΗ [*DEI* Historical Archive Thessa-
loniki] / Folder 7. "Director's correspondence")[64]

The citizen-former politician, with his letter to the director of the service and mainly
with the arguments he uses to support his accusations, showcases the network of
power in which civil servants and citizens are involved, as well as the logic governing
these relationships in the specific political and social context of post-war Greece. The
former member of the parliament puts the focus of his arguments on the moral issue
of the cutoff, and more specifically on his position towards those who believe that the
political commitment to the political party – particularly when this is the governing
party – ensures special privileges.

It is also worth noting that the letter is sent to the Director of *DEI* by the father of
the dentist and not the dentist herself, who suffered the consequences of the actions
of the simple employee of *DEI*. The member of the parliament addresses as a man the
director of *DEI*, who is also a man, about the action of an employee who has a lower
position in the state hierarchy. His negligence cannot be due to a human error, but
seems to conceal an ideological convenience, which threatens from inside the state
apparatus and its post-war objectives.

The distinction between simple employees and famous and not-famous employees of the state service, who claim a better treatment in a state and a governance

---

64   At several points, transcription was not possible because of the oldness of the document.

diving citizens into "patriots" and "dangerous gang communists",[65] showcases the modalities through which the "civilizing" and "development" policy of governing the country is daily assimilated and diffused during this period through high level state employees of an important state service, but also through the employees who choose to implement it or resist to it. The state, having at its disposal a "meta-capital" (Bourdieu, 1999), is able to validate or denounce practices and behaviors through its representatives.

Finally, in this subchapter I used excerpts of short stories of employee disputes identified in the archive of the state service of DEI, to showcase consonance and repetitions regarding the cultural representations of the informants in the filed about the establishment of normative standards in the specific context of post-war conditions. The reproduced discourses must be seen and assessed within the context of the rhetoric of a Gramscian (2006, pp. 71–85) hegemonic "civilization" and "westernization", which was formulated several decades later. In parallel, it should be detected in the informants' representations in relation to the evolution of their personal biography and objective-setting during the first post-war decades in Thessaloniki, as they feel or seek through integration practices to be part of a hegemonic normality that seem to have the stamp of the state.

5.2.1 Settlement of refugees or corruption? The production of benefactor citizen through representations of practices of trespassing of public property

Things, places, and people are interconnected in "networks" of mutual influence and dependence, creating, according to Latour (2005), collectivities and flowing interaction groups (Latour, 2005, as cited in Gialouri, 2012, p. 33). According to several social scientists, (Navaro Yashin, 2009; Latour, 2005; Ingold, 2007b; Knappet & Malafouris, 2008; Miller, 2005; Gell, 1998), "action" can be attributed to people as well as to things, which act and determine people's everyday actions. In the interesting anthropological study by Navaro Yashin (2009) about Northern Cyprus, the anthropologist reveals the relationships and influence networks in the specific context of political and historical condition of the division of the island of Cyprus, as these are produced in the everyday relationships of Turkish Cypriots with the personal belongings and residences that Greek Cypriots left behind. The "sorrow" and "melancholy" they feel is explicitly linked with places and objects that have a negative impact on them through daily practices of dwelling and "illegal" possession. According to Gell (1998, as cited in Gialouri, 2012, p. 38), objects are "active", because of their ability to create feelings

---

in people and actively influence their everyday life. Gell (op.cit) provides the characteristic example about the efficiency of a car or other personal belongings that are considered an extension of the human body, in the sense that we use them, to create, just like we do with our natural characteristics, impressions and achieve goals in the social relationships (Gell, 1998, as cited in Gialouri, 2012, p. 39).

Figure 29: A small icon of the Virgin Mary next to the bust of the former Prime Minister and President of the Hellenic Republic Konstantinos Karamanlis. Both objects were placed on top of the informant's safe.

Source: Photo by Miltiadis Zermpoulis.

How can therefore the bust of a former Prime Minister and President of the Republic be associated with the awards and other honorary distinctions that public actors attributed to a citizen for "illegal"[66] actions but with the ultimate purpose of serving the public interest? How are all these objects used within the context of the informant's representations about his social upward mobility in the post-war era and the practices of his social service to the state, producing in his discourses by analogy the state of development and change and the *noikokyraio* – citizen – "benefactor"?

---

66   This adjective is in quotation marks because in this subchapter an effort is made to problematize it. The aim of the thesis is not to assess the actions of this person, but on the occasion of the archive material to problematize the concept of "legal", at least as this is understood and reproduced within the context of developed states, see Haller and Shore (2004).

Two social associations were installed in places that had been expropriated in 1925[67] aiming at the settlement of refugees through the well-intentioned actions of a citizen who made sure that the "plots are not wasted", taking advantage of his personal friendship with the head of a state service. This state employee informed the citizen-friend of his about article 66 of the royal decree, published on 23 May 1960, which provided for the concession of public plots for "purposes of public benefit". At this point, I provide a characteristic excerpt from my conversation with the informant in Toumba, in which it is interesting to focus on the way in which the informant represents the practices of his "offer" to the Greek state:

> Giorgos: "This did not happen with my own money, actions and time. The local association did not have the money to buy its own premises. Due to my profession, I knew, I had found out which plots belonged to the Social Welfare, meaning to the state!!! I took the necessary actions, submitted the applications, whatever was required, travelled to Athens. Therefore, the concession of one plot to p... and another plot to M... was approved thanks to my actions. But to achieve this – I knew the law –, to achieve the concession on behalf of the Social Welfare, one must have settled in it, should possess it in order to receive a concession. By taking a serious risk, because I was a real estate developer, I hired the required teams and fenced the whole plot of M...; in this way, when the Social Welfare employees would arrive, they would see that the plot was in use, possessed by M.... We also issued false certificates, that we had been possessing the plot for X years, etc."
>
> With this same logic, could other people have fenced plots and take them?
>
> Giorgos: "No, the purpose was social. A childhood friend of mine was a head in the Ministry of Social Welfare and knew about this: "Giorgos, don't leave these plots to land-grabbles, why don't you take action? Do something for social purposes in Toumba. This is how I started, and I knew this was not only one plot, but three or four of them in a row. This was my participation. I have awards at home, what you see here is nothing."

Political anthropology (Gledhill, 2013, pp. 1–27; Sharma & Gupta, 2006; Steinmetz, 1999; Nustad & Krohn-Hansen, 2005) and in particular ethnographies studying state culture and power relationships showed in a particularly enlightening way that the state and its citizens are produced in common through discourses and everyday practices between civil servants and citizens and not as two distinct opposed groups, as they were at least presented in political sciences and economy (Torsello, 2011, p. 3; 2015; Nuijten & Anders, 2007, pp. 1–11; Shore & Haller, 2005, pp. 3–6). Giorgos, son of refugees from Istanbul, born in 1930 in the refugee settlement in Kato Toumba, is proud of the numerous awards and honorary distinctions he received for his social activities in Thessaloniki. The social service for the Greek state and particularly the refugee settlement where he was raised is the constant focus of his narration about the transformation of Kato Toumba. But what does a social activity mean at

---

67   See Government Gazette (Greece) / Minist. Dec. 16314/1925.

moral and cultural level and how can this activity justify the breach of civil law in this specific sociopolitical context of cold-war Greece? Nuijten and Anders (2007, p. 2) stress that corruption or a non-moral or arbitrary action is wrongfully approached as negation or refusal of the law of nation-state. They consider that one can contain the other and finally they can be established correspondingly. The "salvation of Greece" constantly mentioned by Giorgos, was his own priority, as well as the priority of the conservative center-right party he is supportive of. Although he started as an "aetopoulo"[68], he soon realized that "Communists" have different interests from the "peaceful *noikokyraioi* and patriot Greeks that seek for the good of family and home country and perceive Greece as a western and European country.[69] As we saw also in the previous chapters, in the post-war political context, anti-communism is produced in parallel with the positive discourses about the West and Europe, to which the country must belong, while the *noikokyraioi* as an interclass ideal type of Greek citizens are those in charge of the unhindered implementation of this policy that will lead Greece to development. *Noikokyraios* is associated with the urban ethics of self-sacrifice, personal pursuit of prosperity that will contribute also to the development and positive change of society.

Figure 30: The materiality of Power in Post-war Greece. Honorary distinctions and photographs with important politicians of Thessaloniki.

Source: Photo by Miltiadis Zermpoulis.

---

68   Children 8 to 15 years old organized in the United Panhellenic Organization of Youth (EPON) a youth wing of the National Liberation Front (EAM) during the Nazi occupation.

69   This shift can be seen also through the fragmentary model of the collective identity introduced by Papataxiarchis (2006a) trying to explain the ways in which the Greek national cultural homogenization is established. In this case, the informant first as a descendant of refugees from Asia Minor and second as a leftist follows practices that integrate him culturally into the imaginary unified national body fighting for the *prokopi* of the Greek people.

Giorgos became a scout at a very young age and was taught the British principles of volunteering and offer to fellow human beings. His awards, his photographs with the political personalities and authorities of the city, the scout trefoil, the bust of the Ethnarch, the metal safe, it's all gathered in his office, where he spends most of his everyday life hours and meets people from the outside world. The objects decorate the office of the successful real estate developer, providing an important social capital for redemption (Bourdieu, 1999, 2008) in his daily contacts, but also in our own relationship.

In anthropology of material culture, it is often difficult to distinguish the point giving rise to the subject's action: is it one and single subject, separate from the objects through which the subject acts? According to Strathern (1988) and her ethnography about gift exchange in Melanesia, but also according to Gell (1998, as cited in Gialouri, 2012, pp. 37–39), regarding the secondary action factors and more specifically the action of artworks, the subject personality is divided and acts through the objects that constitute human body members, playing an equally important part in social relations.

The reasons for social activities and benefaction, but also the experience itself of everyday contact with the state and its employees seems to produce this specific center-right subject-benefactor. The materiality of the award experience and the tangible acknowledgement of his offer, confirmed by the objects in his office, contribute to the reproduction of his self-image. However, the practices of social activity are associated in his discourses with the achievement of the sought social upward mobility, following "honest" pathways and hard "work". The photographs and objects that represent his relationship with the Greek state participate in our discussion as actors in a network of mutual influence, according to Latour (2005), and are in a position to influence, because of their materiality, my judgment for him as well as our relationship.

In his very interesting text about the ethnography of corruption, Giorgio Blundo (2007, p. 35) stresses that the anthropologist, particularly when he/she studies practices that are difficult to observe and tend to take place secretly, must observe the ways and places in which the informant narrates and represents such practices, combining different techniques and methods of observation in addition to participation. The observation of objects and watching the interactive way in which the informant integrated them into our discussion and relationship were quite revealing about the ways in which the social activity and the choice of what was deemed to be the correct pathway in that era produced and reproduced the *noikokyraios*, peaceful and democratic citizen of middle classes. On the other hand, they helped us perceive the materiality of the offer and benefaction, which, although achieved, as we saw earlier, through "illegal" actions, continues to be experienced differently at the level of representation, because of the action and symbolism of the awards of the state, which legalizes and naturalizes practices of corruption aiming at the common good. In this case, customary law justifies and almost rewards the non-compliance with state laws.

The awards, distinctions, dedication plate outside a public administration building of the refugee settlement, where the informant was raised, are the elements that render him, as he also says, "well-known" in the city and among his fellow citizens, and also the elements and consequently led me to him.

The post-war state of "right-wing governance",[70] which is embodied mainly in the bust of the founder of ERE, Konstantinos Karamanlis, which has been placed on the right of the real estate developer's office on his impressive metal safe, is associated with the social and economic change that took place both in the state and in his personal life. After a hard decade of continuous war and financial disaster, Greece experiences, at least in figures, and in the informants' discourses, the desired development and stability. During this period, the informant manages to overcome the "misery and poverty" that characterized his family life before and during the wars and progressively transform them into today's multi-award-winning, center-right, rich real estate developer, who has in his hands a bundle of *charatsia*,[71] which he has to pay within the context of the current crisis as the owner of lots of properties.

Giorgos's father started working in Greece as an itinerant salesman of *lakerda* (salted mackerel), he continued as a grocer on Charilaou street and ended his working life as a supplier of timber in a rented yard near the old railway station. The informant uses the adjectives "peaceful", "democratic" and *"noikokyraios"* to describe his father, who after the liberation from the Nazi and during the civil war became a member of the "association of nationalists" of Kato Toumba, to avoid the semiotic stigma "Toumba-Stalingrad", which, as we saw in the third chapter, divided the refugee settlement from the "center-right" and "pro-European" city center.[72] He re-

---

70   I use terms that were used in the field or terms that can be found in the Greek bibliography of the political transition, mainly in political sciences, sociology and history (see chapter 2) as well as terms broadly used in the media and public discourse. These terms, such as "rightist", "leftist-lazy", *"koukoues* (supporter of the communist party)", *"noikokyraios"*, *"prokommenos* (diligent)", *"antartosymmoritis"* (guerilla), *"eamovoulgaros"* (offensive term used to indicate people of leftist convictions as enemies of the Greek state), *"mikromesaioi* (lower middle classes)", etc., do not constitute analytical categories that anthropologists bring to the field in order to analyze their empirical material. Words and terms are of emic origin and are used by the informants in the field, by public personalities in mass media and television, and by bureaucrats in public documents I use. Gupta (2006, p. 213) stresses the importance of comparison of the discourses and practices of the informants with the discourses produced and diffused at interterritorial level through newspapers and television. They help us integrate the local into the broader sociopolitical context through which it is shaped and produced.

71   The term is widely used in Thessaloniki and in particular in the context of financial crisis and refers to ENFIA property tax.

72   On the civil war and the different ideological groupings and trends in the city of Thessaloniki, one can consult interesting historical studies examining the establishment and con-

members that during the civil war his father enrolled him to scouting and several times he was a victim of *EPON*[73] youth, who were after him and other scouts to hit them:

> "[...]I was one those young boys who welled up when they saw the Greek flag rais-ing and listened to the national anthem, I had patriot feelings. The Communists, instead of raising the Greek flag, raised the red one."

The dedication plate at the administrative building of Toumba informs people pass-ing-by about the relationship of this citizen with the state, but also about his ac-tivity in a specific context of power relationships. Giorgos is not a random citizen. Besides, because of his acquaintance with administrative state employees, he was able to offer selflessly to his fellow citizens and his city and be honored and distin-guished as a benefactor. According to Nuijten and Anders (2007, p. 2), arbitrary and illegal actions should not be treated individually as practices of a corrupted person. On the contrary – and this is the role and comparative advantage of an ethnography of corruption – these behaviors should be treated as potential institutionalized prac-tices taking place in a grid of power relationships, as well as in a system that makes them feasible. Based on their very interesting ethnography at the border of Mexico and America, Heyman and Campbell (2007, pp. 191–193) concluded that corruption cases do not concern individual and random actions of people but are part of sys-temic processes, which are distinguished by a specific rituality and repetitiveness, undermining the law of the state, and blurring the limits between what is illegal and legally correct.

Giorgos is a citizen, who offered and helped, as we saw at the beginning of this subchapter[74], with the production of public spaces, especially due to his professional quality of real estate developer. The perception of this specific practice as help to-wards the state is not an individual one but is confirmed also by the public servants that acknowledge it as such. All together they form the system that produces state

---

tent of concepts such as *"ethnikofron"*, *"antartosymmoritis"* (guerilla) or *"eamovoulgaros"* (of-fensive term used to indicate people of leftist convictions as enemies of the Greek state), but also the facts themselves that later lent in the post-war context the terminologies of confrontation of the public and popular discourse (see Dordanas, 2006, 2012; Voglis, 2014; Michailidis, Nikolakopoulos & Fleischer, 2006).

73 The United Panhellenic Organization of Youth, abbreviated *EPON*, was a Greek resistance organization that was active during the Axis occupation of Greece; it was the youth wing of the National Liberation Front (*EAM*) organization.

74 Two social associations acquired building infrastructure through the trespassing of pieces of land that had been expropriated by the state with the purpose of settlement of refugees. A royal decree of 1960 and some "illegal" trespassing actions made Giorgos's social activity possible.

works, citizen – benefactor and the welfare state that aids, acknowledges and re-wards:

> "All these awards are for the public buildings I did for free, on my own initiative. They wanted to put me into trouble, but they never managed, I was leading everyone. The palace appointed Karamanlis as prime minister, and if Karamanlis pounded his fist on the table no one protested. As minister of public works, he did a lot of works: Egnatia Odos motorway, roads in Chalkidiki (he saved us from floods by constructing the encircling trench)."

A Weber-inspired rational, unified and administratively efficient state (Herzfeld, 1992, pp. 1–4; Nuijten & Anders, 2007, p. 9) is constantly reproduced in his discourses, "the state of Karamanlis", which is on the opposite side of an anarchical society, in which he is a chosen member, particularly because of his selfless offer. The phrases *"I was leading everyone"* and *"they wanted to put me into trouble, but they never managed"* has a supportive function in relation to the ethics of the person within the framework of a specific social and cultural code of reference of this society, in which it seems that personal involvement or civic engagement aiming exclusively at personal interest are not a virtue.

The modalities of representation of corruption practices and more specifically the reasons that justify them and describe them as something different from their formal content in the public discourse can be particularly revealing, as shown by Heinzpeter Znoj's (2007) ethnography in Indonesia. The focus of corruption practices on the "everyday language" (2007, p. 61) can reveal systemic relationships, power relationships, hierarchy, and logic of duty that influence and delimit people's decisions and actions. According to Heinzpeter Znoj (2007, p. 62), subjects use the language of their class and the identity of the social group to which they feel they belong, to describe practices that are legitimized in the specific social structure.

Giorgos uses very often the same verb, in order to describe the choice of some of his childhood friends from Toumba to "get involved" in parties and the State, e.g. as *Eponites*[75] and later *Elasites*[76] during the civil war or those who cooperated with the "hideous", according to him, *tagmatasfalites* (Security Battalions) or even the police of the region during the critical period at the beginning of the 1960s. His father and himself avoided "such trouble" by remaining neutral in this fight; they were "peaceful" and "democratic", while they were always interested in the salvation of their country, which was threatened by national division.[77]

---

75   Members of *EPON* organization.

76   Members of *ELAS*. *ELAS* was the largest and most significant of military organization of the Greek resistance.

77   On the security battalions in Thessaloniki and their protagonists see Venianakis (2016).

At this point, it is worth reflecting on the issues examined by anthropology of law and anthropology of corruption, and in particular the association of law with ethics on the opposite of which corruption is placed as a "immoral act". The latter turns against public interest, at least in the way it is defined by Eurocentric approaches, but also by discourses of technocrats and development organizations seeking to fight it internationally (Nuijten & Anders, 2007; Pardo, 2004, p. 6). More specifically, the World Bank and Transparency International, non-governmental association founded by the World Bank in 1993, aims at fighting worldwide corruption, which they define "as the abuse of public office for private gain" (World Bank, 2002, as quoted in Haller & Shore, 2005, p. 2). Fighting corruption will lead, according to them, to greater transparency and development (Haller & Shore, 2005, p. 2).

Political anthropologists question the validity and usefulness of such definitions in order to understand under which conditions corruption prospers and how it is finally perceived and represented by people (Nuijten & Anders, 2007, pp. 1–10; Haller & Shore, 2005, pp. 1–6). Its constant association with a non-functional public administration and poor governance is, in their opinion, particularly problematic and rather orientalist, as in this way corruption is associated with specific countries, which, according to development theories, present intrinsic governance problems, which increase poverty and inequality, preventing the unhindered functioning of the free market and competition, but at the same time also the implementation of development and modernization programs (op. cit.). These approaches reproduce without fail the colonialist logic, placing geographically and culturally the corruption practices in the worldwide south and worldwide east, proposing solutions through the comparison of different political systems with that ideal type of bureaucracy and governance described by Weber (Haller & Shore, 2005, p. 71).

In the case of Greece, regarding the discourses about *petty bourgeoisism* and the association of the phenomenon or mentality with the clientelist state and financial underdevelopment[78], the above anthropological observations prove to be particularly useful. They reveal the ways and theoretical schemes through which the Greek society and political system were described as cultural differences, integrated also into Eurocentric and problematic approaches of the "Mediterranean other" (Gilmore, 1982; Herzfeld, 1992). *Petty bourgeoisism* was used as a research scheme, in order to explain the difference of Greek society and economy in relation to central and western European countries.[79]

The "hegemonic ideology of *petty bourgeoisism*", as described by Greek sociologists and political scientists – fast upward social mobility and abrupt urbanization

---

78   On the thories of neomarxists of Greek underdevelopment see second chapter: "'Transformation' and 'petty bourgeoisism'. The Greek class distinctiveness and theories of 'underdevelopment'".

79   Op. cit.

of the until recently rural and pre-modern Greece – was the way in which on the following day of the civil war class inequalities and social turmoil were violently calmed through the prevalence of a "poorly thought out" and non "contractual" urban parliamentarism (Mouzelis, 1978; Charalampis, 1989). The "petty bourgeois self" seems to be shaped in these approaches, and through clientelist relationships, entanglement between public and private, entanglement of pre-modern ethics of honor and shame with a pseudo-urban and modern ethics in the post-war social context, prevents the real capitalist transformation of the country and the accumulation of private capital, which would establish a dynamic and independent national urban class. Therefore, the *petty bourgeoisism*, which is associated with the clientelist non-functional Greek state of corruption, is responsible for the underdevelopment and Greek tragedy or fate, as it is often described.

However, this study, as it can be seen from the analysis of this subchapter, shows that the corruption at the level of explicit communication and representation associated with the social identity of the *noikokyraios* may stand for urban activity and self-sacrifice for the common good. This fact may shape productively, based on a Foucault-inspired conceptualization of production (Foucault, 2006), the European peaceful middle-class citizen and not the non-westernized petty bourgeois subject of an underdeveloped country of the European region.

The informant does not wish to "get in trouble" in a system, which, however, because of his activity, he can also control "from the above" due to his closeness to power. The bust of Karamanlis and the awards in his personal office produce for him the Greek state that honored him and acknowledged his offer, and the state that changed Greece of "poverty" and "misery". The state of *ERE* is produced concurrently with the peaceful, democratic *noikokyraios*, who sought for change at personal and broader social level.

The state that awards and suspends dedication plates creates the feeling of vertical administration, but also that of spatial presence of the upper power, according to Ferguson and Gupta (2002), while at the same time it reminds of the important analysis of Mitchel (2006, pp. 169–186) about the "state effect", according to which the practices and points at which the sense of distinction between society and state is created constitute also exercise of power and social control (Sharma & Ferguson, 2006, pp. 8–9). The honored person is closer to power and for this reason can be a benefactor, therefore the imaginary state of Karamanlis is identified in the informant's discourses with the head of the Ministry of Welfare, who provides him with invaluable information and most probably supervises the implementation of the practices of breach/benefaction, in order to avoid another breach to the interest of unknown people (land grabbers).

The informant's privileged relationship with the power of governors and the production of the place of Toumba differentiates him from his fellow citizens, who "do not have similar relationships and know-how", while justifying the personal growth and prosperity within the post-war context of development. Even in today's socioe-conomic context of crisis, he states that he managed to preserve the property he cre-ated and belong to upper middle classes, living with his wife in a luxurious apart-ment of 250 sq.m., and receiving income from pensions, business activity, savings, and several real estate properties.

5.2.2 "Settlement" of the "benefactor" citizen and public interest

As we saw also earlier, my informant Giorgos, is proud of his achievement to "settle down" and overcome together with other fellow citizens the poverty he used to ex-perience in his family environment because of the refugeeism and the big war that followed and prevented the immediate recovery of the social status that the family enjoyed before the change. Because of a war and a transnational decision, his par-ents were forced to abandon their life and belongings in Istanbul and move to Thes-saloniki, a city that was an equally important urban center of the Ottoman empire for at least five centuries. Both Thessaloniki and the refugees try to integrate into the administrative body of a national state; this is very important to understand the type of state and citizen that is produced in this specific city within the post-war sociopolitical context.

The buildings and places that I visited, the objects about which the informants spoke, but also all other objects that existed in the space and had their own impact on the visitor, constituted the "lines" (Ingold, 2007a) of a web, a thread like the one that, according to Ingold (2008), a spider constructs (SPIDER theory). Ethnography aims at faithfully following the tracks of the lines and reach the points where these are connected and weaved, producing the complex network, in which this person and institutions worked.

As we saw in the above subchapter, a public service with a dedication plate for an "exemplary" descendant of refugees from Asia Minor, a contracting office in an apartment building at the center of Kato Toumba, decorated with the bust of the politician named "Ethnarch", and numerous awards and honorary distinctions for the citizen-benefactor form the knots of the web of a network produced by the ac-tivities of citizens in relation to and within the post-war state, at least at the level of narration and everyday experience and remembrance.

According to social theory, states are "constructed entities", while their ac-tion and influence on social life often relies on symbolic and imaginary/creative tactics (Ferguson & Gupta, 2002, p. 981). The physicalization of the vertical and from the above state authority, perceived as undivided and unified, is produced by everyday spatial and other practices within the context of everyday experiences and social relations between civil servants and citizens (Ferguson & Gupta, 2002, p. 982; Herzfeld, 1992, pp. 43–59; Sharma & Ferguson, 2006, 8–24). According to Foucault, one should seek for the seat of authority elsewhere and not in the state

(Sharma & Gupta, 2006, p. 9). Authority is not static and is not exercised top-down but is diffused and can be found in practices and people that participate in power relationships (Foucault, 1987, p. 24). Authority is therefore productive, crosses things, produces things, entails pleasure, forms of knowledge, produces discourse (Foucault, 1987, p. 21).

The terms "settlement" and "corruption" that I use in the title of the previous sub-chapter[80] are terms that I encountered several times in the field and the archives I studied, in order to collect additional material for the refugee settlement of Toumba and its inhabitants. The "settlement" is a moral act that is associated with the welfare state and successful integration of Christian refugees from the Ottoman empire, who were exchanged as a result of the Treaty of Lausanne (1923). "Corruption" is a negative term, which, in the field, explains the delay of Greece compared to other developed economies of the European Union. As this specific ethnographic example shows, these terms as conceptual systems with a specific content and meaning are often overlapping and often one establishes and allows for the existence of the other.

As it results from the Welfare archives, the Greek state within the context of the "welfare" policy of "settlement" attempted to collect information about the new populations, so that they could be governed in a "productive" way. It used specific legislation that favored the state and the policy of settlement of refugees to bind large private pieces of land, with the intention to grant them against a relatively low price to refugees that had been recently exchanged. The settlement of refugees and its management by the competent state authorities at the beginning of the 20th century mark the transition to the innovative way of governance of a national state through practices of control and discipline of the population, as these are described by Foucault (2006, pp. 131–141). The development of the art of governance and the birth of political economy is associated in our case with the Christian inhabitant of the Ottoman empire, who is progressively established, in the transition to modernity and capitalism, through practices of self-discipline and technologies of self-control of the subject refugee of the Greek national state. Later, in the post-war sociopolitical context of development and cold-war westernization, there is the crystallization of the "peaceful" and "*noikokyraios*-benefactor-productive" citizen, who stands opposite the "communist" and "non-patriot" Greek that threatens the state.

As we saw also in the second chapter,[81] in the case of Toumba, it was the first time that practices of unified urban design and construction had been implemented, aiming at the creation of residences for refugees. The spatial intervention of the state in this case is an absolute one, creating new spatial realities under the supervision of the services of the social welfare state. Families take pictures of

---

80   See 5.2.1 *"Settlement of refugees or corruption? The production of benefactor citizen through representations of practices of trespassing of public property".*

81   See 2.5 *"Space and objects in the discourses and practices of the noikokyraioi from Thessaloniki".*

themselves in front of the houses they acquire, while all their personal and family data are registered and kept in family folders, which are organized by numbers and correspond to the plots of the settlement of Toumba.

As we saw earlier,[82] Giorgos is not a refugee himself, however, a part of his narration during our first meetings was dedicated, as it was the case with all the informants I met in the field, to the story of his parents' recovery and the difficult moments of moving, which justify and establish the required virtue of refugeeism. It is a narration that is quite common in the field of Toumba, which is associated mainly in the post-war era with the positive connotations of being a descendant of refugees and the privileges of "welfare" settlement, meaning acquire with the help of the state a residence or workplace as a refugee and become in this way integrated into the social fabric.[83]

I found accidentally[84] Giorgos's folder in the archive, as Giorgos, not being a refugee himself, should normally be included only in the descendants and protected members of the family folder kept in his father's name. But I found two folders in the archive: the first one concerned the case of settlement of Giorgos's father in the 1930s, while the second one concerned Giorgos himself, who according to the archive of this service, seems to be "settled" in the 1970s by the Ministry of Welfare, based on the provisions of article 85 of royal decree number 330/60 "About the codification of legislation on the settlement of urban refugees". According to the provisions of articles 85 and 86 of the above decree, the concession of two plots in the refugee settlement of Toumba to Giorgos, which had been expropriated based on decision 16314/25 aiming at the settlement of urban refugees, took place because of the long-time arbitrary trespassing of the public property. In this ethnographic example, the arbitrary act of a citizen is associated with a moral and welfare practice of a state that until that moment was applied to people in real need because of refugeeism. The private properties of the residents of Pylaia, which were expropriated by the Greek state in 1925, would be used exclusively for the purpose of the necessary settlement of the refugees from Asia Minor, justifying this action taken by state in that period.[85] The

---

82   See 5.2.1 *"Settlement of refugees or corruption? The production of benefactor citizen through representations of practices of trespassing of public property"*.

83   On a positive assessment of settlement within the context of governance by Venizelos see Voutira (2006, pp. 238–248), but also Hirschon (2006) about the ways of settlement based on the ethnographic example of Kokkinia.

84   As it is shown by several ethnographies regarding corruption, anthropologists do not initially have the intention to study corruption, but they encounter it accidentally in the field and especially in recent years; also because of the international discussion on the topic by organizations and technocrats fighting it, they constitute the topic of everyday discussion and public discourse in the countries where anthropologists conduct fieldwork (see Nuijten & Anders, 2007, p. 5; Blundo, 2007, pp. 36–37).

85   See in detail 3.2.1 *"Poverty, deprivation and strategies to recover a lost world"*.

case of settlement of Giorgos was completely different at moral and legal level from all other settlements I studied in the Welfare archive, since it was the settlement of a citizen because of *"arbitrary trespassing of public property"*. The truth is that the results of my investigation in the archives of Thessaloniki reserved this surprise for me, since Giorgos in his oral interviews, as we saw earlier,[86] concealed the way of getting the plot, on which his office and residence were located, presenting it as the result of a common *antiparochi* within the context of his contracting activity started in the 1970s. The concealment is indicative of the moral code, which, on one hand, prohibits the description of this story, but on the other hand, imposes the reproduction of the story of social offer and benefaction, as we saw in the previous subchapter, which relies on the same law and takes place in the same way.

This story is about two different plots and cases of trespassing, which rely on the same legislation and in which the same person is the key actor. The difference is that one of the stories, which is described as social offer, as we also in the previous subchapter,[87] is represented by himself, while the other one is concealed and accidentally discovered by the anthropologist in the archive. The conceptual distinction between private and public and the negative connotation entailed by its reversal leads the informant to choosing to conceal the illegal practice that is associated with his private interest.

The discourses for the state of development and the representations of the practices of offer and benefaction that produced the citizen benefactor[88] contributed in a crucial way to my processing and understanding the state and the citizen through a different point of view, that of the legal and judicial documents of a state service. The comparison of these two different sources, the discourses of Giorgos and the discourses of the official documents, helped me understand the ambiguity and relativity of concepts, such as "corruption" and "settlement".

Blundo (2007, p. 28) underlines that, if from the legal point of view, it is possible to define what is corrupted and what is not, from the emic point of view it is difficult to define it, since the actions of corruption and their assessment enter a complex cultural system of conceptualization. What is characterized as Anthropology of the Mediterranean Area and in particular the first ethnographies of the 1960s and 1970s showcase the different conceptualizations and cultural uses of practices of patronage, clientelist relationships and gift exchange and their role in the establishment of reciprocity and solidarity relationships, in the adaptation to conditions of intense social inequality, defense and preservation of the family and personal honor

---

86   See 5.2.1 *"Settlement of refugees or corruption? The production of benefactor citizen through representations of practices of trespassing of public property".*

87   See 5.2.1 *"Settlement of refugees or corruption? The production of benefactor citizen through representations of practices of trespassing of public property".*

88   Op. cit.

(Gilmore, 1982, pp. 179–180; Nuijten & Anders, 2007, p. 4). As Nuijten and Anders (2007, p. 7) stress, there are different types of corruption, depending on the political and economic context and political system in which they take place.

On the other hand, several anthropologists look into the polysemy of the concept of morality and try through ethnographic examples to dissociate it from Eurocentric approaches and discourses about development, social trust and contractual civil society (Torsello, 2011, p. 10). Torsello (2011, p. 11) uses the ethnographies by Rivkin-Fish (2005) in Russia and by Olivier de Sardan (1999) in Africa, to show different "moralities" of corruption in societies and sociopolitical systems where the personal relationships and exchanges between citizens and bureaucrats are not perceived as corrupted – and therefore non moral – but on the contrary contribute to the establishment of mutual trust, social relations and a "moral economy" of solidarity (Torsello, 2011, p. 11). In addition, according to de Sardan (1999), actions denying this context are experienced as non-moral, selfish, characterizing people that are not interested in fellow human beings (Torsello, 2011, p. 12).

These analytical tools help us understand that in the Greek sociopolitical context, practices of breaching the law or deceiving the public authorities because of personal acquaintances[89] and contacts with state actors may, at the level of discourses and public representations, be presented and experienced as offer and benefaction, when they serve what is socially and culturally determined as "common good". Giorgos's silence on similar practices used, for personal benefit this time, although they are legally correct, since the Greek law and Greek courts justify the arbitrary trespassing conceding him the plots, renders visible the ambiguity of the concept of legally correct at moral level, preventing Giorgos from mentioning this story. In other words, Giorgos's representations are filtered by the discourses of the

---

89   At this point, I cite once again the excerpt about the practices regarding the type of his social activity through "illegal actions", as it is necessary for the analysis at this: – Informant: *"This did not happen with my own money, actions and time. The local association did not have the money to buy its own premises. Due to my profession, I knew, I had found out which plots belonged to the Social Welfare, meaning to the state!!! I took the necessary actions, submitted the applications, whatever was required, travelled to Athens. Therefore, the concession of one plot to p... and another plot to M... was approved thanks to my actions. But to achieve this – I knew the law –, to achieve the concession on behalf of the Social Welfare, one must have settled in it, should possess it in order to receive a concession. By taking a serious risk, because I was a real estate developer, I hired the required teams and fenced the whole plot of M...; in this way, when the Social Welfare employees would arrive, they would see that the plot was in use, possessed by M.... We also issued false certificates, that we had been possessing the plot for X years, etc."* With this same logic, could other people have fenced plots and take them? Informant: *"No, the purpose was social. A childhood friend of mine was a head in the Ministry of Social Welfare and knew about this: "Giorgos, don't leave these plots to land-grabbles, why don't you take action? Do something for social purposes in Toumba. This is how I started, and I knew this was not only one plot, but three or four of them in a row. This was my participation. I have awards at home, what you see here is nothing."*

western modern morality and correct discourse, which distinguishes public from private associating corruption with the exploitation of the public to the benefit of the private (Nuijten & Anders, 2007, pp. 2–6; Haller & Shore, 2005, pp. 3–6). Finally, the concepts "corruption" and "settlement" are used with a question mark and aim at problematizing research schemes placing corruption on the opposite side of the rational state law, which serves and defends the public interest and correct functioning of a state apparatus that is distant from the society it represents.

In other words, in this subchapter it is concluded that the Greek *petty bourgeoisism* and illegal practices do not entail the underdevelopment and peripheral economic role of Greece. These data contribute to the broader anthropological discussion about the polysemy of corruption practices (Haller & Shore, 2005, pp. 1–28; Nuijten & Anders, 2007, pp. 1–26), and their association with the parallel production of the state and reproduction of middle-class citizens in the sociopolitical context of a European country experiencing an important pace of growth during this period.[90]

During the fieldwork in Thessaloniki, often the informants justified illegal practices and corruption actions in their daily contacts with representatives of the political system, but also with low-level civil servants, using phrases such as "the end justifies the means" or "nice guys finish last". The corruption discourses, as pointed out also by Gupta (1995, p. 226) in his very important ethnography about Nothern India, are productive, producing the state and citizens. It is interesting to note the way in which the corruption discourses in post-colonial India produce the citizen that has rights and the politician or civil servant who bears responsibility within the sociopolitical context of a nationally independent state and a parliamentary democracy, while at the same time citizens in their everyday contacts with low-level civil servants experience corruption in all Indian bureaucracy sectors (p. 225). Giorgos might have not "got in trouble" with the Greek state, since he has never been a civil servant or employee, however he offered his services and knowledge voluntarily, in order to build through trespassing two public buildings on the plots initially destined for the settlement of refugees. The action of trespassing and all practices of corruption and deceit of the Greek state that followed cannot be seen by him as "illegal" actions, since they served the "common good".[91]

In this way, the informant put himself in "moral" and "legal" danger based on a western moral code of honor, which results from the state law, by doing something "illegal" that served the public interest though. As we saw, the support he received from the head of the competent service contributed to some extent to this choice;

---

90   See observations by Blundo (2007, pp. 34–35) about the need for anthropologists to systematize the categories they study in order to contribute to a comparative analysis and avoid an anecdotal approach of corruption phenomena.

91   See 5.2.1 "*Settlement of refugees or corruption? The production of benefactor citizen through representations of practices of trespassing of public property*".

because of his personal friendship with the informant and his relationship with the settlement, he encouraged the citizen's actions.

Legal pluralism (Merry, 1988) has shown that the behaviors of people and the code of ethics in everyday life are not shaped only by the state legal system. Many different codes of values act at the same time, affecting people's practices. As Herzfeld (1992) points out, regarding the way in which bureaucracy works, it has been ascertained that the limits between civil servant and citizen are not clearly determined and inaccessible; they are produced and reproduced through daily contacts between citizens and state representatives. The dual role of the head of the Ministry of Welfare leads him to conceding to Giorgos the important legal information that will activate the citizen "benefactor", who will not hesitate, because of his know-how, to use illegal practices to create the formal conditions required by law, in order to make a contribution to the social associations. The head who gives the idea for the illegal action, Giorgos and the associations who accept to implement it, the audit services of the state who confirm what appears to be a trespassed area and finally the state services and associations who award prizes to the trespasser participate in social relationships producing the state of social welfare and the citizen who is interested in the common good.

5.2.3 The social reproduction of *noikokyraios* through practices of trespassing of public property in the post-war context of reconstruction

As we saw in the previous two sub-chapters,[92] the practices that could be described based on a Weberian logic of public administration and governance[93] as non-western, problematic for the growth of the state and non-moral produced with the direct involvement of civil servants and institutional organs the democratic citizen – benefactor and the western welfare state of settlement in the Greek post-war context. The methodological focus on the everyday practices, the discourses about the state and the representations of the experiences of the citizen's relationship with it, protected us against the reproduction of a unified form of it intermediated with "fantasies" and "wishes" (Aretxaga, 2003, pp. 394–398).

---

92   See 5.2.1 *"Settlement of refugees or corruption? The production of benefactor citizen through representations of practices of trespassing of public property"* and 5.2.2 *"'Settlement' of the 'benefactor' citizen and public interest"*.

93   According to Herzfeld (1992, pp. 1–16), the concept of western bureaucratic function is associated with the Weberian distinction between a fatalistic subject encountered in the East and a western individualized national self that can determine his/her fate. These conceptualizations are associated with the stereotyped establishment of the western as a general category of countries with specific characteristics that differentiate them from the rest of the world.

Giorgos, through the experience of his contact with simple employees of public administration during the years of *ERE* governance, imagines a "powerful state" and a "reasonable and efficient administration", characterized by the spirit of "change" and "growth", which he contrasts often to the subsequent "inefficient governance of *PASOK*" that eventually led the country to the current financial crisis. The informant achieves his personal goals through a successful contact with and understanding of the Greek public administration. Giorgos is on the opposite side of those citizens, who, according to Herzfeld (1992, p. 4), accuse public administration because of their own weakness and personal failure to succeed in their everyday contact with it.

The "successful *noikokyraios*" citizen is produced through the experience of his/her contact with public administration, which is confirmed and reinforces the fantasy of the existence of the "efficient state of Karamanlis". The symbolism of efficient authority and decisiveness as characteristics of his governance – *"when Karamanlis pounded his fist on the table no one protested. As minister of public works, he did a lot of works"*[94] – satisfy the citizen's wish for "safety" and "absolute control" after a troubled era. The intense "anticommunism" of this politician and of the Greek Press,[95] establishes the interior other that in the cold-war context produces the *noikokyraios* citizen, who identifies himself/herself with the cultural construction of the single Greek nation-state that "belongs to the West"[96] and must be protected. It is precisely this "new" reproduction of the form of the powerful state and the wish for more state representation that, as Aretxaga (2003, p. 394) characteristically mentions, helps to maintain civil national conflicts and reproduce the establishing terms of the conflict. Civil servants as well as the citizen justify their actions, by making reference to the general "public interest", which is probably identified with the political and ideological symbolisms that characterize this specific era and serve the interests of the class, to which they feel they belong. The focus on the practices and discourses reveals, by removing the mask of the unified state (Abrams, 1988), the complexity of these power relationships.

The contact with the employees and the experience of the successful outcome produce the special social identity of Giorgos, who is interested in his social progress through selfless actions "of public tidying up/*noikokyrema*" of a country that is threatened by internal and external enemies.

---

94   Excerpt of my conversation with Giorgos in Toumba.

95   See Dordanas (2006, 2012), Voglis (2014) and Michailidis, Nikolakopoulos and Fleischer (2006).

96   I borrow here the phrase of K. Karamanlis from his speech at the Parliament, see (@GorillaGrodd1979, 2013).

Further investigation of the Social Welfare Service revealed that the same "arbitrary" practices,[97] but also the broader experience of exploitation of the ambiguity of the civil law and Greek legislation were used this time by the citizen-benefactor to serve his private interest at the expense of other citizens of the Greek state.

Taking into account this aspect of the ethnographic example, we will focus this time, based on judicial and other public documents, on the blurred limits that separate "legal" from "illegal" as a result of the indeterminacy and ambiguity of the legal texts, which often allows the acting people to take advantage of it, by choosing interpretations that serve their personal objective-setting (Nuijten & Anders, 2007, p. 14). The selective use of the articles of a law can, with the intermediation of different factors, lead to the legalization of practices that are completely different from the initial logic of the legislation.

According to Herzfeld (1992, p. 15), the anthropologist who studies the public administration will meet most of the times civil servants, whose decisions are influenced by symbolic systems originating from the local and personal system of values, but also from the personal and local interests, which oblige them, depending on the circumstance, to escape the commonly accepted interpretations of the law (Herzfeld, 1992, p. 15). The "public" is not independent of the "private" and "individual" interest. In their interesting ethnography about organized crime and corruption in Naples, Holden and Tortora (2007) show the possibilities and margins of a different treatment of what by law is a criminal act, through the powerful effect of different factors that determine the outcome of dispensing justice based on one and only legal code. According to the same authors, (2007, p. 104), corruption is illegal, mainly because it has been defined as such by the law of a country.

In this subchapter, we will show how arbitrary practices are legalized with the excuse of serving the "public interest" at the expense of other people who do not belong to the constructed and imaginary unified national body; through them both the Greek western state of welfare and the *noikokyraios* – middle-class and peaceful citizen are finally established in the informants' discourses and the public and judicial documents.

These documents were included in Giorgos's individual folder, which I studied, among others, in order to collect more information about the settlement of the refugees of Kato Toumba, and about the life of the informants in this specific settlement during the 1950s and 1960s. The informant never shared this story with me; therefore, its discovery was accidental, but quite revealing combined with his oral testimony. The use of the archive as complementary source in the ethnography of Toumba is not aiming at cancelling or double-checking the oral testimonies, but at showcasing the different aspects of establishment of subjectivities, in particular

---

97   See 5.2.1 *"Settlement of refugees or corruption? The production of benefactor citizen through representations of practices of trespassing of public property"*.

that concerning their contact with public administration and civil servants. Besides, in an ethnographic study, as Holden and Tortora (2007, p. 104) correctly point out, it doesn't matter whether the informants are saying the truth or not; what matters is the construction and reconstruction of facts by the social actors.

The Social Welfare archive for Toumba makes it possible to see a fact, like the one described in the previous two subchapters, [98] with the difference that it allows the showcasing of different discourses, like the written discourses produced as a result of a judicial conflict between the state and its citizens.

This archive highlights a different version of Giorgos's family story, while it contradicts the informant's representations about the way of acquiring his residence and office in Toumba. The total concealment of this story is indicative of the imprint that this experience left to the informant. In our private meetings in his office in Toumba, Giorgos never referred to previous dwelling or other previous use of this space prior to its construction.

As it results from the specific archive, the Greek State was in long-lasting dispute with several owners of expropriated land, on which the refugee settlement of Toumba was built. One of these disputes can be entirely represented based on the documents included in Giorgos's individual folder. This folder documents the communication between him and the state, the communication between the denouncing Jewish family and their appointed attorney on one side and the state and Greek justice on the other side, and finally the internal correspondence and communication between the different involved services of the Greek state about this stake for at least two decades, from the mid-1950s to the mid-1970s.

According to the common decision of the Ministries of Welfare and Agriculture number 16..., which was published on 17/2/1925 in the Government Gazette, the Greek state expropriated private land "in Thessaloniki, area of Toumba". Within this huge land, there was, among others, the property of a Jewish family, [99] which the family acquired in 1919, as it results from the notary acts and conveyance record of the district court of Thessaloniki. The Jewish family had bought this land from a

---

98   5.2.1 "Settlement of refugees or corruption? The production of benefactor citizen through representations of practices of trespassing of public property" and 5.2.2 "'Settlement' of the 'benefactor' citizen and public interest".

99   In an effort to protect my informant's anonymity in compliance with the rules governing ethnographic research but also respecting the personal data protection which I promised to the employees of decentralized administration of Macedonia-Thrace and more specifically the department of public property of the Financial Directorate of the Directorate general of internal functioning regarding the judicial and public documents that I was allowed to investigate and use in my thesis, I avoid the use of names or other details that can disclose the identity of the people concerned by the described ethnographic cases.

Muslim family, who in turn had bought this piece of land from a Christian family of the Ottoman Thessaloniki in 1907.[100]

The surface of the piece of land of the Jewish family was one stremma, while there were two one-story warehouses built on it. As described in the Ottoman *tapio* (land registry), this piece of land was located in the area of Kourou Tsesme within the current municipality of Thessaloniki. In 1920 and 1921, the said Jewish family bought another two pieces of land of 2 stemmas and 1 725 cubits respectively in the regions of Kapoutzides, Chamidie and Kourou Tsesme, right next to the first real estate property. The said three real estate properties together with the buildings constituted since then a single fenced piece of land. On this piece of land, the new owners built a two-story house and warehouses, while they also created the relevant sanitary infrastructure. Since then, the land was used as flower garden, while a coffee shop and a dance school operated there. As it is mentioned in the lawsuit of the family against the Greek state, a "high-society hall" well-known to the people of Thessaloniki, operated in this piece of land.

In 1930, part of the plot was transferred to a relative of the Jewish family. But the Municipality of Thessaloniki and more specifically the city plan office expropriated a part of the plot in the subsequent years, in order to open three main roads in the area. In the meantime, after the violent death of the owners in Poland in 1943 during the Nazi occupation, following the persecution of the Jewish citizens of Thessaloniki, their property was inherited by first-grade relatives. According to the heirs, who appear as residents of Israel,[101] the Greek state until 1958, when they requested for the first time to be informed about the trespassing of their property by the Social Welfare Service, had not proceeded to any occupation or use of their piece of land.

As it can be seen in the lawsuits brought against the Greek state in the following years, the family continued using the residence and the huge plot, considering the expropriation of 1925[102] as null and void because of the non-timely occupation of the litigious plot by the state. In a lawsuit in 1963 the family claimed from the Greek state damages of 3 000 000 drachmas, for their charge because of the illegal trespassing and use of a part of the plot by the Greek state.

The family sent similar documents to the Prefecture of Thessaloniki and the Social Welfare Service, in order to communicate the ownership status of this plot, which, according to the family, was illegally trespassed by the state, in order to

---

100   Here we see also the interesting composition of the population of Thessaloniki during the Ottoman empire before the Hellenization of the city in the subsequent years.

101   It is interesting to note the use of terms "enemy citizens, Israeli residents of Tel Aviv" in the public and legal documents issued by the Greek services in their internal communication.

102   At this point, we would like to remind that, as mentioned in the previous chapters, the expropriation of private lands in the region of Toumba in 1925 aimed at the settlement of thousands of refugees that had arrived from Asia Minor, see in detail 3.2.1 "Poverty, deprivation and strategies to recover a lost world".

settle families of refugees: "The other party to the proceedings, the Greek state, in October 1958 started occupying parts of the above-mentioned real estate property of ours, and in this way until December 1959 it occupied a large part of it of an approximate surface of 3 000 square meters, enclosed by two roads [...] . The above part of our plot, which was not occupied legally, was included by the other party into the settlement of Kato Toumba to be constructed, despite our objection and opposition, claiming that we had been deprived of our right of property, while they contest and question our above undeniable rights to it."[103]

After the first petition of the family against the Greek estate, as a reaction to the allegedly illegal use and trespassing of their personal property, the different services and institutions of the Greek state through their employees (Legal Council of the State, Ministry of Finance, Ministry of Social Services, Court of First Instance and State Council) try to examine the case thoroughly and collect the necessary information, in order to deal with the upcoming judicial litigation with these citizens.

During two decades, the Greek state and its representatives tried, as it can be seen in numerous documents, to prove the validity of the expropriation from 1925 onwards and the legal possession of this piece of land, in order to avoid a vicious circle of claims that would threaten the Greek state with huge expenses because of the damages that should be paid to future claimants of land that the state had made available to settle refugees. At least this is one of the two official versions, which is presented in the internal communication of the different departments of the Ministry of Social Services. In the reports and memos of the Ministries to the judicial authorities of the country, the arguments change and rely exclusively on interpretations of civil law, based on which the services acted to take the decision to grant this property to my informant Giorgos. In the discourses produced by the services, in particular at the beginning of the dispute, it is possible to discern the different way of description of this case and the contradictions regarding the ownership status of the specific piece of land. Several years would pass before a common line of handling this dispute in favor of the interests of the Greek state could be found. What is particularly interesting is the fact that the public documents, despite the special and rather complex language used, did not manage to cover elements of orality and often obvious intimacy that characterized the internal communication of the civil servants of the different services involved. Moreover, what was interesting and useful to establish conclusions was the study of language differentiations and the different way of interpreting and using the Greek law in the different discourses produced in the communication of the state representatives with different institutions and recipients.

The ambiguity of the acts and the possibility of misinterpretation is obvious in these specific documents that present an evolving process of establishing arguments

---

103   See Folder of Toumba/ Department of Public Property.

over time, by choosing articles and decisions that are in favor of the Greek state. The parallel readjustment of the arguments of each party is also interesting. This evolving process of establishing the defense line of the state, and the intermediation of numerous factors that will influence the final stake showcase the relativity of the "legally correct" and the inadequacy of absolute definitions of "corruption" placing it on the opposite side of the civil law, identified almost exclusively with random individualized actions of independent subjects (Nuijten & Anders, 2007, p. 2). The different interpretations of the same fact, produced as a result of specific legislation, which informs and shapes the argumentation of the two parties, showcases the indeterminacy of the law, which allows the flourishing of "corruption" (Holden & Tortora, 2007, p. 119).

The questions raised by this ethnographic example are many and concern primarily the distinction between private and public, which is one of the basic principles of the Weberian reasonable public administration, which was until recently the focus of the scientific research on corruption (Torsello, 2011, p. 3). This feature combined with the fact that anthropology studied until recently precapitalist and postcolonial societies contributed to the limited ethnographic research in this field (2011, pp. 3–4). Already in 1992, anthropologist Herzfeld, in an effort to deconstruct the concept of western and its association with a rational bureaucratic administration serving the interests of the modern individualized and non-passive subject, showed that in the origin of the western bureaucratic organization there are symbolic systems and logics, which can be found in the culturally constructed non-western world. In this study, the author stressed the dual quality of the civil servant as an employee and as a citizen, to show the processes and logics that intermediate the practices and decisions of those who represent what is perceived at the level of the imaginary production and reproduction as state.

The exclusive study of the archive material without the experience of the field could reproduce this distinction, in the sense that the "public interest" invoked by unknown civil servants against other parties acting to defend their own private interests, arises effortlessly from the public documents and seems almost self-evident. The symbols of the Greek state through the seals and the gravity of the signatures of state representatives also work as actors and can create the sense of the unified upper power, acting with the aim of the public interest, which is distinguished from the ulterior private one. But the elements from the overall ethnographic research allow the anthropologist to notice details that reveal the gaps and fragmentary nature of the function of public administration, as well as the influence of cultural and social factors affecting the interpretation and dispensing of the law.

In this example, the state legalizes arbitrary actions, which are against the legal right of urban possession and management of the private property.

In 1964 and following a series of lawsuits and judicial disputes between the two parties, Giorgos filed a petition to the Social Welfare Service of Thessaloniki claiming that he had trespassed arbitrarily the said three pieces of land of the Jewish family since 1948 with his father. He also claimed that since 1956 his father had moved to another piece of land, exercising a different craft from him. In his claim of settlement as arbitrary trespasser, Giorgos claims that he built a factory in this piece of land, where he lives with his family.

In our personal meetings, the informant referred several times to the professional course of his father, which marked also his own professional development. Giorgos said that he worked since he was a very young boy with his father, in the first yard he rented at the center of Thessaloniki as well as in the second one at least until he started the profession of real estate developer in the 1970s. In addition, he insisted, in particular in his oral testimonies, on the fact that he lived with his parents in their refugee house in the settlement of Toumba, which he transformed in a "little villa" in the 1960s, by investing the amount of 120 000 drachmas,[104] when the selling price of a typical refugee house in the area was approximately 40 000 drachmas.

In 1967, Giorgos filed a new urban reclamation[105] to claim final concession of the said real estate property, while in 1973 he filed a memo before the Prefectural Housing Council of Thessaloniki, in which he mentions the following:

> "[...] A) Legalization of petition: Since 1948, I have settled arbitrarily in the land property that belonged to the management of the Center of Social Policy of Thessaloniki [...]. Since that year, I have completed the following works: a) I have constructed a permanent building where I installed a small business of manufacturing of x... k..., employing daily approximately 4–5 people, while up to this day I exercise exclusively this profession in this building, b) I renovated, extended and completed the shabby building located there and I settled as arbitrary owner. I have constantly stayed there up to this day quietly and uncomplainingly, and my family has settled there as well without any other person sharing the dwelling. Since 1960 I have made intense efforts, before this Service as well as before the Central Services of the Ministry, to achieve concession through sale to me of the single piece of land where I live and exercise my exclusive profession to earn a living. Within the context of my long-standing and costly actions, although I received support and willingness to satisfy my request, I faced various obstacles, the most

---

104   We observe an interesting consonance between the representation of Kostas and that of Georgia in the fourth chapter. Old houses are transformed with the money of growth into small villas and thus their owners contribute to the broader change and modernization taking place during that period in Greece. See in detail 4.2 *"The counterexample: 'peasants' and 'migrants from Germany' in Toumba of 'eastern suburbs'"*.

105   See Folder of Toumba / Department of Public Property / Memo 26/01/1973 to the Prefectural Housing Council.

important of which was the lack of land development of the unified piece of land where I lived [...]."

A big problem that the Social Welfare Service had to deal with in its defense line against the claims of the Jewish heirs was that part of their arbitrarily trespassed land, according to the informant's allegations, had not been parceled and, at least until 1957, had not been made available for the settlement of refugees, as provided for in the law:

"[...] The said piece of land was occupied by the state together with the whole expropriated property from the moment of the expropriation, in particular its largest part was divided into plots, which were conceded to refugee families, and another part was made available for the creation of road [...] and only a part of 990 square meters of the plot number [...] has not yet been parceled and is possessed by [...], who has in there a timber laboratory for the manufacturing of x.... On this piece of land there is also an old permanent house. For the use of the spaces and buildings Mr [...] stated that he pays a rent to the appointed attorney of the original owners [...]."[106]

The engineering office of the Social Welfare center, following in situ surveying of the situation of the plot in question reports:

"The above-mentioned person has possessed since 1948 the plot with reference A... up to the old buildings, which belong, according to information, to his heirs[107] [...]."[108] [...]XY[109] pays a rent to the appointed attorney of the heirs [...] which amounts to a monthly amount of 2 000 drachmas. In addition to the old buildings [...] in 1948, he constructed metal sheet shelters A... to extend his factory and fenced it with metal sheets and wood. Of the old two-story building, Mr [...] possesses the whole ground floor and of the upper floor the 2 rooms with common use of living room, while the other 2 rooms have been possessed since 1943 the 5-member family of L.S., who also pays a rent to his heirs [...]."[110]

In his memo Giorgos stresses that thanks to his efforts the competent authorities were informed about the burning issue of the pending land development that threatened the fate of the building plot:

"[...] Further to many actions of mine, finally the land development issue reached the central Housing Council, which, in its meeting number [...] decided to parcel

---

106   See Folder of Toumba / Department of public property.
107   This refers to the Jewish heirs living in Israel.
108   See Folder of Toumba / Department of public property.
109   This refers to the trespasser, meaning my informant Giorgos.
110   See Folder of Toumba / Department of public property.

the [...] whole building block and by decision dated 24.... of the secretary general of the Ministry Mr..... the Service was ordered to proceed to their concession to the people who dwelled in the parceled land. In this way, the land I arbitrarily possessed was also parceled; however, in the accompanying cadaster table, it does not appear as a unified plot of land but divided into two plots number [...]."[111]

Then, the informant analyses in his memo the reason why, according to the provisions of R.D. 330/1960 articles 79 to 86 he is absolutely entitled to present a request of concession for both his civil and profession settlement as arbitrary owner, against payment of the legal value of the conceded property.

In March 1969, the department of revenue management of the Municipality of Thessaloniki asked the Social Policy Center for information, to update the family folder with regard to tax debts of the owners – the Jewish family – for the financial year 1966, which at least until then was recognized by this service as the legal debtor for this piece of land. The Legal Council of the State and more specifically the Legal Counsellor's Office, by letter dated 7/7/1970 and addressed to the Social Policy Center, refuses to respond to the request of the Housing Service to cancel the lawsuits of the Jewish owners by mentioning:

"[...] Given that the above-mentioned pieces of land had not been occupied by you until 15/4/57 and no indemnity has been paid for these, on the contrary they have been possessed by the owners or the beneficiaries all along, we believe you must abstain from any action contesting the rights of the owners on them, given that the court of first instance and the court of appeal of Thessaloniki, especially after [...] do not accept a fictitious occupation of the pieces of land included in the expropriation by means of the original delimitation of the whole piece of land, when the owner never desisted from the tenancy of the expropriated part, and the latter is independent with regard to the larger piece of land and within it. Finally, regarding the cancellation from the claims register of long-standing pending claims, the following must be taken into account: first, it cannot be concluded from your above document to what claims you refer. If your refer to the pending claim of heirs (of the Jewish family), to cancel it, it must not, according to article 4 paragraph 2 of Law N. 4697/1930 (single article of Law 309/43) be substantially justified, which means that it must be certified that the occupation of the litigious piece of land took place before 15/4/67, but, according to what your technical service communicated to us orally [...] the occupation of the above piece of land took place in 1958 [...]". (1970, Leg. Couns. of the State to the Social Policy Center."[112]

---

111   Folder of Toumba / Department of public property.
112   Folder of Toumba / Department of public property.

The Ministry of Social Services ascertains in a letter to the Social Policy Center of Thessaloniki the importance of the element of the arbitrary possession of part of the litigious piece of land by Giorgos. Until 1959, the state had made available only 255 square meters of this piece of land to a family of Refugees with the purpose of the family's housing, therefore, the argument of "prior occupation and dispensing" to refugee families lacked legal ground:

> "[...]For these reasons we report to you that for the rest of the piece of land that was not occupied by the Service, as reported to you in this regard, that evidence and information have been provided on the case of... (Giorgos), arbitrary owner of the piece of land with building plot number ..., in the Settlement of Kato Toumba [...]."[113]

The Jewish owners appeared in 1971, immediately after the continuous claims of Giorgos to legalize the arbitrarily trespassed real estate property with an extrajudicial statement against the Directorate of Social Welfare, explaining that because of the judicial dispute between them – which is still pending – they should avoid any concession of the piece of land to any third party, naming also for the first time my informant. They even warned that they intended to terminate the lease contract with him and proceed to his eviction.

Nevertheless, the department of Social Security and Welfare of the Prefecture of Thessaloniki informs the Ministry of Social Services that:

> "[...] The legalization of the applicant, who exercises a profession on this plot, may entail the implementation of the provisions of article 85 paragraph I of R.D. number 330/60 because he meets the required conditions, given that the occupation took place before 30 October 1950, by a non-beneficiary, and on the plot a shop was installed, in which a manufacturing laboratory of k... is operated, submitted in due time together with the legal supporting documents, as the pieces of land are not located in the area where provisional settlements were constructed [...], and for the price of the current value, according to the same article [...]."[114]

However, the Service expressed concerns about the fact that:

> "The service [...] was reluctant to proceed to the concession-legalization of the pieces of land [...], due to the fact that both of them are located on a central street of Thessaloniki, and are of large surface, and for this reason seeks your instructions and advice whether to satisfy or not the claim of [...]."[115]

---

113   Folder of Toumba / Department of public property.
114   Op. cit.
115   Op. cit.

According to Royal decree 330/60 and article 23, the arbitrary occupation of real estate property of the state, whether this concerns a building or a free piece of land of the state, is severely punished with imprisonment and fine up to 20 000 drachmas. This article, which was included in an older relevant law, provided for "the immediate administrative expulsion of any occupier", while it was stipulated that only in exceptional cases, which would be assessed as such by the Housing Council, it would be possible to concede the occupied piece of land instead of demolishing and expulsing the trespasser, who, in this case, would have to pay the applicable value of the real estate property at the moment of the decision of the Council.

In a detailed report addressed by the head of the department of Social Security and Welfare to the Legal Council of the state, he justifies his decision to concede to Giorgos as arbitrary trespasser this unusually large piece of land in the center of Kato Toumba based on the reasoning of the "exceptional case" by which the Social Service of the State could legalize the arbitrary trespassing of public land by issuing a series of orders and laws.

According to the reasoning of the report of the head of the department of Social Security and Welfare, with these laws, the Greek state during the period of the war as well as immediately after the liberation, sought to avoid "the creation of an acute social problem", since the majority of the arbitrary trespassers in question were characterized by an absolute need of housing and therefore their settlement was necessarily taking place for social purposes only. Before the Housing Council finally conceded definitively and irrevocably in 1973 the whole litigious piece of land to this arbitrary trespasser at the expense of the initial owner, the Jewish family, the head of the said Service sent a detailed report to the Public Housing Directorate, specifying the reasons for which the Greek state should expedite the procedures, in order to prevent any new complication, which could entail negative consequences on the interests of the Greek state. In his report, the head describes the risks of the situation, since the original owners

> "filed a claim action, claiming that there has never been an action of occupation by the state, and no indemnity has been paid to them, and that they filed through their appointed attorney constant actions of possession and occupation." [116]

According to the head, these actions could anew put in danger the interests of the state, which

> "parceled and dispenses to refugees, for housing, the largest part of [...] except for the pieces of land under judgment, which were recently parceled as mentioned earlier."[117]

---

116   See Folder of Toumba / Department of public property.
117   Op. cit.

In his letters to his colleagues at the Ministry, the head expressed his fear of the Greek courts not taking a final decision and the possibility of a new action of the Jewish family against the Greek state. In October 1972, in his report to the ministry, he referred to the responsibilities of the Greek Administration, the handling of which put in a big and immediate danger the interests of the Greek state. In this letter, he also expressed his concern about the way in which other parties will act, and in particular the arbitrary trespasser, giving the impression that the Greek administration should be protected, taking specific measures to deal with any likelihood:

> "[...] Besides, obviously the Jewish family, to judge in advance on the dispute with the State (because the case is not urgent and the state has proceeded since then and up to this day to "actions of owner") and obviously to reinforce their prior action, they filed an action against the petitioner, invoking the existence of a renting relationship between him and their appointed attorney, on which decision number ber [...] of the single-member Court of First Instance of Thessaloniki was issued, preliminary ruling, obliged to prove the occupation or not, not fictitious together with K.Z. [...] decisions about the surface of the 2 pieces of land by the state before 15 April 1957. Because of this fact, we deem that the state runs an immediate risk because of these pursuits of the Jewish family, if he (the informant-arbitrary trespasser) files an action against the state, either because he does not have the possibility to prove the raised issue of proof or because he ignores or does not want or for any other reason, given that his father since 1945 and then himself, having a professional business there, know the region, while the latter also acted as a witness for the state, in trials about similar real estate properties. With regard to these properties, we mentioned that near that region we lost two trials for non-occupation (before 15.4.57) of [...], if we lose a third one (when he [...] does not prove occupation for the state before 1957), then there will be claims not only for the two pieces of land under judgment but for all pieces of land of the surface of 6 421 square meters of the alleged property of the claiming heirs, which were conceded, and which fall into the building plots on [...] and [...], and which were conceded to refugee families for housing, with various consequences for the state. The Administration (Ministry and Service) being unaware of the claims and trials of the Jewish family proceeded in the past to successive concessions to refugees, for self-housing, and recently the Ministry, proceeded to street planning, knowing the litigations and while the Legal Counsellor of the Ministry was aware. [...]."[118]

One year after this letter was sent to the Ministry of Social Services, the Prefecture of Thessaloniki and more specifically the department of social policy finally issued a "concession" in the name of the arbitrary trespasser, whom they "settled" for social purposes, at professional and civil level, by conceding to him the total surface of the

---

118   See Folder of Toumba / Department of public property.

two pieces of land together with the two-story house and the shops of the Jewish family, which were included in it.

The Jewish family through their appointed attorney filed an action and report to the Prefect of Thessaloniki but also before the competent service and more specifically the department of social policy, asking the reexamination of the legality of the act of concession of the two pieces of land in the settlement of Kato Toumba, insisting on the allegations that it was not an arbitrary trespassing but normal lease, initially of the warehouses and subsequently of the two-story house and the shops of their mother, who had been murdered in Poland. In its report, the family expresses concerns about the purposes of this concession, which did not respond to the reasons of the initial expropriation of the property that took place in 1925 by the Greek state, allegedly because of the extraordinary circumstances created by the treaty for the exchange of populations. [119] The Jewish family specifically mentions:

> "As you must have noticed, the surface of the conceded piece of land is 1 024.48 square meters. I doubt there is such a generous legal provision for the concession of pieces of land of more than 1 000 square meters in the city of Thessaloniki for the settlement of a refugee. Obviously, there must be a special provision, which I am not aware of, for his so privileged treatment [...]."[120]

Following a discussion that took place before the Prefect on 15.10.1973 with the Housing service, which reiterated the legality and validity of the decision of concession of this real estate property, the Jewish family expressed in a new report their concern about the future purposes of this arbitrary trespasser as well as the likelihood of the future detriment of the Greek state, which chose, in this circumstance of reconstruction and increase of the land value, to dispense such a large public piece of land to a private:

> "We wish to stress that by our statement communicated to the Service on 28.1.1971 we drew its attention to not concede the piece of land of the warehouse to [...]. Instead of this, the Service conceded 1 024.48 square meters to make [...] filthy rich at the expense of the state, because at the end of the day, if, as we hope, we win the trial, the state will be obliged to indemnify us for this illegal action."[121]

The Jewish family through its appointed attorney points out at another point of the report the possibilities created by this concession to this private, who, according to

---

119   On the Treaty of Lausanne and dynamics created by the first compulsory population exchange in the history of Europe, see Tsitselikis (2006).

120   See Folder of Toumba / Department of public property / Letter of Jewish family to the Prefecture of Thessaloniki, 1973.

121   Op. cit.

the family, is not in absolute need of housing as provided for by the law with regard to the illegal occupations of public real estate property:

> "[...] will judge also if it is legal to give it to him on the sole ground, which is a COM-PLETELY FALSE one,[122] that he arbitrarily occupied a surface of 1 024.48 square meters to settle him as a refugee, while a) all others settled from time to time in the surrounding area received pieces of land of 250–360 square meters, as it can be seen from plan ... which the Service will of course submit to the Prefect and b) when this poor refugee IMMEDIATELY pays 1 844 124 drachmas for the value of the land. When a person can pay such an amount of money, this person IS NOT IN NEED of housing. The Service should take into account that, in compliance also with the new General Construction Code, Mr [...] or any other person can build some of the largest apartment buildings of Thessaloniki with dozens of apartments and thousands of built square meters [emphasis by the Author]." [123]

In October 1973, precisely one month after the concession of the piece of land from the state, Giorgos applied, just as the Jewish family had warned, for the immediate utilization of this land through the system of construction by *antiparochi*. In his application to the Prefecture of Thessaloniki and the Directorate of Social Service submitted on the 1st of October 1973 he mentions the following:

> "Because, for the better utilization of the above-mentioned pieces of land, I intend to transfer to a real estate developer apartments by *antiparochi*, and because it is known that there are legal restrictions regarding my free management of these plots, since as I mentioned above the opportunity of utilization of my plots presented to me is of great value, which I could not achieve on my own, this becomes an unavoidable need." [124]

The Prefectural Housing Council of Thessaloniki, by a decision issued ten days later, delivered a unanimous opinion in favor of lifting all prohibitions, to allow the issuing of the required by the Service authorization of divestment of these real estate properties, judging the practice of *antiparochi* as the most advantageous solution for the interests of the arbitrary trespasser.

Many ethnographies about corruption practices showed that the state through its representatives modifies laws, in order to serve their interests, highlighting the problematic distinction between essentialist and Eurocentric approaches of legal and illegal practices (Nuijten & Anders, 2007, p. 13). It is interesting to note that none of the actions described was "illegal", at least not to the extent that the informant could be condemned for an action against the civil law of the country or civil servants

---

122   Use of upper case to stress concepts is mine.

123   See Folder of Toumba / Department of public property.

124   Op. cit.

were proved to act in favor of their private interests. The use of the term "corruption" describes mainly the informant's practices regarding his relationships with high-level and simple employees of the state apparatus and their alleged involvement in the social offer practices described in the previous two chapters.[125] During our meeting, the informant stressed the social activity[126] he performed in the settlement of Toumba, because of his quality of real estate developer but also his acquaintance with the head of the Ministry of Welfare. These cultural representations of benefactor Giorgos in the specific context of Toumba helped me understand the informant's discourses in the present, comparing them with the discourses of the past, as they result from the public documents of the Welfare archive, but also from his own letters to the state. According to Nuijten and Anders (2007, p. 17), corruption practices are characterized by secrecy and discretion of the involved parties, therefore, they tend to remain secret and be publicly disapproved, often even by those who commit them. Therefore, in the explicit communication with me, the informant referred only to those practices who allowed the arbitrary trespassing of public pieces of land with the help of public authorities due to his personal contacts within the context of the discourses of social activity and genuine benefaction, which legalize and justify through the use of different idioms what in a different case would be considered corruption based on the Greek civil law and urban ethics. Moreover, from the internal correspondence of the civil servants, it becomes obvious that not only the informant but also his father kept in touch with this service, which he had supported several times since 1945 in its judicial litigation with the owners of the pieces of land that had been expropriated by the state.

"Corruption" and in general the practices of management and production of social capital, as it is vividly showcased by the anthropological study regarding the practice of Guanxi – particularly in the context of the capitalist transformation of China – require awareness of a culturally and socially updated performativity (Smart & Hsu, 2007, pp. 167–189). The person who takes part in such practices must be aware of the laws and normalities characterizing this social system of relationships and contacts (Nuijten & Anders, 2007, p. 17). According to Holden and Tortora (2007, p. 119), "corruption is illegal merely because it was designated as such by positive law and this definition loses its meaning beyond legal formalism". The authors continue by saying that the "corruption thrives along the shadowy paths of formal legality because law is needed for its very existence." (op.cit.)

---

125   See 5.2.1 "Settlement of refugees or corruption? The production of benefactor citizen through representations of practices of trespassing of public property" and 5.2.2 "'Settlement' of the 'benefactor' citizen and public interest".

126   I mean specifically the practices of trespassing lands that had been expropriated for the settlement of refugees in order to build the important social associations and public buildings in Toumba.

Finally, although the terms "corruption" and "settlement", based on a moralistic and formalistic conceptualization, could never coexist in the context of the Greek welfare policy, however, as the ethnographic example of Giorgos shows, the "corruption" practices could not exist without the legislation framework and the possibilities established by the contingency of its interpretation and implementation.

Conclusions

In this thesis, I tried, with the help of anthropological tools and methods, to study the everyday life of the residents of Kato Toumba, an urban district in the eastern part of the city of Thessaloniki. In the five chapters of the thesis, of which three constitute the ethnography, I tried to showcase the concepts and meanings of the dwelling, decoration, and everyday life practices at lifestyle level, as well as the relationship of my informants in Kato Toumba and the Center of Thessaloniki with the State, as these have been shaped over time within the context of post-war western capitalist development.

More specifically, this thesis, according to the conclusions of the analysis of the ethnographic and archive material, focuses on the following:

a) expansion of the construction of social and cultural identities in expanded *petty bourgeoisism* conditions, as a result of post-war American, Greek and European policies of transformation and further westernization of the Greek State fighting communism and seeking a western growth pace;

b) meanings and symbolic practices of subjects in their interaction with spaces and objects of everyday life in the specific context of post-war *noikokyrmenos* (tidy) way of living. These conceptualizations are investigated, on one hand, within the context of recalling memories of family life and practices in the context of refugeeism and experiences of poverty and deprivation characterizing their life during the Second World War and subsequent civil war, and, on the other hand, within the context of gender-based performances of the modern, according to the code of *noikokyrio* (household), and post-war hegemonic imperative at the level of discourses and actions for a *noikokyrimeni* (tidy) life;

c) relationship of my *noikokyraioi* informants with the State of "development" and "modernization", in an attempt to investigate the construction of identities and power relationships established in the specific context of post-war "development" and "civilization", as this is reproduced in the practices and discourses of simple citizens and representatives of state services in their exchanges.

As explained in the second chapter, the term *petty bourgeoisism* is used to describe mentalities and practices that can be explained within the context of capitalist relations of production. The important expansion of capitalist relations of production that took place in Greece after the end of the civil war led to an important expansion of middle-class strata of the Greek society, which, as the ethnographic material shows, experience drastic changes in their everyday life through their integration into the hegemonic normative way of living of middle-class *noikokyraioi*. More specifically, regarding the paradigm of Thessaloniki, the threat condition of the Northern danger (cf. anti-communism policies) largely shapes the policies of integration and settlement of the big mass of refugees arriving in Greece as a consequence of the Treaty of Lausanne in 1923. The settlement and final integration of these populations into the model of *noikokyremenos* (tidy) way of living in urban centers will be completed to a great extent, as it can be documented by the fieldwork in Toumba, during the post-war period.

In the third chapter, informants reproduce narrations of refugeeism and everyday life in Kato Toumba and the city center. From the point of view of material culture theories, social dimension of space, analytical category of class and analytical category of home as materiality, I attempt to showcase the specific ways in which contrastive identities of poverty and deprivation are established in the specific context of the refugee settlement of Kato Toumba in relation to the identities of the *noikokyraioi* of the city center, who reproduce narrations of the dominant way of living of good homes.

The refugee homes of Toumba, through the policies of welfare settlement and the logic of concessions, express the poverty and deprivation experienced by the informants as children within the specific context of a place specifically made for refugees. Within these first homes, the wish for change and social progress by recovering the lost domesticity is established. This specific identity of the poor but "civilized" refugee is established and reproduced through the memory of the informant's relationship with the materiality of the "old home" and the feelings it triggers to the subject.

Pre-war spatial dimension of Toumba and experiences of dwelling there progressively shape interesting subjectivities of poverty and refugeeism, but also a collective memory, which will be on the opposite side of the collective memory of the city for many years. Toumba is experienced both by its inhabitants and by people living outside it as a special settlement, which historically, culturally, and socially does not belong to the city itself.

Experiences of illness, death and constant loss of living and lifeless things establish Toumba as a place of poverty and deprivation, while the cultural, social, and material distance from the good homes shapes the idea of a border separating the two areas of the city.

The differentiation of the city center from the settlement of Toumba – even though Toumba and the city center jointly form the Municipality of Thessaloniki – lies, based on research, in the broader negative treatment of refugees by the native populations, particularly regarding the paradigm of Thessaloniki, which was in that period in a transition phase of integration into the narrow framework of the Greek state. In addition, the role of many inhabitants of Toumba in the civil war, but also their leftist ideological position establishes the dominant discourses about a "Red Toumba", which contribute in the post-civil-war era to the further isolation and marginalization of the settlement within the context of cold-war capitalism.

Refugee widows cross literally and figuratively the social and cultural border dividing the two areas, functioning as agents of the dominant way of living and behavior in the refugee homes of Toumba. This way is adapted to native cultural values within the context of the model of "Asia Minor *noikokyrio*" and *prokopi*, as this is shaped through policies of modernization and Europeanization of the Ottoman empire at the end of the 19th century.

Modernity imperatives change drastically the space of the imperial city already at the end of the 19th century, contributing to the establishment of new practices and behaviors in the public space. The integration of the city into the Kingdom of Greece intensifies this change, in particular within the context of the Venizelian policy of expansion of capitalist relationships of production and establishment of extended middle classes through the successful integration of refugees. Thessaloniki undertakes to play the part of a modern European Greek big city in the spirit of urban integration that characterizes the governments of Venizelos.

"Good homes" are established by everyday experiences and practices of a Greek western way of living of middle-class strata being able to have a "good" life even in war and non-normality conditions. The informants recall memories of home spaces, their objects, and their social and family relationships within the context of the specific condition created by the Second World War and the civil war. These memories are particularly important for the public urban space and life of an imperial city, which is progressively transformed into the second biggest city of a national state.

Finally, this chapter showcases the modalities in which "poor and marginalized inhabitants of Toumba" are progressively integrated into the normative model of *noikokyraioi*, adopting elements of a lifestyle prevailing in the city during this period. The spatial experience of the excluded and peripheral Toumba is progressively transformed due to infrastructure projects, but also due to the change of the way of dwelling in the area. The state through its services propagandizes the new lifestyle, while the press and cinema depict and impose it. The practice of *antiparochi*, which starts in the city center and much later reaches also Toumba, establishes a new spatial experience shaping subjectivities of "modern" and "contemporary" way of living.

The fourth chapter deals with the relationships of subjects with the objects symbolizing the "modern" way of living. These special consumption practices and objectifications in the context of modernization contribute to establishing the gender-based identity of *noikokyra* woman and *noikokyris* man, who, within the context of seeking a *noikokyremenos* (tidy) way of living, cooperate with the aim to increase the profit of their family and its intergenerational reproduction.

In particular, "becoming a *noikokyra* woman or a *noikokyris* man" within the post-war context of the normative model of the class of *noikokyraioi* is directly linked to the consumption of a modern equipped apartment in an apartment building, and the complementary dimension in the *noikokyrio* management.

Apartments are equipped by *noikokyres* women, using the money earned by the salaried *noikokyris* husband, with the latest domestic appliances, while spaces are created at home intended to the public self-presentation of the tenants. "Noble and aristocratic living rooms" equipped with dark solid furniture, paintings, luxurious dining rooms, display cabinets with European porcelain dinnerware and crystals, are used by the family only on formal occasions, aiming at confirming the status that the tenants have acquired, but also at preserving the social relationships and networks they have created in the city.

The wives of the *noikokyraioi* are those who unite, mainly through the management of the *noikokyrio* (household) money earned by their husbands through salaried work, the public and domestic sphere, aiming at the biggest possible profit for their *noikokyrio* (household). In cooperation with their husbands, they take over economic transactions with services and banks, supplying home with the necessary items, communication with school and university attended by their children. Besides, the social reproduction of this middle-strata class of *noikokyraioi* passes over time through university education and securing a stable job in the public sector, particularly regarding the third generation, meaning the children and grandchildren of my informants. *Noikokyres* women are most of the time sole responsible for the choice of a home, its decoration and finally its correct administration.

Through the everyday life in a modern apartment, which has a bathroom, a kitchen with electrical appliances, an aristocratic living room for celebrations and a casual one for family use, the informants from Toumba perform the specific subjectivites of the modern, while confirming their successful integration into the hegemonic normative way of living a *noikokyremeni* (tidy) life. The full integration into this way of living after the 1960s is experienced in many cases as a return to and recovery of what had been lost because of refugeeism. Through these practices and this lifestyle, the children of refugees contribute to the *noikokyrema* (tidying up) – development of Greece.

Renting a real estate property for dwelling purposes is an indicator of low social status and in the context of a *noikokyremenos* (tidy) way of living it is associated with non-reasonable waste of money. Home ownership, in particular by *antiparochi*, allowing for 1) dwelling, 2) settling down children, and 3) increasing the financial capital by renting apartments to others constitutes the most appropriate choice in this specific frame of reference.

Particularly within the context of Kato Toumba, the choice to dwell in the refugee home – even after the extended implementation of the practice of *antiparochi* – is a reason for social conflict, even between members of the same family, providing an indicator of social failure and low social status.

Immigration to Germany is a strategic solution for some informants from Toumba, in order to raise the required financial and social capital to integrate into the normative model of everyday living in the settlement and eventually meet the requirements created by the expansion of capitalist relations of production in Greece.

However, both internal and external migration are indicators of social failure and are seen in a negative way in the context of developed Toumba, because of the movement of these people for financial reasons. Nevertheless, "peasants" and "*Lazogermanoi*" are those who contribute, by investing their capitals, to the enlargement of Toumba and its population after the 1970s. Within the context of the normative way of living, they establish alternative subjectivities that do not completely match the dominant ones. Different experiences, such as life at the factory, rural life, immigration and life abroad contribute to different performances of the modern, which presents "gaps", upsetting the hegemonic cultural perceptions in the region.

The informants from Toumba oppose the narrations of the "old refugee home" to those of the "modern apartment", documenting in this way the change that occurred in the settlement as well as in themselves.

By consuming the modern, they feel they are "humanized" and "civilized" in relation to the experiences of general loss that characterized the previous phase of life. The objects they possess create feelings of joy, pride and satisfaction. However, in the context of financial crisis prevailing in the country since 2010, objects and home materiality create stress to their owners regarding the possibility of their maintenance and use by future generations. Children and grandchildren migrate, capitalizing the cultural and financial capital they raised within the context of a *noikokyremenos* (tidy) way of living and seek to experience nostalgically the true development, where it truly takes place.

Finally, the fifth chapter investigates the way in which post-war state and *noikokyraios* citizen are established as a result of their everyday contact. With the help of material culture theories, network theory and theories of state and power relationships, this chapter seeks to show how the "modern" post-war state is established through practices and discourses of society "civilization". In addition, with the help of the ethnographic material and historical archives, an effort is made to problematize concepts and practices, such as corruption and clientelist relationships, which were associated in the post-war era with the functioning of the Greek bureaucracy, and the ethics of *petty-bourgeoisized* subject, as this is shaped in an underdevelopment system of a peripheral capitalist economy. With the help of anthropological tools and methods, an effort is made to showcase the modalities, through which corruption practices or simply illegal actions can be conceptualized and experienced differently by subjects because of the cultural values and constructions intermediating the relationships of citizens with state employees.

The "modern" post-war Greek state cannot be understood without the hegemonic cultural constructions regarding the *noikokyraioi* citizens and their practices in the specific context of performing the national-collective purpose of reconstruction of Greece that was destroyed by the war.

The "modern" state is a transfer of modernization experiences that *noikokyraioi* have from their homes and neighborhoods. "Modern" describes the contemporary state emerging from reconstruction, modernization of the Greek administration, extended electrification of the country, construction of modern infrastructure and, finally, transformation of the legislation and customary law. Citizens follow step by step in their everyday life the "civilizing" and modernizing imperative to establish the identity of a *noikokyraios* citizen, who is characterized by social upward mobility through: 1) a successful professional course, mainly in the private sector, 2) the possibility of building a privately owned house, furnished and decorated to meet not only the vital need of family housing, but also the social life requirements regarding especially the family image in the broader social group.

The establishment of the *noikokyraios* identity in Toumba is associated with the experiences of an improved public space through infrastructure and electrification projects taking place in the region, but also the everyday life in the modern apartment of the apartment building, in which men and women through their contact with modern life objects feel they are "humanized" and "civilized". By means of these experiences, Kato Toumba overall as a district is transformed from "Red Toumba" of leftist refugees into a modern middle-strata district of eastern Thessaloniki.

DEI, through advertising campaigns and formal speeches of *DEI* representatives, shapes the normative images of modern and contemporary, seeking the biggest possible integration of a part of society into the lifestyle it suggests. "Progress" and *"prokopi"* must characterize the objective-setting of the state, its employees and also simple citizens, who will contribute through the performance of a *"noikokyremenos* (tidy) but modern way of living" to its further development. Through practices of saving money and appropriate consumption of the modern goods suggested by *DEI* (fridge, cooker, etc.), *noikokyris* man and *noikokyra* woman are established, serving in this way native cultural values of the model of *noikokyrio* (household) that characterizes the Greek paradigm over time.

DEI advertising campaigns promote a different standard of family life from the one that prevailed in pre-war Greece. The campaigns focus on the woman, who is showcased as the exclusive handler of the modern appliances. The *noikokyra* woman through the appropriate use of appliances takes the responsibility to improve the family's living conditions at home and to increase the family's profit by means of the transformations (saving of time, energy and money) that the appliances bring to the traditional distribution of housework.

The campaigns suggest adopting modern ways of living at home, based on the reproduction of normative cultural values, such as saving money and time, and meeting the family needs, drawing from the model of the Greek *noikokyrio* (household) and code of *noikokyrosyni*.

The modern Greek *noikokyra* must be stylish (dressed in modern fashionable clothes) throughout the day, even when she cooks or does the laundry at home. Appliances can ensure this right to a comfortable, easy and happy everyday family life at home.

Within the context of post-war development and modernization, it is culturally likely that "illegal" practices and "corruption" actions, particularly those serving the imperative of reconstruction and production of a public space for social purposes, be experienced by the actors as social activity. In these cases, the subject as citizen-benefactor, through a close relationship with state representatives, knows how to undermine civil law and avoid bureaucratic obstacles, to serve in the best possible way, through offer and self-sacrifice, the state and its citizens, as distinct essences, which were reproduced and continued to exist as such by means of these practices.

The citizen who takes social initiatives to offer projects to fellow citizens and contributes to the "salvation" and *"prokopi"* of Greece is established as opposed to the subjectivity of lazy communist, who, in the cold-war context of a city such as Thessaloniki, bordering with the "Northern danger", is the one who puts its course in danger.

The objects that are found in the subjects' spaces, functioning as a framework within and through which the various subjectivities are produced, can be revealing of the action and function of the social networks in which people participate. Moreover, the way they are placed in the informant's home is indicative of their importance in relation to the subject's practices, revealing his/her interesting pathways.

The successful *noikokyraios* citizen is produced through the experience of contact with the public administration, which, through its function, confirms and reinforces the fantasy of existence of an "efficient state". The symbolism of efficient authority and decisiveness as characteristics of governance in the post-war context of capitalist development fulfil citizens' desire for safety and absolute control after a turbulent period. The intense anti-communism establishes the interior other producing in the cold-war context the *noikokyraio* citizen, who is identified with the cultural construction of the unified nation-state that belongs to the West and must be protected to prosper.

State employees and citizens justify their actions, invoking the public interest, which probably matches the political and ideological symbolisms that characterized this period, but eventually serving their own personal interests. The new reproduction of a form of powerful state and the desire for more state representativeness helps maintain civil national conflicts and reproduce the terms establishing conflict.

The symbols of the Greek state by means of the seals and the weight of the signatures of state representatives also work as actors and can create the sense of the unified upper power, acting with the aim of the public interest, which is distinguished from the ulterior private one. But the elements from the overall ethnographic research allow the anthropologist to notice details that reveal the gaps and fragmentary nature of the function of public administration, as well as the influence of cultural and social factors affecting the interpretation and dispensing of the law.

Like other ethnographies of corruption, this study showcases the problematic distinction between essentialist and Eurocentric approaches of legal and illegal practices. The ambiguity of the laws and the possibility of misinterpretation showcase the relativity of the legally "correct" and the inadequacy of absolute definitions of "corruption" placing it on the opposite side of the civil law, identified almost always with random individualized actions of independent subjects.

In conclusion, this thesis as a whole – following the processing of the ethnographic material that resulted from my meetings and discussions with ninety informants – brought up four paradigms of social acknowledgement and development that mark after the end of the 1960s the change and transformation of Kato Toumba into a middle-strata settlement in the eastern side of the city:

a) possibility to live in a privately-owned modern apartment in an apartment building, built either through the practice of *antiparochi* or individually by purchasing a plot or an apartment in an apartment building;
b) possibility of the wife-mother to stay home, in charge of home financial management, raising children, maintaining and extending social relationships and the family's network;
c) possibility to have spaces in the apartment, such as living room with all necessary household goods, which are used only within the context of the family's social commitments, while for the rest of the time they remain closed and are not used;
d) possibility for next generations to study at university and be professionally settled by being appointed as state employees. Children getting married and having offspring, as well as children's appointment as state employees or children finding permanent employment in the private sector, which was guaranteed by a university degree, established for most families from Toumba the "normality" that ensured their intergenerational social reproduction.

References

Abrams, Ph. (1988). Notes on the Difficulty of Studying the State (1977). *Journal of Historical Sociology*, 1(1), 58–89. https://doi.org/10.1111/j.1467-6443.1988.tb00004. x

Abrams, L. (2014). *Θεωρία προφορικής Ιστορίας* [Oral History Theory]. Plethron.

Althusser L. (2006). Ideology and Ideological State Apparatuses (Notes towards an Investigation). In A.Gupta & A. Sharma (Eds.), *The Anthropology of the State* (pp. 86–111). Malden: Blackwell.

Anastasiadis, G. (1997). Τα ντοκυμαντέρ της πόλης και η ιστοριογραφία της. Οι κινηματογραφικές ταινίες ως πηγή της Ιστορίας [Documentaries and historiography of the city. Cinematography movies as source of history]. *Thessalonikeon Polis* [City of Thessalonians], 2, 126–129.

Anastasiadou, M. (2002). 'Δια λόγους τιμής': Βία, συναισθήματα και αξίες στη μετεμφυλιακή Ελλάδα ["For reasons of honor": Violence, emotions and values in post-civil-war Greece]. Nefeli.

Anastasiadou, M. (2008). *Θεσσαλονίκη 1830–1912: Μια μητρόπολη την εποχή των οθωμανικών μεταρρυθμίσεων* [Thessaloniki 1830–1912: A metropolis in the era of Ottoman reforms]. Politia.

Anderson, B. (1991). *Imagined Communities: Reflections on the Origin and Spread of Nationalism*. Verso.

Angelopoulos, G. (2003). Πολιτικές πρακτικές και πολυπολιτισμικότητα: η περίπτωση της Θεσσαλονίκης Πολιτισμικής Πρωτεύουσας της Ευρώπης 1997 [Political practices and multiculturalism: the case of Thessaloniki European Capital of Culture 1997]. *O politis*, 107, 35–43.

Antonopoulou, S. (1991). *Ο Μεταπολεμικός μετασχηματισμός της ελληνικής οικονομίας και το οικιστικό φαινόμενο 1950–1980* [Post-war formation of the Greek economy and the residential phenomenon 1950–1980]. Papazisi.

Appiah, K. A. (2016, November 6). There is no Such Thing as Western Civilization. *The Guardian*. https://www.theguardian.com/world/2016/nov/09/western-civilisation-appiah-reith-lecture.

Appadurai, A. (1988). *The social Life of Things. Commodities in Cultural Perspective*. University Cambridge Press. (1996). *Modernity at large*. University of Minnesota Press.

Aranitou, V. (2018). *Η Μεσαία τάξη στην Ελλάδα την εποχή των μνημονίων. Μεταξύ κατάρρευσης και ανθεκτικότητας* [Middle classes in Greece in the era of memorandums. Between collapse and resilience]. Themelio.

Aretxaga, B. (2003). Maddening States. *Annual review of Anthropology*, 32, 393–410. https://doi.org/10.1146/annurev.anthro.32.061002.093341

Arvidsson, A. (2001). From Counterculture to Consumer Culture: Vespa and the Italian youth market, 1958–1978. *Journal of Consumer Culture, 1*(1), 47–71. Doi: 10.1177/146954050100100104

Athanasatou, G. (2001). *Ελληνικός κινηματογράφος (1950–1967). Λαϊκή μνήμη και ιδεολογία* [Greek cinema (1950–1967). People's memory and ideology]. FINATEC.

Athanasiou, E. (Ed.). (2001). *Η κόκκινη Βιέννη, το Pruitt-Igoe και η πολυκατοικία της αντιπαροχής* [Red Vienna, Pruitt-Igoe and antiparochi apartment building]. *He Architektonike os Techni* [Architecture as art], 5, 20–22.

Athanasiou, E. (2016). *Εισαγωγή. Για μια κριτική αναθεώρηση της έκκεντρης νεωτερικότητας* [Introduction. For a critical review of off-center moderity]. In A. Athanasiou (Ed.), *Αποδομώντας την Αυτοκρατορία. Θεωρία και πολιτική της μεταπολεμικής κριτικής* [Destructuring the Empire. Theory and politics of post-war criticism] (pp. 9–21). Athens: Politis.

Attfield, J. (1999). Bringing modernity home. In I. Cieraad (Ed.), *At Home. An Anthropology of domestic Space* (pp. 73–82). New York: Syracuse University Press.

Avdela, E. (1995). *Η κοινωνική τάξη στη σύγχρονη ιστοριογραφία: από το οικονομικό δεδομένο στην πολιτισμική κατασκευή* [Social class in modern historiography: from the financial setting to the political construction]. *Istorika*, 22, 173–204.

Axelos, K. (2010). *Η Μοίρα της σύγχρονης Ελλάδας* [The fate of modern Greece]. Nefeli.

Bachelard, G. (1994). *The Poetics of Space*. Beacon Press.

Bade, C. P., & C. Sant (1992). *The making of the Modern Greek family*. Cambridge university Press.

Bada, K. (2011). *Σημείωσεις για τον Υλικό πολιτισμό (18ος -20ος αιώνας)* [Notes on material culture (18th-20th century)]. Univ. of Ioannina.

Bhabha, K. H. (1994). *The Location of Culture*. Routledge.

Bailey, P. (2013). *Leisure and Class in Victorian England*. Rootledge. https://doi.org/10.4324/9781315870748

Bakalaki, A. (1994). *Εισαγωγή. Από την Ανθρωπολογία των γυναικών στην Ανθρωπολογία των φύλων* [Introduction. From women anthropology to gender anthropology]. In A. Μπακαλάκη (Ed.). *Ανθρωπολογία, γυναίκες και φύλο* [A. Bakalaki (Ed.) Anthropology, women and gender] (pp. 13–74). Athens: Alexandria.

Bakalaki, A. (2008). *Λόγοι για το Φύλο και αναπαραστάσεις της πολιτισμικής ιδιαιτερότητας στην Ελλάδα του 19ου και 20ου αιώνα* [Discourses about gender and representation of cultural specifics in Greece of the 19th and 20th century]. In D. Gkefou-Madianou (Ed.) *Ανθρωπολογική θεωρία και Εθνογραφία, Σύγχρονες τάσεις* [Anthropological Theory and Ethnography: Modern Trends] (pp. 519–582). Athens: Ellinika Grammata.

Bakalaki, A. (2003a). Χρήσεις και καταχρήσεις του Κοινωνικού Φύλου στην Ανθρωπολογία [Uses and abuses of social gender in anthropology]. In *Το Φύλο, τόπος συνάντησης των επιστημών. Ένας πρώτος ελληνικός απολογισμός* [Gender, where science fields meet. A first Greek review] (pp. 1–22). Mytilene: University of the Aegean.

Bakalaki, A. (2003b). Locked into security, keyed into modernity: The selection of burglaries as source of risk in Greece. *Ethnos: Journal of Anthropology, 68(2)*, 209–229.

Balibar, E. (1995). *The Philosophy of Marx*. Verso.

Banks M., & Zeitlyn D. (2015). *Visual Methods in Social Research*. Sage Publications.

Beaudrillard, J. (1996). *The System of Objects*. Verso.

Beaudrillard, J. (2000). *Η καταναλωτική κοινωνία* [The Consumer Society]. Nisides.

Berstein S., & Milza, P. (1997). *Ιστορία της Ευρώπης 2. Η ευρωπαϊκή συμφωνία και η Ευρώπη των εθνών 1815–1919* [History of Europe 2. The European agreement and Europe of Nations 1815–1919]. Alexandria

Blunt, A., & Dowling, R. (2006). *Home: Key Ideas in Geography*. Routledge.

Blundo, G. (2007). Hidden Acts, Open Talks. How Anthropology Can 'Observe' and Describe Corruption. In Nuijten M. & Anders, G. (Eds.), *Corruption and the Secret of Law. A Legal Anthropological Perspective* (pp. 27–52). Burlington: Ashgate.

Bountidou, Ath., & Stergioudis, D. (Eds.). (2002). *Η Τούμπα των Προσφύγων* [Toumba of Refugees]. KITH.

Bourdieu, P. (1999). Rethinking the State: Genesis and Structure of the Bureaucratic Field. In G. Steinmetz (Ed.), *State/Culture, State-formation after the Cultural Turn* (pp. 53–75). http://www.jstor.org/stable/10.7591/j.ctv1nhjcg

Bourdieu, P. (2006). *Η αίσθηση της πρακτικής* [The logic of practice]. Alexandria.

Bourdieu, P. (2008). *Η Διάκριση. Κοινωνική Κριτική της καλαισθητική Κρίσης* [Distinction: A Social Critique of the of the Judgement of Taste. Patakis.

Brüggemeier, F., & Kocka, J. (Eds.). (1985). *Geschichte von unten- Geschichte von innen. Kontroversen um die Alltagsgeschichte. Fernuniv.* Hagen.

Buchli, V. (2002). Introduction. In V. Buchli (Ed.), *The Material Culture Reader* (pp. 1–23). Oxford – New York: Berg.

Buchli, V. (2010). Households and Home cultures. In D. Hicks & M. Beaudry (Eds.), *The Oxford Handbook of Material Culture Studies* (pp. 502–520). Oxford: University press.

Burchell, G., Gordon, C., & Miller, P. (1991). *The Foucault Effect studies in Governmentality*. Harvester Whealboor.

Burgel, G. (1976). *Αθήνα: Η ανάπτυξη μιας μεσογειακής πρωτεύουσας* [Athens: The development of a Mediterranean capital city]. Exantas.

Butler, J. (2009). *Αναταραχή Φύλου. Ο Φεμινισμός και η ανατροπή της Ταυτότητας* [Gender Trouble: Feminism and the Subversion of Identity]. Alexandria.

Carrier, J. G., (2015). The concept of Class. In G. J. Carrier & D. Kalb (Eds.), *Anthropologies of Class. Power, Practice and Inequality* (pp. 28–40). https://doi.org/10.1017/CBO9781316095867

Chatzigakis, S. (2015, November 11). Η γενναία υπέρβαση που χρειάζεται η ΝΔ [The brave overcoming that New Democracy needs]. To Vima. https://www.tovima.gr/2015/10/10/opinions/i-gennaia-yperbasi-poy-xreiazetai-i-nd/

Charalampis, D. (1985). *Στρατός και πολιτική εξουσία: Η δομή της εξουσίας στην μετεμφυλιακή Ελλάδα* [Army and political power. The structure of power in post-civil-war Greece]. Exantas.

Charalampis, D. (1989). *Πελατειακές Σχέσεις και Λαϊκισμός. Η εξωθεσμική συναίνεση στο ελληνικό πολιτικό σύστημα* [Clientelism relationships and Populism. Extra-institutional consent to the Greek political system]. Exantas.

Chastaoglou V. (2008). Προσφυγική εγκατάσταση. Κοινωνικοί και πολεοδομικοί μετασχηματισμοί [Refugee settlement. Social and urban transformations]. In E. Ioannidou (Ed.), *Η Μεταμόρφωση της Θεσσαλονίκης. Η εγκατάσταση των προσφύγων στην πόλη (1920–1940)* [Transformation of Thessaloniki. Settlement of refugees in the city (1920–1940)] (pp. 43–88). Athens: Epimetro.

Chatziiosif, Chr. (1993). Η περίοδος της ανασυγκρότησης 1945–1953 ως στιγμή της Σύγχρονης Ελληνικής και Ευρωπαϊκής Ιστορίας [The reconstruction period 1945–1953 as a moment of Modern Greek and European History]. In *Η Ελληνική Κοινωνία κατά την πρώτη μεταπολεμική περίοδο (1945 – 1967): 4° Επιστ. Συνέδριο/ Πάντειο Πανεπιστήμιο 24–27 Νοεμβρίου 1993 –* [Greek Society in the first post-war period: 4.Conference/ Panteion University 24–27 November 1993] (pp. 23–33). Athens: Idryma Saki Karagiorga.

Christianopoulos, D. (2008). *Θεσσαλονίκην, ου μ᾽εθέσπισεν... Αυτοβιογραφικά Κείμενα* [To Thessaloniki, where He sent me.... Autobiographical texts]. Ianos.

Chevalier, S. (1999). The French Two-Home Project. Materialization of Family Identity. In I. Cieerad (Ed.), *At home. An Anthropology of domestic space* (pp. 83–94). https://doi.org/10.2307/j.ctv1w36pj9

Chevalier, S. (2002). The Cultural Construction of Domestic Space in France and Great Britain. *Signs*, 27(3), 847–856. https://doi.org/10.1086/337929

Cieraad, I. (Ed.). (1999). *An Anthropology of domestic Space.* Syracuse University Press. https://doi.org/10.2307/j.ctv1w36pj9

Cieraad, I. (1999). Anthropology at home. In I. Cieraad (Ed.), *An Anthropology of domestic Space* (pp. 1–12). New York: Syracuse University Press.

Clifford, J., & Marcus, G. E. (Ed.). (1986). *Writing Culture: The poetics and politics of Ethnography*, Berkeley. University of California Press.

Collard, A. (1993). Διερευνώντας την Κοινωνική Μνήμη στον Ελλαδικό χώρο [Investigating social memory in the Greek territory]. In E. Papataxiarchis & Th. Paradellis (Eds.), *Ανθρωπολογία και Παρελθόν: Συμβολές στην Κοινωνική Ιστορία της Νεότερης Ελλάδας* [Anthropology and Past: Contributions to the Social History of Modern Greece] (pp. 357–389). Athens: Alexandria.

Colonas, V. (2005). *Greek Architects in the Ottoman Empire*. Olkos.

Csikszentmihalyi, M., & Rochberg-Halton, E. (1999). *The meaning of things. Domestic Symbols and the self*. Cambridge University Press.

De Certeau, M. (1988). *The practice of everyday Life*. University of California Press.

Deltsou, E. (1995). *Praxes of Tradition and Modernity in a village in Northern Greece* [Doctoral Dissertation, Indiana University].

Deltsou, E. (2004). Ποντιακοί σύλλογοι και πολιτική: Η δημόσια διαμόρφωση και η σημασία της μνήμης των ποντίων προσφύγων του 1922 στη Θεσσαλονίκη του 2000" [Pontic associations and politics: the public shaping and importance of the memory of Pontic refugees of 1922 in Thessaloniki of 2000]. In V. Gounaris & I. Michailidis (Eds.), *Πρόσφυγες στα Βαλκάνια. Μνήμη και ενσωμάτωση* [Refugees in the Balkans. Memory and integration] (pp. 252–285). Thessaloniki: Patakis.

Dertilis G.V., & Kostis, K. (1991). *Θέματα Νεοελληνικής Ιστορίας (18^ΟΣ-20^ΟΣ αιώνας)* [Modern Greek History Issues 18th-20th century]. Sakoula.

Dertilis, G. (2015). *Ιστορία του Ελληνικού Κράτους 1830–1920* [History of the Greek State 1830–1920]. Univ. Editions of Crete

Dertilis, G. (2016). *Επτά Πόλεμοι, Τέσσερις Εμφύλιοι, Επτά Πτωχεύσεις 1821–2016* [Seven wars, four civil wars, Seven Bankruptcies]. Polis.

Diamantouros, N. (2000). *Πολιτισμικός δυϊσμός και πολιτική στην Ελλάδα της Μεταπολίτευσης* [Cultural Dualism and Politics in Greece of political transition]. Alexandria.

Dimitriadis, D. (2003). *Πεθαίνω σαν Χώρα* [Dying as a country]. Agra.

Dimova, R. (2006). *Ethno-Baroque: Materiality, Aesthetics and Conflict in Modern Day Macedonia*. Berghahn.

Dordanas, S. (2006). *Έλληνες εναντίον Ελλήνων* [Greeks against Greeks]. Epikentro.

Dordanas, S. (2012). Η γερμανική στολή στη ναφθαλίνη. Επιβιώσεις του δοσολογισμού στη Μακεδονία [The German uniform in mothballs. Survival of Kollaboration in Macedonia]. Epiekntro.

Donner, H. (2015). Making middle-class families in Calcutta. In G. J. Carrier & D. Kalb (Eds.), *Anthropologies of Class. Power, Practice and Inequality* (pp. 131–148). Cambridge University Press.

Drazin, A., & Frohlich, D. (2007). Good Intentions: Remembering through Framing Photographs in English Homes. *Ethnos* 72(1), 51–76. https://doi.org/10.1080/001 41840701219536

Dubisch, J. (translation by Moustri, D.) (Ed.). (2019). *Το θρησκευτικό προσκύνημα στη σύγχρονη Ελλάδα. Μια εθνογραφική προσέγγιση* [In a Different Place. Pilgrimage, Gender, and Politics at a Greek Island Shrine]. Alexandria.

Dubisch, J. (Ed.). (2019). *Gender and Power in Rural Greece*. Princeton.https://doi.org/1 0.2307/j.ctvcmxs7q

Du Boulay, J. (1974). *Portrait of a Greek Mountain Village*. Clarendon Press.

Edwards, E. (2009). Photography and the Material Performance of the Past. *History and Theory*, 48(4), 130–150. http://www.jstor.org/stable/25621444

Edwards, E. (2012). Objects of Affect: Photography Beyond the Image. *Annual Review of Anthropology*, 41, 221–234. https://doi.org/10.1146/annurev-anthro-092611-1457 08

Elefantis, A. (2002). *Μας πήραν την Αθήνα. Ξαναδιαβάζοντας μερικά σημεία της Ιστορίας 1940–1950* [They have taken Athens away from us. Rereading some 1940–1950 History aspects]. Vivliorama.

Elias, N. (translation by Loupasakis, Th.) (1997). *Η διαδικασία του Πολιτισμού. Μια Ιστορία της κοινωνικής Συμπεριφοράς* [The Civilizing Process. The History of Manners]. Alexandria.

Elias, N. (2000). *The Civilizing Process: Sociogenetic and Psychogenetic Investigations*. Blackwell.

Federici, S. (2011). *Ο Καλιμπάν και η μάγισσα. Γυναίκες, σώμα και πρωταρχική συσσώρευση* [Caliban and the Witch: Women, the Body and Primitive Accumulation]. Editions Xenon.

Ferhevary, K. (2002). American Kitchens, Luxury Bathrooms, and the search for a 'Normal' Life in Postsocialist Hungary. *Ethnos Journal of Anthropology* 67(3), 369–400. https://doi.org/10.1080/0014184022000031211

Ferguson, J. (2005). Decomposing Modernity: History and Hierarchy after Development. In A. Loomba, S. Kaul & M. Burton (Eds.), *Postcolonial Studies and Beyond* (pp. 166–181). Durham: Duke University Press.

Ferguson, J., & Gupta, A. (2002). Spatializing States: toward an ethnography of neoliberal governmentality. *American Ethnologist*, 29(4), 981–1002. http://www.jsto r.org/stable/3805165

Filias, V. (1974). *Προβλήματα κοινωνικού μετασχηματισμού* [Social transformation problems]. Papazisis

Foucault, M. (translation by Sarikas, Z.) (1987). *Χώρος, γνώση και εξουσία. Συζήτηση με τον Paul Rabinow τον Μάρτιο του 1982* [Space, Power, and Knowledge. An interview with Paul Rabinow in March 1982]. In Foucault, M., *Εξουσία, γνώση και ηθική* [Power, Ethics and Knowledge] (pp. 51–60). Athens: Ypsilon.

Foucault, M. (2002). *The order of things*. Routledge.

Foucault, M. (2006). Governmentality. In A. Sharma & A. Gupta (Eds.), *The Anthropology of the State: a Reader* (pp. 131–142). Malden: Blackwell.

Friedl, E. (1962). *Vasilika: A Village in Modern Greece*. Holt, Rinehart and Winston.

Friedl, E. (1963). Lagging Emulation in Post-Peasant Society: A Greek Case. In J. G. Peristiany (Ed.), Contributions to Mediterranean Sociology (pp. 93–106). Paris: Mouton.

Frykman, J., & Löfgren, O. (1987). *Culture Builder: A historical Anthroplogy of Middle-Class Life.* Gers University Press.

Gampbell, J.K. (1964). *Honour, Family, and Patronage: A Study of Institutions and Moral Values in a Greek Mountain Community.* Oxford University Press.

Garvey, P. (2001). Organized Disorder: Moving Furniture in Norwegian Homes. In *Home Possessions: the Material Culture of the Home* (pp. 47–68). Oxford: Berg.

Gazi, E. (1999). Οριενταλισμός. Το κείμενο ως γεγονός [Orientalism. Text as fact]. *Mnimon, 21,* 237–246.

Gell, A. (1998). *Art and Agency. An Anthropological Theory.* Clarendon Press.

Gkefou-Madianou, D. (1999). *Πολιτισμός και Εθνογραφία. Από τον Εθνογραφικό Ρεαλισμό στην πολιτισμική Κριτική* [Culture and Ethnography. From Ethnographic Realism to Cultural Critique]. Ellinika Grammata.

Gkefou-Madianou, D. (2006). "Στο πρόσωπο του άνδρα μου εμένα βλέπουν": το "δημόσιο" και το "ιδιωτικό" ως τόποι κατασκευής της έμφυλης ταυτότητας ["In my husband's face they see me": "public" and "private" as places of construction of gender-based identity]. In D. Gkefou-Madianou (Ed.), *Εαυτός και "άλλος". Εννοιολογήσεις, ταυτότητες και πρακτικές στην Ελλάδα και την Κύπρο* [Self and "other". Conceptualizations, identities and practices in Greece and Cyprus) (pp. 111–181). Athens: Ellinika Grammata.

Gkefou-Madianou, D. (2008). Εισαγωγή: Από την ολιστική προσέγγιση στις μερικές αλήθειες [Introduction: From a holistic approach to partial truths]. In D. Gkefou-Madianou (Ed.), *Ανθρωπολογική θεωρία και Εθνογραφία, Σύγχρονες τάσεις* [Anthropological Theory and Ethnography: Modern Trends] (pp. 11–66). Athens: Ellinika Grammata.

Gkefou-Madianou, D. (Ed.) (2009). *Όψεις ανθρωπολογικής έρευνας. Πολιτισμός, Ιστορία, Αναπαραστάσεις* [Aspects of anthropological research. Culture, History, Representations]. Ellinika Grammata.

Giakoumakatos, A. (2003). *Στοιχεία για τη Νεότερη Ελληνική Αρχιτεκτονική. Πάτροκλος Καραντινός* [Elements on Modern Greek Architecture. Patroklos Karantinos]. MIET.

Gialouri, E. (Ed.). (2012). *Υλικός πολιτισμός, Η ανθρωπολογία στη χώρα των πραγμάτων* [Material culture: Anthropology in the land of things]. Alexandria.

Giannakopoulos, K., & Giannitsiotis G. (Eds.). (2010). *Αμφισβητούμενοι χώροι στην πόλη. Χωρικές Προσεγγίσεις του πολιτισμού* [Questionable places in the city. Spatial approaches of culture]. Alexandria/Univ. of the Aegean.

Giannakopoulos K. (2001). Ανδρική ταυτότητα, σώμα και ομόφυλες σχέσεις. Μια προσέγγιση του φύλου και της σεξουαλικότητας [Male identity, body and same-sex relationships. An approach of gender and sexuality]. In D. Sotiriou (Ed.) *Ανθρωπολογία των Φυλων [Anthropology of Genders]* (pp. 161–187). Athens: Savvalas.

Giannakopoulos K. (2006). Ιστορίες σεξουαλικότητας [Sexuality Stories]. In K. Giannakopoulos (Ed.), *Σεξουαλικότητα: Θεωρίες και Πολιτικές της Ανθρωπολογίας* [Sexuality: Theories and Policies of Anthropology] (pp. 17–102). Athens: Alexandria.

Giannitsis, T. (1985). *Η Ελληνική Βιομηχανία. Ανάπτυξη και Κρίση* [The Greek Industry: Development and Crisis]. Gutenberg.

Giannoulopoulos, G. (1992). *Ο Μεταπολεμικός Κόσμος. Ελληνική και Ευρωπαϊκή Ιστορία (1945–1963)* [Post-ward World. Greek and European History (1945–1963). Papazisi.

Gilmore, D. (1982). Anthropology of the Mediterranean Area. *Annual Reviews* 11,175–205. http://www.jstor.org/stable/2155780

Gledhill, J. (2013). *Οι μεταμφιέσεις της εξουσίας. Ανθρωπολογικές οπτικές για την πολιτική* [Power disguise. Anthropological aspects of politics]. Alexandria.

Goffman, E. (1975). *Frame Analysis.* Penguin.

Gombrich, E. (1979). *The sense of Order: A Study in the psychology of Decorate Art.* Phaidon Press.

Gounaris B. C. (1989). Railway Construction and Labour Availability in Macedonia in the Late Nineteenth Century. *Byzantine and Modern Greek Studies, 13*(10), 139–158. https://doi.org/10.1179/byz.1989.13.1.139

Gramsci A. (2006). Selections from the Prison Notebooks. In A. Gupta and A. Sharma, *The Anthropology of the State* (pp. 71–85). Malden: Blackwell.

Godelier, M. (1977). *Perspectives in Marxist Athropology.* Cambridge University Press.

Goldin, I., Cameron G., & Balarajan, M. (2013). *Αυτοί δεν είναι σαν εμάς. Το παρελθόν και το μέλλον της μετανάστευσης* [They are not like us. Past and future of immigration]. Univ. Editions of Crete.

Gounaris V. (1995). *Θεσσαλονίκη 1917–1967 η ταυτότητα της πόλης μέσα από το δημοτικό αρχείο* [Thessaloniki 1917–1967, the identity of the city through the municipal archives]. Thessaloniki History Center.

Gullestad, M. (1984). *Kitchen-table society: a case study of the family life and friendships of young working-class mothers in urban Norway.* Norwegian University Press.

Gupta A., & Sharma, A. (2006). Blurred Boundaries: The discourse of Corruption, the culture of politics, and the imagined State. In A. Gupta and A. Sharma (Eds.), *The Anthropology of the State: The Reader* (pp. 211–242). Malden: Blackwell.

Habermas, J. (1991). *The structural transformation of the public space. An inquiry into a category of Bourgeois Society.* MIT Press.

Halbwachs, M. (2013). *Τα κοινωνικά πλαίσια της Μνήμης* [Social Frameworks of Memory]. Nefeli.

Haller, D., & Shore, Ch. (Eds.). (2005). *Corruption: Anthropological Perspectives.* Pluto Press. https://doi.org/10.2307/j.ctt18fs7ts

Hansen T. B., & Stepputat, F. (Eds.). (2001). *States of Imagination: Ethnographic Explorations of the Postcolonial State*. Duke University Press. https://doi.org/10.2307/j.c tv11smxxj

Hantzaroula, P. (2002). The making of subordination: Domestic Servants in Greece, 1920–1945 [Doctoral Thesis, European University Institute]. file:///C:/ Users/pp019937/Downloads/Hantzaroula_2002.pdf

Hantzaroula, P. (2012). Σμιλεύοντας την υποταγή: έμμισθες οικιακές εργάτριες στην Ελλάδα το πρώτο μισό του εικοστού αιώνα [Carving submission: salaried domestic workers in Greece in the first half of the twentieth century]. Papazisi.

Hastrup K. (2008). Ιθαγενής ανθρωπολογία: Μια αντίφαση στους όρους [Anthropological Advocacy. A contradiction in terms]. In D. Gkefou-Madianou (Ed.) *Ανθρωπολογική θεωρία και Εθνογραφία, Σύγχρονες τάσεις* [Anthropological Theory and Ethnography: Modern Trends] (pp. 337–364). Athens: Ellinika Grammata.

Haralovich, M.B. (1988). Suburban family sitcoms and consumer product design: Addressing the social subjectivity of homemakers in the 1950s. In P. Drummond & R. Paterson, *Television and its audience*. https://dx.doi.org/10.4135/97814462800 41

Hecht, A. (2001). Home Sweet home Tangible Memories of an Uprooted Childhood. In D. Miller (Ed.), *Home Possessions. Material Culture behind Closed Doors* (pp. 123–145). Oxford and New York: Berg.

Hegel, G.W.F (1977). *Phenomenology of Spirit*. Oxford University Press.

Herzfeld, M. (1982). *Ours Once more: Folklore, Ideology and the making of Modern Greece*. University of Texas Press.

Herzfeld, M. (1987). *Anthropology through the Looking-Class: Critical Ethnography in the Margins of Europe*. Cambridge University Press.

Herzfeld, M. (1993). *The social production of Indifference. Exploring the Symbolic Roots of Western Bureaucracy*. The University of Chicago Press.

Herzfeld, M. (1997). *Cultural Intimacy. Social Poetics in the Nation-State*. Rootledge.

Herzfeld, M. (2002). The Absence Presence: Discourses of Crypto-Colonialism. *The South Atlantic Quarterly*, 101(4), 899–926. https://www.muse.jhu.edu/article/3911 2.

Herzfeld, M. (2008). Η κοινωνική ποιητική: Όψεις από την ελληνική εθνογραφία" [Social poetics: Aspects of Greek ethnography]. In D. Gkefou-Madianou (Ed.) *Ανθρωπολογική θεωρία και Εθνογραφία, Σύγχρονες τάσεις* [Anthropological Theory and Ethnography: Modern Trends] (pp. 447–518). Athens: Ellinika Grammata.

Herzfeld, M. (2019). Within and Without: The Category of 'Female' in the Ethnography of Modern Greece. In J. Dubisch (Ed.), *Gender and Power in Rural Greece* (pp. 215–234). https://doi.org/10.2307/j.ctvcmxs7q

Hetherington, K., & Munro, R. (Eds.). (1997). *Ideas of Difference. Social Spaces and the Labour of Division*. Sociological Review Monographs. Oxford, UK: Blackwell.

Heyman J., & Campbell, H. (2007). Corruption in the US Borderlands with Mexico: The 'Purity' of Society and the 'Perversity' of Borders. In M. Nuijten & G. Anders (Eds.), *Corruption and the Secret of Law. A Legal Anthropological Perspective* (pp. 191–219). Burlington: Ashgate.

Hicks D., & Beaudry M. C. (Eds.). (2010). *Material Culture Studies*, Oxford: Oxford University Press.

Hirschon, R. (1978). Open Body/ Closed Space: The Transformation of Female Sexuality. In S. Ardener (Ed.), *Defining Females: The Nature of Women in Society* (pp. 66–88). London: Croom Helm.

Hirschon, R. (1981). Essential Objects and the Sacred: Interior and Exterior Space in an Urban Greek Locality. In S. Ardener (Ed.), Woman and Space (pp. 72–88). London: Croom Helm.

Hirschon – Filippaki, R. (1993). Μνήμη και ταυτότητα. Οι Μικρασιάτες πρόσφυγες της Κοκκινιάς [Memory and Identity: The Asia Minor Greeks in Kokkinia]. In E. Papataxiarchis & E. Paradellis (Eds.), *Ανθρωπολογία και Παρελθόν: Συμβολές στην Κοινωνική Ιστορία της Νεότερης Ελλάδας* [Anthropology and the Past: Contributions to Social History in Modern Greece] (pp. 327–356). Athens: Alexandria.

Hirschon, R. (2006). *Οι Κληρονόμοι της Μικρασιατικής Καταστροφής. Η κοινωνική ζωή των Μικρασιατών προσφύγων στον Πειραιά* [Heirs of the Greek Catastrophe: The Social Life of Asia Minor Refugees in Piraeus]. MIET.

Holden, L., & Tortora, G. (2007). Corrupted Files: Cross-fading Defense Strategies of a Vesuvian Lawyer. In M. Nuijten and G. Anders (Eds.), *Corruption and the Secret of Law. A Legal Anthropological Perspective* (pp. 99–124). Burlington: Ashgate.

Hurdley, R., (2006). Dismantling Mantelpieces: Narrating Identities and Materializing Culture in the Home. *British Sociological Association*, 40(4), 717–733. https://doi.org/10.1177/0038038506065157

Ingold, T. (2007a) *Lines: A brief History*. Rootledge

Ingold, T. (2007b). Materials against materiality. *Archaeological Dialogues*, 14(1), 1–16. doi:10.1017/S1380203807002127

Ingold, T. (2008). When ANT meets SPIDER: Social Theory for arthropods. In C. Knappet & L. Malafouris, (Eds.), *Material Agency: Towards a Non-Anthropocentric Approach* (pp. 209– 215). New York: Springer.

Ioannidou, A. (2004). Έμφυλες ταυτότητες στο περιθώριο. Η περίπτωση της Καλκάντζας [Gender-based identities in the margins. The case of Kalkantza] [Doctoral Thesis, University of the Aegean]. https://www.didaktorika.gr/eadd/handle/10442/15638

Ioannidou, E. (Ed.). (2008). *Η Μεταμόρφωση της Θεσσαλονίκης. Η εγκατάσταση των προσφύγων στην πόλη (1920–1940)* [Transformation of Thessaloniki. Settlement of refugees in the city (1920–1940)]. Epimetro.

Iatridis, G. (Ed.) ([1981] 1984) *Η Ελλάδα στη δεκαετία 1940–1950. Ένα έθνος σε κρίση* [Greece in the decade of 1940–1950. A nation in crisis]. Themelio.

Kalb, D. (2015). Introduction: Class and the new anthropological holism. In G. J. Carrier & D. Kalb (Eds.), *Anthropologies of Class. Power, Practice and Inequality* (pp. 1–28). doi:10.1017/CBO9781316095867

Karagianni S., & Nikolaou A. (1993). Βιομηχανική πολιτική στις πρώτες μεταπολεμικές δεκαετίες: χωρικές και κλαδικές διαστάσεις [Industrial policy in the first post-war decades: spatial and sectoral dimensions]. In *Η Ελληνική Κοινωνία κατά την πρώτη μεταπολεμική περίοδο (1945 – 1967): 4° Επιστ. Συνέδριο/ Πάντειο Πανεπιστήμιο 24–27 Νοεμβρίου 1993* – [Greek Society in the first post-war period: 4.Conference/ Panteion University 24–27 November 1993] (pp. 94–114). Athens: Idryma Saki Karagiorga.

Karadimou-Gerolympou A. (1995). *Η ανοικοδόμηση της Θεσσαλονίκης μετά την πυρκαγιά του 1917. Ένα ορόσημο στην ιστορία της πόλης και στην ανάπτυξη της ελληνικής πολεοδομίας* [Reconstruction of Thessaloniki after the fire of 1917. A milestone in the history of the city and the development of Greek urban planning]. University Studio Press.

Karadimou-Gerolympou A. (1997). *Μεταξύ Ανατολής και Δύσης. Θεσσαλονίκη και Βορειοελλαδικές πόλεις στο τέλος του 19ου αιώνα* [Between East and West. Northern Greece cities at the end of the 19th century]. University Studio Press.

Karadimou-Gerolympou A. (2008). *Ο αστικός χώρος της Θεσσαλονίκης. Μακρές διάρκειες και γρήγοροι μετασχηματισμοί, με φόντο την βαλκανική ενδοχώρα* [The urban space of Thessaloniki. Longue durée and fast transformations, against the backdrop of the Balkan continent]. In G. Kafkalas, L. Lambrianidis, & N. Papamichos (Eds.), *Η Θεσσαλονίκη στο μεταίχμιο. Η πόλη ως διαδικασία αλλαγών* [Thessaloniki on the threshold. The city as a process of changes]. Athens: Editions Kritiki.

Karadimou-Gerolympou A. (2013). *Η ανάδυση της σύγχρονης Θεσσαλονίκης. Ιστορίες, πρόσωπα, τοπία* [Emergence of modern Thessaloniki. Stories, people, landscapes]. University Studio Press.

Karalidou, F. (2008). *Κοινωνικές σχέσεις, ταυτότητες και τοπική αυτοδιοίκηση στο δήμο Αξιούπολης και στο δήμο Χέρσου του νομού Κιλκίς: η εφαρμογή του Ν.2539/97. Καποδίστριας* [Social relations, identities and local administration in the municipality of Axioupoli and in the municipality of Herso of the perfecture of Kilkis: implementation …] [Doctoral Thesis, Aristotle University of Thessaloniki]. https://thesis.ekt.gr/thesisBookReader/id/35010#page/1/mode/2up

Karapostolis, V. (1983). *Η καταναλωτική συμπεριφορά στην ελληνική κοινωνία. 1960–1975* [Consumption behavior in Greek society. 1960–1975]. EKKE.

Katsikas, I. (2000). Το κοινωνικό περιεχόμενο της αντιπαροχής και οι οικονομικές του προεκτάσεις [The social content of antiparochi and its economic repercussions]. *Epitheorisi koinonikon Erevnon, 103*(3), 3–26.

Knappet, C., & Malafouris, L. (2008). Material and nonhuman Agency: An Introduction. In C. Knappet & L. Malafouris, (Eds.), *Material Agency: Towards a Non-Anthropocentric Approach*, ix–xix. New York: Springer.

Kojève, A. (1947). Introduction to the Reading of Hegel: Lectures on the Phenomenology of Spirit. Cornell University Press.

Kokot, W. (1994). Kognition und Soziale Identität in einem Flüctlingsviertel: Kato Toumba, Thessaloniki [Cognition and social identity in a refugee quarter of Salonica, Greece] [Habilitation, Universität zu Köln].

Kokot, W. (1996). Kleinasienflüchtlinge in Thessaloniki: Zur Verarbeitung von Fluchterlebnissen in Biographischen Erzählungen (Asia Minor Refugees in Thessaloniki: Revising Experiences of Escaping in Biographical Narratives). In W. Kokot & D. Drackle (Eds.), *Ethnologie Europas:Grenzen, Konflikte, Identitäten* (pp. 259–271). Berlin: Reimer.

Kolonas, V. (2012). *Η αρχιτεκτονική μιας Εκατονταετίας* [The architecture of a century]. University Studio Press.

Kondylis, P. (1991). *Der Niedergang der bürgerlichen Denk- und Lebensform: Die liberale Moderne und die massendemokratische Postmoderne*. VCH – Acta Humaniora.

Kondylis, P. (1995). *1943–1998. Η παρακμή του αστικού πολιτισμού: Από τη μοντέρνα στη μεταμοντέρνα εποχή και από το φιλελευθερισμό στη μαζική δημοκρατία* [1943–1998. The decline of urban culture: from modern to post-modern era and from liberalism to massive democracy]. Themelio.

Kondylis, P. (2011). *Οι αιτίες της παρακμής της σύγχρονης Ελλάδας* [Reasons of decline of modern Greece]. Themelio.

Kornetis, K. (2015). *Τα παιδιά της Δικτατορίας* [The children of dictatorship]. Polis

Korre-Zografou, K. (2007). Η καθημερινή ζωή των Νεοελλήνων (1700–1950) [Everyday life of Modern Greeks (1700–1950)]. *Ta Istorika*, 24(46), 227–232.

Kremmydas, V. (1993). Η Ελλάδα του 1945–1967: Το ιστορικό πλαίσιο [Greece of 1945–1967: The historical context]. In *Η Ελληνική Κοινωνία κατά την πρώτη μεταπολεμική περίοδο (1945 – 1967): 4° Επιστ. Συνέδριο/ Πάντειο Πανεπιστήμιο 24–27 Νοεμβρίου 1993* – [Greek Society in the first post-war period: 4.Conference/ Panteion University 24–27 November 1993] (pp. 16–19). Athens: Idryma Saki Karagiorga.

Kuper, A. (2008). Ιθαγενής εθνογραφία, πολιτική ευπρέπεια και το σχέδιο μιας κοσμοπολιτικής ανθρωπολογίας [Indigenous ethnography, political decency and the project of a cosmopolitan anthropology]. In D. Gkefou-Madianou (Ed.), *Ανθρωπολογική θεωρία και Εθνογραφία, Σύγχρονες τάσεις* [Anthropological Theory and Ethnography: Modern Trends] (pp. 297–336). Athens: Ellinika Grammata.

Kyriakidou-Nestoros, A. (1993a). Folkloric Studies II. Poria.

Kyriakidou-Nestoros, A. (1993b). *Λαογραφία και Προφορική Ιστορία* [Folklore and Oral History]. In A. Kyriakidou-Nestoros, *Λαογραφικά Μελετήματα II* [Folkloric Studies II] (pp. 227–270). Athens: Poria.

Laclau, E. & Mouffe, Ch. (2001). *Hegemony and Socialist Strategy. Towards a Radical Demokcratic Politics*. Verso. https://files.libcom.org/files/ernesto-laclau-hegemo ny-and-socialist-strategy-towards-a-radical-democratic-politics.compressed. pdf

Latour, B. (1993). *We have never been modern*. Harvard University Press.

Latour, B. (2005). Reassembling the Social: An Introduction to Actor-Network Theory. Oxford University Press.

Lefebvre H. (1991). *The production of space*. Blackwell.

Liakos A. (2001). The Construction of National Time: The Making of the Modern Greek Historical Imagination. *Mediterranean Historical Review, 16*(1), 27–42. http s://doi.org/10.1080/714004571

Liakos A. (2004). Modern Greek Historiography (1974–2000). The Era of Tradition from Dictatorship to Democracy. In U. Brunbauer (Ed.), *(Re) Writing History, Historiography in Southeast Europe after Socialism* (pp. 351–378). Münster: LIT Verlag.

Liodakis, G. (1993). Κοινωνικο-θεωρητικές βάσεις και πρακτικές οικονομικού προγραμματισμού στην Ελλάδα κατά την πρώτη μεταπολεμική περίοδο" [Social and theoretical basis and practices of financial planning in Greece in the early post-war eara]. In *Η Ελληνική Κοινωνία κατά την πρώτη μεταπολεμική περίοδο (1945 – 1967): 4° Επιστ. Συνέδριο/ Πάντειο Πανεπιστήμιο 24–27 Νοεμβρίου 1993 –* [Greek Society in the first post-war period: 4.Conference/ Panteion University 24–27 November 1993], 77–94. Athens: Idryma Saki Karagiorga.

Löfgren, O. (1987). Decostructing Swedishness: Culture and Class in Modern Sweden. In A. Jackson (Ed.), *Anthropology at Home* (pp. 74–94). London: Tavistock.

Loukos, Chr. (1992). *Οικονομικές συμπεριφορές, ψυχολογία και βιοτικό επίπεδο ενός Συριανού τοκιστή: Στέφανος Δ. Ρήγας* [Economic behaviors, psychology and living standard of a moneylender from Syros]. EMNE.

Low, S., & Lawrence-Zúñiga, D. (2007). *The Anthropology of Space and Place: Locating Culture*. Blackwell.

Maloutas, Th. (1990). *Αθήνα, Κατοικία, Οικογένεια: Ανάλυση των μεταπολεμικών πρακτικών στέγασης* [Athens, Residence, Family: Analysis of post-war housing practices]. Exantas.

Marcus, G. E. (1995). Ethnography in/of the World System: The Emergence of Multi-Sited Ethnography. Annual Review of Anthropology, 24, 95–117. http://www.jst or.org/stable/2155931

Marcus, G. E., & Fischer M. M. J. (1986). *Anthropology as Cultural Critique: An Experimental Moment in the Human Sciences*. The University of Chicago Press.

Marcus, G. E. (2008). *Τα μετά την κριτική της Εθνογραφίας* [After the critique of ethnography]. In D. Gkefou-Madianou (Ed.), *Ανθρωπολογική θεωρία και Εθνογραφία, Σύγχρονες τάσεις* [Anthropological Theory and Ethnography: Modern Trends] (pp. 67–108). Athens: Ellinika Grammata.

Martin, V. (1997). Illusions of the City. Journal of Urban History, 23(6), 760–769. http s://doi.org/10.1177/009614429702300606

Marx, K., & F. Engels (Eds.). (1962). *Das Kapital: Kritik der Politischen Ökonomie, Der Produktionsprozeß des Kapitals, vol. 1, book 1.* Berlin: Dietz Verlag.

Marx, K. (1964a). Manifest der Kommunistischen Partei. In K. Marx & F. Engels (Eds.), *Ausgewählte Schriften in zwei Bänden* (pp. 25–57). Berlin: Dietz Verlag.

Marx, K. (1964b). Zur Kritik der Politischen Ökonomie. In K. Marx & F. Engels, *Ausgewählte Schriften in zwei Bänden*, vol. 1, (pp. 334–338). Berlin: Dietz Verlag.

Marx, K. (1964c). Der achtzehnte Brumaire des Louis Bonaparte. In K. Marx & F. Engels (Eds.), *Ausgewählte Schriften in zwei Bänden*, vol. 1, (pp. 222–316). Berlin: Dietz Verlag.

Marx, K. (2009). *Das Kapital: Kritik der Politischen Ökonomie*. Anaconda.

Maurer, M. (Ed.). (2003). Historische Anthropologie. In *Aufriss der historischen Wissenschaften. Neue Theme und Methoden des Geschichtswissenschaft* (pp. 294–391). Stuttgart: Reclam.

Mazower, M. (2006). *Θεσσαλονίκη: Πόλη των φαντασμάτων* [Salonica: City of ghosts]. Alexandria.

McCracken, G. (1989). 'Homeyness', a cultural account of one constellation of consumer goods and meaning. In Hirshmann, E. (Ed.), *Interpretative consumer research*, (pp. 168–183). Provo: Association for Consumer Research.

Merry, S. E. (1988). Legal Pluralism. Law & Society Review, 22(5), 869–896. https://d oi.org/10.2307/3053638

Merten, K. (2014). *Untereinander, nicht nebeneinander: Das Zusammenleben religiöser und kultureller Gruppen im Osmanischen Reich des 19. Jahrhunderts* [Among each other, not side by side : the coexistence of religious and cultural groups in the Ottoman Empire of the 19th century]. Lit Verlag.

Michailidis, I. Nikolakopoulos, I., & Fleischer, H. (Eds.). (2006). *Εχθρός' εντός των τειχών. Όψεις του Δωσιλογισμού στην Ελλάδα της Κατοχής* [Enemy Intramuros. Aspects of collaborationism in Greece of Nazi occupation]. Ellinika Grammata.

Mihailescu, V. (2014). Something nice. Pride Houses, Post/Peasant Society and the Quest for Authenticity. *Cultura*, (2)11, 83–107. https://doi.org/10.5840/cultura20 1411216

Miller, D. (1987). *Material Culture and Mass Consumption*. Blackwell.

Miller, D. (1998). *Material Cultures. Why Some Things Matter*. University of Chicago Press.

Miller, D., Jackson, P. Thrift, N., Holbrook, B., & Rowlands M. (1999). *Shopping, Place and Identity*. Routledge.

Miller, D.. (Ed.). (2001). *Home Possessions. Material Culture behind Closed Doors*. Berg.

Miller, D. (2005). *Materiality*. Duke University Press.

Miller, D. (2008). *The Comfort of Things*. Polity Press.

Miller, D. (2010). *Stuff*. Polity Press.

Mitchell, T. (2006). Society, Economy and the State Effect. In A. Sharma & A. Gupta (Eds.), *The Anthropology of the State: A Reader* (pp. 169–186). Oxford: Blackwell.

Mouzelis, N. (1978). *Νεοελληνική Κοινωνία: όψεις υπανάπτυξης* (μτφρ. Μαστοράκη, Τζ.) [Modern Greek Society: underdevelopment aspects (translation by Mastoraki, Tz.)]. Exantas.

Murphy, K. M. (2013). A cultural geometry: Designing political things in Sweden. *American Ethnologist*, 40(1), 118–131. http://www.jstor.org/stable/23357960

Mylonaki, A. (2012). *Από τις αυλές στα σαλόνια. Εικόνες του αστικού χώρου στον ελληνικό δημοφιλή κινηματογράφο (1950–1970)* [From courtyards to lounges. Images of urban space in Greek popular cinema (1950–1970)]. University Studio Press.

Naguib, N., (2008). Storytelling: Armenian Family Albums in the Diaspora. *Visual Anthropology*, 21(3), 231–244. https://doi.org/10.1080/08949460801986228

Naidoo, L. (2012). Ethnography: An Introduction to Definition and Method. In (Ed.), *An Ethnography of Global Landscapes and Corridors*. IntechOpen. https://doi.org/10.5772/39248

Navaro-Yashin, Y. (2009). Affective spaces, melancholic objects: ruination and the production of anthropological knowledge. *Willey Online Library*, 15(1), 1–18. https://doi.org/10.1111/j.1467-9655.2008.01527.x

Niethammer, Lutz (Ed.). (1980). *Lebenserfahrung und kollektives Gedächtnis. Theorie und Praxis der „Oral History"*. Syndikat.

Nikolaidis A. (2008). *Die Griechische Community in Deutschland. Von transnationaler Migration zu transnationaler Diaspora. Eine Studie zum Paradigmenwecsel am* Fall *der griechischen studentischen Community in Bochum*. Dr. Müller.

Nikolaidou, S. (1993). *Η κοινωνική οργάνωση του αστικού χώρου* [Social organization of urban space]. Papazisi.

Nitsiakos, V. (2003). *Χτίζοντας το χώρο και το χρόνο* [Building space and time]. Odysseas.

Nuijten M., & Anders, G. (Eds.). (2007). *Corruption and the Secret of Law. A Legal Anthropological Perspective*. Ashgate.

Nustad K. G., & Krohn-Hansen C., (2005). *State Formation: Anthropological Perspectives*. Ann Arbor, MI, Pluto Press.

Oikonomou D. (1987). Η στεγαστική πολιτική στη μεταπολεμική Ελλάδα. Βασικές ερμηνευτικές υποθέσεις, πιστοδότηση της στέγης και πολιτική ενοικίων [Housing policy in post-war Greece. Basic interpretative hypotheses, housing credit and policy of rents]. *Epitheorisi koinonikon Erevnon*, 64, 56–129.

Oikonomou, L. (1999). *Η γέννηση ενός αθηναϊκού προαστίου. Όψεις της κοινωνικής και πολεοδομικής ιστορίας της Βούλας* [Birth of an Athenian suburb. Aspects of social and urban history of Voula]. private edition.

Oikonomou, L. (2008). *Η κοινωνική παραγωγή του αστικού χώρου στη μεταπολεμική Αθήνα. Η περίπτωση της Βούλας* [Social production of urban space in post-war Athens. The case of Voula]. Ellinika Grammata.

Olivier de Sardan. J. P. (1999). A Moral Economy of Corruption in Africa? *The Journal of Modern African Studies, 37*(1), 25–52. http://www.jstor.org/stable/161467

O'Reilly, K. (2007). *Ethnographic methods.* Routledge.

Panagiotopoulos, P. (2021). *Περιπέτειες της μέσαιας τάξης. Κοινωνιολογικές καταγραφές στην Ελλάδα της ύστερης Μεταπολίτευσης* [Adventures of the middle classes. Sociological records in Greece of the late political transition]. Epikentro.

Panourgia, N. (2013). *Επικίνδυνοι πολίτες. Η ελληνική αριστερά και η κρατική τρομοκρατία* [Dangerous citizens. The Greek left wing and state terrorism]. Kastanioti.

Pantelakis, N. (1991). *Ο εξηλεκτρισμός της Ελλάδας. Από την ιδιωτική πρωτοβουλία στο κρατικό μονοπώλιο (1889–1956)* [Electrification of Greece. From private initiative to state monopoly]. MIET.

Papailia, P. (2016). Ανθρωπολογία και Μεταααποικιακές Σπουδές: Από τη μεταποικιακή κριτικής της Ανθρωπολογίας στην Ανθρωπολογία της αποικιοκρατίας [Anthropology and post-colonialism studies. From post-colonialism critique of Anthropology to Anthropology of colonialism]. In A. Athanasiou (Ed.), *Αποδομώντας την Αυτοκρατορία. Θεωρία και πολιτική της μεταποικιακής κριτικής* [Destructuring the Empire. Theory and politics of post-colonialism critique] (pp. 23–73). Athens: Politis.

Papamichos, N. (2000). Η μεταπολεμική πόλη, πόλη της αντιπαροχής" [Postwar city, city of antiparochi]. In *Επιστημονικό Συμπόσιο 1949–1967–Η εκρηκτική Εικοσαετία (10–12 Νοεμβρίου 2000)* [Scientific Symposium 1949–1967–An explosive twenty-year period (10–12 November 2000)] (pp. 79–86).

Papanikolaou, D. (2018). *Κάτι τρέχει με την οικογένεια: έθνος, πόθος και συγγένεια την εποχή της κρίσης* [Something is going on with family: nation, desire and relatives in the crisis era]. Pataki.

Papataxiarchis, E., & Paradellis Th. (Eds.). (1993). *Ανθρωπολογία και Παρελθόν: Συμβολές στην Κοινωνική Ιστορία της Νεότερης Ελλάδας* [Anthropology and Past: Contributions to the Social History of Modern Greece]. Alexandria

Papataxiarchis, E. (1992). Από τη σκοπιά του Φύλου. Ανθρωπολογικές θεωρήσεις της σύγχρονης Ελλάδας [From the point of view of Gender. Anthropological considerations of modern Greece]. In E. Papataxiarchis and Th. Paradellis (Eds.), *Ταυτότητες και Φύλο στη σύγχρονη Ελλάδα. Ανθρωπολογικές προσεγγίσεις* [Identities and Gender in Modern Greece. Anthropological approaches] (pp. 11–98). Athens: Editions Kastanioti / University of the Aegean.

Papataxiarchis, E. (2003). Η κοινωνική ανθρωπολογία στη μεταπολεμική Ελλάδα: Τα πρώτα βήματα [Social anthropology in post-war Greece: first steps]. In I. Lampiri-Dimaki (Ed.), *Κοινωνικές Επιστήμες και Πρωτοπορία στην Ελλάδα* [Social sciences and Innovation in Greece], 1950–1967 (pp. 115–154). Athens: Gutenberg & EKKE.

Papataxiarchis, E. (2006a). Το 'νοικοκυριό', ναι, σε εισαγωγικά: 'Οικονομική Ανθρωπολογία', 'Ελληνική Εθνογραφία' και η πολιτισμική συγκρότηση της οικιακής εργασίας ['Noikokyrio', yes, in inverted commas: 'Economic Anthropology', 'Greek Ethnography' and cultural establishment of domestic work] (pp. 1–17). http://www1.aegean.gr/gender-postgraduate/Documents/Fylo_Chrima_Antallagi/Fylo%20kai%20oikiaki%20ergasia-10-edraft.pdf

Papataxiarchis, E. (2006b). Εισαγωγή. Τα άχθη της ετερότητας: Διαδικασίες διαφοροποίησης στην Ελλάδα του πρώιμου 21ου αιώνα [Introduction. The burdens of otherness: Differentiation processes in Greece of early 21st century]. In Περιπέτειες της ετερότητας: Η παραγωγή της πολιτισμικής διαφοράς στη σημερινή Ελλάδα [Adventures of otherness: the production of cultural difference in Greece of today] (pp. 1–85). Athens: Alexandria.

Papataxiarchis, E. (2006c). Το καθεστώς της διαφορετικότητας στην ελληνική κοινωνία. Υποθέσεις εργασίας [The status of diversity in Greek society. Working hypotheses.]. In Περιπέτειες της ετερότητας: Η παραγωγή της πολιτισμικής διαφοράς στη σημερινή Ελλάδα [Adven-tures of otherness: the production of cultural difference in Greece of today] (pp. 407–469). Athens: Alexandria.

Pardo I., & Prato G. (Eds.). (2018). *The palgrave handbook of urban ehnography*. Palgrave Macmillan.

Pardo, I. (2004). (Ed.) *Between Morality and the Law: Corruption, Anthropology and Comparative Society*. Rootledge.

Paschalidis G. & Vamvakas V. (Eds.). (2018). *50 Χρόνια ελληνική τηλεόραση (πρακτικά συνεδρίου)* [50 years of Greek television (conference proceedings)]. Epikentro.

Passerini, L. (1987). *Fascism in popular memory: the cultural experience of the Turin working class*. Cambridge University Press.

Passerini, L. (2004). *Autobiography of a generation: Italy, 1968*. Wesleyan University Press.

Petridou, E. (2001). The Taste of Home. In Miller, D. (Ed.), *Home Possessions* (pp. 87–104). Berg.

Poulantzas, N. (1975). *Classes in Contemporary Capitalism*. NLB.

Poulantzas, N (1978). *Political Power and Social Classes*. NLB.

Poulantzas, N (1985). *Πολιτική εξουσία και κοινωνικές τάξεις* [Political power and social classes].Themelio.

Potamianos, N. (2015). *Οι Νοικοκυραίοι. Μαγαζάτορες και Βιοτέχνες στην Αθήνα 1880–1925* [Noikokyraioi shop owners and manufacturers in Athens 1880–1925]. Univ. Editions of Crete.

Potiropoulos, P. (2001). Νέα Μηχανιώνα Θεσσαλονίκης: Προσφυγική συνείδηση και συλλογική ταυτότητα [Nea Michaniona, Thessalonoki: Refugee consciousness and collective identity]. In C. Chatzitaki-Kapsomenou (Ed.), *Ελληνικός παραδοσιακός πολιτισμός. Λαογραφία και Ιστορία (Συνέδριο στη μνήμη της Άλκης Κυριακίδου-Νέστορος)* [Greek traditional culture. Folklore and History (Conference in memoriam of Alki Kyriakidou-Nestoros)] (pp. 262–272).

Potiropoulos, P. (2003). *Νέα Μηχανιώνα. Από 'χαμένες πατρίδες' στην πατρίδα του 'Σήμερα'* [Nea Michaniona. From 'lost homelands' to the homeland of 'Today']. University Studio Press.

Putnam, T. (1999). Postmodern' home life. In I. Cieraad (Ed.) *At Home. An Anthropology of domestic Space* (pp. 144–154. https://doi.org/10.2307/j.ctv1w36pj9

Rivkin-Fish, M. (2005). Bribes, Gifts and unofficial payments: rethinking corruption in post-soviet Russian health care. In D. Haller & Ch. Shore (Eds.), *Corruption: Anthropological Perspectives (pp. 47–64)*. https://doi.org/10.2307/j.ctt18fs7ts

Said, E., (1978). *Orientalism*. Random House.

Salamone, S.D., & Stanton, J.B. (2019). Introducing the Nikokyra: Ideality and Reality in Social Process. In J. Dubisch (Ed.), *Gender and Power in Rural Greece* (pp. 97–120). Princeton: Princenton University.

Seremetakis, K. N. (2018). *Αναγνωρίζοντας το καθημερινό. Διαλογική Ανθρωπολογία, θεωρία και πράξη* [Recognizing the everyday. Dialogical Anthropology, theory and practice]. Pedio.

Sharma, A. & Gupta, A. (Eds.). (2006). *The Anthropology of the State: A Reader*. Blackwell.

Smart, A & Hsu, C. (2007). Corruption or Social Capital? Tact and the Performance of Guanxi in Market Socialist China. In M. Nuijten & G. Anders (Eds.), *Corruption and the Secret of Law. A Legal Anthropological Perspective* (pp. 167–190). Burlington: Ashgate.

Steinmetz, G. (Ed.). (1999). *State/Culture, State-formation after the Cultural Turn*. Cornell University Press.

Strathern, M. (1988). *The Gender of the Gift: Problems With Women and Problems With Society in Melanesia Studies in Melanesian*. University of California Press.

Sutton, D., & Vournelis, L. (2009). Vefa or Mamalakis? Cooking up Nostalgia in Contemporary Greece. *South European Society and Politics*, 14(2), 147–166.

Thompson, E.P. (1966). *The making of the English working class*. Random House.

Thompson, M. (2017). *Rubbish Theory. The creation and destruction of value*. Pluto Press.

Thompson, P. (2008). *Φωνές από το παρελθόν: Προφορική Ιστορία* [The Voice of the Past: Oral History]. Plethron.

Tebbe, J. (2008). Landscapes of Remembrance: Home and Memory in the Nineteenth-Century Bürgertum. *Journal of Family History*, 33(2), 195–215.

Torsello, D. (2011). The ethnography of corruption: research themes in political anthropology. In *QoG working paper series*,1 – 24. Gothenburg: University of Gothenburg. http://hdl.handle.net/2077/39023

Torsello, D., & Venard, B. (2016). The Anthropology of Corruption. *Journal of Management Inquiry*, 25(1), 34–54. https://doi.org/10.1177/1056492615579081

Tsibiridou, F. (1999). "Μας λένε Πομάκους!": Κληρονομιές και πολιτικές κατασκευές και βιώματα σε μειονοτικές, περιθωριακές ταυτότητες ['They call us Pomaks!': Heritage and political constructions and experiences in minority, marginal identities]. *Mnemon*, 21, 163–182.

Tsibiridou, F. (2006a). "Πομάκος σημαίνει άνθρωπος του Βουνού." Εννοιολογήσεις και βιώματα του 'τόπου' στις κατασκευές και τις πολιτικές μειονοτικών περιθωριακών ταυτοτήτων [Pomak means man of the mountains. Conceptualizations and experiences of 'location' in the constructions and policies of minority marginal identities]. In Th. Malkidis & N. Kokkas (Eds.), Μετασχηματισμοί της συλλογικής ταυτότητας των Πομάκων [Transformations of the collective identity of the Pomaks] (pp. 131–160). Xanthi: Spanidi.

Tsibiridou, F. (2006b). Writing about Turks and Powerful Others: Journalistic Heteroglossia in Western Thrace, South European Society and Politics, (1)11, 129–144. DOI: 10.1080/13608740500470380

Tsibiridou, F. (2013). Προς μία δημιουργική κριτική του 'ανθρώπινου': εμπειρίες επισφάλειας, συμμόρφωσης και υπονόμευσης του 'κυρίαρχου' από μια τραβεστί κούρδισσα φεμινίστρια καλλιτέχνη της πόλης [Towards a creative critique of 'human': experiences of vulnerability, compliance and undermining of the 'dominant' by a Kurdish transvestite feminist artist of the city], Epitheorisi koinonikon Erevnon, 140, 133–151.

Tsibiridou, F. (2015). Lifestyle and Consumerism: Neoliberal biopolitics and Islamist Experiences in the Muslim World. In G. Paschalidis & L. Yoka (Eds.), Semiotics and Hermeneutics of the Everyday (pp. 60–81). Cambridge Scholars Publishing.

Tsibiridou, F. (2017). Πέρι της πολιτικής και εργαλειακής χρήσης των συνόρων μεταξύ ισλάμ και Δύσης [On the political and instrumental use of the borders between Islam and the West]. In Ventoura, L., Karydas, D., & Kouzelis, G. (Eds.), Σύνορα/'Ορια [Borders/Limits] (pp. 117–138). Athens: Society for the Study of Human Sciences.

Tsibiridou, F. (2018). An Ethnography of Space, Creative Dissent and Reflective Nostalgia in the City Centre of Global Istanbul. In I. Pardo & G. Prato (Eds.), The Palgrave Handbook of Urban Ethnography (pp. 405–426). Kent: Palgrave-Macmillan.

Tsibiridou, F., & Deltsou, E. (2016). Introduction. Semiotics and Fieldwork: On critical Ethnographies. Punctum, Journal of Semiotics, 2(2), 5–13. DOI: 10.18680/hss.2016.0011

Tsitselikis, K. (Ed.). (2006). Η Ελληνοτουρκική Ανταλλαγή Πληθυσμών. Πτυχές μιας εθνικής σύγκρουσης [Population exchange between Greece and Turkey. Aspects of a national conflict]. KEMO

Tsotsoros, St. (1995). Ενέργεια και Ανάπτυξη στη μεταπολεμική περίοδο. Η Δημόσια Επιχείρηση Ηλεκτρισμού 1950–1992 [Energy and Development in the post-war era. The Public Power Corporation]. Centre for Modern Greek Research of the National Hellenic Research Foundation

Tsoukalas, K. (1977). Εξάρτηση και αναπαραγωγή. Ο κοινωνικός ρόλος των εκπαιδευτικών μηχανισμών στην Ελλάδα [Dependence and reproduction. The social role of educational mechanisms in Greece]. Themelio

Tsoukalas, K. (1981). *Η ελληνική τραγωδία. Από την απελευθέρωση ως τους συνταγματάρχες* [The Greek tragedy. From liberation to Colonels]. Nea Synora –A.A. Livani

Tsoukalas, K. (2005). *Κράτος, Κοινωνία και Εργασία στην μεταπολεμική Ελλάδα* [State, Society and Labor in post-war Greece].Themelio.

Selekou, O. (2004). *Η καθημερινή ζωή των Ελλήνων της διασποράς. Δημόσιος και Ιδιωτικός βίος (19ος -Αρχές του 20ου αιώνα)* [Everyday life of the Greeks of diaspora. Public and private life (19th-Beginning of 20th century)]. EKKE.

Skouteri-Didaskalou, N. (1984). *Ανθρωπολογικά για το γυναικείο ζήτημα* [Anthropological considerations of the women issue]. Politis.

Skouteri-Didaskalou, N. (1988). *Ιστορία και Ανθρωπολογία; Ένα σημείωμα με αφορμή την ελληνική περίπτωση* [History and Anthropology: A note on the Greek case]. *Sychrona Themata*, 35–36-37, 230–232.

Skouteri-Didaskalou, N. (1994). *Φωτογραφίζοντας την προσφυγική Ελλάδα: Μνήμη και Ιστορία"* [Taking a picture of refugee Greece: Memory and history]. *Entefktirio* 25, 85–92.

Stathakis, G. (2000). *Η απρόσμενη οικονομική ανάπτυξη στις δεκαετίες του '50 και '60: Η Αθήνα ως αναπτυξιακό υπόδειγμα"* [The unexpected economic growth in the 1950s and 1960s: Athens as development model], in *Επιστημονικό Συμπόσιο 1949–1967-Η εκρηκτική Εικοσαετία (10–12 Νοεμβρίου 2000)* [Scientific Symposium 1949–1967-An explosive twenty-year period (10–12 November 2000)] (pp. 43–65).

Stavridis, St. (Ed.). (2006). *Μνήμη και εμπειρία του χώρου* [Memory and experience of space]. Alexandria.

Stavridis, St. (1990). *Η συμβολική σχέση με το χώρο* [The symbolic relationship with space]. Kalvos.

Valoukos, S. (1998). *Φιλμογραφία του Ελληνικού κινηματογράφου* [Filmography of Greek cinema]. Aigokeros.

Vamvakas, V., & Panagiotopoulos, P. (2014). *Η Ελλάδα στη Δεκαετία του '80. Κοινωνικό, πολιτικό και πολιτισμικό Λεξικό* [Greece in the 1980s. Social, political and cultural dictionary]. Epikentro.

Van Boeschoten, R, Vervenioti, T., Lambropoulou, D., Mouliou, M., & Hantzaroula, P. (Eds.). (2016). *Η μνήμη αφηγείται την πόλη. Προφορική ιστορία και μνήμη του αστικού χώρου* [Memory narrates the city. Oral history and memory of urban space]. Plethron.

Van Laak, D. (2003). Alltagsgeschichte. In M. Maurer (Ed.), *Aufriss der historischen Wissenschaften* (pp. 14 – 80). Stuttgart: Reclam.

Veikou, Hr. (1998). *Κακό μάτι: Η κοινωνική κατασκευή της οπτικής επικοινωνίας* [The Evil Eye: The Social Construction of Visual Communication]. Ellinika Grammata.

Venianakis, A. (2016). *Δάγκουλας, ο Άρδκος' της Θεσσαλονίκης. Συμβολή στην Ιστορία των Ταγμάτων Ασφαλείας επί Κατοχής (1941–1944)* [Dangoulas, the "Dragon" of Thessaloniki. Contribution to the History of Security Battalions during the Nazi occupation (1941–1944)]. Epikentro.

Vergeti, M. (2000). Η ποντιακή ταυτότητα στον ελληνικό χώρο και ο γεωγραφικός χώρος αναφοράς της, ο ιδιαίτερος δεσμός τριών γενιών με το γεωγραφικό χώρο αναφοράς τους [Pontic identity in the Greek area and their geographical area of reference, the special link of three generations with their geographical area of reference]. In M. Bruneau (Ed.), Η διασπορά του ποντιακού ελληνισμού [The diaspora of Pontic hellenism] (pp. 273–288). Thessaloniki: Irodotos.

Vlachos, X. (1978). Κατοικία και κοινωνικές τάξεις στον Ελληνικό αστικό χώρο [Residence and social classes in Greek urban space]. In D. Fatouros, A., Papadopoulos & L., Tentokali, (Eds.), Μελέτες για την κατοικία στην Ελλάδα [Studies on residence in Greece] (pp. 73–132). Thessaloniki: Paratiritis.

Vlachoutsikou, Ch. (1999). Περί κατανάλωσης, ορίων και πολιτικής ή: Διαμέρισμα με νοίκι και τα δύο συνολάκια [On consumption, limits and politics or: Apartment with rent and two sets of clothes]. In R. Kaftantzoglou & M. Petronoti (Eds.), Όρια και Περιθώρια: Εντάξεις και Αποκλεισμοί [Limits and margins: integrations and exclusions] (pp. 169–194). Athens: EKKE.

Voglis, P. (2014). Η αδύνατη επανάσταση [The impossible revolution]. Alexandria.

Voukelatos, G. (2003). Γερμανία 1960–1974. Κβελλενστρασε 2. Αγώνες και Παρασκήνια [Germany 1960–1974. Quellenstraße 2. Fights and backstage]. Libro.

Voutira, E. (1997). Population Transfers and Resettlement Policies in inter-war Europe: The case of Asia Minor Refugees in Macedonia from an International and National Perspective. In P. Mackridge & E. Yanakakis (Eds.), Ourselves and others: The Development of a Greek Makedonian Cultural identity since 1912 (pp. 111–131). Oxford – New York: Berg.

Voutira, E. (1994). Προσφυγική Ελλάδα: Παράδειγμα προς Μίμηση; (Βιβλιογραφικό άρθρο) [Greece of refugees: An example to follow? (Bibliographical paper)]. Istor, 7, 175–183.

Voutira, E. (2006). Η 'επιτυχής' αποκατάσταση των Μικρασιατών προσφύγων [The successful settlement of refugees from Asia Minor]. In K. Tsitselikis (Ed.), Η ελληνοτουρκική ανταλλαγή πληθυσμών. Πτυχές μιας εθνικής σύγκρουσης [Population exchange between Greece and Turkey. Aspects of a national conflict] (pp. 238–248). Athens: KEMO.

Voutira, E., & Harrell – Bond, B. (2006). Successful refugee settlement: are past experiences relevant?. In M. Cernea & Chr. McDowell (Eds.), Risks and Reconstruction. Experiences of Resettlers and Refugees (pp. 56–76). Washington: World Bank.

Weber, M. (2006). Bureaucracy. In A. Sharma & A. Gupta (Eds.), The Anthropology of State: A Reader (pp. 47–70). Malden: Blackwell Publishing.

Weber, M., (1948). Essays in sociology. Oxford University Press.

Westwood, S., (2002). Power and the Social. Routledge.

Wierling, D. (2003). Oral History. In M. Maurer (Ed.), Aufriss der historischen Wissenschaften, (pp. 81–151). Stuttgart: Reclam.

Williams, R. (1994). Κουλτούρα και Ιστορία [Culture and Society]. Gnosi.

Wolf, P. R. (1984). *Understanding Marx: A reconstruction and Critique of Capital*. Princeton University Press.

Wright E. O. (1978). *Class, Crisis and the Sate*. NLB

Zermpoulis, M. (2017). Heuristic displays of photographic images inside the home: Greek family photographs as efficient agents of an appropriate past, proper present and inspired future. *Revue Science and Video* 6, 1–31. https://scienceand video.mmsh.fr/n-06/

Znoj, H. (2007). Deep Corruption in Indonesia: Discourses, Practices, Histories. In Nuijten M. & Anders, G. (Eds.), *Corruption and the Secret of Law. A Legal Anthropological Perspective* (pp. 53 –76). Burlington: Ashgate.

Zourgos, I. (2005). *Στη σκιά της πεταλούδας* [In the shadow of the butterfly]. Pataki.

Archives

Thessaloniki History Center

Social Welfare Archive (Decentralized Administration of Macedonia-Thrace, Department of Public Property)

DEI Historical Archive Thessaloniki

Greek TV series

Nemeas, V. (Writer), & Koutelidakis, N. (Direktor). (1989–1991), *The Afthairetoi* [Arbitrary people] [TV Series], Machi TV Productions.

Dalianidis, G. (Writer & Director). (1992–1993), *The Mikromesaioi* [middle classes] [TV Series]. Tsebelis Productions.

Dalianidis, G. (Writer & Director). (1990–1992), *Retire* [Penthouse]. Tsebelis Productions.

Journalistic articles

Karali, M. (2015, March 6). "Ο πρόεδρος βλέπει τσόντα;" [Does the president watch porn?]. Lifo. https://www.lifo.gr/arxeio/blepei-tsonta-o-proedros-tis-boylis.

Paridis, C. (2015, January 23). "Ο μικροαστισμός είναι η μόνη ιδεολογία που έχει παραγάγει η Ελλάδα. Ο κοσμήτορας του Πανεπιστημίου του Σίδνεϊ και καθηγητής Ελληνικών και Βυζαντινών Σπουδών Βρασίδας Καραλής μιλά στη Lifo" [Petty bourgeoisism is the only ideology Greece has produced. The Dean of the University of Sydney and Professor of Greek and Byzantine Studies Vrasidas Karalis

speaks to Lifo]. Lifo. https://www.lifo.gr/now/greece/o-mikroastismos-einai-i
-moni-ideologia-poy-ehei-paragagei-i-ellada.

Filmography

Tsavellas, G. (Writer & Director). (1965). "Η δε γυνή να φοβήται τον άνδρα" ["And the
Wife Shall Revere Her Husband"] [Film]. Damaskinos-Michailidis.

Electronic resources

(1957). Έρευνα οικογενειακών προϋπολογισμών 1957 [Research of family budgets
1957"]. National Statistical Service. Retrieved November 25, 2022, from http://dl
ib.statistics.gr/portal/page/portal/ESYE/yeararticles?p_topic=10008049&p_ca
t=10008049&p_catage=1957
(2010). Agnosti Thessaloniki [Unknown Thessaloniki]. Facebook. Retrieved November 25, 2022, from https://www.facebook.com/groups/agnosti.thessaloniki/?re
f=bookmarks
(2012). Thessaloniki 2012. Municipality of Thessaloniki. Retrieved May 20, 2013, from
http://www.thessaloniki2012.gr/.
(2012). Νεοκλασικά Θεσσαλονίκης project [Neoclassical buildings of Thessaloniki].
Facebook. Retrieved November 25, 2022, from https://www.facebook.com/grou
ps/504888489524433/
(2012). "Θεσσαλονίκη: μια πόλη σε μετάβαση, 1912–2012" [Thessaloniki: a city in transition,
1912–2012]. Program of conference. Retrieved November 25, 2022, from http://www.tch.
gr/default.aspx?lang=el-GR&page=3&season=2012-2013&tcheid=1142
(2013). Μνήμες Θεσσαλονίκης – Σύνδεση με το Παρόν [Memories of Thessaloniki –
Link with the present]. Facebook. Retrieved November 25, 2022, from https://w
ww.facebook.com/groups/395469423904836/
@GorillaGrodd1979. (2013, August 5). Κωνσταντίνος Καραμανλής – Η Ελλάς ανήκει
εις την Δύσιν (12 Ιουνίου 1976) [Konstantinos Karamanlis – Greece belongs to the
West (12 June 1976)] [Video]. YouTube. https://www.youtube.com/watch?v=-51D
bXntglI
(2015, November 22). Νίκος Νικολόπουλος: Το κόμμα των νοικοκυραίων έγινε κόμμα
των... μοιραίων [Nikos Nikolopoulos: The party of the Noikokyraioi" became the
"party of... the fatalists"]. The Best. Retrieved November 25, 2022, from https://
www.thebest.gr/article/364633-
Paridis, C. (2015, January 23). "Ο μικροαστισμός είναι η μόνη ιδεολογία που
έχει παραγάγει η Ελλάδα": Ο κοσμήτορας του Πανεπιστημίου του Σίδνεϊ και
καθηγητής Ελληνικών και Βυζαντινών Σπουδών Βρασίδας Καράλης μιλά στη

LifO ["Petty bourgeoisism is the only ideology Greece has produced" The Dean of the University of Sydney and Professor of Greek and Byzantine Studies Brasidas Karalis speaks to LifO. Lifo. Retrieved November 22, 2022, from https://www.lifo.gr/now/greece/o-mikroastismos-einai-i-moni-ideologi a-poy-ehei-paragagei-i-ellada

Albums

Άσυλο του Παιδιού [Children's Asylum] (Album) (1994).

Megas G. & Chorbos N. (2002, *Η Θεσσαλονίκη μέσα από τον φακό του Γιώργου Λυκίδη* [Thessaloniki throught the camera of Giorgos Lykidis]. Ianos.

Σύνδεσμος Αποφοίτων Βαλαγιάννη [Valagianni Alumni Association] (Λεύκωμα) [(Album)] (1996), *Μνήμες και Αφιερώσεις* [Memories and Dedications]. Chronos.

List of Figures

GPSR Authorized Representative: Easy Access System Europe, Mustamäe tee 50, 10621 Tallinn, Estonia, gpsr.requests@easproject.com